THE EAST-WEST CENTER—officially known as the Center for Cultural and Technical Interchange Between East and West—is a national educational institution established in Hawaii by the U.S. Congress in 1960 to promote better relations and understanding between the United States and the nations of Asia and the Pacific through cooperative study, training, and research. The Center is administered by a public, nonprofit corporation whose international Board of Governors consists of distinguished scholars, business leaders, and public servants.

Each year more than 1,500 men and women from many nations and cultures participate in Center programs that seek cooperative solutions to problems of mutual consequence to East and West. Working with the Center's multidisciplinary and multicultural staff, participants include visiting scholars and researchers; leaders and professionals from the academic, government, and business communities; and graduate degree students, most of whom are enrolled at the University of Hawaii. For each Center participant from the United States, two participants are sought from the Asian and Pacific area.

Center programs are conducted by institutes addressing problems of communication, culture learning, environment and policy, population, and resource systems. A limited number of "open" grants are available to degree scholars and research fellows whose academic interests are not encompassed by institute programs.

The U.S. Congress provides basic funding for Center programs and a variety of awards to participants. Because of the cooperative nature of Center programs, financial support and cost-sharing are also provided by Asian and Pacific governments, regional agencies, private enterprise and foundations. The Center is on land adjacent to and provided by the University of Hawaii.

East-West Center Books are published by The University Press of Hawaii to further the Center's aims and programs.

Communication Research—
a Half-Century Appraisal

Communication Research—
a Half-Century Appraisal

Edited by
DANIEL LERNER
LYLE M. NELSON

ℑ *AN EAST-WEST CENTER BOOK*
from the East-West Communication Institute

Published for the East-West Center
by The University Press of Hawaii
Honolulu

This book was made possible in part by a grant from the Earhart Foundation, Ann Arbor, Michigan.

The "Postscript" by Paul F. Lazarsfeld was first published in *An Introduction to Applied Sociology,* edited by Ann Pasanella, and is reprinted by permission of Elsevier North-Holland, Inc.

Manufactured in the United States of America

Library of Congress Catalog Card No. 77–89616

ISBN: 0-8248-0566-6

This book is dedicated to
Wilbur Schramm
by his colleagues, friends, and admirers

Contents

II. A LIFE IN COMMUNICATION RESEARCH

Communication Research—
a Half-Century Appraisal

Introduction

The first half-centennial of the study of communication is being celebrated in 1977. Wilbur Schramm is one of three leading men who have shaped the field of communication as it is understood today. It is therefore appropriate that this book, which reviews the field's past and evaluates its prospects, should be dedicated to him.

The half-century of systematic communication study can be traced through the creative work of three great scholars: Harold Dwight Lasswell, Paul Felix Lazarsfeld, and Wilbur Lang Schramm. All of us concerned with the field of communication are greatly pleased that the work of all three men is represented in this book.

The story of communication research begins with the publication in 1927 of Lasswell's *Propaganda Technique in the World War*. This pioneering book was the first to set out the theoretical framework of communication research that was to be elaborated and applied over the next fifty years. It set forth the dominant paradigm: "Who says what to whom, through what channels, with what effects?" Lasswell's collation of propaganda themes foreshadowed his later invention of content analysis; his differentiation of propaganda audiences provided the framework for subsequent audience research; his in-depth interviews brought psychoanalysis into the center of communication research.

If Lasswell was the preeminent theorist of the field, Lazarsfeld was the predominant methodologist. From the time of his arrival in

America in the mid-thirties, Lazarsfeld turned his fertile imagination to the problems that arise whenever two or more people try to communicate with each other. Using the Bureau of Applied Social Research at Columbia University as his chosen instrument, Lazarsfeld initiated studies of every field in which communication occurs—that is, of every field of human interaction. No experience was too specialized or too insignificant to escape his methodological penetration. His bureau poured forth pioneering studies that ranged from the daytime reveries of a housewife listening to soap operas to the professional codes underlying relations between doctors and their patients. Lazarsfeld was the first to see that market research was a gold mine of data for those methodologically sophisticated enough to use it. With Dr. Frank Stanton, subsequently president of the Columbia Broadcasting System, he developed the Program Analyzer to study the effects of the content of radio programs on their audiences. He converted voting studies from wildly erratic straw polls to the finely honed pre-election research we know today. He worked out the mathematics—a gargantuan task—of Latent Structure Analysis.

Building on the work of theorist Lasswell and methodologist Lazarsfeld, Schramm became the principal researcher of the field. Virtually no aspect of communication escaped his scrutiny. He examined psychological warfare (in *The Reds Take a City*), communication in development, the effects of television on children, the use of audiovisual media and programmed instruction in schools, and the responsibilities of communicators.

No researcher could have accomplished all that Schramm has done. He had to be theorist and methodologist as well as researcher. Schramm's unique combination of these skills is evidenced by his two great anthologies, as well as by his *Handbook of Communication,* which provided the intellectual coordination needed in a field that, at various times, seemed to be growing exponentially in all directions.

Schramm was also a born organizer of the systematic research effort. Realizing at an early age that he could not do all the communication studies himself, Schramm organized three of the greatest institutes of communication research in the United States—the first at the University of Illinois, the second at Stanford University, and the third at the East-West Center in Hawaii. Illinois and Stanford have produced many, perhaps most, of the new generations of scholars who have sustained communication research as an intellectual focus of the social sciences over the past quarter-century, and the East-West Center has contributed significantly to the volume and importance of such studies.

Schramm's personal accomplishments will be described more fully in the intellectual biographies of Part II of this book, where his personal activity and the professional development of communication research are shown to be nearly synonymous. We are certain that all of the contributors to this book and all people engaged in communication research, past and future, will be pleased that the three giants of this field are represented in this collection. As editors of the book, and as two of Wilbur Schramm's oldest friends and colleagues, we are especially happy to dedicate this volume to him.

DANIEL LERNER
LYLE M. NELSON

I
STATE OF THE ART

Communication and Education

Yesterday's and Tomorrow's Television Research on Children

HILDE T. HIMMELWEIT

In a book honoring one of the intellectual giants in the field of communication, an examination with today's hindsight of his famous studies in *Television in the Lives of Our Children*, the field work for which was completed almost two decades ago (in 1961), seems appropriate. Wilbur Schramm's findings and theoretical perspectives were almost identical to those of the British studies (Himmelweit *et al.*, 1958).[1] The close correspondence testifies to the demand characteristics of the problem despite differences in the culture and broadcasting systems of the two countries. Similar results were obtained when the British cross-sectional and before-and-after studies were repeated in Japan between 1959 and 1961, using many of the same instruments. (Furu [1971] reports on these studies alongside others carried out in the late sixties).

Roberts (1973) and Comstock (1975) have provided comprehensive reviews of the many excellent studies of children and television carried out in the intervening years. For this book, then, I will not repeat this exercise but will discuss in Part 1 of this article the implications of selected theories from these early studies. These theories have stood the test of time and may help predict how viewers will react when, within the next ten or twenty years, a different media mix will become available in their homes.[2]

In Part 2 of this article, I examine the principles derived from a longitudinal study that reaches from the pretelevision to the posttelevision era. Schramm (1962) ended his book with the plea for "studies extensive in time and intensive in treatment." I found an opportunity to do just such work by building on a study begun in the greater London area in 1951 that was concerned with the interplay of social background and type of school on the outlook and behavior of adolescent boys. The initial study took place at a time when less than 10 percent of the subjects had television at home. To study the development of outlook, attitudes, and behavior between adolescence and adulthood, the subjects were reinterviewed eleven years later at age 25, when over 90 percent had television at home, and again eight years later at age 33. The research made it possible to develop principles concerning usage and taste in adolescence and in adulthood, and the relation of the two to one another. The full report is published elsewhere (Himmelweit and Swift, 1976); in this article, I single out certain aspects for discussion.

The research differs from two important longitudinal studies about the media (Lefkowitz, *et al.* [1972]; Heller and Polsky [1975]) in that it has a longer time perspective (eleven and twenty years) and that it focusses not on a particular type of content but on media usage and taste generally.

In Part 3 of this article, suggestions are made for types of research which have been relatively neglected, with special emphasis on the need for improved two-way traffic between communication research and the social sciences, on the one hand, and broadcasting, on the other.

PART 1: THEORETICAL PERSPECTIVES AND PRINCIPLES DERIVED FROM THE EARLIER STUDIES

For both sides of the Atlantic, the assignment to study television's effect upon children proved difficult. The fact that policy makers might be influenced by our findings proved an intoxicating challenge. The rapid rate of purchase of sets forced the pace, particularly in Britain, since our research orientation required maximum comparability in life style and school and home experience of viewer and control. In the case of the United States, a control group had to be searched for beyond her borders. Above all, the problem arose of knowing where to draw the line, given the ubiquitous character of the medium and the lack of conceptualization about children's use of leisure into which to fit the advent of television.[3]

Wilbur Schramm in *Television in the Lives of Our Children* describes in his customary vivid style our respective research orientation:

To understand the conditions of effect, we have to understand a great deal about the lives of children. Something in their lives makes them reach out for a particular experience on television. This experience then enters into their lives, and has to make its way amidst the stored experience, the codified values, the social relationships, and the immediately urgent needs that are already a part of those lives. As a result, something happens to the original experience. Something is discarded, something is stored away, perhaps some overt behaviour occurs. This is the "effect of television." What we are really trying to understand, then, is the part which the television experience plays in the lives of children.

The general orientation of the studies was, as is also true of studies today, *essentially interactionist, seeing usage and response to the media as a dynamic process, to be studied in context.* This process reveals development and change with time, with changing circumstances in the individual's life, and with changes in the position that the media occupy in society.

Kurt Lewin's dictum that nothing is as practical as a good theory is no less true for having been so frequently quoted. It applied with particular force at a time when television had not yet settled into a pattern, nor had society solidified its response. That the theoretical perspectives[4] derived from these studies have stood the test of time to a remarkable extent is, I believe, due to four reasons: (1) the stress in the research orientation on context and on the active role of the viewer; (2) the interdisciplinary approach used—the pioneer studies of Maccoby (1951) and Riley (1951) had alerted Schramm and me to the need for both a sociological and a psychological approach, requiring information about the child's background and schooling, as well as about his ability, adjustment, outlook, and needs; (3) the use of sufficiently large samples so that the effects of the characteristics could be studied singly and in interaction; and (4) the timing of the studies, which made it still possible to use a traditional research paradigm (matching viewers with controls),[5] supplemented in Britain and Japan by a before-and-after study from which causal inferences could be drawn.[6]

The British government even provided an "experimental variation." The opening of a second channel during the period of our research made it possible to compare viewers' behavior in a monopoly and a choice situation. Also, the relative novelty of the medium led to a degree of cooperation by teachers, parents, and children on a scale difficult to obtain today.[7]

Size of sample and, in the case of the British study, the emphasis on individual matching brought a further dividend for theory. A comparative analysis could be made not only of the television addict matched by age, sex, social class, and ability with someone who viewed less frequently but also of the controls of cinema addicts and of those who went to the cinema less frequently. In this way, generalizations concerning excessive use of a readily accessible medium could be developed (Himmelweit, 1958).

One might argue that in the case of Britain and Japan the before-and-after study alone would have been sufficient for teasing out causal relations. Still, a cross-sectional study was needed, in addition. We found that novelty tends to overlay individual differences when we did a comparative analysis of recent and established viewers (three or more years of availability of television in the home) and their controls. Also, since one cannot control who buys a set, a before-and-after study alone is unlikely to yield a sufficient number of cases for the influence of relevant characteristics (singly and in interaction) to make themselves felt.

I have selected for discussion five of the propositions or theories:[8]

1. The influences of television is the result of *two distinct types of effects: displacement effects* and *stimulation effects.* Stimulation effects are due to the content of television itself, minus the content of those activities or entertainments now less sampled.[9] The two types of effects may be orthogonal to one another; more often, they represent two ends of a continuum or they interact to produce a given effect. A play on television based on a book may increase the likelihood that the book will be read. Television in the British study reduced the demand for reading material similar in content—that is, for comics and for serials in women's magazines—but did not reduce overall time devoted to reading.

2. Certain types of activities are likely to be displaced: *The principle of functional equivalence* predicts that an entertainment or activity will be displaced by the newer one provided it serves the same needs as the established activity but does so more cheaply or conveniently. The distinction between objective and functional equivalence[10] is fundamental in this context, as is the notion that an activity can serve many needs. For this reason the displacement value of an activity can vary from individual to individual or, for the same individual, it can vary at different periods of his life.

It is important to bear in mind that this process is always in flux because of the interplay of four factors: (1) changes in the capabilities, needs, and interests of the user (especially changeable in the case of young people); (2) changes within the medium (such as the introduction of a new, more specialized, channel)—for example, good public broadcasting may, in the case of those who generally view little, increase the overall amount of viewing, not merely distribute it differently; (3) the close interdependence of the media—to survive, a medium has to become functionally dissimilar from the new medium to which it is losing clients; since media borrow each other's successes, this process is continuous,[11] accelerated by the technologies (for example, video cassettes) or by change in the availability of each medium (for example, in Britain a few years ago the government lifted its restriction on the number of hours a channel could broadcast); (4) changes in the availability or attractiveness of accessible alternatives, such as the opening of a swimming pool or a change in management of a youth club on the decline.[12]

Marginal or fringe activities will be reduced to make room for viewing. Leisure became more organized; television, despite its structured character and the many hours devoted to it, today may well represent such a marginal activity—a tap turned on upon coming home, more a habitual response than an enjoyed event. Television as mass entertainment is therefore vulnerable to reduction in the future.

3. *Viewing may be a choice behavior.* Schramm (1961) and Himmelweit (1958) suggest that the principles that apply in decision making are relevant. Schramm studied the ratio of expected reward to effort required; Himmelweit looked at a series of pulls toward and away from the medium, depending on the utility function of accessible alternatives. These utility functions include the needs these activities serve (see Schramm's [1961] extensive list, which includes escape, social reality testing, information seeking, and the like). Habit, home, neighborhood, and school exert facilitating or restraining influences. These considerations apply not only to how much the individual views and what is given up to make room for viewing but also to what the viewer chooses to view where choice exists. When the second channel was opened in Britain, it offered more attractive programs (western and crime) than did the British Broadcasting Corporation (BBC), yet the overall amount of viewing did not increase. Television's attractiveness was not sufficiently great to encroach further on other leisure pursuits. The second channel did, however, alter what children chose to view, since they could now switch from channel to channel in pursuit of favorites.

These data suggest that *choice reduces exposure to the novel* simply because the risk of turning to an untried program becomes greater where known attractive alternatives exist than where the choice, as in the one-channel situation, is between viewing and switching off. This fact explains the paradox that greater choice of channels often leads to greater sameness of diet.

To choose to spend time on viewing does not require, if our theory is correct, that television is liked, only that it is marginally more satisfying than other alternatives.

The increase in viewing reported recently is not in itself inconsistent with the reduction of enjoyment, noted by Bower (1973) for adults in the United States between 1963 and 1970, or for Britain between 1971 and 1975 as noted by the BBC Audience Research Department (1976). The BBC study points to a steady decline in overall satisfaction with television: the average index of satisfaction in 1975 was only a little over 40 (out of 100), compared with radio which has remained at 68. Radio used to be the tap that was turned on. Now it is more selectively used and apparently more enjoyed. One aspect of the choice behavior lies in the relative allocation of time between reading, the cinema, radio, and television. Schramm's typology of print versus television (1961) is an important one, as is his finding that, at a given age, hunger for material beyond the child's immediate experience makes the abler child consume all media more, while, at a later stage, the same hunger leads to decreased use of the stereotyped and predictable (for example, television) and to an increased use of print. Clearly, therefore, this balance depends on the content of the two media which might well change if books were to become so expensive to produce as to require a mass market, with cable television making the provision of minority programs economically viable.

Himmelweit's (1958) comparison of television addicts and of cinema addicts drawn from the controls showed that *absolute* amount of viewing is no indication of the role television plays in a particular child's life; to determine this role, one must consider viewing relative to the modal pattern for the child's age, sex, and ability group. Where viewing is excessive, it is a response to insufficient or inadequate peer or other interpersonal relations, and to tension or unhappiness. Increased environmental opportunities or lessening of tension, or both, led to reduced viewing, a further indication of the also-ran and multi-purpose uses including that of providing undemanding, vicarious companionship, to which television is put.

4. *Under certain principles, a medium is likely to have maximal impact on outlook and values.*[13] In the late sixties, we carried out a study of the social and personality factors associated with taste for televison programs among 10- and 11-year-old children (Harper, Munro, Himmelweit, 1970). The television fan[14] who liked everything he or she viewed was like the television addict studied ten years earlier, when we had measured amount of viewing, not enjoyment. Any excessive involvement with the medium relative to that of the viewer's age and ability group may be an indicator of immaturity and poor adjustment.

Displacement effects could be predicted on the basis of decision theory; the principles are those which apply to the process of socialization, generally making it virtually impossible to single out the impact of any one influence or socializing agent over the impact of others. When we engage in discussions about the effects of television violence, we must consistently recall that to have found any consistent trend across studies is already remarkable. The difficulty of testing general principles about television's influence on values, outlook, and information is the ready circularity into which it leads us: How much an individual views and what he or she chooses to view, especially of entertainment programs, is also an expression of the viewer's needs and outlook. While this problem is readily recognized in political campaigns, it applies equally to exposure to entertainment programs. Thus the forced-feeding paradigm (enforcing a restricted diet on viewers) adopted by Feshback and Singer (1971) is not an adequate solution, nor are the laboratory studies in which the influence is tested almost immediately.

The situation that existed in Britain in the fifties provided one of the last opportunities for examining the role of television on outlook, through comparison of viewers and matched controls. Four conditions are needed for maximum impact to occur: (1) The subject needs to be emotionally ready for the message to impinge on his awareness. (2) His or her attitudes and views should be as yet relatively unformed, that is, not already firmly shaped through the more powerful direct socializing influences of school, home, and neighborhood.[15] (3) The values need to be repeatedly presented, preferably in dramatic and implicit rather than explicit form. (We termed this the principle of the *drip effect,* unnoticable at first until at a given time cognitive and attitudinal restructuring occurred [Feather, 1971]). (4) The setting needs to be such that emotional identification becomes easy.

The fewer the alternatives sources of information and the greater the consistency of existing information, the stronger the influence will be. Parents, teachers, and peers—the entire personal influence network— carry greater sway than do the media. Impact will therefore vary depending on the child and the setting. Striking in the early studies was the extent to which, where personal experience was lacking, television's choreography and implicit values were learned and introjected.

Asked for a description of a living room of an ordinary family, children drew on their personal experiences; when asked to describe that of a rich family, they drew on the emblems of wealth traditionally displayed in television drama.[16] Similarly, when asked to describe a Frenchman or a German, they chose the manner in which these people were identified and presented on television. The Frenchman was seen as lighthearted and gay (viewed during the Maurice Chevalier era), the German as cruel (during the era of films about the Nazis).

Television will have a maximal impact on viewers' perceptions of outgroups, depending on whether evaluative descriptions are given or implied. But both fiction and news programs tend to use evaluative adjectives, the latter because only conflict or disaster makes a group or category of persons newsworthy. Thus much of the concern about, for example, the media's presentation of labor–management relations or about the presentation of minority groups is justifiable.

I contend that in the absence of contrary information, persistent labeling by the media will create attitudes about people and events which, once formed, will become part of the individual's value orientation and then may be as difficult to dislodge as those values acquired through personal experience. Some may consider this view an exaggerated one. I do not, particularly with regard to children who, with fewest alternative resources, view up to six hours a day. Their view of society comes from television. For this reason, Gerbner's (1976) content analyses are so important for understanding the culture to which the child is exposed.

5. *The distinction between reality and fantasy is effected.* Schramm (1961), fully aware of the complexity of the problem, found that analyzing content with regard to reality or fantasy yielded a number of insights: for instance, he found a relation of interest in reality to cognitive maturity and to home and school influences. Although fantasy throughout was preferred to reality, Schramm showed, as did Harper (1970), a relatively greater withdrawal into fantasy to be characteristic of children for whom, due to social or psychological factors, daily life offered few rewards. Sophistication in analysis has

grown considerably in this area over the years. Distinctions might be drawn at many levels. First, the ability exists to distinguish between the real and the fictional (Leifer, 1975). Further, differences occur due to presentation, with the dramatic often underplayed where it is real, as in the news, and emphasized (even underlined through music) where it is fiction. In that case, are we dealing with different levels of arousal (Tannenbaum, 1974)? Does the knowledge that a situation is true more than compensate for its undramatic presentation? Further, does this factor vary depending on the sophistication of the viewer or on the reinforcement that the real is given through newspapers, conversations, and so on? What is retained longer? What do we mean by impact or influence in this context: precise knowledge, the understanding of an event in broad outline, or the creation or reinforcement of an attitude or belief?

Peterson and Thurstone (1933) showed that attitudes to war (that is, to the reality of war) were affected by the presentation of fictional films about war. This effect is not surprising, considering that much of drama is based on arousing emotion as an aid to reconstruction of the social reality through identification and analogy (as in the plays of Bertolt Brecht). One or two attempts have been made in the research literature to distinguish between the influence of the real and the fictional, but much more needs to be done, preferably not by immediate recall but by the study of influence over time in environments designed to reinforce or modify. The school setting, experimentally varied, could be used for that purpose rather than as now, only for the presentation of the initial stimulus. Suffice it to say that this aspect gets at the very heart of what constitutes symbolic representation of society, or what Peter Hall, the director of the British National Theatre, describes as "the plastic reality of television." According to him, news is also presented in a plastic format. The efforts of Leifer (1975) to develop children's abilities to distinguish between the real and the fictional are important, but they need to be coupled with a detailed study of the differential impact, if any, that results from such distinction.

We already know that small children, apart from their inability to distinguish between the real and the fictional, respond to isolated familiar incidents of a story. Given their stage of cognitive development, the impact of a program must of necessity be different from that on a child for whom the same episodes represent part of the tapestry that makes up the theme.

The principles outlined above, governing media usage and its influence on attitudes, provide useful guidelines. A subtler analysis of the content of what is offered is now needed, and a relationship of it to an equally subtle analysis of types of social influence and their interaction. Gerbner's work (1976) points the way and should be linked to advances made in the understanding of people's cognitive maps, and the way in which these relate to attitudes and beliefs (Fishbein and Ajzen, 1975; Moscovici, 1972).

PART 2: A LONGITUDINAL STUDY OF MEDIA USAGE AND TASTE

The longitudinal study was an offshoot of a larger study aimed at charting the influence of different socializing experience (home, school and later higher education, work, and marriage) on educational and job attainments, adolescent and adult outlook and personality (Himmelweit and Swift, 1969, 1972). A total of 365 middle- and working-class adolescents from two different types of secondary schools[17] were reinterviewed eleven years after the original study, and 246 of them were interviewed again twenty years later (in 1970) when they were aged 33 to 24. The study obtained information about background, educational and occupational history, relation to family and peers, and measures of personality and outlook at these three points in time.[18] These measures, more comprehensive than is customary in media studies, provided a good opportunity for examining the interaction between social or context, and psychological or need, factors and the extent to which such interaction varied depending on the user, the medium, and its content.

The following measures of media, usage, and taste were obtained from the subject as adolescent and adult. In adolescence, frequency of cinema visits and number of books and comics read were evaluated. From questions about leisure activities and about the content of comics, books, films, and radio programs, three taste indices were computed, reflecting taste across media: (1) liking for strong stimulation (with the emphasis on adventure and violence); (2) "highbrow" taste;[19] and (3) liking for sport (as participant and spectator). At age 24 to 25, the measures consisted of frequency of television viewing, cinema visits, and number of books read; of enjoyment of reading and television as well as two favorite television programs (these questions were repeated at age 33). In addition, based on a factor analysis of answers to a questionnaire about sixty different types of book, we obtained three measures of reading taste: taste for the serious and "highbrow," for the technical, and for thrillers. The research orientation was the same as the discussed in Part 1. The availability of multivariate statistical computer programs permitted better tests of the propositions than had been possible in the late fifties.[20]

Fourteen principles were formulated, some stemming directly from the earlier work, others from findings of the longitudinal study itself, which will require confirmation from other samples. These principles concern the place of the media in leisure; perceptions of the media and their value; the relative importance of background, intelligence, outlook, and personality in influencing usage and taste, and their continuity across time. I shall draw attention only to some main issues and their implications for policy and research.

As in the early studies, media—though much used—were part of the background of the leisure life of the subjects in adolescence and in adulthood. The foreground was occupied by activities in which the individual was more actively involved such as sport or hobbies, or those activities that satisfied needs for companionship and interaction.

Heavy use of the popular, "on-tap" medium of the day was characteristic of those with fewest resources—that is, those with lower ability, nonselective schooling, and a working-class background. The on-tap medium in adolescence for which we had any measures was the cinema (we did not think it possible to obtain accurate measures of amount of listening to the radio). In adult life, it was television. The unmarried of both classes spent little time at home and so viewed little. Once a subject married, viewing increased, particularly among the working class, especially the unskilled, but relatively little among the middle class. In the middle class, varied and home-centered interest had been built up in adolescence so that television did not take over as easily.

High ability, good education, and a middle-class environment led to selective use of the popular medium. Within similar ability and educational groups, personality and outlook influenced usage and taste. Gregariousness and low need achievement predisposed individuals toward the medium aimed at mass audiences. Adjustment had an impact in both periods, the less well-adjusted tending to seek escape in strong stimulation (thrillers). High interest in achievement resulted in a turning away form the popular medium in adolescence. In adult life, the interest in achievement was related to interest in news, information, documentaries, and books which informed. A positive outlook and a nonauthoritarian view of society were each associated with high interest in varied, demanding, or factual material, while those who saw themselves as powerless preferred stereotyped material: thrillers and light fiction.

These factors together suggest a continuum, at the one end of which is success, adjustment, and a positive outlook and at the other end of which is withdrawal, lack of success, and maladjusted passivity. The more positive subjects were selective in the material they viewed or read, while the unsuccessful and more passive ones seemed to retreat into the media, using the least demanding part of what they offer. The picture presented represents ideal types and needs to be seen against the background of the varied tastes of our subjects.

The medium most on tap—television, for example—was the least enjoyed. Only 12 percent of the subjects as adults enjoyed television very much compared with 55 percent who claimed to enjoy reading very much, a marked difference even allowing for the halo effect that surrounds reading, and the guilt about frequent viewing noted by Steiner (1963), Furu (1971), and Himmelweit (1976). Television viewing, even among those brought up without it, appears to have become a habit which, rather like bland food, evoked no strong reaction of any kind.

The relationship between usage and enjoyment of television and reading threw light on the way television was used. Those bored by reading spent more time viewing than those who enjoyed books, but they enjoyed television no more. Indeed those who watched little television were more clear-cut in their program likes and dislikes than were those who viewed a great deal.

The search for a fit between the contexts of one's life and one's needs and the media continues from early childhood until old age. Changes in preferences provide valuable insights into changing needs in the course of the life cycle. Adolescent tastes, like leisure tastes in general, were centered on the adventurous and the exciting and on sport. Taste for strong stimulation showed itself particularly in heavy comic reading but also in the subjects' preferences in books and films. In adult life, tastes became more differentiated and shifted from fantasy to reality. As adults, the men were more interested in technical and nonfiction books than in westerns and detective stories. On television, news, documentaries, and sports programs were their favorites rather than thrillers and westerns. As television became established, use of it as a main news source and trust in its reporting, relative to radio, increased dramatically between 1962 and 1970.

Media create as well as reflect tastes, for both adults and children. For this reason, tastes in a single medium are little guide to an individual's wider interests, particularly where the content of a medium is narrowly focussed, as in the case of material provided for adolescents with its heavy diet of adventure and excitement. Nor are tastes within a single medium stable.

So far we have demonstrated with a different sample, at a different period, and with a different media mix, the validity of the propositions outlined in Part 1. In trying to explain usage and taste, we need first to know the stage of cognitive development the individual has reached, then the type of environment in which the subject lives. Outlook and personality play a part at the second level of explanation, their contribution varying depending on the taste.[21] We have also demonstrated the importance of interaction effects between social and personality factors.

The above analyses were necessary to establish the nature of adolescent and adult media behavior. We now turn to the question of prediction. How far were tastes and usage in adolescence precursors of adult media behavior? It is worth recalling that the time span between interviews is eleven years and that we predicted from radio, film, and books to reading preferences and to viewing and television tastes. The findings are clear: Both positive and significant correlations occur across time.

The adolescents who favored the cinema—the most popular medium of the pre-television era—tended as adults to be the most heavy users of television, the medium that supplanted the cinema in popularity and easy availability. This fact strikingly demonstrates the principle of *functional equivalence*. Despite their objective equivalence, no correlation existed between cinema going at the two points in time.

In three distinct areas, adolescent tastes carried over to adult tastes in books, newspapers, and television. These areas were: preference for *"highbrow"* content (the serious, literary and informative, which implies both liking for, and skills in, coping with cognitively difficult content); preference for *strong stimulation*[22] (enjoyment of adventure and violence); and liking for *sport*.[23] These relationships across time held even when the effects of background, schooling, education, and occupation were partialled out.

Adolescent taste was not simply another way of expressing background and outlook; if so, then it would add nothing to the prediction of adult media behavior over and above social and outlook factors.

However, the multiple regression analyses showed that media behavior in adolescence had an independent effect. When adolescent tastes were added to social and outlook variables, the percentage variance for the frequency of reading as an adult increased from 14 percent to 20 percent; for liking of highbrow books from 12 percent to 14 percent, and for thrillers, from 9 percent to 11 percent. These increases are small but consistent.

Television favorites at age 24 to 25 were predicted as well by measures of adolescent tastes as by data about social background, outlook, and personality factors as an adult. Interestingly, the attitude as adult to the policy issue of cutting down on violence on television was predicted as well by adolescent measures (with taste for strong stimulation playing an important role) as by measures of outlook and relevant social data obtained at age 25.

Prediction across eight years from tastes in adult life at age 24 to 25 to age 32 to 33 showed a similar pattern of influences. Television favorites at age 32 to 33 were best predicted ($R^2 = .18$) from a combination of television favorites, reading habits and preferences at age 24 to 25, and tastes at age 13 to 14. Tastes from each development stage made a significant and independent contribution.

The evidence strongly suggests that during a critical period in adolescence, some children are attracted to or learn to like media content and leisure pursuits that are more demanding and more varied than the normative, age–culture preferences of their peers. Further, irrespective of subsequent educational attainment and occupational status, which may reinforce them, such tastes have continuity over time.

The study also has implications for gratification research. Through its historical perspective, it points to some of the environmental factors which influence not only choice behavior but also the significance of the choices. Those which deviate from typical choices made by others of similar age and position in society tell us more about satisfaction of deep-seated individual needs than do normative choices.

The study's historical perspective also emphasizes that not all individuals have access to the full range of media content, nor the same opportunity to select other activities which might gratify their needs better than the on-tap medium (television). Gratifications, therefore, must be assessed in the light of what alternatives are effectively within the individual's reach—that is, those which form part of that individual's repertoire of leisure pursuits.

The study has implications for the strategy of media research. It illustrates the advantage and problems of studying individuals *in depth* rather than merely in large numbers. Through a longitudinal approach, we can establish the importance of past experiences, estimate the independent effect of past media behavior over and above past socializing experiences, and examine the extent to which a medium creates preferences as well as reflects existing normative tastes.

Hopefully this study will be the first of many longitudinal studies; perhaps reliable media questions (tested for their suitability for different age groups) may be built up which could be added to suitable longitudinal studies carried out for other purposes. Wilbur Schramm was certainly correct in saying that it is important to collect a great deal of data about the same individual. These data are indeed of value, provided they cover social data, measures of ability and education, and personality orientation and outlook. They should also contain the subject's reactions to several media, for only in juxtaposition can the significance of each factor be assessed.

The results also have policy implications. For parents and educators, they point to the importance of education in the skilled use of leisure time, including leisure time spent at home. For television producers, the study results imply that more can be done with the medium than is being done. They often fail to understand that; by offering so much that is stereotyped, they have encouraged the use of television merely to pass the time, leading the active and forward-looking in particular to spend time on things which provide more challenge.

PART 3: RESEARCH POSSIBILITIES AND NEEDS

In Parts 1 and 2, I have indicated certain research directions, emphasizing the importance of obtaining a great deal of data about each boy and girl. These data would include information about each child's personality, cognitive style, and needs, and about his or her relation to the main socializing agents of family, school, and peers.

By contrast with studies of adults, which by-and-large have followed an epidemiological model using representative samples and are primarily concerned with prevalence and its variation across populations and time, studies with children have focussed on *process*. They have tended to be more theoretically oriented, drawing on theories of child development, notably those of Piaget (1953) and Bruner (1966) and, more recently, on theories of cognitive social psychology (Harvey, 1967; Bieri, 1966; McGuire, 1973). I do not intend to present a list of research priorities—the reader is referred to the list prepared by Comstock (1975), based on his evaluation and that of researchers in the field. Instead I should like to discuss some broader implications that would follow if closer links than now exist were established between research done on adults and that done on children, between research on instructional and on general broadcasting, and between communication research and the social sciences on which it draws.

First, I should like to bury once and for all the distinction so frequently made between policy- and theory-oriented research (Comstock, 1975). Such a distinction is meaningless, but it is harmful to the field. I can think of no useful policy-oriented research that does not build on existing theories or attempt new formulations, nor of any theory-oriented research that has no potential implication for policy. The media are powerful institutions which, like the public they serve, influence and are influenced by what happens in society. Like other organizations, what they offer, how they offer it, and how it is received changes over time. The period that elapses between the commissioning of research and its completion may coincide with changed circumstances which make the need for the research less urgent.

The history of the British study reported in Part 1 is a case in point. The BBC had asked the Nuffield Foundation to sponsor a study, stressing that it would take note of its recommendations. By the time the study was reported, the scene had changed dramatically; none of the recommendations were implemented because they might have adversely affected what had become the overriding priority—namely, to stand up to the competition of the second channel which had come into existence after the study had begun. Under the circumstances this policy research, as any other, should correctly have been planned to provide a conceptual model of relevant parameters and their interaction. Only in this way can policy-makers be provided with the tools to monitor the present and, more important, to rehearse likely effects if changes in one or another parameter were to be introduced.

This view, once taken, has implications for the conduct of policy research, shifting the focus from prevalence to process. For example, both Himmelweit (1958) and Schramm (1961) saw television as a competitor among other leisure pursuits for the child's time and involvement. This view required asking as many questions about other leisure activities as about television since only by juxtaposition could television's role and influence be understood—that is, the shift from concern with particular findings to a conceptual model required the original objectives to be redefined within a broader framework. But the same is true for theory-oriented research, as for example in the case of Tannenbaum's (1974) propositions that the effects of programs of violence depend more on their excitatory quality than on their content.

With increased specialization, research on children has tended to use a different conceptual framework from that used in research on adults—partly because studies of children have been done primarily with a psychological orientation, building on theories of child development, while studies of adults tend to have a more sociological slant. While specialization is unavoidable in practice, I should like to see more cross-fertilization through borrowing of each other's perspectives and through doing research on the same programs with both adults and children. Broadcasters, after all, provide a rare opportunity, hard to come by in the social sciences, where adults and children of different ages voluntarily select and often enjoy the same stimuli. Let me give two examples. In the program series "All in the Family," itself an offshoot of the original British program "Till Death Do Us Part," socially disapproved hostile sentiments against certain groups within society are expressed as are taboo racialist statements. Indeed, were these remarks made in earnest—that is, not in fictional programs— they might in Britain well offend against the Race Relations Act which forbids statements designed to incite hatred against racial groups. The intention of the producers is clear: By showing, through the reactions of other members of the family within the program, that the character who makes these statements is bigoted, the producers intend to make the viewer more critical of the holders of such views, and possibly more aware of his or her own prejudices. The study on these programs done in Britain (BBC Audience Research Report, 1973), and those done in the United States by Vidmar and Rokeach (1974), Surlin and Tate (1976), Brigham and Giesbrecht (1976), as well as the study in Holland by Wilhoit and de Bock (1976), teach us much about the conditions under which the intended discount or reversal occurs. The majority of studies were done on adults; Vidmar and Rokeach's included adolescents.

I should like to see such a program studied across the age groups, not only because of its social significance, but because it involves a relatively complex intellectual operation. In the case of adults, little learning occurred; the program served to reinforce existing attitudes, including the prejudice of those so disposed (thus confirming the famous study by Cooper and Jahoda [1947]). The situation may be very different with younger children whose attitudes about outgroups may not yet have been formed and whose ability to separate source from message may not be highly developed. If such a study were done, I should like to see it examine the impact on the parents and their offspring, drawing on children not only of different ages, but also those who come from homes differing in the type of discussion that takes place between parents and children (Chaffee and McCleod, 1972) and also in the racial attitudes held by the parents. A carefully planned study of this kind would not only extend the knowledge of the broadcasters as to the impact of their program, but would in turn contribute to our understanding of cognitive development.

The second example is rather different: In a recent as-yet-unpublished study, we show that the images of Britain which adults hold (examined by means of semantic differentials) are far more differentiated than their images of France or Germany—that is, proximity or personal knowledge leads to the making of finer distinctions that in the case of issues about which personal experience is lacking. For children, compared with adults, more situations or issues shown on television, whether in the news or in fictional programs, have no counterpart in their everyday experience. As part of the longitudinal study discussed in Part 2, we showed that in adolescence, fewer gradations occurred in the subjects' responses and more agreement with positively worded authoritarian statements, compared with answers to the same questions given by the subjects as adults. At adulthood, the above differences due to intelligence, pronounced in adolescence, had disappeared (Himmelweit and Swift, 1971). At first, we saw this result as one further example of the growth with age of the ability to handle cognitive complexity. However, when we contrasted the adolescents' replies to attitude statements about home and school with those about the wider society (of which the authoritarian statements were one instance) in the former case there were neither differences due to intellectual ability nor a tendency to agree with positively worded statements. That is, we were witnessing in adolescence precisely the same process which we had demonstrated among adults in the comparative study of the images of Britain and other countries. Television, particularly where it displays the same themes repeatedly, may increase familiarity with situations and issues beyond the child's immediate environment.

I should like to see studies of adults and children of different ages to see how far such discrimination occurs in describing or evaluating the behavior and values portrayed in television programs, and how far this varies depending on the frequency with which the programs are shown and viewed—that is, to what extent, irrespective of subject matter, does television provide an extension of experience that would show itself in subtler evaluations than might be expected on the basis of age, leading additionally to a reduction of differences due to ability? Such a study would be one way of examining the extent to which broadcasting "teaches" not in terms of information gained but in terms of increased differentiation. A study is required in which differentiation of the familiar—the immediate environment which offers first-hand experience—is contrasted with that reflected in the children's replies which draw on the content of television programs.

Essentially, broadcasting acts as a potential socializing agent for both adults and children. After all, socialization continues throughout an individual's life. In many instances, both one's birth and the manner of one's dying are influenced by cultural norms and expectations. Psychologists like Bandura (1969), Kohlberg (1969), Erikson (1959), and others have suggested ways in which social learning occurs: Cognitive maps are drawn and redrawn, and changes in perception, evaluation, and behavior take place. Because broadcasting is only one of the socializing agents, its influence will vary with the topic, the manner of its exposition, and the way in which the subject relates to broadcasting. A kind of *systems approach* is required, one with which research on instructional broadcasting is far more familiar than are researchers of broadcasting received in the home. For this reason, I should like to see increased collaboration between the two branches of research. In the case of instructional television, the role that the school system plays, the contrast between style of teaching of the broadcast and that of the teacher, and any follow-up lessons are all elements which have been shown to enhance, modify, and nullify the influence of the broadcast itself.

Wilbur Schramm's brilliant pioneer researches in this field in the United States, and indeed in different parts of the globe, which have been continued by his colleagues, testify to the value of this approach. In one study, in Colorado, Schramm showed that the same television program teaching Spanish yielded quite different results, depending on whether the teachers who were doing the follow-up lessons enjoyed teaching (this variable turned out to be the most significant, since neither teacher nor pupil knew Spanish). Furthermore, when volunteer teachers developed their own follow-up lessons, the greatest gains in knowledge were made, even though the techniques they used differed widely. In this example, the relevant components in the system were varied and their influence was examined. Such a systems approach helps explain the success of "Sesame Street" with American children and its rather striking lack of success, despite adaptations, when it was tried on Mexican children.

The need for a fit between content and pace of a program and the culture in which the child lives is powerfully brought home. But for general television, as well, the impact will vary depending on the fit between what is viewed and what is experienced in the immediate environment. In this area, too, field studies could be done using the teacher as experimenter. Taking "All in the Family" as an example again, I should like to see field studies in which the prior preparation and subsequent discussion of such a program by the teachers were systematically varied and its influence on different age groups examined. At one extreme, the teacher might simply encourage discussion after the series is completed; at the other, the teacher might underline the ridiculous or bigoted character of Archie Bunker to see how far this emphasis influences recall, evaluation, and acceptance of his statements. Since the program is viewed at home, the family's attitude to the program and to the outgroups attacked in it ought also to be ascertained. Because the series has a similar approach, though changing the outgroup under attack, intervention could be studied either at the beginning, after the first program, or later in the series.

Similarly, teachers could be used, this time by bringing television programs into the school, to study the effect of labeling a program. The introduction of the same program could be varied systematically to examine how far the relative influence of content or the induction of a prior mental set varies with the topic and the age of the child.

My intention in citing these examples is not to provide an exhaustive list of what might be done but to illustrate how much could be learned about the impact of what is presented by the broadcasters by systematically varying the other relevant parameters which we know to have a bearing. This approach is very similar to the one discussed in Part 1, where we showed that the role of television could be understood only when juxtaposed with other competing leisure activities. We are again extending the argument and suggesting that the impact of a program or a program series can be understood only by juxtaposing it with other influences which bear on the child, except that, in this case, experimental variations can more readily be introduced.

I should like to take this argument one step further. For some reason, communication researchers have been preoccupied with examining the impact of television and with carrying out research aimed at increasing any positive and reducing any harmful effects. But more work needs to be done, if—unlike the children in the late fifties and early sixties who spent between two and three hours viewing—children of today, especially in the United States, may spend between four to six hours of their free time in front of the screen. While the original studies stressed the importance of displacement as well as stimulation effects, the tide in the intervening years has been in the direction of examining the effects of content—that is, the stimulation effects. I believe we need to go back to displacement effects and examine, possibly by repeating some aspects of these earlier studies, how and why children spend so much time in front of the screen. To devote time to viewing requires not that viewing is enjoyed, but only that it is marginally more liked, or less disliked, than other ways of occupying one's time. If, in most households, a child coming into the home turns the television set on, or finds it already on with members of the family watching, we should therefore ask not why do children view, but why do they *not* view? What are the other competing interests? I should like to see an ecological study, in the mode of Barker's, in which the behavior of children once home from school is observed, including the extent to which television, and also radio, is treated as background that can become figure when a favorite program comes on or when some noise or other incident arouses momentary interest. Do children talk about what they see during or after the program? Do they do other things while viewing? Do they become emotionally involved? Do they refer to the programs at some later stage? Or do they treat television as a kaleidoscope, shaken by someone else, which presents from time-to-time a picture that gives pleasure, arouses fear, or creates involvement?

If the figures of between four to six hours' viewing are accurate—and good figures are difficult to come by—it is unlikely that this practice constitutes a healthy way to grow up. We already know that an excess of vitamins, so good when taken in small doses, can harm; a television diet has none of the vitamins' potential health-giving properties.[24] Consumed in excess, a steady diet of television viewing may do harm, not because of its stimulation but because of its displacement effects. After all, television can provide only vicarious experience and may reduce, because of the time it involves, direct interaction with peers and others, or the experience presented by the challenge of sports or other activities. It may also offer too easy a withdrawal from problems that need to be faced.

It seems to me, therefore, incumbent on communication researchers to concern themselves with understanding what factors in the child's environment make—within a given social class, ability, and age group—for lesser, rather than greater, viewing. We should look for variations in viewing, not only in terms of the usual indicators of age, ability, and social class, but within these parameters to the variations due to the facilities provided by the neighborhood. Comparative field studies should be carried out in which places are selected which are known to have differing provision in extramural activities organized by the school or in opportunities provided by climate, landscape, or other sources.

I must add a brief comment about further areas where promising work has begun but where a more comprehensive and concerted effort is needed. The work on visual literacy begun by Gaby Salomon (1973) encompasses the understanding not only of the methods of production but also the learning of discrimination and the understanding of perspective, gradients, and movement through frequent viewing.

Studies are also being done with regard to the relation of television content as ''symbolic culture'' to its effects on the viewer. Gerbner, who coined the phrase, has done the important pioneer work with adults; he shows, for instance, that the frequency with which certain situations or trades occur in television programs led to a similar estimation of their frequency in real life—that is, a direct translation from the world of fiction to that of reality. In the case of children, this aspect would also be worth studying but an even more important study would be that of the progression in comprehension that occurs with age: from the understanding of isolated incidents to that of theme or plot, and from an understanding of the action to that of motivation, causes, and consequences. Likely this progression occurs in some regular relationship, with cognitive maturity, family background, and familiarity with the program or its genre playing a part. We know little about the relative contribution of each of these factors, singly or in interaction.

For those concerned with cognitive development, the study of children's comprehension—immediate and delayed—of television programs provides many challenging research opportunities. What makes television so suitable for such a study is its visual element, which makes it far more independent than is verbal material (whether read or spoken) of the limits imposed by the child's vocabulary which, in turn, is so dependent on social background, age, and ability. Disadvantaged children spend more time viewing than do children from more advantaged homes. We ought to find ways of studying how far this fact has led to greater knowledge and understanding of the motivation of characters and of the workings of institutions which are so frequently portrayed on television. I am concerned not with how far such presentation matches real life (as is implied in some of Gerbner's work) but in seeing how correct the viewers' understanding is of what is offered on television. If repeated exposure on television to information leads to greater differentiation, this might emerge when comparing accounts of those who view a great deal with those who view little, provided always that subjects are matched by age and ability.

Broadcasting and books represent important aspects of a country's culture. The continuing neglect by teachers of the fare provided by television is indefensible. No one would let children loose in a library without seeking to inform them or to help them find books which stretch rather than restrict imagination and enrich rather than impoverish. Yet I do not know many teachers who feel impelled to do the same as far as children's viewing is concerned, rarely informing when some outstanding performance or event takes place.

Finally, I must add two more comments. The study of communication, as Schramm has frequently pointed out, is not a discipline but an important field of inquiry which draws for its strength on the advances made in psychology, sociology, political science, and literature. That those working in the field do not become too specialized, talking mainly to one another and publishing solely in their own specialist journals, is important, therefore. Great effort must be made to form strong links between research institutes and the relevant university departments. That scholars move in and out of the field is also important. All parties would benefit from such exchange.

Finally, I feel a need for more active collaboration between broadcasters, or the makers of programs, and researchers. It is absurd that we cannot draw on the experienced producer for the development of different versions of programs systematically varied to test our predictions about conditions favoring comprehension, modeling, or attitude change. For many years, broadcasters and researchers have met in combat rather than partnership, an understandable situation given the industry and its pressures. I should like to see us move to a new partnership where some producers become interested in the challenge that our research requirements offer and would be prepared to make programs suited to our needs, which, unlike our homemade efforts, would bear the hallmark of the creativity that is a producer's trade.

NOTES

1. The British study had been published before we learned of the American research. Likewise, Schramm first learned of the British inquiries when his study was already well advanced. Today crossnational communication has fortunately increased a great deal.
2. Increased availability of cable television will allow a massive increase in choice of channels as well as video cassettes and discs. Printed material will be projected on the screen; prototypes of up to 100 continuously updated pages are being shown in Britain today, with the viewer dialing the page he wishes to read.
3. The British researchers faced the additional problem that when they accepted the assignment, they had neither television at home nor had viewed regularly.
4. For a summary of these theoretical perspectives, see introduction and chapter 9 in Schramm, chapters 8 and 9 in Furu, and chapters 3, 21, and 35 in Himmelweit, whose chapter 36 deals with implications for social and child psychology.
5. Matching in Britain was done on an individual basis: A child with television at home was matched with one of the same age, sex, ability, and social background who had no set and little access to television elsewhere. A factorial design of forty-eight cells using equal numbers was used: Each cell comprised a treatment versus a control group. Within each group were two social class, two age, two sex, and three ability groups.
6. In a medium-sized British town before television was due, all school children aged 10 to 11 and 13 to 14 were tested; a year later, all those whose families had since acquired a set were reexamined along with a matched control group—an expensive but rewarding exercise. In the first wave, 2,200 children were tested, yielding a year later less than 10 percent, or 185 matched pairs.
7. In Britain, 4,500 children in five regions each completed for one week a daily diary of how they spent their time after school on each previous day; during the second week, they kept a diary of viewing and listening. In addition, each child was tested for about seven hours—that is, three school mornings were given over to the study, and teachers provided data from the records and carved out comparative ratings of performance and behavior of the television pupils and their controls. Matching within classrooms by age, sex, social background, and IQ yielded 1,854 pairs of matched viewers and controls.
8. The word *theory* seems very loosely used these days; at best, some of the work in communication research constitutes middle-range theory. Since

terminology is subject to fashions, I leave the reader to choose the formulation most to his or her liking.

9. Supposing television replaces reading; its stimulation effect then depends on the content of the television diet and on the book or comic diet displaced or reduced.

10. For the 10- to 11-year-old, television was the equivalent of free cinema at home, so he or she cut down on cinema visits; not so the 13- to 14-year-old, for whom cinema was also the place for dating and was useful as a means for getting away from home. Radio listening, however, was functionally equivalent for both, and so sharply reduced. For a fuller discussion, see Himmelweit (1958, p. 363).

11. The film industry, for instance, responded at that time by concentrating on intimate analysis of character and also on large-scale biblical spectaculars. Today films become increasingly horrific and pornographic. Both types of films would be difficult to show on television; both gain some of their impact from the wide screen. Women's magazines have cut down on serials (demand for which was well catered for by television) and increased their information content.

12. Even in the heady days when television first became available, few children mentioned in their daily diaries television or any of the other media as their more enjoyed leisure activity.

13. Himmelweit (1958), chapters 17–21.

14. For each of sixty programs, the subject was asked to indicate how much he had liked those he had viewed (on a 5-point scale). An index of overall attitude to television was calculated by dividing the sum of ratings of all programs by the number viewed.

15. In their evaluation of the prestige of jobs, the 13- to 14-year-old were influenced, not the 11-year-olds, while a reduction in prejudiced attitudes about foreigners was found only in the younger age groups. The older ones had already relatively well-articulated attitudes, which rendered them immune to the implicit values conveyed by television drama and news.

16. Chandeliers, drink cabinets, and so on.

17. In Britain's divided secondary school system, the ablest 20 percent are selected for grammar school education which provides, compared with the nonselective secondary modern school, a more academic curriculum, requiring more homework; its pupils stay longer at school and go on to white-collar jobs, or obtain further education. The effects of ability can therefore be examined only in interaction with different school environments.

18. Measures of neuroticism, gregariousness, academic achievement orientation, authoritarianism, and preferences for change rather than the status quo. The same types of measures were obtained for the subject as adult except that achievement orientation now covered success goals, and the measure of forward looking outlook included both preference for change and a feeling of being in control of one's life rather than powerless to influence events.

19. "Highbrow" in relation to a 13- to 14-year-olds refers to liking for serious, "adult" content in books, magazines, radio, films, and so forth.
20. By means of analysis of variance, metric and nonmetric regression and path analyses.
21. In the case of sport, for instance, the adolescent's background or the type of school attended counted for little; the well adjusted and gregarious, not the academically inclined, proved the keenest. In the case of "highbrow" taste, background and ability accounted for most of the variance with academic orientation adding relatively little—that is, this type of taste requires stimulation through home and school. Taste for strong stimulation was normative for boys attending nonselective schools and coming from working-class homes. Among groups where such tastes were less frequent, the liking of strong stimulation was related to a particular outlook (antiachievement) and a high level of tension.
22. The cross-time correlation was almost exclusively due to the able grammar school boys for whom such tastes had been an expression of personality needs.
23. For example, taste for sport in adolescence correlated .31 and .25 with the selection of sports programs as their favorites at age 25 and 33, respectively.
24. Even if the prosocial programs were to have an impact, for this impact to be lasting requires that the model behavior needs to be practiced and then reinforced by its own success.

REFERENCES

Bandura, A. "Social-learning Theory of Identificatory Processes." In D. A. Goslin (ed.), *Handbook of socialization theory and research.* Chicago: Rand McNally, 1969.

Bieri, J. "Cognitive Complexity and Personality Development." In O. J. Harvey (ed.), *Experience, Structure and Adaptability.* New York: Springer, 1966.

Bower, R. *Television and the Public.* New York: Holt, Rinehart & Winston, 1973.

Brigham, J. C., and L. W. Giesbrecht. "'All in the Family:' Racial Attitudes." *Journal of Communication, 26,* Autumn, 1976.

British Broadcasting Corporation. "'Till Death Us Do Part' as Anti-prejudice Propaganda," *Audience Research Report,* March, 1973.

British Broadcasting Corporation. Audience Research Department. *BBC Audience Research Findings Annual Review,* 1974/5.

Bruner, J. S., R. R. Olver, and P. M. Greenfield. *Studies in Cognitive Growth.* New York: Wiley, 1966.

Chaffee, S. H., and J. M. McLeod. "Adolescent Television Use in the Family Context." In G. A. Comstock and E. A. Rubinstein (eds.), *Television and Social Behavior, vol. III: Television and Adolescent Aggressiveness.* Washington D.C.: U.S. Government Printing Office, 1972.

Comstock, G. *Television and Human Behavior: The Key Studies.* Santa Monica, Calif.: The Rand Corporation, 1975.

Comstock, G., and G. Lindsey. *Television and Human Behavior: The Research Horizon, Future and Present.* Santa Monica, Calif.: The Rand Corporation, R-1748-CF, 1975 (b).

Cooper, E., and M. Jahoda. "The Evasion of Propaganda: How Prejudiced People Respond to Anti-prejudiced Propaganda." *Journal of Psychology, 27,* 1947.

Erikson, E. H. "Identity and the Life Cycle." *Psychological Issues, 1,* 18, 1959.

Feather, N. T. "Organization and Discrepancy in Cognitive Structures." *Psychological Review, 78,* 355–379, 1971.

Feshbach, S., and R. D. Singer. *Television and Aggression.* San Francisco: Jossey-Bass, 1971.

Fishbein, M., and I. Ajzen. *Belief, Attitude, Intention and Behavior.* Reading, Mass.: Addison-Wesley, 1975.

Furu T. *The Function of Television for Children and Adolescents.* Tokyo: Sophia University, 1971.

Gerbner, G., and L. Gross. "Living with Television: The Violence Profile." *Journal of Communication, 26,* 173–199, 1976.

Harper, D., J. Munro, and H. T. Himmelweit. "Social and Personality Factors Associated with Children's Tastes in Television Viewing—Summary of Study." *Media Sociology,* Constable, 1970.

Harvey, O. J. "Conceptual Systems and Attitude Change." In C. W. Sherif and M. Sherif (eds.), *Attitude, Ego-involvement and Change.* New York: Wiley, 1967.

Heller, M. S., and S. Polsky. In Lieberman Research Inc., *Overview.* Five-year review of research sponsored by the American Broadcasting Company, 1970–1975.

Himmelweit, H. T., A. N. Oppenheim, and P. Vince. *Television and the Child.* London: Oxford University Press, 1958.

Himmelweit, H. T., and B. Swift. "A Model for the Understanding of School as a Socializing Agent." In P. Mussen, J. Langer, and M. Covington (eds.), *Trends and Issues in Developmental Psychology.* New York: Holt, Rinehart & Winston, 1969.

Himmelweit, H. T., and B. Swift. "Adolescent and Adult Authoritarianism Reexamined: Its Organization and Stability Over Time." *Eur. J. Soc. Psych.,* 357–384, 1971.

Himmelweit, H. T., and B. Swift. "Social and Personality Factors in the Development of Adult Attitudes toward Self and Society." *Report to the U.K. Social Science Research Council,* 1972.

Himmelweit, H. T., and B. Swift. "Principles of Continuities and Discontinuities in Media Usage and Taste: A Longitudinal Study of Adolescents Re-examined at Ages 25 and 33." *J. Soc. Issues, 31,* 1977.

Kohlberg, L. "Stage and Sequence: The Cognitive-developmental Approach to Socialization." In D. A. Goslin (ed.), *Handbook of Socialization Theory and Research.* Chicago: Rand McNally, 1969.

Lefkowitz, M. M., L. D. Eron, L. O. Walder, and L. Rowell Huesman. "Television Violence and Child Aggression: A Follow-up Study." In *Television and Social Behavior, vol. III. Report to the Surgeon General.* New York: U.S. Department of Health, Education and Welfare, 1972.

Leifer, A. D. "Teaching with Television and Film." In *Seventy-fifth Yearbook of the National Society for the Study of Education.* Chicago: University of Chicago Press, 1975.

Maccoby, E. E. "Television: Its Impact on School Children." *Public Opinion Quarterly, 15,* 1951.

McGuire, J. "Persuasion, Resistance and Attitude Change." In I. de Sola Pool and W. Schramm (eds.), *Handbook of Communication,* Chicago: Rand McNally, 1973.

Moscovici, S. In J. Israel and H. Tajfel (eds.) *The Context of Social Psychology.* London: Academic Press, 1972.

Peterson, R. C., and L. L. Thurstone. *Motion Pictures and the Social Attitudes of Children.* New York: Macmillan, 1933.

Piaget, J. *The Origins of Intelligence in Children.* London: Routledge & Kegan Paul, 1953.

Riley, M. A., and J. W. Riley. "A Sociological Approach to Communication Research." *Public Opinion Quarterly, 15,* 1951.

Roberts, D. F. "Communication and Children: A Developmental Approach." In I. de Sola Pool and W. Schramm (eds.), *Handbook of Communication,* Chicago: Rand McNally, 1973.

Salomon, G. "What Is Learned and How It Is Taught: The Interaction between Media, Message, Task, and Learner." In D. R. Olsen (ed.), *Media and Symbols: The Forms of Expression, Communication, and Education,* Seventy-third Yearbook of the National Society for the Study of Education, Part I. Chicago: University of Chicago Press, 1974.

Schramm, W., J. Lyle, and E. B. Parker. *Television in the Lives of Our Children.* Stanford: University Press, 1961.

Schramm, W., and D. F. Roberts (eds.). *The Process and Effects of Mass Communication* (rev. ed.), Urbana: University of Illinois Press, 1971.

Schramm, W. (ed.). *Quality in Instructional Television.* Honolulu: University Press of Hawaii, 1973.

Steiner G. A. *The People Look at Television.* New York: Alfred A. Knopf, 1963.

Surlin, S. H., and E. D. Tate. " 'All in the Family': Is Archie Funny?" In *Journal of Communication, 26,* no. 4, Autumn, 1976.

Tannenbaum, P. H., and D. Zillman. "Emotional Arousal in the Facilitation of Aggression through Communication." In L. Berkowitz (ed.), *Advances in Experimental Social Psychology.* New York: Academic Press, 1974.

Vidmar, N., and M. Rokeach. "Archie Bunker's Bigotry: A Study in Selective Perception and Exposure." In *Journal of Communication, 24* (1), 1974.

Wilhoit, G. C., and H. de Bock. " ' All in the Family' in Holland." In *Journal of Communication, 26,* no. 4, Autumn, 1976.

On Mass Communication Experiments and the Like

Arthur A. Lumsdaine

INTRODUCTION
PURPOSE AND SCOPE

This chapter presents, as a historical and methodological essay, some issues and developments over the course of the last few decades in the use of well-controlled field experiments for gauging the effects of mass media programs and other socioeducational innovations or treatments. "Experiments" is a key referent, as it was in the title of the 1949 book coauthored with Carl Hovland and Fred Sheffield, of which the title of this paper is an obvious permutation. The main kinds of experiments to be considered are field trials designed to ascertain the impact or effects produced by various educational or informational communication programs and by social programs such as those in the economic, legal, and sociomedical or health-care (including fertility-control) areas.

These experiments are typically *mass* experiments (in the title, "mass" can modify either communication or experiment or both). By mass experiments, I mean social experiments to determine the effects of programs or treatments for which the relevant recipients are commonly the masses—or some human subpopulation, and the samples for study must often, in order to represent fairly the typical reactions of a population, be chosen for assignment to experimental and control groups by a mass sampling procedure. In such a procedure, intact population units, rather than single individuals one at a time, are, generally by some random (or, in any event, unbiased) procedure, assigned en masse to one of the two or more contrasting conditions whose outcomes are to be compared in the experiment.

By *field* experiments (or field tests or field trials) I refer to a determination of treatment effects or impacts under the usually complex and rather variable conditions which in fact are (and, also, are so perceived by recipients) as "real life" experiences, rather than simplified laboratory arrangements which are perceived as artificial or contrived "guinea pig" situations by subjects who know they are being experimented upon. The use by Mosteller and associates (1973, 1975) of the term "field trial" also suggests the possibility of considerable variation in program operation and/or impacts from one place, site, or institution to another.

The purpose of the present chapter, unlike most earlier reviews of social and educational program effects, is not primarily to survey experimental literature with respect to substantive results or findings as such. Rather, its main concern is with purpose or role, approach or conceptualization, and—in the broadest sense—*methodology* in controlled social experimentation. My aim is to suggest some lessons of general applicability to experiments, on programs of communication, education, and other social interventions, that may help us to conduct more informative experimentation in the future.

In general, substantive findings of past experiments are cited only to illustrate methodological points or approaches. In contrast, most of the earlier, more substantive reviews have emphasized research findings concerning the effect of operationally or theoretically defined program variables on the outcomes of instructional or other communication programs. Among these reviews should be noted those by Schramm (1962a and b, 1964b, 1971, 1972), Lumsdaine and May (1965), Gilbert, Light, and Mosteller (1975), and McKeachie (1974). In addition to the background provided by these reviews, I am especially indebted for the help provided by Wilbur Schramm in furnishing advice, references, and documentation (for example, Schramm, 1971) concerning the experiments on fertility control (family planning, and the like) utilized in analyzing the methodology of such experiments (Hilton and Lumsdaine, 1975; Lumsdaine *et al.*, 1976) and employed as examples in this section and the section of this chapter entitled "Sampling Issues in Selection of Program Recipients."

EXPERIMENTATION AND INNOVATION

The concept of an "experiment" goes beyond scientists' concern with field experiments or controlled field trials as a definitive method for ascertaining program impacts. In most instances, any new program or treatment being evaluated is per se necessarily an "experiment" in at least the general sense of exploratory intervention or innovation. In this lay sense, an "experiment" is not merely a method for assessing a program's impact but is the essence of what is to be assessed; in this broad sense, experimentation thus embraces creative innovation and informal tryout of new approaches, as well as scientifically designed experimental trials capable of ascertaining with some precision the outcomes produced by such innovations or of identifying the factors responsible for the outcomes observed.

Because the term "experiment" is frequently used in both of these ways, Mosteller and his collaborators (1971, 1973, 1975) have referred to the controlled scientific experimental studies as "controlled field trials," and when these trials employ the special precaution of randomization, they prefix the word "randomized." True (or veridical) experiments, in the sense I am using these terms, are roughly though not exactly synonymous with what Mosteller and his associates call "randomized controlled field trials." The latter, or "true experiments," can be contrasted with other sorts of planned, less-well-controlled field comparisons of experimental programs or treatments, which have been identified by the Campbell-and-Stanley (1963, 1966) label of "quasi-experiments."

HISTORICAL PERSPECTIVES

A benchmark for the initiation of sociobehavioral experiments in the area of attitude change, communication, and instructional media is often taken as the World War II mass-communication experiments reported in the 1949 Hovland-Lumsdaine-Sheffield book which formed the third volume of *The American Soldier,* a series of studies of social psychology in World War II. The World War II experiments developed originally as extensions of, and in the milieu of, cross-section surveys of soldier opinions, directed by Samuel A. Stouffer. The experimental studies, under Carl Hovland, extended the survey's concern with the *status* of opinion, attitude, and information, to engage the question of causative factors in producing *changes* of opinion, and so forth.

Stouffer expressed the critical role of experiments in a memorandum written in June 1942 to General Osborn, head of the Army's Information and Education Division (quoted in Stouffer *et al.,* Vol. 1, pp. 12–18, 1949), noting that "the only certain way to demonstrate that A has the effect B is by controlled experiment." The supplementing of static correlational techniques by the introduction of actual controlled experiments was generally regarded at the time as a significant departure in the social sciences. (Historical precedent for experiments on the impact of educational films on soldier attitudes actually goes back even further, however, to a little-known study of film effects in World War I reported by the pioneer behaviorists Karl S. Lashley and John B. Watson, in 1922.)

Single-program versus comparative impacts. We should note a distinction between two different kinds of program-impact studies. First, "program evaluation" studies are limited to ascertaining a single program's effects. In contrast are "comparative" experiments, in which the effects produced by two or more programs are compared. In much research on social program effects, emphasis has been limited to ascertaining and interpreting the effects ascribable to a particular social program, rather than attempting comparison of alternative programs or variant treatments with each other. However, the importance of ascertaining comparative effects is increasingly recognized.

The now well-recognized distinction between evaluative and analytic experiments was noted in Stouffer's 1942 memorandum,

> In experimental studies, two quite different classes of problems may be seen. One may be called program testing, the other hypothesis testing, although the two are not always separable. An example of program testing is investigation to determine what effects a given film had. This may or may not involve explicit use of scientific theory in the form of hypotheses. An example of hypothesis testing is investigation to determine which of two scientific theories seems to be tenable in the light of a given set of experimental evidence. (Stouffer *et al.,* 1949, pp. 50–51)

One of the initial World War II experiments was a comparison of two methods of physical training; another was a comparison of motion pictures and lectures in education. These initial studies led to a number of further studies from 1942 to 1946 (later reported by Hovland, Lumsdaine, and Sheffield, 1949) for ascertaining rather precisely and in great detail the effects on soldiers' knowledge, opinions, attitudes, and motivation produced by the Army orientation films, training films, and related informational media. (In this context, the now-fashionable term "evaluative research" [cf. Suchman, 1967] appears to

have originated for designating studies of the effects of particular programs—films, in this case—as differentiated from more analytic studies
aimed at identifying the effects of specific input variables.)

The World War II studies presaged a long series of postwar studies
on variables governing the effects of communication and instructional
media programs—continuing in programs at Yale under Mark May
and Carl Hovland starting in the 1940s and 1950s (for example, Hovland, Janis and Kelley, 1953; May and Lumsdaine, 1958), in the
Navy-sponsored program at Pennsylvania State College under C. R.
Carpenter in the 1940s and 1950s (for example, Carpenter and
Greenhill, 1958), and in the Air Force programs during the 1950s (for
example, Lumsdaine, 1961). Later analytic experiments on instruc-
tional/communication variables under Office of Education and other
auspices at centers such as the American Institute for Research and at
Stanford, UCLA, and other universities (for example, Gropper et al.,
1961; Maccoby and Comstock, 1965; Cochran, 1966; Maccoby and
Sheffield, 1961) have been complemented by more recent work on the
evaluation of instructional media programs at UCLA, Northwestern,
Stanford, and elsewhere (for example, Wittrock and Wiley, 1970;
Cook et al., 1975; Maccoby and Farquhar, 1975; Allendoerfer, 1969).

Many of the program evaluation studies (see reviews by Perloff et
al., 1975; Wortman, 1975; Gilbert, Light, and Mosteller, 1975; Hilton and Lumsdaine, 1975) have employed quite rigorous experimental
designs, and in some cases they canvass a wide range of possible outcomes as dependent variables. Concern by psychologists and other behavioral scientists with program-evaluation studies to assess the effects
of mass media communication and instruction has by now expanded
to encompass the entire range of educational, economic, and other
social programs involving key aspects of public policy and the expenditure of billions of dollars in public funds. Meanwhile, the methodology of experimental and quasi-experimental studies to ascertain the
impact of educational and communication and other social programs
has received increased attention recently through the works of social
scientists such as Donald Campbell, Henry Riecken, Marcia Gutten-
tag, Frederick Mosteller (who had been a statistical consultant on our
World War II studies), and numerous others.

Although the immediate raison d'être for program-evaluation studies is limited and specific to decisions concerning the operation,
modification, continuance, or termination of a particular circum-
scribed, programmatic effort, both methodological and the substantive implications of any program evaluation actually may be of much

wider compass. An important recent example in terms of the comparative validity, feasibility, efficiency, and cost of quasi-experimental versus randomized designs is the comparative analysis made by Mosteller and associates (1973, 1975). Such methodological considerations as their analysis explicates in the case of program-evaluation studies seem equally applicable to multitreatment field experiments for comparing the effects of theoretically relevant treatment variations.

PATTERNS OF COMPARISON IN FIELD STUDIES OF PROGRAM EFFECTS

Experiments (or quasi-experiments) generally permit three basic types of comparisons:

Single treatment, plus nontreatment control group, thus showing the "absolute" effect of that one treatment by comparing results for treated versus control groups (symbolized "*x-c*").

Two or more treatments compared, but no *nontreatment control group,* thus showing the *difference* in effectiveness between the two treatments but, lacking a control to furnish a zero baseline, not measuring the "absolute" effect of either treatment—symbolized "*x-y*" (or "*x* versus *y*").

Two (or more) treatments with a nontreatment control group (symbolized "*x-y-c,*" and so forth), so as to show the absolute effects of each treatment as well as the difference between their effects.

Several examples from studies of fertility-control experiments that exemplify these three patterns are shown in Table 2–1. The three patterns of comparison distinguished are of particular relevance in more rigorous experimental comparisons employing unbiased (for example, random) assignment of treatments to recipients, but appear also in less-well-controlled quasi-experimental comparisons that attempt to identify the impact of a given program or the comparative effects of alternative programs.

EXPERIMENTAL REQUIREMENTS
THE NEED FOR CONTROLLED EXPERIMENTS

Why do we need experimental data from planned field trials to assess the impact of social innovations, programs, or treatments? One forceful answer to this question has been given by, among others, Gilbert, Light, and Mosteller (1975): "A knifelike truth that the policy maker, the economist, the social scientists, the journalist, and the layman . . . need to learn to handle is that we often do not know

TABLE 2–1. Three Basic Experimental Patterns, Illustrated in
Family-Planning Studies*

---

1. *Hong Kong reassurance* (Chan, 1971). Unbiased assignment (by alternation) of individual IUD acceptors (client at a clinic) was made either to a single treatment condition (reassurance visit by field worker) or to a nontreatment control condition. (The clinic staff was "blind" to which condition was given.) *c* versus *x* (simple program evaluation) pattern.

2. *Bogota mail/visits* (Simmon, 1973). Random assignment of indiviudals was made either to a no-treatment control or to one of two treatments (mailing versus home visits). *c-x-y* comparison pattern.

3. *Hong Kong visit types* (Mitchell, 1968). Random assignment of individuals was to one of two treatments (type of field worker visit) or to control. *c-x-y* pattern.

4. *IUD checkups* (Bang, 1970). Unbiased (alternated) assignment of successive ad hoc groupings of individuals (successive day's contingents of IUD acceptors at a Korean clinic) to one of three treatments (differing in how soon acceptor was to return for checkup). x_1-x_2-x_n pattern: two or more treatments compared, but without a nontreatment control group.

---

*Further examples of the incorporation of such comparisons in somewhat more complex experimental designs are included in Table 2–2.

which is the best of several possible policies and, worse yet, that we may not know if any of them betters what we are now doing. . . . *we still will not know how things will work in practice until we try them in practice.*" (Emphasis added.)

Moreover, in the World War II "Why We Fight" film studies and many other programs on which firm experimental data have been obtained since the early 1940's, one general conclusion that emerges is that the actual effects demonstrably produced by programs have often been very far indeed from the expectations of the producers, sponsors, or even users. Generally, the demonstrated effects of social interventions have been less marked than anticipated, though not always (see Gilbert, Light, and Mosteller, pp. 113, 175). Also, in addition to intended effects, data have sometimes revealed important and sizable unintended effects, either desirable or, in other cases, undesirable.

THE IMPORTANCE OF RANDOMIZATION

Preferred basis for ascertaining the impact of programs or treatments. As previously indicated, our concern is primarily with aspects of field-study design and execution that influence the validity and efficiency of data for ascertaining program/treatment impacts or effects. It is generally agreed that, other things equal, the optimal basis for such a determination is afforded by controlled experimental field trials which are designed to eliminate any systematic bias in assigning treatment conditions to the program recipients (individuals or population units). Normally such a design includes suitable use of randomization and associated procedures. Further argument by several authorities in support of such designs (Gilbert, Light, and Mosteller, 1975; Campbell and Boruch, 1975; Deniston and Rosenstock, 1973; and others) is summarized below. The crucial advantage of randomized designs is in their ability to isolate unambiguously those changes that actually are a result of each treatment being studied, so that its impact is not confounded with changes that would result from other causes.

Randomized versus nonrandomized trials. Mosteller and associates (1973, 1975) emphasize that the results of quasi-experimental, nonrandomized, and other poorly controlled trials and observational studies are shown, by the record of numerous studies they examined, to have been frequently misleading. This finding was well illustrated in several medical studies they describe, as well as in studies of housing, nutrition delivery, educational "performance contracting," and others. They note (1975, p. 176) that nonrandomized studies may or may not lead to a correct conclusion but that "without other data the suspicion will persist that their results reflect selection effects" not only undermining a decision maker's own confidence in some evaluations but also inhibiting his action in other cases where his clients are not convinced by the findings. They further point out that while "observational studies are rarely successful in resolving a controversy about causality . . . few controversies about the effects of new programs survive a series of carefully designed randomized controlled trials." The same authors also review a very instructive analysis by Grace *et al.*(1966) on the relation (in this case inverse!) between the strength of evidence and the credence accorded it by practitioners convinced of the efficacy of medical treatment.

Gilbert, Light and Mosteller conclude, after reviewing nonrandomized field studies of both social and medical programs:

> The review of these studies leads us to the conclusion that randomization, together with careful control and implementation, gives an evaluation a strength and persuasiveness that cannot ordinarily be obtained by other means. We are particularly struck by the troublesome record that our examples of nonrandomized studies piled up. Although

some nonrandomized studies gave suggestive information that seems reliable, we find it hard to tell which were likely to be the misleading ones, even with the power of hindsight to guide us. (p. 44)

And they add:

> This weakness of uncontrolled trials poses a particularly difficult problem for the policy maker faced with what appears to be more and more evidence in favor of a particular course of action when he knows that he may just be seeing the same biases again and again. (p. 134)

Similarly, Deniston and Rosenstock (1973, pp. 163–164) stated as follows their conclusions from another comparison of alternative research designs for evaluating health-service programs:

> In this, the first of a series of papers concerning the validity of nonexperimental or quasi-experimental designs in estimating program effectiveness, the use of two single group before–after designs without controls, and the use of two designs using nonequivalent control groups were shown to yield invalid estimates of program effectiveness when compared with the experiences of a true control group.
>
> The single-group before–after designs overestimated program effectiveness while the nonequivalent comparison groups underestimated-program effectiveness.

Donald Campbell, in collaboration with Robert Boruch (1975), recently has also further strengthened the argument for true, randomized experiments in a way that may somewhat surprise readers of his well-known series of earlier papers coauthored with J. C. Stanley (1963, 1966) and others:

> It may be that Campbell and Stanley . . . should feel guilty for having contributed to giving quasi-experimental designs a good name. There are program evaluations in which the authors say proudly, "We used a *quasi*-experimental design." If responsible, Campbell and Stanley should do penance, because in most social settings there are many equally or more plausible rival hypotheses than the hypothesis that the puny treatment indeed produced an effect. . . . The arguments presented in this chapter [Campbell and Boruch, 1975] continue the strategy of justifying randomized experiments by making explicit the costs in equivocality and the burdens of making additional estimations of parameters that result from a failure to randomize. . . . There is, in particular, one plausible rival hypothesis that invalidates most social experiments of a quasi-experimental design nature: that is, there is a profound underlying confounding of selection and treatment. . . . If an experiment is not randomized, assumptions must be made that are often untenable and are even more frequently unverifiable. . . . [invoking] problems in themselves . . . sufficiently formidable . . . to

justify eliminating them at the outset, by assuring through randomization that groups are identical to one another with respect to unknown parameters. (1975, pp. 202–203, 208)

Later on, Campbell and Boruch conclude, after reviewing in detail half a dozen sources of underadjustment bias in studies of compensatory education (1975, pp. 275–277):

In the absence of more reliable information about the grouping effect, randomization is a relevant vehicle for our ignorance. . . . Where randomization is not possible, we should, of course, seek quasi-experimental approaches which avoid or reduce the bias. . . . But until such data [are] analyzed and the parameters of the feedback process known in detail, randomization of treatments seems essential.

. . . In compensatory education, the few existing randomized experiments have produced optimistic, encouraging, and informative results. Had those same experiments not been randomized, in most cases they would have produced estimates of effect that were biased in a pessimistic direction.

CONTINUANCE OF VERIDICALITY

The categorical notion of a "true" absolutely veridical experiment, while it may be demarcated fairly clearly, can also be thought of as a region or zone in a multivariate continuum, in regard to features of randomization and the like. This view applies in recipient sampling or treatment assignment, as well as in procedural control in the field and appropriateness of data analysis in relation to these features of research design and conduct. Obviously, any actual experiment may approach or fall short, by various degrees, of an ideal of perfection with respect to (1) features of sampling-assignment design, (2) physical conduct, including procedural control of extraneous influences in the application of treatments in the field, (3) reliability and other desirable qualities of criterion measures, or (4) the degree of exactitude with which the statistical bases of causal inference (significance tests, estimates of error) adhere precisely to the logical implications of the first of the above.

Obviously, in the absence of better data, one makes the best judgments one can as to what program emphases will be effective. But, second, one should be aware that such judgments are commonly quite fallible, so one will need to obtain firm data to see what effects a program is actually producing on desired objectives after a reasonable period of operation. Meanwhile, one should seek to get as much informal (though less definitive) observational data as possible in order to correct flaws that might otherwise decrease the actual impact of the program. Finally, in assessing the evidence as to the effectiveness of the program, one must give very serious consideration—even at the top decision-making level—as to the adequacy of the data that purport to indicate program impact. In doing so, one will be recognizing that what might seem somewhat academic refinements in the design of a study can, in fact, make the difference between its being worth full credence or, at the other extreme, being a substantially worthless source of misleading information. (Most current studies seem to fall somewhere in the middle along this continuum of credibility or validity.)

Mixed random/nonrandom designs. A special class of examples of this variation in the "trueness" of design is found in some experiments that include multiple treatment groups; simple characterization of a study as a "randomized" or "nonrandomized" field trial sometimes may give a misleading impression of the design's implications for valid attribution of outcomes to treatment difference as causal factors. For example, in the Taichung City fertility-control study (Freedman and Takeshita, 1969), population units were randomly assigned to *some* of the experimental conditions, but other treatment variations were assigned *non*randomly. Specifically, in this complex design, randomized assignment was made within city sectors, to 2,200 neighborhoods *(lins)* of three treatments—mailings, and home visits including or not including husband—plus a no-treatment control condition. However, a "density" variable (proportion of *lins* receiving treatments) was assigned by city sector, just one sector to each treatment, thus leaving, strictly, no degrees of freedom on the density variable. Thus, even within a single experiment the safeguard afforded by randomization may apply to some of the comparisons, but not to all of them. This important difference can easily be overlooked when conclusions are later drawn from the experimental data.

FEASIBILITY OF FIELD EXPERIMENTS

A factor that has led to underemployment of true experimental designs in the field is the rather prevalent assumption that clean-cut experiments are prohibitively costly and time-consuming. On the contrary, excellent field experiments often can, in fact, be accomplished rather expeditiously and may also be surprisingly low in cost when planned by experienced experimenters. For example, a Thailand fertility experiment (see Table 2-2) required only a simple administrative decision, a randomization process to choose the provinces which would receive the experimental treatment, and a single day's training for the midwives in the experimental provinces. (The data collection and analysis were already being conducted, requiring no additional expenditures.) The cost of good small-to-medium-scale experiments often may, in fact, be much less in the long run than less satisfactory ways of trying to determine the effects of a program, and may be more than paid for by savings in not continuing a noneffective program.

Feasibility, of randomized trials. Mosteller and associates (1973, 1975) show that randomized field experiments can be (and have been) conducted even when complicated by ethical as well as technical problems and despite inevitable political problems that make evaluations hard to carry out. For example, they conclude (1975, p. 179) that the Salk vaccine field trials "show that society is willing to apply randomization to its children when the issues at stake are well known." While they recognize that some experimental field trials could be impractical or counterindicated as unethical, they point to regulations which will continue to be developed to protect the public. They also suggest the use of appropriate incentives to encourage participation, and that some flexibility is available when those participating are willing to accept either one of available alternative treatments. They further indicate how a randomized field trial often can be conducted even though local units (cities, schools, or the like) retain a veto on treatments they consider unacceptable.

Cook and Campbell (1976) list a number of circumstances that help meet some of the objections that may be raised to the conduct of randomized field experiments, and may thus increase their feasibility— for example, when demand for a treatment exceeds available capability and allocation by lot seems the fairest way to decide who gets the scarce commodity, when experimental units are spatially isolated, and so on. Methodological aspects of assignment of treatments to separated units en bloc is further considered below.

The feasibility of conducting true field experiments can also be supported simply by looking at the record of ones that have, in fact, been conducted as well as by considering arguments such as the preceding to overcome objections sometimes raised to the feasibility of conducting true experiments in real-life social settings. Let us look briefly at part of the record of what has been done.

During the past three or four decades, at least several hundred formal educational experiments on short instructional programs have been carried out and reported. In terms of small or middle-size programs (that is, those programs of short or medium duration and scope—for example, a few minutes to an hour or two of instruction), a considerable share of our experience comes from military and civilian experiments for assessing the effects of informative and educational or instructional communication programs, particularly those implemented through the educational media of films, television, and recordings. (I have personally participated in some fifty or more of these experiments, mostly in the educational media field, following the systematic experimentation for the Army during World War II.) Some of these studies—or "mini" programs—are of short duration, but a number of others concern larger-scale educational programs. Good illustrations of experimental field trials of such "macro" programs are furnished by the summaries by Mosteller and associates (1973, 1975) of randomized field trials of the Emergency School Assistance Programs (ESAP) and Harvard "Project Physics" program. Other examples of "macro" programs of a number of months' or even years' duration are found in the dozen or so true experiments (including appropriate use of randomization) for gauging the effects of fertility-control programs in Third World countries identified by Hilton and Lumsdaine (1975), out of several dozen studies that attempted to assess such program effects. (A few of the simpler or these studies were cited earlier to illustrate each of three types of experimental comparison types, "cx," "xy," and "cxy.") A further long-duration experiment was the Taiwan free-IUD study (Chen and Chow, 1973). The treatment (an offer, good for a three-month period, of a free IUD insertion) was rotated during the two-year study in turn to each of seven groups of thirty townships apiece, while the remaining six groups of townships at each time period served as a control. (This special rotation design in the free-IUD study afforded counterbalancing of the treatment groups, and also provided time-series data prior to and following the treatment period for the various groups of townships.)

An appendix to the previously cited 1975 paper by Campbell and Boruch lists a number of other randomized field experiments for evaluating educational programs, including programs of medium to large scope and duration in fields such as teacher training, curriculum and communication, counseling systems, and educational systems. Most of the references they give concern completed field experiments incorporating a randomized design, though the quality of the design and its implementation seem to have considerable variation.

Abstracts of a few of these references were included in the appendix to Riecken and Boruch (1974), which lists references to, and abstracts of, illustrative randomized experiments for appraising the effects of various social programs. This appendix furnishes empirical evidence that randomized experimental tests are feasible in a wide variety of settings.

The social programs tested experimentally include about a dozen experiments in delinquency and criminal reform, experimental tests in each of half a dozen law-related programs or procedures and of rehabilitative programs in mental health, ten experimental assessments of special educational programs, and several each in sociomedical and fertility control, communication-methods effectiveness, and "experimental" (innovative) economic programs.

The abbreviated Campbell and Boruch bibliography for educational studies includes some six dozen studies, with the number of referenced studies distributed as follows: curriculum and other learning conditions (ten studies), instructional objectives (eight), electronic and mechanical assistance for instruction (eight), compensatory education, preschool and primary grades (fifteen), special training, disadvantaged groups, including manpower training and career education (six), postsecondary training, education, communications (eight), school-based systems for social and psychological adjustment (five), systems for improving quality of educational measurement (nine), and aptitude-trait interaction (eleven).

Secondary Evaluation. An important recent example in which large resources were devoted to seeking to assess the effects of major instructional communication programs is found in the studies of the "Sesame Street" programs of the Public Broadcasting System (PBS). The recent 400-page volume on Sesame Street by Cook *et al.* (1975) is one of the most exhaustive attempts to date at post hoc reanalysis of the effects attributed to a physically reproducible (videotaped) instructional mass communication program. It thus exemplifies a growing trend for "secondary evaluation," or reevaluation in detail, by an independent researcher following an initial evaluation of program outcomes. The evidence on program effects was in this case from a quasi-experimental rather than randomized design, and a good deal of reassessment of the initial evaluation was concerned with the adequacy of the extent to which selection artifacts were or were not sufficiently corrected for by the data-analysis methods used.

This major reevaluation effort by Cook, and the earlier one by

Hawkridge and DeWitt (1969) on the Ellson programmed-tutoring program in elementary reading further discussed later in this chapter, did not stop with weighing the validity of imputed effects of the program; they also attempted to deal with the even more difficult question of assessing the worth of such outcomes, in the sense of cost-benefit balance. Some of the methodological problems involved clearly transcend those involved in most theoretically oriented research on instructional/communication variables, which generally stop with weighing the support for attributed effects and commonly leave untouched the questions of outcome worth and its relation to input cost.

EVOLUTIONARY EXPERIMENTATION
THE NEED FOR PILOT PROGRAMS AND FORMATIVE EVALUATION

A crucial issue in social experimentation or program evaluation and evolution is whether a program is implemented at the outset on a full-scale basis, or whether it is first tried out on a limited basis as a pilot program. Only with such a pilot program, subject to modification and revision before wider adoption, can the function of experimental field testing be maximally useful for improving the program or for making decisions about its use. Moreover, the samples of recipients needed for a control group in most cases may be rendered unavailable if a new program is disseminated widely instead of on a limited pilot basis for evaluation. However, since experience teaches that the effects of most social innovations are uncertain and may be disappointingly small at first, pilot experiments are needed that are large enough and thus sensitive enough to reveal fairly small effects at the pilot-experiment stage. Further, such experiments should indicate as fully as possible what features of a program or treatment produced any observable good or bad effects, so that the program can be redesigned in a way that is likely to augment good effects and ameliorate bad effects before it goes into full-scale implementation. The general case for pilot-program or "prototype" evaluation in social innovation has been well put by Neal E. Miller (1967, pp. 114–115):

> In spite of all the practical and theoretical knowledge in the automobile industry, no one of the large manufacturers ever considers putting out a radically new model without extensive road tests of a prototype model. . . . Similarly, one can never be certain whether a new social program actually will be a cure or whether it will have unexpected undesirable side effects. . . . It is understandable, but ironic that it is only with the new sciences, such as those dealing with behavior, that

the would-be users often are so impatient for quick results of practical value that they will not support the long program of developmental research and field-testing that often is especially needed in just these cases.

The resources devoted to developing and field testing any program should depend on how and where the program is to be later used. For example, extensive and costly experimentation may be fully warranted for programs that are essentially reproducible (or "exportable") and for those which are large in scale (in terms of the extent of benefits anticipated for large numbers of recipients of the program's activities or products) but not for limited or nonreproducible programs.

The concept of the pilot program has been well utilized in some cases of family-planning programs (but in other cases, unfortunately, has been completely ignored). The Khanna studies (Wyon and Gordon, 1971) and Singur study (Mathen, 1962) provide good examples of using pilot programs. A further recent example is the Thailand auxiliary midwife experiment (Rosenfield and Limcharoen, 1972) in which major policy decisions were based on evidence from pilot-program data. Various other examples might be cited which bring out the costly consequences of initiating a program precipitously on a wide scale without a tryout on a pilot basis. A critical need exists for proper understanding and appreciation of pilot-program experimentation. That behavioral scientists recognize this need is not enough; that the capabilities of experimental field trials be well understood is also important, so they may be taken adequately into account by policy makers and social program managers at all levels.

EMPIRICAL EVIDENCE ON BENEFITS FROM REVISION BASED ON DIAGNOSTIC PROGRAM EVALUATION

Considerable evidence has accumulated to document the extent of improvement that can be produced by empirically based program revision. One of the first such demonstrations was in experiments done some years ago in Pittsburgh at the American Institute for Research (Gropper *et al.*, 1961). Data from junior high school students who took tests after seeing a preliminary version of a television program were used as a basis for revising the program. Students in a sample class watched a preview lesson televised to them, and the item-by-item data from their responses on a comprehensive post test of the lesson content were provided to the television instructor. These data indicated to the instructor which points were adequately covered and which ones were inadequately covered for that particular kind of audience.

The new or revised lesson, prepared on the basis of this feedback to the instructor, was then administered later to one group, while simultaneously a parallel group, also randomly chosen, saw the initial, unrevised version on a different television channel. This procedure was followed in two separate experiments on two different television lessons. Analysis of results, comparing preview and revised versions, showed in both experiments that the students who watched the revised version scored significantly higher on achievement tests than those who watched the original version. Improvement for various test items ranged from 6 percent to 76 percent, as measured in terms of the difference between percentages of correct answers for students watching the revised versus unrevised versions of the program.

Several further studies are described by Flanagan (1969). One of these further studies of the use of evaluation data in developing improved instructional materials was done by David Markle (1967) at the American Institute for Research. The objective of Markle's project was to develop a seven-hour course in basic first aid. The objectives of the course were based on a large number of incidents posing first aid needs. These incidents helped to define the competence needed and thus the aims of the training. The data for a group without any specific prior training in first aid showed less than 30 percent correct answers, while individuals who had received training from a previously developed first aid course answered some 40 to 50 percent correctly. In developing the new, data-based course, the programmers prepared, for each of a series of topical units, a preliminary version of the program, trying it out on typical trainees one at a time and testing their achievement of the objectives. After some weeks of work of this type, further tryouts were made with small groups, and those parts of the material shown by tests to be ineffective were revised and the new units tried out again. Frequently the cycle was repeated with another filming, editing, and tryout of the films. The final seven-hour training program resulted in the trainees answering 80 percent of the items correctly on the average.

A later study was concerned with the improvement of a series of programs on mathematics originally developed under the National Science Foundation by Allendoerfer (1969). The effectiveness of these programs was improved by use of test data on the extent to which use of the programs met various defined objectives. However, the use of these data made necessary the redefinition of the objectives in much more precise terms than had been done originally. The work with the Allendoerfer mathematics program involved some interesting methodological features. Not only was it a "retrofit" kind of evaluation in which typically the objectives had only been defined in broad terms until after the materials were developed, but it also exemplified a situation in which material had already been revised several times on nondata grounds and so was presumably quite good *before* the use of empirical tryout data as a basis for further revision. The fact that, under these circumstances, substantial gains in the effectiveness were still achieved can be attributed partly to the use of the data and partly to refinement of relevant content resulting from a thorough reanalysis of objectives.

It was not possible in the Allendoerfer project, though, to separate out clearly the effects of the *objective-refinement* process on the one hand, and the *use of data* for identifying weak spots on the other (though subjective impressions indicated that both were of considerable assistance). However, in another study using a shorter program, Marvin Rosen (1968) made an experimental analysis which would separate out the contribution made by refinement of objectives from the additional help gained from having data on the effectiveness of each specific point. In brief, Rosen's results showed that use of data yielded more improvement than revision made without the quantitative data from the earlier tryout. It also showed that instructions to revise on the basis of detailed objectives could be followed by programmers so as to result in rather consistently and significantly better programs. (I will refer again to this aspect of Rosen's study in considering the generality of the independent variables in societal experiments.)

The above examples represent "formative" program development based on empirical trials. The terminology of "formative" evaluation, currently applied to a quite diverse range of practices, includes informal pretesting of reactions to a program or proposed treatment as well as major sequential tryouts, such as the above, to ascertain the impacts demonstrably produced by successively modified programs in the spirit of "evolutionary development" (Gilbert, Light, and Mosteller, 1975) or "evolutionary operation." The concern of evolutionary program development can include not only successive improvement of programs by sheer empiricism but also identification of those program features associated with the more successful outcomes. However, a reasonably definite pinning down of "features associated with success" requires not only an evolutionary succession of revisions but an *actual comparison of program variants* randomly assigned and exemplifying alternative program features. Such experiments have less often been done with very large-scale social programs than with instructional media, although a number of examples of randomized field tests of treatment alternatives are reviewed by Hilton and Lumsdaine (1975) and by Gilbert, Light, and Mosteller (1975).

SAMPLING ISSUES IN SELECTION
OF PROGRAM RECIPIENTS
RANDOMIZATION IN SAMPLE SELECTION
AND EXPERIMENTAL ASSIGNMENT

Authorities in the field of sampling and experimental design generally recognize, as indicated earlier, that some form of randomization in the selection or assignment of people to treatments (or treatments to people) is a crucial safeguard for assuring lack of bias in survey or experimental samples. By randomization we mean a process of selecting a sample, or assigning samples to experimental treatments, by an essentially *chance procedure* which ensures that each unit in a population has an equal chance of appearing in the sample or of being assigned to one treatment rather than to an alternative treatment. The units thus assigned in laboratory experiments usually are individuals but in field experiments often are larger population units such as classrooms, schools, neighborhoods, towns, and so forth.

Randomization can have two principal functions in field studies. These functions need to be distinguished, since they are often confused and have different degrees of importance in different kinds of studies; one or both may fail to be employed in a given study. The first function is that of random or representative sampling to select a subpopulation or pool of potential treatment recipients that is representative of a specified larger population. This function is particularly important in the use of surveys to provide a representative picture of the status of a total population based on a sample; also, it fosters external validity in an experiment. The second function is random assignment of population units within the pool or subpopulation used in a given study, such that the particular samples assigned to different treatments are comparable to each other—that is, equivalent except for chance fluctuations. Only if groups assigned to different treatments are thus comparable can we assure internal validity in order that selection and treatment are not confounded. Otherwise, posttreatment difference in the behavior of the experimental groups will not be unambiguously attributable to differences in treatment but rather may be ascribed to irrelevant, prior differences between the samples that were assigned to the alternative treatments.

IMPLICATIONS OF UNIT SAMPLING

As noted earlier, assignment to programs or treatments in true experiments or other controlled field studies is commonly made by preformed social units, such as schools, classrooms, regions, neighborhoods, villages, towns, counties, or the like, rather than by assigning individuals randomly to the treatments. In such cases it is important to deal with unit-to-unit variability in comparing treatments given to population groups that are taken as sampling or assignment units in the experimental design.

The need for unit assignment may arise from administrative or political constraints; assigning a treatment to all members of a community, school, or other population unit may make an experiment more acceptable than giving it some people and withholding it from others within the unit. Also, en bloc unit assignment may be required in order to achieve realistic conditions to insure that individuals who are within such a societal unit, and thus in close contact with each other, will not be caused to respond in an atypical fashion by their perception of themselves as being specially or differentially treated. If individuals in an experimental work group, for example, realize they are receiving new and special treatment, that very realization, rather than normal treatment benefits as such, may lead them to exert extra effort as the familiar "Hawthorne effect" and thus spuriously boost their performance. An opposite kind of spurious artifact (the "John Henry effect") may result if control-group subjects put forth extra effort to compensate for an innovative benefit they feel they are being deprived of. While conceivably these effects might cancel each other out, one or the other of the "contaminating" influences more likely will predominate and result in our underestimating or overestimating, perhaps grossly, the size of any true inherent effects of the treatment itself.

Analysis of unit data. Not only must care be exercised in considering assignment procedures to assure that randomization precludes bias and thus assures pretreatment equivalence to allow a fair comparison between experimental groups, but it is also important that the data reported and the analyses performed take adequate account of the way in which the randomization was accomplished. Of particular importance is the need, when population units (as opposed to individuals) are in fact what are randomly assigned to program treatments, for reporting and analysis of data in a way that accurately reflects the amount of unit-to-unit variability rather than merely individual-to-individual variability within units.

An optimal rigorous analysis for a group-assignment experiment thus should preferably use groups, rather than individuals, as the unit of analysis for estimating chance variability or experimental error in determining the reliability ("significance") of treatment differences or program impacts. The unit data provides considerably more stable measures than that for single individuals, but also it involves a smaller "sample size" or "N," in terms of the number of independent random assignments of population units to treatments.

In any case, a condition for such a logically rigorous experimental test (cf. Fisher, 1935, *et seq.*, section 19), is that the estimate of experimental error be based on the operations that actually determine experimental error. To this end, analysis in terms of unit-to-unit variance, later suggested as an option by Lindquist in 1953, had been recommended in the 1949 Hovland, Lumsdaine, and Sheffield book (p. 326):

> As indicated earlier, a frequent reason for nonrandom sampling is that the experiment must be administered to units rather than individuals. . . . In such a case the population units may often be randomized and the statistical tests made in terms of the obtained variance among means of units rather than responses of individuals. This is a very efficient procedure if a sizable number of units is possible.

Basing degrees of freedom on the number of independent acts of randomization means, in practical terms, that errors of omission or commission in attribution of effects will seldom result from the frequent situation in which group-to-group (for example, village-to-village) variability may grossly differ from what would result from random sampling of equivalent-sized groups.

At present it is, unfortunately, a common occurrence in reports of field experiments in all areas, including instruction and education as well as in studies of the impact of the various psychosocial variables, for the number of *individuals* and variation among them to be made the basis for estimating the stability of the findings, rather than using the *unit-to-unit* variability as a measure of stability or error, as is logically implied in the case where the sampling or assignment to treatment was done on a unit basis rather than by individuals. (See also Lumsdaine, 1963, p. 657.)

A considerable number of field experiments on the effects of instructional and other program variants have employed random en bloc assignment of treatments to intact population units (schools, classes, and so on), and some have then appropriately made use of the means of the assignment units as the units of analysis, as suggested by Hovland, Lumsdaine, and Sheffield. Studies that illustrate the potential advantages of such unit-variance analysis include, for example, experiments by Michael and Maccoby (1953), May and Jenkinson (1953), May and Lumsdaine (1958, chapter 5), Roshal (1961), Gropper *et al.* (1961), Maccoby and Comstock (1965), and Patel (1976).

In some cases the number of units assigned to each treatment is so small, and/or the sample for each unit is so small as to render unit-by-unit analysis quite insensitive. Where unit sampling has been employed with only *one* population unit (for example, a single town, district, school) assigned to each treatment, formally, no degrees of freedom exist for estimating unit-to-unit variability, and thus no intrinsic estimate of unit-to-unit error is afforded for a test of statistical significance—for example, one of the Freedman and Takeshita comparisons, Salcedo's 1954 Philippines nutrition study, discussed by Mosteller and associates (1975, pp. 118–119), and the heart-disease educational media experiment by Maccoby and Farquhar (1975). In such cases, the reliability or significance of imputed differences must be defended on a priori or extrinsic grounds (which commonly involve unverified assumptions) that are generally less elegantly convincing than a straightforward estimate of error deriving directly from the unit-to-unit variance and based squarely on the experimental randomization operations actually performed in the experiment.

Finally, in some cases the data, though readily amenable to unit-by-unit analysis, have in fact instead been analysed only as aggregates with error estimated from within-unit variance. In some of these cases (for example, Lumsdaine and Janis, 1953), a unit-by-unit analysis was also added by the experimenters. And, in some other cases, at least some of the unaggregated unit-level statistics have been preserved, permitting reanalysis by later investigators.

In many comparisons presented in available reports on experimental studies of the effects of social or educational programs, the reviewer's task in assessing the reliability or dependability of differences between treatment groups compared is aggravated by incomplete reporting. Of the numerous studies that employ unit or group sampling with treatments assigned to groups rather than to individuals, many fail either to give much if any indication of the degree of consistency for the different groups or to present the basis on which any "significance" figures given were calculated. This latter situation is doubly unfortunate in that the investigators usually do not provide the unit-by-unit data on the basis of which the reviewer might be able to determine for himself the consistency or dependability of suggested superiority of one treatment group over another.

Of the twelve true experimental population-planning studies Hilton and Lumsdaine (1975) were able to locate, eight had geographic units assigned to treatments (see some simple examples in Table 2-2). However, in only one instance, the Taiwan free-IUD-offer study

TABLE 2-2. Some Simple Examples of Random Unit Assignment
(by Villages, Counties, or Provinces)
in Family-Planning Experiments*

Taiwan group meetings. (Lu, Chen, and Chow, 1967)—"x versus y" pattern: Random assignment of thirty-seven Taiwan *villages* was made to either of two treatments—group meetings in every neighborhood of the village versus in every other neighborhood; no nontreated control group.

Taiwan agent incentives. (Chang, Cernada, and Sun, 1972)—"c versus x" pattern: Random assignment of ten Taiwan *counties* was made to treatment (incentives to field workers for each acceptor obtained), and ten nontreated control counties; assignment by smaller units (townships) was rejected to avoid contamination.

Thailand midwife. (Rosenfield and Limcharoen, 1972)—"c versus x" pattern: Assignment of treatment (pills prescribed by auxiliary midwives) was made to four randomly chosen Thai *provinces* out of a total of seventeen provinces studied; the other thirteen provinces served as an untreated control.

Korean Mothers' Club support. (Yang, 1972)—"c, x, and y" pattern: Within three equal-size subgroups of Korean *townships*—each group relatively homogeneous on several demographic and program indices—the townships were randomly assigned to one of two treatments (differing in amount of financial support given for mothers' club) or to nontreated control.

---

*A more complex example is the Puerto Rico communications study (Hill, Stycos, and Back, 1959) in which villages from an "eligible" pool of villages (those that had a meeting hall) were randomly assigned to an untreated control condition or to one of nine treatment conditions, comprising all 3 × 3 combinations of two treatment factors: (a) type of communication program—mailing versus large versus small meetings, and (b) kind of educational content presented, also having three variations.

(Chen and Chow, 1973), were they able, through correspondence with one of the investigators, to obtain adequate unit-by-unit data, which evidently have not been published elsewhere.

In this context, it is worth noting the importance not only of the correctness of the basis for inference concerning reality (that is, the statistical "significance"—or nonchanciness—of differences between treatments) but also the clarity and directness with which the basis for determining such "significance" can be expressed, so that it is clearly apparent to nontechnicians such as administrators who need to appreciate the force of the evidence in making important programmatic decisions. The latter purpose of communication perhaps might often be facilitated by displaying, in simple tabular or perhaps graphical form, the degree of overlap or nonoverlap of contrasted distributions (for example, for control versus experimental conditions), particularly when each of the distributions compared represents a rather small number of rather stable observations, such as the means for each of a set of population subunits that were assigned as whole units to treatment conditions. For illustrative graphical contrasts, see the reanalysis of Roshal's data in Lumsdaine (1961, chap. 11, p. 169), or the presentation by Hilton and Lumsdaine (1975, p. 382) of the unit-by-unit data from the 1973 Chen and Chow experiment.

EXTERNAL VALIDITY AND REPLICABILITY
VALIDITY AND DEPENDENT-VARIABLE CHARACTERISTICS

In field experiments on communication and other program effects, dependent variables used are commonly verbal measures of attitude or opinion, rather than more basic behavioral outcomes which it is hoped the program will change. For example, in studies of the effects of family-planning programs, requested use or acceptance of a contraceptive often is the primary dependent variable employed, though continued effective use leading to ultimate reduction in fertility rates represents the ultimate impact hoped for. Though some family-planning experiments do go a step further to observe continued use rather than merely acceptance, in most of the well-designed experiments on family-planning programs, actual resulting fertility decline was not directly observed. Conversely, in the field studies of family planning reviewed by Hilton and Lumsdaine (1975), the studies which made the strongest attempts to measure fertility outcomes were not controlled experiments.

Strength in sampling/assignment design and analysis in a study of course does not offset weakness in the validity of the dependent variables, or vice versa: serious flaws on either count will weaken the inferences possible. As seen above, a study that is strong in one of these essential respects often is flawed in the other. An interesting early example is in Hartmann's pioneering (1936) field experiment on political persuasion, which compared the effect of leaflets using "emotional" appeals in three wards versus "rational" appeals in four other wards of a small city. Despite faults in the design and analysis of this nonrandomized unit-sampling study, it had the merit of using as a dependent variable actual vote counts in an election, rather than relying on subjects' self-reports of how they voted.

In a more recent example, the initial outcome measures reported by Maccoby and Farquhar (1975) on the effects of a Stanford communication campaign aimed at reducing heart disease were verbal reports by the subjects of the behaviors it advocated (for example, improved dietary habits); however, the experimenters subsequently took pains to supplement these verbal indicators with follow-up data, including physiological measures such as blood-cholesteral levels from the subjects in the control town and the two experimental towns.

Some important and sometimes vexing problems in the measurement of outcomes of other kinds in field experiments for assessing social program impacts are examined in the recent book by Rossi and Lyall (1976), which is devoted to an extensive critique of the New Jersey–Pennsylvania "negative income tax" experiment.

EXPORTABILITY

A question needing an answer before an initially successful pilot program is expanded is whether the program is essentially reproducible or "exportable." For example, if a rural family-planning program works successfully using five particular field workers, do we necessarily know that the program will be successful using different field workers? The resources (money, personnel, facilities, and the like) available for pilot testing may be of higher quality than those available for a wider-scale program. Thus, in the Khanna fertility-control studies (Wyon and Gordon, 1971), the pilot program utilized field personnel who were later to become supervisors of the larger field staff used in the field program. The small cadre of people were probably better trained, more highly motivated, and so forth, than the field workers they later had to depend on. It is therefore not surprising to find the original level of performance not reached by the wider-scale program—a finding that parallels the more general findings of a relatively low proportion of programs in the social and medical fields that Mosteller and associates (1973, 1975) judged could be classified as "highly effective" on the basis of impact data yielded by controlled randomized field trials (only about one-fifth of some thirty innovations they thus examined).

REPLICABILITY OF TREATMENTS

A vexing problem in experimental research on social program effects concerns the extent to which the independent variables named by the investigator are idiosyncratic to that investigator. For example, in experiments on "student participation" or "headstart" or "group counseling" (or you name it), the program/treatment as an independent variable is seldom defined in terms sufficiently operational to provide reasonable assurance that someone else would be doing essentially the same thing if that investigator said he or she were implementing the nominally "same treatment." For most or the treatments or variables derived from either common societal practice or from theory, the *specific way* in which a "variable" is implemented can turn out to be a great deal more important than *what* variable it nominally is. We, therefore, get experimental findings in which the "same" kind of treatment (for example, "permissive supervision" or "ease of access") turns out to produce one result when explored by one investigator and another result when implemented by another investigator. The conclusion would seem to be that, pending such time as we are better able to define what our treatment variables mean in more reproducible, operational terms, we may wish to assume the burden of explicit, empirical demonstration of the generalizability of our findings. The critical point can be summarized simply by saying that we ought to be able to show, in a scientifically acceptable fashion, that *someone else* can manipulate and implement the variable under consideration. At present, this demonstration is not easy, for many treatment variables at least, except by brute empirical demonstration.

A possible further deduction from this conclusion is that in an experiment in which one manipulates a named variable or procedure, the critical number of "degrees of freedom" on which generalization from the experiment depends is a function of the number of independent replications (for example, at different sites or with different teams) rather than just the number of recipients or groups of them. Put another way, if we are really going to say that we have found a dependable or generalizable social treatment or procedure, we ought to be able to show that we can write a "recipe" or a set of instructions which will allow *another* experimenter, program manager, teacher, or the like to create effects substantially similar to those we obtained.

To answer the question of reproducibility or "exportability" in the case of a larger-scale field example—the Ellson programmed-tutoring program in basic reading (Ellson *et al.*, 1968)—a field study was made of the tutoring behavior of forty-four tutors in six cities. The purpose was to see whether new personnel in a new site could repeat in essence what had been done in pilot trials by the program developers—that is, whether the effectiveness in pilot trials could be applied usefully to the prediction of future effectiveness in wide-scale application. The tutors' behavior was categorized so that comparisons could be made between the original model, initially tested in four major evolutionary trials from 1964 to 1968 in Indianapolis, with later replications with different supervising personnel in the other five centers. A conclusion drawn by Hawkridge and DeWitt (1969) in their secondary analysis of the "exported" use of the Ellson program was that, on the input side, the original model was replicated in each of the five centers visited with only minor deviations, without changes in overall procedure and with no aspects of it grossly modified. On the output side, experimental results on reading achievement in the decentralized operation, at new sites and under new supervision, likewise bore out the essential pattern of results obtained by the original.

To show empirically that the relative effectiveness of two particular programming procedures was generalizable across a population of programmers (and thus to afford an initial example of this needed approach, in which programmers are used as the experimental units), Rosen (1968) compared two procedures for revising a "draft" version of an instructional program: one based upon an analysis of the program's behavioral objectives; the other, using this same analysis but also using test data obtained following a trial run of the "draft" program. A short, fixed-pace program on "English Money" was prepared using slides and tape. Test-generating statements of the program's objectives were prepared, as well as a specific sample of posttest items. Twenty programmer-subjects, selected from a population of teachers, were then randomly assigned to two treatment groups, and each was directed to develop a fifteen-minute supplementary lesson intended to augment the "draft" program and thereby improve its effectiveness. The programmers in one group were instructed to study data showing the percentage of sixth-graders who passed each of the posttest items following a trial of the "draft" program. The programmers in the other group were asked to study the program's general objectives in relation to the "draft" program as a basis for planning their supplementary lessons, but did not see any data. Videotapes of the twenty lessons they prepared, ten representing each of the two treatment groups, were then tested in randomly assigned sixth-grade classes using the mean posttest score in each class as the measure of each program's effectiveness.

Both types of revisions were significantly more effective than the original "draft" version of the program, and the revisions based upon an objective analysis of test data were significantly more effective than the revisions based solely upon a subjective analysis of the objectives alone.

The experimental model employed in this study appears to be a viable procedure for assessing the relative effectiveness of alternative programming techniques.

A CONCLUDING COMMENT

This chapter has discussed historical developments, current practices and needs, and future potentialities in assessing the impact of educational and social programs, with reference to paradigms historically employed for determining causal relationships in field studies of treatment effects. The author has argued for the importance and feasibility of a thoroughgoing commitment to controlled, randomized field trials—that is, "true" not "quasi" experiments—to determine the impact of social programs, employing individuals or population units (districts, towns, and the like) as the units of randomized assignment. Properly conducted, reported, and cost-accounted, such true experiments are, contrary to the conventional view, in the long run generally *less* costly, as well as more definitive, than quasi-experimental or correlational survey studies. Our concern with the appropriateness of the experimental paradigm for ascertaining demonstrable program effects, as a critical (though not sole) input to programatic and policy decisions, is in contradistinction to other aspects of program evaluation such as assessment of program goals, priorities, and net merit of program impacts.

A fundamental need in the utilization of experimental field trials is that impact be determined for progressively improved programs in an evolutionary sequence. It is essential for impact studies to learn not only whether, but how, improvement is being made, and for impact data to be used as a tool for realistic guaging of progress toward defined goals that are commensurate with the realities of critical societal problems. We need not only better *data* on program impact, but rapid evolution of more effective, more ambitiously conceived *programs* for which such data will indeed show substantially increased social gains. At present, to mount such programs in many of the developing countries (cf. Schramm, 1964a; Myrdal, 1970) seems likely to require financial as well as technical assistance from more affluent nations that is substantially greater, possibly by an order of magnitude, than that currently being supplied. Such assistance must almost certainly include strong support for increasing socieconomic development and attendant motivation for substantial reduction in population growth rates.

REFERENCES

Allendoerfer, C. B. *An Experiment in the Evaluation and Revision of Text Materials.* Seattle: University of Washington, 1969.

Bang, Sook. "Can IUD Retention Be Improved by Prompt Check-up Visits?" In *Population and Family Planning in the Republic of Korea* (vol. 1), Ministry of Health and Social Affairs, Republic of Korea, pp. 130–135, March, 1970.

Bennett, C. A., and A. A. Lumsdaine, eds. *Evaluation and Experiment: Some Critical Issues in Assessing Social Programs.* New York: Academic Press, 1975.

Campbell, U. T., and R. F. Boruch. "Making the Case for Randomized Assignment to Treatments by Considering the Alternatives." Chapter 3 in Bennett and Lumsdaine, *op. cit.,* 1975.

Campbell, D. T., and J. C. Stanley. "Experimental and Quasi-experimental Designs for Research on Teaching." In N. L. Gage, ed., *Handbook of Research on Teaching,* Chicago: Rand McNally, pp. 171–246, 1963. (Also published as *Handbook of Research,* Chicago: Rand McNally, 1966.)

Carpenter, C. R., and L. P. Greenhill. "Instructional Television Research." Report No. 2, University Park, Pennsylvania: Pennsylvania State University, 1958.

Chan, K. C. "Hong Kong Report of the IUD Reassurance Project." *Studies in Family Planning,* 2, pp. 225–233, 1971.

Chang, M. C., G. P. Cernada, and T. H. Sun. "A Field-worker Incentive Study." *Studies in Family Planning,* pp. 270–272, 1972.

Chen H. C., and L. P. Chow. "Strategies for the Introduction of Contraceptive Methods: The Taiwan Experience." In G. W. Duncan, E. J. Hilton, P. Kreager, and A. A. Lumsdaine, eds., *Fertility Control Methods: Strategies for Introduction,* New York: Academic Press, pp. 141–156, 1973.

Cochran, D. L. *The Effects of Practice Schedules and Perceptual Variables on Learning from a Filmed Demonstration.* Unpublished doctoral dissertation, University of California, Los Angeles, 1966.

Cook, T. D., *et al.* *"Sesame Street" Revisited.* New York: Russell Sage, 1975.

Cook, T. D., and D. T. Campbell. "The Design and Conduct of Quasi-experiments and True Experiments in Field Settings." In M. D. Dunnette, ed., *Handbook of Industrial and Organizational Research,* Chicago: Rand McNally, pp. 223–336, 1976.

Deniston, O. L. and I. M. Rosenstock. "The Validity of Nonexperimental Designs for Evaluating Health Services." *Health Service Reports, 88,* pp. 153–164, Feb. 1973.

Ellson, D. G., P. Harris, and L. Barber. "A Field Test of Programed and Directed Tutoring." *Reading Research Quarterly, 3* (3), pp. 307–367, 1968.

Fisher, R. A. *The Design of Experiments* (1935 or later editions). New York: Hafner, 1960.

Flanagan, J. C. "The Uses of Educational Evaluation in the Development of Programs, Courses, Instructional Materials and Equipment, Instructional and Learning Procedures and Administrative Arrangements." *Yearbook of the National Society for the Study of Education,* 1969.

Freedman, R., and J. Takeshita. *Family Planning in Taiwan: An Experiment in Social Change.* Princeton, New Jersey: Princeton University Press, 1969.

Gilbert, J., R. J. Light, and F. Mosteller. "Assessing Social Innovations: An Empirical Base for Policy." Chapter 2 in Bennett and Lumsdaine, *op. cit.,* 1975.

Grace, N. D., H. Muench, and T. C. Chalmers. "The Present Status of Shunts for Portal Hypertension in Cirrhosis." *Gastroenterology, 50,* pp. 684–691, 1966.

Gropper, G. L., *et al. An Evaluation of Television Procedures Designed to Stimulate Extracurricular Science Activities* (Studies in televised instruction, Report No. 6). Pittsburgh: Metropolitan Pittsburgh Educational Television Stations WQED-WQEX and American Institute for Research, 1961. (Abstract in *Audio-Visual Communication Review,* USOE Installment 2, pp. 54–55.)

Hartmann, G. N. "A Field Experiment on the Compatative Effectiveness of "Emotional" vs. "Rational" Political Leaflets in Determining Election Results." *Journal of Abnormal and Social Psychology, 31,* pp. 99–146, 1936.

Hawkridge, D. G., and K. M. DeWitt. *An Evaluation of the Programmed Tutoring Technique.* Palo Alto: American Institute for Research, Report No. AIR-822-3/69-FR, 1969.

Hill, R., J. M. Stycos, and K. W. Back. *The Family and Population Control: A Puerto Rican Experiment in Social Change.* Chapel Hill, North Carolina: The University of North Carolina Press, 1959.

Hilton, E. T., and A. A. Lumsdaine. "Field Trial Designs in Gauging the Impact of Fertility Planning Programs." Chapter 5 in Bennett and Lumsdaine, *op. cit.,* 1975.

Hovland, C. I., I. L. Janis, and H. H. Kelley. *Communication and Persuasion: Psychological Studies of Opinion Change.* New Haven: Yale University Press, 1953.

Hovland, C. I., A. A. Lumsdaine, and F. D. Sheffield. *Experiments on Mass Communication*. Princeton, New Jersey: Princeton University Press, 1949.

Lashley, K. S., and J. B. Watson. *A Psychological Study of Motion Pictures in Relation to Venereal Disease Campaigns*. Washington: U. S. Interdepartmental Social Hygiene Board, 1922.

Light, R. J., F. Mosteller, and H. S. Winokur, Jr. "Using Controlled Field Studies to Improve Public Policy." Chapter 6 in Volume 2, *Federal Statistics: Report of the President's Commission*. Washington, D.C.: U.S. Government Printing Office, pp. 367–402, 1971.

Lindquist, E. F. *Design and Analysis of Experiments in Psychology and Education*. New York: Houghton Mifflin, 1953.

Lu, L. P., H. C. Chen, and L. P. Chow. "An Experimental Study of the Effect of Group Meetings on the Acceptance of Family Planning in Taiwan." *The Journal of Social Issues, 23*, pp. 171–177, 1967.

Lumsdaine, A. A., ed. *Student Response in Programmed Instruction*. Washington, D.C.: National Academy of Sciences, National Research Council, 1961.

Lumsdaine, A. A. "Instruments and Media of Instruction." Chapter 12 in N. L. Gage, ed., *Handbook of Research on Teaching*, Chicago: Rand McNally, 1963.

Lumsdaine, A. A., E. T. Hilton, and D. L. Kincaid. "Evaluation Research Methods." Chapter 2 in E. M. Rogers and R. Agarwala-Rogers, eds., *Evaluation Research on Family Planning Communication*, Paris: UNESCO, 1976.

Lumsdaine, A. A., and I. L. Janis. "Resistance to Counter-propaganda Produced by One-sided and Two-sided Propaganda Presentations." *Public Opinion Quarterly, 17*, pp. 311–318, 1953.

Lumsdaine, A. A., and M. A. May. "Mass Communication and Educational Media." *Annual Review of Psychology, 16*, pp. 475–533, 1965.

Maccoby, N., and G. Comstock. *The First Year of Peace Corps Educational Television in Colombia*. Stanford University: Institute for Communication Research, 1965.

Maccoby, N., and J. W. Farquhar. "Communication for Health: Unselling Heart Disease." *Journal of Communication, 25:3*, pp. 114–126, Summer, 1975.

Maccoby, N., and F. D. Sheffield. "Combining Practice with Demonstration in Teaching Complex Sequences: Summary and Interpretation." In Lumsdaine, *op. cit.*, pp. 77–85, 1961.

Markle, D. G. *The Development of the Bell System First Aid and Personal Safety Course*. Report No. AIR-E81-4/67-FR. Palo Alto: American Institutes for Research, 1967.

Mathen, K. K. "Preliminary Lessons Learned from the Rural Population Control Study of Singur." in C. V. Kiser, ed., *Research in Family Planning*, Princeton: Princeton University Press, 1962.

May, M. A., and N. L. Jenkinson. "Developing Interest in Reading with Film. *Audio-Visual Communication Review, 1*, pp. 159–166, 1953.

May, M. A., and A. A. Lumsdaine. *Learning from Films*. New Haven: Yale University Press, 1958.

McKeachie, W. J. "Instructional Psychology." *Annual Review of Psychology*, *25*, pp. 161–193, 1974.

Michael, D. N., and N. Maccoby. "Factors Influencing Verbal Learning from Films under Varying Conditions of Audience Participation." *Journal of Experimental Psychology*, *46*, pp. 411–418, 1953.

Miller, N. E. "Some Contributions of Behavioral Science." In E. Hutchings and E. Hutchings, eds., *Scientific Progress and Human Values*, New York: American Elsevier Publishing Company, Inc., 1967.

Mitchell, R. E. "Hong Kong: An Evaluation of Field Workers and Decision Making in Family Planning Programs." *Studies in Family Planning*, *1*, pp. 7–12, 1968.

Mosteller, Frederick. "Assessing Social Innovations by Controlled Field Trials." (Paper presented at a symposium at Battelle Institute's Seattle Research Center, July, 1973). See the later-published expanded version coauthored by Gilbert, Light, and Mosteller (1975); see also the related paper by Light, Mosteller, and Winokur (1971).

Myrdal, G. *The Challenge of World Poverty*. New York: Random House, 1970.

Patel, C. B. *To Develop Auto-instructional Programmes in Geometry and Find Out Their Effectiveness*. Ph.D. thesis, A. G. Teachers' College, Navrangpura, Ahmedabad, India, 1976.

Perloff, R., E. Perloff, and E. Sussna. "Program Evaluation." *Annual Review of Psychology*, *27*, pp. 569–594, 1975.

Riecken, H. W., and R. F. Boruch, eds. *Social Experimentation: A Method for Planning and Evaluating Social Intervention*. New York: Academic Press, 1974.

Rosen, M. J. *An Experimental Design for Comparing the Effects of Instructional Media Programming Procedures*. Unpublished doctoral dissertation, University of California, Los Angeles, 1968.

Rosenfield, A. G., and C. Limcharoen. "Auxiliary Midwife Prescription of Oral Contraceptives: An Experimental Project in Thailand." *American Journal of Obstetrics and Gynecology*, *114*, pp. 942–949, 1972.

Roshal, S. M. "Film-mediated Learning with Varying Representations of the Task: Viewing Angle, Portrayal of Demonstration, Motion, and Student Participation." Chapter 11 in Lumsdaine, *op. cit.*, pp. 155–176, 1961.

Rossi, P. H., and K. C. Lyall. *Reforming Public Welfare: A Critique of the Negative Income Tax Experiment*. New York: Russell Sage, 1976.

Salcedo, J., Jr. "Views and Comments on the Report on Rice Enrichment in the Philippines." In *Food and Agriculture Organization of the United Nations*, Report Number 12, Rome, Italy, pp. 101–106, March, 1954.

Schramm, W. "Mass Communication." *Annual Review of Psychology*, *13*, pp. 251–284, 1962(a).

_____. *Programed Instruction: Today and Tomorrow*. New York: Fund for the Advancement of Education, The Ford Foundation, 1962(b).

_____. *Mass Media and National Development*. Stanford, California: Stanford University Press, 1964(a).

_____. *The Research on Programed Instruction: An Annotated Bibliography*. Washington, D.C.: U.S. Department of Health, Education, and Welfare, Office of Education, 1964 (b).

———. "Communication in Family Planning." *Reports on Population/Family Planning,* April, 1971.

———. "What the Research Says." In W. Schramm, ed. *Quality in Instructional Television.* Honolulu: University Press of Hawaii, pp. 44–79, 1972.

Simmons, A. B. "Information Campaigns and the Growth of Family Planning in Colombia." In J. M. Stycos, ed., *Clinics, Contraception, and Communication,* New York: Appleton-Century-Crofts, pp. 116–171, 1973.

Stouffer, S. A., *et al. The American Soldier:* Vol. 1, *Studies in Social Psychology in World War II.* Princeton: Princeton University Press, 1949.

Suchman, E. A. *Evaluative Research: Principles and Practice in Public Service and Social Action Programs.* New York: Russell Sage Foundation, pp. ix and 186, 1967.

Wittrock, M. C., and D. C. Wiley, eds. *The Evaluation of Instruction.* New York: Holt, Rinehart and Winston, 1970.

Wortman, P. M., "Evaluation Research." *American Psychologist, 30,* pp. 562–575, 1975.

Wyon, J. B., and J. E. Gordon. *Khanna Study: Population Problems in the Rural Punjab.* Cambridge, Massachusetts: Harvard University Press, 1971.

Yang, J. M. "Studies in Family Planning and Related Programs in Rural Korea." In *Social Evaluation of Family Planning Programs and Research Activities in Korea.* Seoul, Korea: Korea Sociological Association, pp. 122–135, 1972.

Communication and Education in Open Learning Systems

DAVID G. HAWKRIDGE

PROLOGUE

In May 1975, Wilbur Schramm stood in Bristol, England, to receive the honorary degree of Doctor of the University from Sir Walter Perry, Vice-Chancellor of the Open University. A large audience of graduates and their children celebrated the occasion, a day of fine achievement for all. The man from the former British Sandwich Islands who had done much for open learning was honored before them, and the clapping was long and loud. What could have been more fitting?

To write now for Wilbur's *festschrift* is a pleasure, and it seems entirely appropriate to focus on those studies which have increased our understanding of how open learning systems can be set up and can operate successfully. By no coincidence, Wilbur Schramm's name will appear rather frequently.

DEFINITIONS, CHARACTERISTICS, AND EXAMPLES

"The Open University is magical. It means to each what he wants it to mean." So said a distinguished visitor to the Open University. Much the same might be said about the words "open learning systems": They are magical in that they carry widely varying connotations both among different groups of academic specialists and among the general public.

"Open learning" means for some the activities of children incarcerated in open-plan classrooms. For others, it means the freedom for students to explore their physical and intellectual environment. For still others, it means access to learning resources that were formerly inaccessible, for whatever reason. This last meaning will be used in this chapter.

For cyberneticians, "learning systems" are systems that learn. For educators, they are systems that aid learning by humans. In the context of this chapter, macrosystems set up by ministries of education, perhaps as national or regional institutions, are of special interest, although the microsystems involving only a handful of humans must never be neglected.

"Open learning systems" are therefore systems that aid human learning by offering many people access to learning resources that were formerly inaccessible.

The purpose of this chapter would be suited if this definition were watertight. It is not. One might say, correctly, that a mobile library is an example of an open learning system, yet I write not about mobile libraries. The best way to refine the definition is to identify the characteristics of the particular sort of open learning system, now evolving in many countries, on which the rest of this chapter is based. Alternative definitions have been attempted by MacKenzie, Postgate, and Scupham (1975), and by the National Association of Educational Broadcasters (1974); in both cases, the authors resorted to listing characteristics rather than providing precise definitions.

First, as we have said, these systems increase educational opportunity. As a rule, they do so in part by a liberal admissions policy. They employ more than one medium to communicate with learners, in the hope of increasing learners' chances of learning. They bring learning resources to the learner rather than expecting the learner to come to the resources. They serve large numbers of students and can usually increase these numbers without increasing costs proportionately. In them, control of production is centralized, but distribution of the products is at least partly decentralized. They are capital-intensive rather than labor-intensive. They are complex, often highly integrated, and require sophisticated technical skills for their operation. Frequently, but not always, they demand a well-developed infrastructure from the country or region in which they operate: they ride "piggy-back" on other social institutions, including educational ones. Because they are highly centralized in production, they are vulnerable to political interference. They offer rich resources to learners but not on an individualized basis; some say they are not learner-oriented. Finally, they frequently catalyze reform in adjacent educational systems—sometimes in dramatic ways, sometimes in subtle fashion.

These open learning systems belong entirely to the twentieth century—indeed, to the second half of that century. They are new phenomena, made possible through technological advances.

Examples of open learning systems abound. In Table 3-1, more than fifty such systems are mentioned, ranging from those which provide African village people opportunities to learn about farming to those which provide university studies for people in westernized countries.

Wilbur Schramm was particularly closely associated with three examples from Table 3-1: those systems in American Samoa, El Salvador, and Israel. For American Samoan and Salvadorian systems, his principal role was that of evaluator; for Israel, he was leader of the commission which drew up proposals for the system.

In American Samoa, an open learning system was built using instructional television. Three channels started broadcasting in 1964 to primary schools, covering all grades. The following year, three more channels were added to broadcast a complete high school curriculum (Schramm, 1973a). Up to 6,000 live instructional programs a year were produced for broadcasting. Almost at a stroke, the learning opportunities for children in American Samoa were transformed. Only one island was unable to receive the transmissions. In recent years, adults and preschool groups as well as school children have been receiving broadcasts.

The American Samoan open learning system was established deliberately with the intention of upgrading Samoan education far more quickly than could have been done by conventional means. According to Schramm, its existence enabled the Samoans to "overleap the time required to train teachers adequately" and to speed up the mastery of English by primary school children. By 1973, although the system was serving only 8,100 pupils, their education was being radically affected. The programs were no mere "add on" to classroom instruction and were supplemented by teachers' guides and pupils' workbooks.

Today, instructional television is being used to complement rather than transform education in American Samoan schools. The open learning system's catalytic purpose has been served. Some proponents of open learning express disappointment that the heyday of instructional television there has apparently passed, and the learning system is becoming more closed, more conventionally based on classroom instruction. Those who see open learning systems as contributing to deschooling, in Ivan Illich's sense, may feel that the American Samoan experiment failed. They would be wrong in thinking this way. Within the objectives set up in American Samoa, an open learning system succeeded amid numerous problems (Cooney, 1973).

In El Salvador, too, instructional television was the basis for an open learning system aimed at catalyzing educational reform. In the 1960s, political leaders in that country came to view educational reform as essential if the nation's social and economic ills were to be cured. The five-year reform plan put forward in 1968 proposed the installation of a national instructional television system for grades 7 through 9. American aid was sought, and broadcasting began in 1969 for grade 7. Again, the programs were aimed at direct instruction, not merely enrichment. Texts, closely interpreted with the programs, were distributed to teachers and pupils.

Salvadorean educators insisted that curriculum reform and teacher retraining should run ahead of the televised instruction. Since the pacing effect of the television project was relentless, these and other changes took place speedily, if inadequately. Indeed, Salvadorean leaders claimed that the Educational Reform, as the project was called, would not have taken place at all without the catalytic effect of television.

As examples of changes brought about in El Salvador between 1968 and 1973, Schramm's evaluation team quoted the following factors in their final report: a tripling of numbers of students in grades 7 through 9, a reduction in dropouts and repeaters, an increase in numbers of disadvantaged children entering grade 7, a reduction in per capita cost for the system as more students entered, and an increase in class numbers without a decline in the quality of education (Hornik et al., 1973). Not all of these factors can be ascribed to the introduction of an open learning system in the form of television, but the team's report asserts that without television, the quality of education would certainly have *declined* in the schools.

Clearly, the El Salvador open learning system indirectly and directly brought opportunities for learning to many who would have been the poorer educated but for it.

When Schramm went to Israel in 1972, he found a rather different situation from that in American Samoa or El Salvador. Israel already had a highly developed if somewhat traditional education system, including seven excellent universities. As a modern state, partly in-

TABLE 3-1. Examples of Open Learning Systems

Africa

Ghana	Radio Rural Forum
Ivory Coast	Schools television
Kenya	Teacher training by radio and correspondence (CCU)
Niger	Radio Club Association; Télé-Niger
Nigeria	National Teachers Institute; University of the Air
Rhodesia	Schools television, radio and correspondence
Senegal	Téléclubs
South Africa	Radio and correspondence, schools for remote areas
Tanzania	Radio Farm Forum
Togo	Radio Rural Forum
Zambia	Schools television, radio and correspondence; radio farm forum

Asia

India	Radio Rural Forum
Japan	NHK Gakuen High School; National Broadcasting University (proposed)
Pakistan	People's Open University
Thailand	Radio for schools

Australasia and Pacific

American Samoa	Instructional Television Project
Australia	Radio-correspondence schools; National Institute for Open Tertiary Education (proposed); University of New England

Europe

East Germany	Television Academy
France	Télé-CNAM
Great Britain	The Open University; National Extension College
Italy	Telescuola
Netherlands	Teleac
Poland	Television Polytechnic; Television Agricultural High School
Spain	National University of Long Distance Education
Sweden	TRU (Committee for Television and Radio in Education)
USSR	Northwest Polytechnic, Leningrad
West Germany	Deutsches Institut für Fernstudien; Bavarian Telekolleg; Funkkolleg; Fernuniversität

Latin America

Colombia	Radio Sutatenza; Schools television project
Costa Rica	Radio Rural Forum
El Salvador	Instructional Television Project
Mexico	Radioprimaria; Telesecundaria

TABLE 3–1. (Continued)

Middle East	
Iran	Free University
Israel	Everyman's University
North America	
Canada	Quebec Téléuniversité; Athabaska University
USA	State University of Nebraska; Chicago TV College; Alaskan Satellite Project; Sesame Street and The Electric Company; Open University for Massachusetts; Hawaii Open Program

dustrialized, Israel needed many well-educated people. Yet large numbers of children—and adults—mostly Oriental Jews and Arabs were failing in the conventional education system, with few chances of ever remedying that failure.

Everyman's University, as the open learning system in Israel is now called, is intended to serve the socially and educationally disadvantaged both by providing courses for adults who wish to gain or upgrade qualifications and by undertaking inservice teacher training to improve classroom instruction in the schools.

Unlike the American Samoan and El Salvador examples, Everyman's University may not depend much on television. Correspondence materials, including kits and other equipment, will be sent to students, who will probably be able to meet tutors in local study centers. Radio may be important, if the suggestions of the inquiry commission headed by Schramm are accepted (Schramm, Hawkridge, and Howe, 1972). The costs of installing an additional television channel to serve the open learning system would be great, but an extra radio channel would cost far less.

By late 1975, Everyman's University was still in its early development stage. Backed by money from Hanadiv (The Rothschild Family Foundation) and by the Government's Council for Higher Education, its staff was busy producing the first six courses. No indication was yet apparent of how many thousands of students would enroll in October 1976, when teaching was due to begin.

These three examples, from American Samoa, El Salvador, and Israel, illustrate well the characteristics of open learning systems. We can point to the way Everyman's University will bring courses to the kibbutz, or to how in El Salvador the existing schools were used to provide the "study centers," or to the combination of media employed in

American Samoa. A change of government in El Salvador might wipe out the open learning system there, just as Telescuola disappeared almost overnight in Italy. In Israel, the hope is that the high initial cost of making courses in Tel Aviv will be set against the low recurrent cost of distributing them to thousands of students up and down the country. In American Samoa, technical expertise from the mainland may be required for a few more years to keep the open learning system running. Thus these three examples display well the principal features of open learning systems, including their strengths and weaknesses.

STUDIES OF OPEN LEARNING SYSTEMS AND THEIR COMPONENTS

Now that we have established what open learning systems are like, the next step is to consider studies that have been made of them. These studies can be divided into those undertaken *before* any decision had been taken to set up an open learning system and those done afterwards *in* an existing system.

Among the preliminary feasibility studies are those of political context, of academic milieu, of social needs, of likely demand, of alternative systems of delivery and communication, and of costs.

To catalog the studies of existing systems is more difficult: broadly, they fall into design and development studies, on the one hand, and evaluative studies on the other. Within the first category are studies that have implications for closed learning systems as well as open ones, but all the studies in this category have an evaluative flavor. They include, for example, studies of student characteristics, of teaching and learning styles, of the structure of course content, of media selection, of testing techniques and formats, of tutoring and counseling of students. Many of these studies merge into evaluative studies of the effectiveness of open learning system course components, including television, radio, print, tutoring, and so on. Other studies examine the impact of open learning systems on students' lives or upon adjacent educational systems. Costs and benefits are the subject of still further studies.

To try to separate these studies into basic and applied research or some similar dichotomy might be desirable, but the inadequacies of these categories have been amply demonstrated (see, for example, Taylor, 1973). Instead, we shall identify as many studies as possible, using a series of simple headings, within each of the two major classes: feasibility studies and studies in existing open learning systems.

SOME FEASIBILITY STUDIES

Political context. Open learning systems are capital-intensive, as we have said. Before governments take the plunge and set them up, the political factors must be weighed carefully. The final decision to establish an open learning system is always a political one, as Peters, Bierfelder, and Lörcher (1973) show in their discussion of the Japanese University of the Air or National Broadcasting University, and as Rau (1974) points out for the Rhine–Westphalian Distance University. Official reports, such as that of the Iranian Ministry of Higher Education (1972) on the Free University of Iran, the Report of the Worth Commission on Educational Planning in Alberta (Commission on Educational Planning, 1972), and the Karmel Report and Falk Report on open tertiary education in Australia (Committee on Open University, 1974; Falk and Anwyl, 1973; Northcott, 1975) are essentially political context studies, although they also cover much else. The Worth Report led to political decisions on Athabasca University's distance teaching system, while in Australia the political debate continues over the National Institute for Open Tertiary Education (Braithwaite and Batt, 1975). Similarly, the New England Open University Steering Committee (Smith, 1972) conducted a political analysis as part of its preparation for proposing a regional institution for that part of the United States. The State University of Nebraska (1973) obtained the collaboration of State Governors and undertook careful studies of its political context, leading to its proposals for the University of Mid-America, serving several states. In Japan, the Preparatory Study Committee for the University of the Air (1970) incorporated within its membership politicians as well as educators, broadcasters, and industrialists.

Needless to say, in Britain the political context was of great importance during discussions in parliament on the University of the Air, later to become the Open University (see, for example, Ardagh, 1966, and Jackson, 1967). In Israel, Schramm's commission was also bound to take political factors into account during its consultations (Schramm, Hawkridge, and Howe, 1972).

We might cite many other examples of this kind of assessment of what is politically feasible. When an open learning system is proposed, wide-ranging inquiries into the needs as perceived by political authorities of different character appear to be the standard pattern, even in relatively authoritarian countries. MacKenzie, Postgate, and

Scupham (1975) offer some useful checklists of the sources that should be consulted. Exceptions to this pattern will probably be found in a few totalitarian countries, where an open learning system is set up with the deliberate aims of the central government in mind—namely to avoid providing other educational facilities, to dominate education with a particular ideology, or to claim the prestige of having an open learning system (along with a national airline). Sometimes all three aims are served.

Academic milieu. Many of the existing open learning systems were set up following studies of their future academic milieu. By "academic milieu" we mean the relationships the systems bear to other educational institutions in the country concerned. If the open learning system is intended to serve adults, for example, and to prepare them for degrees as in the case of the Open University, then considerable thought has to be given to what is already being done by other institutions preparing students for degrees. Duplication is to be avoided, complementarity enhanced. This concern is reflected in the report of the Open University Planning Committee (1969). Similarly, the Preparatory Study Committee for the University of the Air (1970) in Japan consulted widely among academics when considering the content of the future curriculum. In the State University of Nebraska project, the question of academic acceptance of the credit courses to be offered by the proposed University of Mid-America had to be tackled, in the context of a declared open admissions policy (Wedemeyer, 1975). I have cited just a few examples; others will be found in the reports quoted already.

Social needs. In addition to arriving at a political consensus and studying the academic milieu, some countries and institutions have tried to carry out studies of the social needs. It is one thing for politicians to say in the legislature that the country needs an open learning system, or for the unions to demand one, as in Belgium (see Childs, 1973). It is quite another to carry out a social survey to obtain the opinions of a sample of the population. Gooler (1975) has provided a discussion of the conceptual problems of needs assessment for open learning systems within the consumer-oriented American economy, but he does not approach the basic questions of which needs ought to be recognized and served by such systems and of how these needs can be identified. Nearly all the studies of social needs done to date have been academic and theoretical, as for example in Israel (Schramm, Hawkridge, and Howe, 1972), where demographic data provided the principal basis. In Canada, the newly-constituted Ontario Educational Communications Authority held a Round Table Conference in 1971 (Duggan and Waniewicz, 1972) which focussed its attention for some time on the question of matching the new media to social needs but did not come up with any prescription.

A careful survey for the same Authority by Jacobs (1971) yielded a list of the educational, not social, needs expressed by respondents in the Toronto region. This study was carried out to provide a firmer foundation for the exploitation of the available and planned open learning facilities in that area. It appears to be one of the few "consumer surveys" of social needs undertaken before the setting up of an open learning system, although Lefranc (1967) reported that in the early days of Télé-Niger, a study was made of twenty villages into which television was to be introduced.

Likely demand. Although few attempts have been made to use social science methods to provide a more objective basis for deciding on the social needs to be served by a new open learning system, studies have been made of what clients would like among certain options and how great the demand is likely to be. For example, future clients have been surveyed to discover what courses they think they would probably take. The institution which has undertaken more of this kind of work than any other is the State University of Nebraska. A series of surveys, reported by Ross, Brown, and Hassel (1972), Central Surveys (1973), Flinn (1973), Brown (1974), Sell (1975), and Eggert (1975), provided data from representative panels of adults at state and regional levels. Sell's summary indicated that three of the surveys were aimed at establishing the likely demand for particular courses to be offered by the university: Psychology and accounting were named as top choices. Other questions related to the award of credit, the reasons adults take courses, where they wished to study, how much direction they wanted while studying, what media they would prefer, and the obstacles they perceived to studying. Data were also collected on each respondent's age, sex, and educational and occupational background. Eggert's paper compared the survey results with similar data from students actually studying the first two courses offered by the State University of Nebraska.

Elsewhere, the Japanese Ministry of Education published two surveys on the University of the Air, carried out among young people; over a million people seemed likely to take courses if the University were to come into being (Sakamoto, 1971). Takasaki (1973) carried out surveys among adult education students during his feasibility studies for the proposed Hawaii State College, another open learning system. A survey made before the Open University was established led to the estimate that a pool of 35,000 to 184,000 people existed in Britain from which the university would draw its students. The error of measurement was large.

These surveys, conducted primarily by questionnaire but sometimes supplemented by face-to-face or telephone interviews, have not provided the answers that planning committees require. Faced with the problem of whether or not to recommend to government that an open learning system should be set up, such committees want to know above all else whether demand will be sufficient for the courses provided through the system. The cost-effectiveness argument is such a strong one, for or against the proposed system as the case may be. In carrying out surveys of this kind, however, the researchers have to send a confused message: Do you want to study through this Whatsit? We can't describe it to you in detail, we don't know what the course will be, and we are not sure if it will ever exist in this country. But do you want to study through it? Yes or no.

This caricature of how the surveys have been carried out underlines the basic problem of communication. In fact, some of the surveys have asked whether people have television and radio (if these media are thought to be parts of the potential system), have asked about people's access to education at present or about their hopes and frustrations regarding becoming literate or professionally qualified, and so on. Much can be discovered that is useful to planning committees and to the new institution once it is established. McIntosh's (1970) studies on the British National Extension College students and their courses, for example, provided basic data for the Open University's guidance.

The surveys have taken place only where the relevant planning committee has a client-oriented model in mind. Elsewhere, attempts have been made to use a society-oriented model—that is, a manpower planning model. Governments decide demand will be made for a particular course offered through an open learning system, and may even enhance the demand by offering rewards of money or promotion to those who complete that course. In Kenya, a firm decision was made to use an open learning system based on correspondence and radio to upgrade teachers' qualifications (see Edington et al., 1974; Kinyanjui, 1975). In Poland, the Television Polytechnic was set up specifically to help remedy the shortage of engineers and technicians (Vanderheyden, 1973). In Iran, the Free University has been established with specific manpower needs in mind—for instance to upgrade teachers and paramedicals—although it will probably serve many others (Iranian Ministry of Higher Education, 1972; Beardsley, 1975). In Pakistan, the People's Open University was first planned with the vocational education of elementary teachers and members of the National Literacy Corps in mind, together with the promotion of rural and community development activities (Shah, 1973).

Alternatives for delivery and communication. Decisions about whether or not to use various alternatives, such as radio or the telephone, for delivery of learning resources and for communication between the learners and their teachers are often based on the availability of these alternatives and their costs, rather than upon the pedagogical advantages of each. For example, the lack of a second television channel in Israel has already been mentioned as being likely to determine how much television is used in Everyman's University. In Iran, the problems of delivering printed materials seem almost insuperable at present: Students will have to come to study centers to collect their texts.

Feasibility studies have been carried out in a few places, but the reports have not been published. For example, long before any courses were being taught, the Open University sent test packages through the mail to various parts of the country and had them returned to ascertain delivery times. Bates (1973a) has discussed alternative audiovisual delivery systems, although not as part of a feasibility study for a *new* open learning system. Gallagher and Marshall (1975) reported on a pilot project introducing video-cassette recorders into Open University study centers; again, this project was testing the feasibility of an addition to an existing system. Schramm (1973b) drew comparisons between alternative systems, resting the debate on the costs and general benefits. In these few studies, little of the data generated would be directly useful to planning committees.

Costs. All planning committees for new open learning systems have asked questions about costs, but we have to face the fact that very seldom have they called for financial feasibility studies. Instead, they have drawn upon evidence from three sources: costings of media, prescriptions for cost-benefit analysis, and historical data from existing systems. In the case of costings of media, they have had available general studies of educational media and media components. For instance, a massive study was made by General Learning Corporation

(1968); Miller in a paper (1969) gave rough estimates of the costs per student hour of different media; and a survey was made by the National Council for Educational Technology (1973) in Britain. Schramm (1973b) depends heavily on the first of these three studies in making his analyses of open learning systems costs. An economist's study by Jamison (1971) examined the costs of using radio in Indonesian education.

In the case of prescriptions for cost-benefit analysis, planning committees may have had access to theoretical prescriptions laying down ways of choosing between alternatives on the basis of cost (for example, Carpenter *et al.*, 1970; Lumsden and Attiyeh, 1974; Doughty, 1974; Jopling and Avery, 1975).

In the case of historical data from existing systems, planning committees have sometimes turned to a growing list of evaluative studies which have cataloged and analyzed the costs of existing open learning systems in several countries. More will be said of these studies later, but Lefranc (1967), Combs (1967), Schramm *et al.* (1967), Speagle (1972), Wagner (1972, 1973), Jamison and Klees (1973), Schramm (1973b), and Laidlaw and Layard (1974) have reported such studies. None of these studies is of much use to a planning committee wanting simple, global answers on costs, since every country offers a different economic and educational environment. On the other hand, taken together they offer plain evidence of the variables that ought to be taken into account, of some of the relationships between these variables, and of the underestimating that has wittingly or unwittingly accompanied the birth of each of the existing systems. Lessons learned about costs in the Open University were useful to the commission on Everyman's University, although conditions in Israel are very different from those in Britain. Heavy dependence on television, as in the State University of Nebraska, can seemingly be achieved only at the expense of some other component. Building new study centers is expensive, as the Free University of Iran is discovering, but may be essential in remote areas where few existing buildings are suitable and available. Using already published materials is cheaper than preparing one's own, but doing so holds hidden costs, as the Open University now knows. Radio programs without local discussion groups seem to be relatively ineffective, as several countries have found with their Radio Farm Forums; therefore the cost of paying discussion leaders must be taken into account. Yet these factors are only a few which must be considered by planning committees costing new open learning systems.

Summary. We can say fairly that no great mass of empirical evidence has been gathered from feasibility studies commissioned by such committees. This verdict applies to all aspects of feasibility but more to some than to others. Planning committees may still learn as much by looking at existing foreign systems as by conducting studies for themselves in their own countries.

STUDIES OF EXISTING SYSTEMS AND THEIR COMPONENTS

It is a far cry from the macroplanning of a more-or-less distinguished commission, soon to be disbanded, to the microplanning of a hard-pressed team appointed as the staff of a new open learning system. For the team, every day brings demands for answers to questions the commission probably never considered, or at best skirted. At first, the questions are basic ones. Staff needs answers in order to get the operation moving. Tested design principles are in short supply. Later, once some students are in the system, learning through it, a host of further questions are raised by staff *and* students. Studies must be undertaken, and research staff appointed to do them.

Almost all the open learning systems listed in Table 3-1 have some kind of research or evaluation group. These groups form a very loosely knit network; they exchange information slowly, fitfully, and cautiously. Many of their publications are not really published. These internal documents may be hidden, sometimes for political reasons, but more often because the words that have been written are seen as first approximations of ideas or solutions. Data are sometimes marked "provisional," because the data collection systems are not yet to be trusted. Research reports are headed "for limited distribution," because they may be misunderstood, the authors fear, if they are read outside the institution.

In spite of difficulties in procuring information about current studies by groups internal to open learning systems, sufficient reports have been identified for a patchy review in which the Open University figures rather prominently. In addition, quite a large literature is now growing up based on the work of external evaluation teams, such as those Schramm himself sometimes led. Enough studies have been generated from these two sources for us to cluster them under headings, as in the previous section.

Students' characteristics and attitudes. No matter how heterogeneous the student body may be in educational level, occupational background, age, sex, motivation, and so on, the staff of new open learning systems is obliged to face the question of who they will be trying to help to learn and what these people are like. As Schramm once said in a lecture on the Voice of America, "The technology of mass communication has been developed primarily to assist the *sender* and has given only secondary attention to the problems of the *receiver.*" In open learning systems both sets of problems must be faced.

Elementary studies along the lines of traditional audience research came first, and British ones were listed by Coppen (1967). These studies were chiefly surveys of the size of audience (was anyone viewing or listening to broadcasts?); sometimes questions were asked to find out what the learners thought. For example, Barath and Sandor (1966) reported a simple survey of the use of educational radio in Hungarian schools. Dubost (1968) carried out a similar study of the students viewing the programs of the Conservatoire National des Arts and Matiers (Télé-CNAM). At Nippon Hoso Kyokai's (NHK) Gakuen High School, according to Schramm *et al.* (1967), several studies of students yielded data on numbers enrolling and their attitudes toward courses. Moore (1969) and McNamara (1973) reported a study of attitudes of students toward off-campus television courses at Memorial University, Newfoundland. The students of Télé-CNAM were again surveyed, this time by Lesne (1970), to investigate their motivation, attitudes, study habits, and social backgrounds. In the Netherlands, van Erde and van Gent (1970) conducted a study of student attitudes for Teleac. Wagner (1971) reported on the characteristics of students taking an Austrian radio-plus-correspondence course. Hoffbauer (1971) described the characteristics, attitudes, and motivation of Quadriga-Funkkolleg students of pedagogy in West Germany.

Edfeldt (1970) and Anderson and Bohlin (1971), reviewing the "extensive research" of the Swedish Committee for Television and Radio in Education (TRU), stated that adult students had been questioned on their previous education, occupations, reasons for taking the courses, study habits and techniques, attitudes toward the television and radio programs, and their satisfaction with times of broadcasts. Rosenbaum (1971) reported on studies of Telekolleg students in Bavaria. Analyses were developed of characteristics such as age, sex, occupation, geographical location (rural/urban), educational level, distance from work, and vocational or other motivation for taking the courses. Tymowsky (1971), Garnier (1971), and Wermer (1971) reviewed similar studies for their respective organizations: the Polish Television Polytechnic, the French Radio-Télévision Scolaire, and the

Dutch Teleac. Egly (1972), in writing a report on the first seven years of the Tele-Niger project, included some analyses of audience characteristics. In Poland, studies have also been made of students in the Television Agricultural High School (see Frentzel-Zagorska and Wyka, 1973; Stone, 1975) reporting on age, sex, occupation, schooling, attitudes to the courses, and motivation. Kempfer (1973) analyzed home-study students in Illinois by age, sex, occupation, and educational level. For the Mexican Telesecundaria, Mayo, McAnany, and Klees (1973) reported student characteristics. Schramm (1973a) gave details of an attitude survey of students in American Samoa. Zigerell (1974) noted a series of studies of students of Chicago's TV College and quoted data on student backgrounds.

The most extensive studies to date on a particular student body are those by McIntosh at the Open University. McIntosh and Bates (1972) carried out studies on the students and courses of the National Extension College, as we mentioned earlier; then McIntosh began studying the first cohort of students in the Open University. She collected a massive file of data from the students' application forms and questionnaires; analyses of these data have been appearing for several years as the students' progress (and that of later cohorts) is followed. Published accounts will be found in, for example, McIntosh (1973), McIntosh and Woodley (1974), McIntosh and Morrison (1974), McIntosh (1975a and 1975b), and particularly McIntosh and Calder (1975). The same research group has also been responsible for studies of Open University students' attitudes toward their courses and progress within them; most of these reports are internal, being statistical data summaries derived from an extensive reporting system used on many courses (see Blacklock, 1972, 1975). Still further inquiries have related to potential students (those who inquire but do not apply, and those who are offered a place but do not accept it), to forecasting demand for courses, to the use of study resources provided for students, to students' financial problems, to aspects of student motivation, and so on. In all these cases, few reports have yet been published outside the Open University, although the published accounts referred to above contain some data.

Curriculum and course design. The staff of a new open learning system has a natural tendency to wonder whether or not they ought to redesign curricula. On what basis can they decide upon a particular section of courses? Whatever they decide to do about curricula, sooner or later they have to design courses. Then they discover that all the problems encountered by designers for closed systems are simply written large in open learning systems. The selection of subject matter, the structuring of knowledge to be taught, and the specification of objectives appear to be all the more necessary, because students in open learning systems are frequently learning at a distance from the coursemakers. Clear communication is even more essential than in closed learning systems.

At the Open University, Neil (1970a, 1970b) put forward proposals for course planning and the use of conceptual models to convey the structure of course units to students, based on his work for a science course team. The developmental testing of course units, using applicants to the Open University as subjects, was described by Connors (1971). Lewis (1971a, 1971b, 1971c) wrote a series of papers dealing with problems of course production at the Open University. He paid particular attention to the activities of Open University course teams, analyzing the problems of interaction and scheduling of tasks. Kaye (1972) derived a list of learning tasks in the natural sciences from the work done in Open University science course teams on specifying learning objectives for students. Hawkridge (1972) used the course production process at the Open University as a model for interuniversity collaboration in preparing instructional materials. Lewis (1973a) reviewed the problem of quality control in course production and the difficulties in assessing students' grasp of the courses.

Other important studies at the Open University have included Macdonald-Ross' (1973) critical review of behavioral objectives, and proposals for stronger methods of curriculum design from Lewis et al. (1973). The Lewis proposals, evolved under a Ford Foundation grant, were written from the Open University perspective but could be used widely. They were based on ideas put forward by Pask (for a recent account, see Pask, 1975a), who has applied these ideas to an analysis of an Open University course (Pask, 1975b). In addition to these reports, numerous internal studies have been undertaken by the Open University's Institute of Educational Technology (for details, see Hawkridge and Coryer, 1975).

Similar activities have been going on in other open learning systems, no doubt, but details are difficult to secure, as we have said. Hoffbauer (1971) discussed some of the methods used and factors taken into account in constructing the course "letters" or units of the course in pedagogy for the Quadriga-Funkkolleg in West Germany.

For Teleac in Holland, Wermer (1971) gave a brief account of the techniques used for producing courses. Cavert (1974) reported on the evolving course design process at the State University of Nebraska. Forman (1975) and Cashell, Lent, and Richardson (1975) provided detailed accounts of needs assessment studies for a particular course of that same university. Grimmett (1975) gave a summary of course design at Memorial University, Newfoundland, while Beardsley (1975) analyzed some of the difficulties facing course design teams in the Free University of Iran.

Learning by correspondence. In many, but not all, of the open learning systems we have been discussing, students learn by correspondence. That is, they learn by receiving textual material, usually by mail, and by returning to tutors a number of written assignments spread over the duration of their courses. Although a long tradition exists of teaching and learning by correspondence, it is not backed by much research, as Mathiesen (1971) showed. Recently established multimedia open learning systems, wishing to provide learning opportunities by correspondence, have had remarkably little upon which to base their designs. Thus a study by Baath and Flinck (1973) in Sweden, to be completed by 1976, appears to examine comparatively trivial variables such as frequency of assignments as well as potentially more important ones such as the supplementation of written contact with telephone instruction and group meetings.

The Open University has taken seriously the questions raised by correspondence learning, although it does not have the answers yet. For example, in its texts it has stressed participative exercises (see Harrison, 1971). A primer for its tutors has been published (Grugeon, 1974), incorporating results of studies of students' manuscripts and tutors' comments. The tutors' roles were discussed by MacKenzie (1974) in the light of a small study of a sample of tutors. The format of the texts has also received attention: Developmental work by Macdonald-Ross and Waller (1975a, 1975b) was aimed at improving the readability of text and diagrams.

If similar studies are in progress elsewhere, to know of them would be valuable. Meantime, this section remains apologetically sparse.

Learning through broadcast and other electronic media. In almost all the open learning systems listed in Table 3-1, students learn through receiving broadcasts of television or radio or both. An extensive literature about broadcasting includes many research studies, and Schramm contributed more than his own share in this field (see, for example, Schramm, 1964; Schramm *et al.*, 1964; Chu and Schramm, 1967; Schramm, 1969; Schramm, 1971). In most of these publications, Schramm was concerned with instructional television; he wanted to assess the results of using television for helping learners in many different circumstances. He also analyzed the problems and costs.

We ought also to mention several important publications that contributed to the fund of knowledge available later for the study of broadcasting in open learning systems. For example, Halloran (1966) studied the problems of measuring attitude change in television audiences. Lefranc (1966) identified four areas in which research was required: problems of motivating students learning through broadcasts; problems of making programs (particularly of expressing concepts in visual form); problems of audience participation, either in the course of the program or afterwards through written work or the activities of the teacher; and problems arising from the physiological, psychological, and sociological contexts of educational broadcasts. Trenaman (1967) carried out a study comparing reception of the same message in matched versions by television, radio, and print, concluding that the differences in response attributable to the medium were insignificant compared with differences attributable to content. Belson (1967) provided a survey of methods of research applicable to broadcasting. Pihl (1967) reported on Danish experiments employing print, radio, and television; within the constraints of these trials, no significant difference was shown between the results achieved through the different media.

A number of studies of educational broadcasting were reported at the International Conference on Educational Radio and Television in Paris in 1967 (see European Broadcasting Union, 1967), but few of them were rigorous. The French have held out hopes that broadcasts could be analyzed structurally and linguistically (Burgelin, 1968) and that through such analyses new ways would be discovered to improve learning. Scupham and MacKenzie (1968), in reviewing the research to date, noted that the Conference in Paris had recommended "practical research in the form of production-testing, try-out and revision" almost along the lines of developmental testing used in programmed learning, and "basic research." The latter was to consist of testing the validity of proposed rules or principles of program construction and use through well-controlled scientific experiments. In time, this work would lead to a tested guide for the producer in choosing between available alternatives when new programs were being designed or produced. Evaluation of broadcasts in traditional ways was also recommended, using questionnaires, tests, observations, and interviews. Scupham and MacKenzie also listed the limiting factors in such studies: their nongeneralizable findings; the results from large-scale studies often being more useful to administrators than producers; the fact that programs do not lend themselves to research unless specially constructed; the limitations of cognitive tests; and the methodological problems of attitude studies in general.

From this summary we may be able to judge that the literature on learning through broadcasts contained more question marks than solutions for those wishing to design open learning systems incorporating television and radio. Little enough was available in either of the first two Paris categories, although evaluation studies were made. Seldom had any of these studies examined broadcasting being used in a multimedia system such as the Open University, in which print, television, and radio were supposed to be closely integrated.

We might say that one of the first major examples of studies aimed at providing formative evaluation data for an open learning system's broadcasting was that of ''Sesame Street'' (see, for example, Bogatz and Ball, 1971). In West Germany, a few biology broadcasts of Telekolleg were carefully evaluated, as reported by Bedall (1971). For Britain, we have already mentioned the studies of the National Extension College courses carried out by McIntosh and Bates (1972); these studies included reports of students' reactions to broadcasts. Bates went on to carry out research on the Open University's use of broadcasts. He studied the effects of testing students' learning through broadcasts in a system which normally tested only their learning through print (Bates, 1973b). He set up a feedback network to obtain opinions of broadcasts from tutors (Bates, 1974), in addition to the network already established among students by McIntosh. He then began a series of in-depth *post hoc* evaluation studies of individual programs together with Gallagher (see Bates, 1975a; Gallagher, 1975). Each study gathered considerable data from students and tutors, and examined the broadcasts and how they had been used within the context of the total course to which they belonged. Bates (1975b) also completed a massive survey of student use of Open University broadcasts, involving a sample of over 10,000 students. This survey dealt with matters such as student access to the broadcasts, viewing and listening figures for every course, viewing and listening times, how students valued broadcasts in relation to other aspects of the Open University's teaching, and significant differences between student audiences on characteristics such as age, sex, occupation, educational level, and so on. Alternatives to open-circuit broadcasting have also been studied within the Open Univeristy context: Gallagher and Marshall (1975) reported an investigation of the need for replay facilities for students of the university (see also Marshall and Gallagher, 1975). Cooperman (1974) examined the use of audiovisual media in an Open University study center.

The State University of Nebraska (1973) took a very different approach to broadcasts in its early days. During 1972 and 1973, the university designed and produced three experimental television, radio, and print units or modules, two of which dealt with accounting and one with psychology. These units were prepared following the principles laid down by Cavert (1973) and were intended to exemplify different styles. They were field-tested using more than 200 subjects in panels of about twenty. Changes were made on the basis of the reactions of the first groups of subjects. The production and research team reported a number of conclusions; regrettably, these conclusions suffer greatly from the limitations identified by Scupham and MacKenzie.

Again we are obliged to note that other, unreported studies must have been undertaken in open learning systems elsewhere. All that remains to be mentioned is work on the design problem of selecting media for different learning tasks. This problem has been addressed by several researchers in open learning systems: Dohmen (1972), Hawkridge (1973), and Heidt (1974). Clearly, only simplistic algorithms can be devised. Most media choices are likely to be made not on pedagogical or psychological grounds but for logistical and financial reasons.

Learning through discussion, tutoring, and counseling. Many open learning systems encourage face-to-face contact between their students, who provide each other with mutual encouragement and support and who learn from each other. In many such systems, provision is also made for students to meet a tutor or counselor for diagnostic and remedial purposes or to engage in group discussions. Sometimes, but by no means invariably, the tutor is the same person who comments on written assignments sent in by the group of students he or she meets.

In spite of the fact that all face-to-face encounters have taken place within more-or-less integrated systems involving other learning resources such as print and television, relatively little research has been done on how the encounters should be organized. Prescriptions have been laid down about how tutors should behave; for example, Grimm (1971) wrote on the role and functions of the tutor in the Bavarian Telekolleg, which holds regular "College Days" for its students in a number of centers. Her advice and description was not based on any kind of research study, however, and held a tacit assumption that the tutors knew best what to do.

At the Open University, no research basis existed on which to build the tutorial and counseling activities when the first students arrived in 1971. The first published study of Open University counseling was that of Thomas (1974), who examined what were regarded as successful and unsuccessful practices. In 1975 a similar study of tutors was reported internally. Evaluations were also made of attempts to use specific techniques for fostering learning through discussion in study center groups (Northedge, 1975; Watkins, 1975). Sewart (1975) surveyed study groups set up by the students themselves without tutors. In addition, McIntosh (1975c) analyzed the objectives for summer schools, a most important component of some courses in the Open University, providing a whole week of tutorial contact in a residential university.

Because of the difficulties presented by distance to some students who wish to attend tutorial groups, the use of the telephone to aid learning has been studied. Flinck (1974) surveyed the limited literature, while Pinches (1975) discussed some of the technical aspects.

Assessing learning. When an open learning system operates in collaboration with schools, as in American Samoa or El Salvador, standards of achievement are customarily set by teachers in the classrooms, although some use may also be made of standardized tests. Usually, no special study is made of the problems of student assessment in such settings unless an external evaluation has been called for.

In an open learning system for adults, a different approach may be required. Adults learning through open systems request assurances that the grading of their work is both valid and reliable, if the system awards grades at all—Radio Farm Forum programs do not, for example. Where grading occurs, the mechanisms are either totally impersonal as in the case of computer-graded assignments, or personal in a limited sense, through a tutor who is seen only occasionally. Where grading is used, the staff is also under some pressure to demonstrate the quality of the credits they award. Questions about the value of diplomas and degrees from such systems are raised by employers as well as students and colleagues in other educational institutions.

In spite of these pressures, very little has been published about techniques of assessment in open learning systems for adults. Lewis (1972) analyzed the problems as seen from the Open University angle, and Connors (1974) described the computer-graded assignment system of the Open University. Likely many unpublished studies have been made in this field, since some twenty exist for the Open University alone, covering mainly technical aspects, such as standardization, item analysis, and question-banking. These matters are not peculiar to open learning systems, and the extensive literature of educational measurement is available for those seeking to improve assessment of student learning in an open system.

Students' performance. No such poverty of reports exists with regard to the results of students' work in open learning systems. By and large, administrators and researchers have been conscientious in reporting both successes and failures. Evaluation teams' reports supply figures of students graduating and of students dropping out. American-sponsored studies may also give data from standardized tests.

Thus Schramm *et al.* (1967) provided drop-out and graduation data for the NHK Gakuen High School. Wagner (1971) reported the examination results for students enrolled in a radio and correspondence course in economics in Austria. Anderson and Bohlin (1971) gave drop-out figures for TRU courses by radio, television, and correspondence in Sweden. Tymowsky (1971) showed how the performance of students in the Polish Television Polytechnic had been affected by various factors and gave data on the numbers achieving certain standards. For the Bavarian Telekolleg, Bedall (1971) reported on the examination results and the drop-out rate for the first group of students.

In Africa, Treydte (1972) discussed students' difficulties and drop-out rates in the Correspondence Course Unit in Kenya, while Kinyanjui (1975) mentioned analyses carried out by the same unit on student pass rates and questions directed at candidates who had failed. The Kinyanjui study also made some attempt to assess the impact of the courses on the day-to-day work of the students, all teachers.

In Latin America, Mayo *et al.* (1973) summarized student performance in the Mexican Telesecundaria in terms of numbers of graduates. Hornik *et al.* (1973) used standardized tests of general ability and reading, plus curriculum-related achievement tests, in evaluating the El Salvador system. The radio schools of the remote Tarahumara region of Mexico were studied by De Sotelo (1973), who reported on student achievement and drop-out, while Spain (1973) reported similar data for the radio schools of San Luis Potosi State in the same country.

In North America, Zigerell (1974) quoted figures on award of college credit as well as the "retention rate" (he preferred this term to "drop-out") of the Chicago TV College. Grimmett (1975) reported the academic results of students studying at a distance in Memorial University, Newfoundland.

For the Open University, official reports contain the basic data on drop-out pass rates, and the award of degrees (see Perry, 1975, for example), but more interesting analyses have been carried out by McIntosh and others in the studies already referred to. A number of unpublished studies also exist, such as those attempting to relate drop-out rates to given factors in course design.

Community reaction. Studies in a number of open learning systems have been aimed at gauging the response of the community served. Some of these studies have been polls asking whether people know about the system: For example, the Open University commissioned Louis Harris polls in Britain for this purpose (See McIntosh, 1975a, and McIntosh and Calder, 1975, for recent accounts). Bedall (1971) reported similar surveys for the Bavarian Telekolleg. Tymowsky (1971), on the other hand, emphasized the marginal audience of nonregistered students who followed the programs and purchased the written materials of the Polish Television Polytechnic. Hornik (1975) analyzed some of the community variables and referred to studies undertaken in El Salvador of community reaction to the educational reform which was a concomitant of the open learning system there.

These examples are few. Diffusion of innovative resources offered by an open learning system can take place only as awareness of the system rises in the community, yet little evaluation appears to have been made of community reaction.

Costs. We are not concerned in this chapter with published financial accounts. These records may be obtained from many open learning systems, although their publication tends to be delayed. More interesting are the analyses and comparisons of costs carried out by economists and other researchers.

In this field, Schramm *et al.* (1967) probably set the fashion. In their summary of the three volumes published by UNESCO on using the new media (particularly in open learning systems, although that term was not used then), Schramm and his colleagues carried out analyses of the costs—initial and recurrent. Schramm's evaluation teams in Latin America were expected to examine costs as well as benefits of the open learning systems they were to evaluate. Thus Speagle (1972) reported on costs and benefits of the El Salvador system, to be followed by Hornik et al. (1973), who repeated and added to Speagle's data in their final report on the same system. Schramm (1973a) summarized the cost data for the system in American Samoa and followed up the 1967 study for UNESCO with a report to the U.S. Agency for International Development (Schramm, 1973b) in which he provided data comparing costs in a number of open learning systems using various media.

For the Open University, Wagner, an economist, undertook the first analysis (Wagner, 1972) that included comparisons with costs in conventional British universities. He took his studies further in a later paper (Wagner, 1973), and a more detailed study was carried out by a team from the London School of Economics (Laidlaw and Layard, 1974). Two Scottish economists used 1973 data to undertake what they termed an economic analysis of the Open University (Lumsden and Ritchie, 1975).

No doubt these studies indicate the complexity of any analysis of costs of open learning systems. As we mentioned at the beginning of this paper, such systems are usually highly dependent upon other systems of various kinds. They cannot operate without access to delivery systems, for example. Yet in most countries the broadcasting and postal systems are nationalized and subsidized. Open learning systems like the Open Univeristy may not be required to pay the true cost of services. Similarly, students in conventional systems may be subsidized by the provision of housing, transport, food, and other resources which are not, as a general rule provided by open learning systems to their students.

In spite of these complexities, politicians in particular will continue to look for economic justification for the existence and expansion of open learning systems. As we have said, one of the characteristics of these systems is that they can increase the number of students they serve without proportionate increases in costs. This argument is powerful, even with politicians who have little interest in widening access to education.

CONCLUSION

This survey probably represents the first attempt to draw together the published studies on open learning systems worldwide. As such, it must be regarded as a first approximation. Enough material is available to fill a book.

Still, this survey may omit a good many accounts. Regretfully, within the space available, detailed results of the studies reported cannot be provided. With few exceptions, comment on the nature of the studies—whether they are contemplative or empirical, for example—has not been possible, nor has an evaluation of their worth. These tasks remain for the future. Reports are appearing more and more frequently—a trend indicated by the number of 1974 and 1975 references in this chapter. To prepare a definitive account, offering a firm base to countries and commissions considering open learning systems, should soon be possible. Wilbur Schramm will like that!

REFERENCES

Anderson, G., and E. Bohlin. "Adult Education by Radio and TV (TRU)." *Multi-media Systems in Adult Education.* Munich: Internationales Zentralinstitut, 1971.

Ardagh, J. "University off the Air." *Sunday Telegraph,* July 3, 1966.

Baath, J. A., and R. Flinck. *Two-way Communication in Correspondence Education.* Lund (Sweden): Institute of Education, University of Lund, 1973.

Barath, A., and G. Sandor, eds. *Hungarian School Radio and Television.* Budapest: Hungarian Radio and Television, 1966.

Bates, A. W. "Educational and Cost Comparisons between Open-network, Cable and Cassette Systems of Multi-media Teaching." *Proceedings of the Eighth Diorama.* Blankenberge (Belgium): Kingdom of Belgium Ministry of Employment and Labour, 1973*a*.

———. "An Evaluation of the Effects of Basing an Assignment on Broadcast Material in a Multi-media Course." *Programmed Learning and Educational Technology, 10,* 348–359, 1973*b*.

———. "The Role of the Tutor in Evaluating Distance Teaching." *Teaching at a Distance, 1,* 35–40, 1974.

———. *Broadcast Evaluation Report: T291 TV6.* Milton Keynes (England): The Open University, 1975*a*.

———. *Student Use of Open University Broadcasting.* Milton Keynes (England): The Open University, 1975*b*.

Beardsley, J. R. "The Free University of Iran." In N. MacKenzie, R. Postgate, and J. Scupham. *Open Learning: Systems and Problems in Post- secondary Education.* Paris: UNESCO, 1975.

Bedall, F. K. "The Telekolleg." In *Multi-media Systems in Adult Education.* Munich: Internationales Zenralinstitut, 1971.

Belson, W. A. *The Impact of Television: Methods and Findings in Program Research.* London: Crosby Lockwood, 1967.

Blacklock, S. "Course Feedback: A Pilot Study." Unpublished report for the Open University, 1972.

_____. "T262 Man-made Futures: Design and Technology." Unpublished report for the T262 course team at the Open University, 1975.

Bogatz, G. A., and S. Ball. *The Second Year of Sesame Street: A Continuing Evaluation*. Princeton, N.J.: Educational Testing Service, 1971.

Braithwaite, B., and K. Batt. "Open Learning: the Australian Contribution." In N. MacKenzie, R. Postgate, and J. Scupham. *Open Learning: Systems and Problems in Post-secondary Education*. Paris: UNESCO, 1975.

Brown, R. D. "An Open University for the Midlands: Why and for Whom?" *Research in Higher Education, 2,* 45–55, 1974.

Burgelin, O. "Structural Analysis and Mass Communications." *Studies in Broadcasting 6,* 143–168, 1968.

Carpenter, M. B., L. G. Chesler, H. S. Dordick, and S. A. Haggart. *Analyzing the Use of Technology to Upgrade Education in a Developing Country*. Santa Monica, Calif.: Rand Corporation, 1970.

Cashell, J., R. Lent and P. Richardson. "The Utility of Needs Assessment Data for Designers, Content Specialists and Evaluation." *Rhetoric and Practice: Needs Assessment in a Major Development Effort*. Working Paper No. 5. Lincoln, Neb.: University of Mid-America, 1975.

Cavert, C. E. *A Systematic Approach to Instructional Design*. Washington, D.C.: AECT Publications, 1973.

Cavert, C. E., ed. *Conference Proceedings: The First Annual National Conference on Open Learning in Higher Education*. Lincoln, Nebraska: State University of Nebraska and Great Plains National Instructional Television Library, 1974.

Central Surveys. *A Public Opinion Survey Conducted in Five Midwest Markets for State University of Nebraska*. Lincoln, Neb.: State University of Nebraska, 1973.

Childs, K. "Unions Press for Open University." *Times Educational Supplement,* March 23, 1973.

Chu, G. C., and W. Schramm. *Learning from Television: What the Research Says*. Washington, D.C.: National Association of Educational Broadcasters, 1967.

Combs, M. "Chicago's Television College." In International Institute for Educational Planning, *New Educational Media in Action: Case Studies for Planners*. Vol. II. Paris: UNESCO-International Institute for Educational Planning, 1967.

Commission on Educational Planning. *A Choice of Futures*. The Worth Report. Edmonton (Canada): Commission on Educational Planning, 1972.

Committee on Open University. *Open Tertiary Education*. Canberra (Australia): Australian Universities Commission, 1974.

Connors, B. "Testing Innovation in Course Design." *British Journal of Educational Technology 3,* 48–51, 1971.

_____. "Objective Testing at a Distance: The Open University's Computer-marked Assignment System." In R. Budgett, and J. Leedham, eds., *Aspects of Educational Technology VII.* London: Pitman, 1974.

Cooney, S. "American Samoa: In Our Own Image." *Audiovisual Instruction, 18,* 26–27, 1973.

Cooperman, M. H. *Media Accessibility and Use in an Open University Study Centre.* Milton Keynes (England): The Open University, 1974.

Coppen, H. *Bibliography of Published Reports on Research in Sound Broadcasting and Television Completed in Great Britain between 1945 and 1966.* Paris: European Broadcasting Union, 1967.

De Sotelo, S. S. *The Radio Schools of the Tarahumara, Mexico: An Evaluation.* Stanford, Calif.: Institute for Communication Research, Stanford University, 1973.

Dohmen, G. "Mediendidaktik." Paper presented at a Council of Europe symposium at Bad Godesberg, Germany, 1972.

Doughty, P. "Cost-effectiveness Analysis Alternatives for Open Learning Programs." In G. R. Sell, ed., *Preliminary Cost-Effectiveness Considerations for UMA/SUN.* Working Paper No. 4. Lincoln, Neb.: University of Mid-America, 1974.

Dubost, M. *Etude sur L'auditoire des emissions Tele-CNAM, 1966–67.* Paris: Ecole Normal Superieure de St. Cloud, 1968.

Duggan, K., and I. Waniewicz, eds. *Educational Communications and the New Technologies.* Toronto: Ontario Educational Communications Authority, 1972.

Edfeldt, A. W. TRU. Lecture to the Fourth Study Course of the Council of Europe on Multi-media Systems. Munich, Germany, 1970.

Edington, A. B., G. V. H. Grimmett, D. Graves, and F. Marriott. *New Media in Education in the Commonwealth.* London: Commonwealth Secretariat, 1974.

Eggert, J. *An Examination of Goals of Potential and Actual Learners.* Working Paper No. 1. Lincoln, Neb.: University of Mid-America, 1975.

Egly, M. "The End of a Period for Tele-Niger (1964–71)." Unpublished report, 1972.

European Broadcasting Union. *Third E. B. U. International Conference on Educational Radio and Television.* Paris, 8–22 March. Paris: Office de Radiodiffusion-Television francaise 1967.

Falk, B., and J. Anwyl. *The Desirablity and Feasibility of an Australian Open Type University.* Melbourne (Australia): University of Melbourne, 1973.

Flinck, R. *The Telephone as an Instructional Aid in Distance Education: A Survey of the Literature.* Lund (Sweden): Department of Education, University of Lund, 1974.

Flinn, G. *SUN study.* Lincoln, Neb.: State University of Nebraska, 1973.

Forman, D. C. "Needs Assessment of the Course on the Cultural History of the Great Plains." In *Rhetoric and Practice: Needs Assessment in a Major Development Effort.* Working Paper No. 5. Lincoln, Neb.: University of Mid-America, 1975.

Frentzel-Zagorska, J., and A. Wyka. *Research on Effects of Adult Education.* Warsaw: Centre of Public Opinion and Broadcasting Research, 1973.

Gallagher, M. Broadcast Evaluation Reports: M231, E221 and S24-. Unpublished reports to the course teams at the Open University, 1975.

Gallagher, M., and J. Marshall. "Broadcasting and the Need for Replay Facilities at the Open University." *British Journal of Educational Technology, 6,* 35–45, 1975.

Garnier, R. "RTS/Promotion." In *Multi-media Systems in Adult Education.* Munich: Internationales Zentralinstitut, 1971.

General Learning Corporation. *Cost Study of Educational Media Systems and Their Equipment Components.* Vols. I–III. Final Report. Washington, D.C.: U.S. Office of Education, 1968.

Gooler, D. D. "Is There a Need for Needs Assessment?" In *Rhetoric and Practice: Needs Assessment in a Major Development Effort.* Working Paper No. 5. Lincoln, Neb.: University of Mid-America, 1975.

Grimm, S. "The function of the 'Kollegtag' teacher in Telekolleg." in *Multi-media Systems in Adult Education.* Munich: Internationales Zentralinstitut, 1971.

Grimmett, G. "Improving the Skills of Remote Teachers—A Project of the Memorial University of Newfoundland, Canada." In N. MacKenzie, R. Postgate, and J. Scupham, *Open Learning: Systems and Problems in Post-secondary Education.* Paris: UNESCO, 1975.

Grugeon, D., ed. *Teaching by Correspondence in the Open University.* Milton Keynes (England): The Open University, 1974.

Halloran, J. D. *Problems of Television Research.* Leicester (England): Leicester University Press, 1966.

Harrison, R. D. "The Instructional System (of the Open University)." In D. Packham, A. Cleary, and T. Mayes, eds., *Aspects of Educational Technology V.* London: Pitman, 1971.

Hawkridge, D. G. "Applications of the Systems Approach to Teaching and Learning." In H. M. Good and B. Trotter, eds., *Frontiers in Course Development: System and Collaboration in University Teaching.* Toronto: Council of Ontario Universities, 1972.

————. "Media Taxonomies and Media Selection." In R. Budgett, and J. Leedham, eds., *Aspects of Educational Technology VII.* London: Pitman, 1973.

Hawkridge, D. G., and J. C. C. Coryer. *A Bibliography of Published and Unpublished Work by Members of the Institute.* Institute of Educational Technology Monograph No. 2. Milton Keynes (England): Institute of Educational Technology, the Open University, 1975.

Heidt, E. U. "Klassifikationsprobleme in der Mediendidaktik." Unpublished paper, 1974.

Hoffbauer, H. "The Quadriga-Funkkolleg in Pedagogy." *Multi-media Systems in Adult Education.* Munich: Internationales Zentralinstitut, 1971.

Hornik, R. C. "Television, background characteristics and learning in El Salvador's educational reform." *Instructional Science, 4,* 293–302, 1975.

Hornik, R. C., H. T. Ingle, J. K. Mayo, E. G. McAnany, and W. Schramm.

Television and Educational Reform in El Salvador. Final report. Stanford, Calif.: Institute for Communication Research, Stanford University, 1973.

Iranian Ministry of Higher Education. "The Free University: A Combined-media System of Education." Unpublished working draft, 1972.

Jackson, B. "The College of the Air." *Guardian,* February 10, 1967.

Jacobs, D. E. *Study of Educational Needs and Interests in the Channel 19 Coverage Area.* Toronto: Department of Adult Education, Ontario Institute for Studies in Education, and Research and Development Branch, Ontario Educational Communications Authority, 1971.

Jamison, D. *Alternative Strategies for Primary Education in Indonesia: A Cost-effectiveness Analysis.* Research Paper No. 46. Stanford, Calif.: Graduate School of Business, Stanford University, 1971.

Jamison, D., and S. Klees. *The Cost of Instructional Radio and Television for Developing Countries.* Stanford, Calif.: Institute for Communication Research, Stanford University, 1973.

Jopling, S. H., and D. C. Avery. "Cost-benefit Methodology for Instructional Television: A Report to the California Instructional Television Consortium." Unpublished report, 1975.

Kaye, A. R. *A Set of Learning Tasks in the Natural Sciences.* Strasbourg: Council of Europe, 1972.

Kempfer, H. *Private Home Study Schools in Illinois.* Springfield, Ill.: State of Illinois Advisory Council on Vocational Education, 1973.

Kinyanjui, P. E. "Kenya: The Use of Radio and Correspondence Education for the Improvement of Teaching." In N. MacKenzie, R. Postgate, and J. Scupham, *Open Learning: Systems and Problems in Post-secondary Education.* Paris: UNESCO, 1975.

Laidlaw, B., and R. Layard. "Traditional Versus Open University Teaching Methods: A Cost Comparison." *Higher Education Review, 3,* 439–468, 1974.

Lefranc, R. "Pedagogic application of research in educational broadcasting." *EBU Review, 100B,* 55–59, 1966.

———. "Educational Television in Niger." In International Institute for Educational Planning, *New Educational Media in Action: Case Studies for Planners.* Vol. II. Paris: UNESCO-International Institute for Educational Planning, 1967.

Lesne, M. "Tele-CNAM." In F. Gaudray, ed., *International Compendium: Multi-media Systems.* Munich: Internationales Zentralinstitut, 1970.

Lewis, B. N. "Course Production at the Open University 1: Some Basic Problems." *British Journal of Educational Technology, 2,* 4–13, 1971*a.*

———. "Course Production at the Open University 2: Activities and Activity Networks." *British Journal of Educational Technology, 2,* 111–123, 1971*b.*

———. "Course Production at the Open University 3: Planning and Scheduling." *British Journal of Educational Technology, 2,* 189–204, 1971*c.*

———. "Course Production at the Open University 4: The Problem of

Assessment." *British Journal of Educational Technology, 3,* 108–128, 1972.

_____. "Course Production at the Open University: An Approach to the Problem of Quality." *British Journal of Educational Technology, 4,* 188–203, 1973*a.*

Lewis, B. N., C. Byrne, C. Hawkridge, M. Neil, G. Pask, and O. Roberts. *New Methods of Assessment and Stronger Methods of Curriculum Design.* Milton Keynes (England): Institute of Educational Technology, The Open University, 1973.

Lumsden, K., and R. Attiyeh. "Economic Analysis of the UMA/SUN Open Learning Program." In G. R. Sell, ed., *Preliminary Cost-effectiveness Considerations for UMA/SUN.* Working Paper No. 4. Lincoln, Neb.: University of Mid-America, 1974.

Lumsden, K. G., and C. Ritchie. "The Open University: A Survey and Economic Analysis." *Instructional Science, 4,* 237–292, 1975.

Macdonald-Ross, M. "Behavioural Objectives: A Critical Review." *"Instructional Science, 2,* 1–52, 1973.

Macdonald-Ross, M., and R. Waller. *Open University Texts: Criticism and Alternatives.* Milton Keynes (England): The Open University, 1975*a.*

_____. "Criticisms, Alternatives and Texts: A Conceptual Framework for Improving Typography." *Programmed Learning and Educational Technology, 12,* 75–83, 1975*b.*

MacKenzie, K. "Some Thoughts on Tutoring by Written Correspondence in the Open University." *Teaching at a Distance, 1,* 45–51, 1974.

MacKenzie, N., R. Postgate, and J. Scupham. *Open Learning: Systems and Problems in Post-secondary Education.* Paris: UNESCO, 1975.

McIntosh, N. "An Integrated Multi-media Educational Experience. . . ." *Educational Television International, 4,* 229–233, 1970.

_____. "The Response to the Open University—Continuity and Discontinuity." *Higher Education, 2,* 186–195, 1973.

_____. "Institutional Research: Needs and Uses." *Teaching at a Distance, 2,* 35–48, 1975*a.*

_____. "Open Admissions—An Open Door or a Revolving Door?" *Universities Quarterly, 29,* 171–181, 1975*b.*

_____. "The Place of Summer Schools in the Open University." *Teaching at a Distance, 3,* 48–60, 1975*c.*

McIntosh, N. E., and A. W. Bates. "Mass-media Courses for Adults." *Programmed Learning and Educational Technology, 9,* 188–197, 1972.

McIntosh, N. E., and J. A. Calder. *A Degree of Difference: A Study of the First Year's Intake of Students to the Open University of Great Britain.* Milton Keynes (England): The Open University, 1975.

McIntosh, N., and V. Morrison. "Student Demand, Progress and Withdrawal." *Higher Education Review, 7,* 37–68, 1974.

McIntosh, N., and A. Woodley. "The Open University and Second Chance Education." *Paedagogica Europaea, 10,* 85–100, 1974.

McNamara, W. C. *A Study of Off-campus TV Courses in Geography and Attitudes towards This Course.* St. John's (Newfoundland): Memorial University, 1973.

Marshall, J., and M. Gallagher. "A Cassette-replay System for Students?" *Teaching at a Distance, 3,* 32–38, 1975.

Mathiesen, D. E. *Correspondence Study: A Summary Review of the Research and Development Literature.* Syracuse, N.Y.: Syracuse University, 1971.

Mayo, J. K., E. G. McAnany, and S. J. Klees. *The Mexican Telesecundaria: A Cost-effectiveness Analysis.* Stanford, Calif.: Institute for Communication Research, Stanford University, 1973.

Miller, J. G. *Deciding Whether and How to Use Educational Technology in the Light of Cost-effectiveness Evaluation.* Cleveland, Ohio: Cleveland State University, 1969.

Moore, D. L. *Psychology 341—Off-campus ETV Project.* St. John's (Newfoundland): Memorial University, 1969.

National Association of Educational Broadcasters. *Open Learning.* Washington, D.C.: National Association of Educational Broadcasters, 1974.

National Council for Educational Technology. *A Survey of Video Distribution Systems for Educational Purposes.* London: National Council for Educational Technology, 1973.

Neil, M. W. "A Systems Approach to Course Planning at the Open University," *Visual Education,* 27–29, August/September, 1970*a.*

————. "The Nature, Roles and Construction of Conceptual Models in Higher Education." In A. C. Bajpai and J. F. Leedham, eds., *Aspects of Educational Technology IV.* London: Pitman, 1970*b.*

Northcott, P. "Open Tertiary Education in Australia: A Viewpoint." *Teaching at a Distance, 4,* 21–30, 1975.

Northedge, A. "Learning through Discussion in the Open University." *Teaching at a Distance, 2,* 10–19, 1975.

Open University Planning Committee. *The Open University.* London: Her Majesty's Stationery Office, 1969.

Pask, G. *Conversation, Cognition and Learning.* Amsterdam: Elsevier, 1975*a.*

————. *The Systemic Analysis of an Open University Course on the Subject of the Sociology of Education.* Milton Keynes (England): Institute of Educational Technology, The Open University, 1975*b.*

Perry, Sir W. *Report of the Vice-Chancellor 1974.* Milton Keynes (England): The Open University, 1975.

Peters, O., W. Bierfelder, and S. Lörcher. *Die Offene Universitat in Japan.* Tubingen: Deutsches Institut fur Fernstudien, 1973.

Pihl, B. "Researching the Research: Danish Experiments in the Analysis of the Results of Educational Programmes." *EBU Review, 106B,* 13–15, 1967.

Pinches, C. "Some Technical Aspects of Teaching by Telephone." *Teaching at a Distance 3,* 39–43, 1975.

Preparatory Study Committee for the University of the Air. *University of the Air in Japan.* Tokyo: Preparatory Study Committee for the University of the Air, 1970.

Rau, J. *Die neue Fernuniversitat.* Dusseldorf: Econ Verlag, 1974.

Rosenbaum, H. "Telekolleg and Other Multi-media Systems of the Bavarian Broadcasting Corporation." In K. Duggan, and I. Waniewicz, eds., *Educational Communications and the New Technologies.* Toronto: Ontario Educational Communication Authority, 1971.

Ross, G. R., R. D. Brown, and M. Hassel. *Clientele Study*. Lincoln, Neb.: State University of Nebraska, 1972.

Sakamoto, T. "The Development of the University of the Air." *Multi-media Systems in Adult Education*. Munich: Internationales Zentralinstitut, 1971.

Schramm, W., ed. *The Effects of Television on Children and Adolescents*. Paris: UNESCO, 1964.

_____. "The New Educational Technology," Working Paper for the International Education Conference, October, 1969.

_____. "The Research on Content Variables in ITV." Unpublished paper, 1971.

_____. *ITV in American Samoa—After Nine Years*. Stanford, Calif.: Institute for Communication Research, Stanford University, 1973*a*.

_____. *Big Media, Little Media: A Report to the Agency for International Development*. Stanford, Calif.: Institute for Communication Research, Stanford University, 1973*b*.

Schramm, W., I. Amagi, K. Got, M. Hiratsuka, and Y. Kumagai. "Japan's Broadcast-correspondence High School." In International Institute for Educational Planning, *New Educational Media in Action: Case Studies for Planners*. Vol. I. Paris: UNESCO-International Institute for Educational Planning, 1967.

Schramm, W., P. H. Coombs, F. Kannert, and J. Lyle. *The New Media: Memo to Educational Planners*. Paris: UNESCO-International Institute for Educational Planning, 1967.

Schramm, W., D. Hawkridge, and H. Howe. An *"Everyman's University" for Israel*. Geneva: The Rothschild Foundation, 1972.

Schramm, W., K. E. Oberholzer, and others. *The Context of Instructional Television: Summary Report of Research Findings, the Denver-Stanford Project*. Stanford, Calif.: Institute for Communication Research, Stanford University, 1964.

Scupham, J., and N. MacKenzie. "Television and Education: Research Findings, Bibliographies and Sources of Information." Unpublished report to the EVR Partnership, 1968.

Sell, G. R. "Needs Assessment in the Broad Content of an Open Learning Program." *Rhetoric and Practice: Needs Assessment in a Major Development Effort*. Working Paper No. 5. Lincoln, Neb.: University of Mid-America, 1975.

Sewart, D. "Some Observations on the Formation of Study Groups." *Teaching at a Distance, 2*, 2–6, 1975.

Shah, S. H. "The People's Open University Project." Unpublished report to the Government of Pakistan, Ministry of Education and Provincial Coordination, 1973.

Smith, M. D. "Open Teaching/Learning Systems: A Prospectus." Unpublished report to the New England Open University Steering Committee, 1972.

Spain, P. L. *A Report on the System of Radioprimaria in the State of San Luis Potosi, Mexico*. Stanford, Calif.: Institute for Communication Research, Stanford University, 1973.

Speagle, R. E. *Educational Reform and Instructional Television in El Salvador: Costs, Benefits and Payoffs.* Washington, D.C.: Academy for Educational Development, 1972.

State University of Nebraska. *Post Secondary Education Through Telecommunications.* Lincoln, Neb.: State University of Nebraska, 1973.

Stone, G. "The Television Agricultural High School (Telewizyjne Technikum Rolnicze), Poland." In N. MacKenzie, R. Postgate, and J. Scupham, *Open Learning: Systems and Problems in Post-secondary Education.* Paris: UNESCO, 1975.

Takasaki, R. S. "Proposal for a Non-campus, Public Service College for Hawaii—Hawaii State College of the University of Hawaii." An unpublished report to the President of the University of Hawaii, 1973.

Taylor, W., ed. *Research Perspectives in Education.* London: Routledge and Kegan Paul, 1973.

Thomas, A. B. "Success and Failure in Open University Counselling." *Teaching at a Distance, 1,* 9–34, 1974.

Trenaman, J. *Communication and Comprehension.* London: Longmans, 1967.

Treydte, K. P. *Evaluation of the Radio/Correspondence Preparatory Course for KJSE of the Correspondence Course Unit.* Nairobi: Institute of Adult Studies, 1972.

Tymowsky, J. "Politechnika Telewizynja." *Multi-media Systems in Adult Education.* Munich: Internationales Zentralinstitut, 1971.

Vanderheyden, K. *University at Home.* Montreal: Universite du Quebec, 1973.

Van Erde, H., and B. van Gent. *Looking at Teleac.* Amsterdam: University of Amsterdam, 1970.

Wagner, G. "Austria: The Radio Course 'Lebendige Wirtschaft.' " *Multi-media Systems in Adult Education.* Munich: Internationales Zentralinstitut, 1971.

Wagner, L. "The Economics of the Open University." *Higher Education, 1,* 159–183, 1972.

————. "The Open University and the Cost of Expanding Higher Education." *Universities Quarterly, 27,* 394–406, 1973.

Watkins, R. "Cooperative Learning in Discussion Groups." *Teaching at a Distance, 2,* 7–9, 1975.

Wedemeyer, C. "UMA/SUN: The Nebraska Approach to a Regional University of Mid-America." In N. MacKenzie, R. Postgate, and J. Scupham, *Open Learning: Systems and Problems in Post-Secondary Education.* Paris: UNESCO, 1975.

Wermer, F. E. "Teleac." *Multi-media Systems in Adult Education.* Munich: Internationales Zentralinstitut, 1971.

Zigerell, J. J. "Chicago's TV College: A Television-based Open Learning Model." In S. A. Harrison, and L. A. Stolurow, *Productivity in Higher Education.* Washington, D.C.: National Institute of Education and U.S. Office of Education, 1974.

How Should a University Be?

CHARLES E. OSGOOD

This chapter is a very brief, personal, undocumented statement of one man's view of how a university ought to function today. I start with a simple question: "Why is the morpheme *universe* the base of the word we use to refer to our highest educational institution?" Potentially, a university is expected to be involved in the study of *all* aspects of the universe, including astronomy, biology, chemistry, horticulture, psychology, politics, sculpture, and zoology, to mention just a few of the fields covered in university departments. My thesis will be that all "professors" (a term that presupposes knowing), by the very nature of their own training, are *specialists*—they "know" only a little about a few small bits of the "universe"—yet their students are demanding *relevance* in what they teach. I find a fundamental misconception in this situation, one that digs deep into the structure and function of a university.

SPECIALIZATION

Toward the end of the nineteenth century, Herbert Spencer tried to bring together all that was known about the universe; no one in his right mind would try to do that today. In the early 1950s, I wrote *Method and Theory in Experimental Psychology* for the Oxford University Press, trying, in my own smaller way, to bring together what was known in this more limited part of the universe; no psychologist in his right mind would try to do that today, only twenty years later. Now I am under contract with the same publisher to write *Method and Theory in Psycholinguistics*, an attempt to bring together what is known of a still tinier part of the universe—and if I do not hurry, I shall be rightly accused of not being in *my* right mind. I'm sure that my personal history is replicated by most scholars and scientists in any university. Given the explosion in population and (in part because of it) the explosion of information about the universe, individual human beings have no choice but to "profess" about sections of the universe which are narrowing exponentially.

RELEVANCE

Yet professors today are under great pressure from their students to be relevant in what they teach—relevant, presumably, to the problems of society as students, usually quite correctly, perceive them. We see departmental committees hustling about trying to rename, redesign, and streamline old courses, as well as to create new courses and programs which will, indeed, be relevant. Although I have been reasonably radical in my own life, I think that *this* demand is both misconceived and misplaced. Professors, by the very nature of their specialized training, are literally incapable of relevance in the sense demanded. If they try to achieve it, they are likely to dilute what they *do* know and profess about what they do *not* really know and should not try to profess—or they may even prostitute themselves by professing what they *think* they know in the jargon and style of a generation not their own.

Achievement of relevance is the problem of the student, not the professor. The student must select from among the cafeterial offerings of a university those servings which are relevant *for him or her;* the student must search for the interrelationships among these servings; the student must strive to integrate the chosen menu into a developing specialization of his or her own. Again, using myself as the source of illustration with which I am most familiar, nothing in my training in perception at Dartmouth, in learning theory at Yale, or in anthropology at both schools explicitly "put it all together" for my work on the nature and measurement of meaning or, for that matter, in trying to devise a strategy of calculated deescalation in international conflicts—but I did get many of the bits and pieces.

MODULES

Let me adapt—from architecture, I believe—the notion of "modules of knowing." Professors in a university, being of necessity specialists, know a lot (relatively) about a few things and very little about most other things. The few things they do know something about, and can profess, we may call their "modules of information about the universe." Again, speaking for myself, I think I can provide such modules in (1) the nature and measurement of meaning, (2) the behavior theory approach to psycholinguistics, (3) cross-cultural research into subjective culture and its universals, and (4) interpersonal and international conflict and its resolution. Some of these modules might be relevant for a student majoring in linguistics, some for a student in psychology, some for a political science major, and some even for students in philosophy, rhetoric, and aesthetics.

Surely each professor in a university could provide a similar module profile—listing rather specific things about which he or she knows something and can profess with reasonable competence. In some cases, these modules would correspond to existing courses, but in many cases they would not (for example, introductory and survey courses). The validity of the professor's claim to competence would be, as it is now, some joint function of the judgments of superiors, colleagues, and, ultimately, students.

Each student in a university, in seeking to achieve an education relevant to his or her own interests or the problems of society as he or she sees them, must select from among the modules available some personal pattern. These patterns would range from the relatively standardized (present departmental programs) to the highly unique (inter- and multidepartmental). But in each case the student would be assembling a set of modules deemed relevant—and, in effect, *moving along a line toward a particular, inevitable specialization.* This method is as it should be, I think. Although at any particular point in time the number of functions demanded of individuals by their societies is limited, these functions are potentially modifiable and expansible in terms of new forms of specialization (the ombudsman, a pollution monitor, a television color-music creator). Those who are expected (*by* society) to generate new knowings experience a continual process of recombining and applying old knowings, and the more well-formed the modules of existing knowledge about the universe, the better able will be the new specialist to integrate them into novel and fruitful contributions of his or her own. But obviously *the student's freedom to select among available modules must be maximized,* which implies some radical changes in the structure and function of universities.

SPHERES AND PYRAMIDS

If my arguments so far have some validity—that "professors" are of necessity conveyors of specialized modules of knowing and that "students" are by nature, if not by necessity, integrators of such knowings into new specializations—then seemingly higher education should be essentially a matter of continuous and fluid recombining of old into new clusters of modules. Out of the interactions within the new clusters of "knowing"—particularly when they happen to be clustered within the mind of some genius—entirely new "knowings" about the universe are generated, and knowledge is thus extended.

At any point in time, fields of knowledge appear as *spheres* of these modules, and such spheres have a way of becoming "departments" in a university. These spheres of knowing have reasonable dense and clear cores of tightly interlocked molecules but very fuzzy borders where their molecules overlap with those of many other spheres of knowing. *In the overlapping boundary regions, the most exciting developments of knowledge within universities have usually taken place.* As a new focus or core forms, it comes to define a new sphere of knowing—as in the case of astrophysics, biochemistry, ecology, urban development, psycholinguistics—and, in the nature of things, it tends in time to become a new "department" in the university.

But in the shift from a field of knowing to a departmental division of an institution, a dramatic structural transformation takes place— from a sphere into a pyramid. Whereas the analogy of fluidly merging and expanding spheres seems "natural" for fields of knowing about the universe, it does not seem natural for organizations of human beings. Viewing individuals as elements within social systems, human organizations characteristically develop from replication of functions among individuals, through specialization of these functions, to pyramidal, hierarchical specialization of functions by individuals in terms of unequal distributions of power (as broadly conceived). Departments within a university are no exception: They typically have broad, amorphous bases at which highly replicated teaching assistants and junior professors teach large numbers of equally replicated undergraduate students; within the middle regions, departments become better defined in terms of knowledge molecules, with more senior and specialized faculty teaching more senior and specialized undergraduate and graduate students; near their apices they become very sharply and professionally defined, with highly specialized senior professors teaching increasingly specialized graduate students.

The higher one goes in one of these departmental pyramids, the more remote becomes the field of knowing *it* represents from the fields of knowing of other departments, the more inaccessible become its modules for outsiders because of prerequisites, and the less accessible for its insiders become modules into other departments, both because of *their* prerequisites and because of heavy within-department program requirements. Thus undergraduates at freshman and sophomore levels typically have more freedom of selection than juniors and seniors with departmental majors, and the juniors and seniors in turn have more freedom than departmental graduate students. Supraordinate to departments are colleges, professional schools, and even whole campuses—across whose manmade boundaries the integration of modules of knowing becomes incredibly difficult.

This pyramidal system actually reaffirms and maintains *existing* clusters of modules of knowing (specializations along departmental lines) and greatly constrains the fluid recombining of modules into *new* clusters and hence new specializations. Thus I consider the pyramidal departmental structure of universities to be inappropriate to the nature of knowing about the universe. But is the departmental system inappropriate for a university, which is, after all, a human insitution?

ARE DEPARTMENTS NECESSARY?

Contemporary universities are very large organizations, involving thousands of administrating, teaching, learning, and supporting personnel. Such massive and complex systems have to be divided into more manageable subsystems, more knowledgeable about their human individual elements, for efficient and humane operation. This need is one justification for the existence of departments and their supraordinate structures in a university. Departments (of geology, of psychology), colleges (of communications, of engineering), and professional schools (of law, of medicine) also correspond reasonably well to the functions educated individuals can perform in contemporary society—getting jobs as bankers, entertainers, lawyers, politicians, teachers, and so on. This response is another justification for the existence of these structures. Furthermore, schools, colleges, and departments also do divide up the university into administrative, teaching, and learning segments that at least *roughly* correspond to spheres of knowing about the universe as these are contemporarily defined. This correspondence is also justification for the existence of the structure. But we must realize that all these justifications more often look backward toward *past* structures of knowledge and functions in society than toward potential *future* structures and functions.

I conclude that these justifications of departmental organization of universities—efficiency and humaneness of operation, correspondence with the needs of contemporary society, and at least rough correspondence with existing spheres of knowing about the universe—are sufficient. But I conclude as well that departmental organization does encourage the perseveration of past specializations and discourage the development of future specializations by severely constraining the freedom of choice of students. Then the problem becomes: How can the organizational advantages of the pyramidal departmental *structuring* of a university be retained, while at the same time guaranteeing that the *functioning* of a university will encourage the fluid recombining of spheres of knowing and serve to maximize the student's freedom to determine his or her own new integrations? Or, put quite simply, how can a departmentalized university satisfy the needs of creative students and their desires to find relevance?

This question has no simple answer. Rather, the juxtaposition of necessary departmental structure and needed educational function implies changes in emphasis at all levels and across all segments of the university. Further, I realize that each modification in the system would have ramifications throughout the system. The following suggestions are made with these complications in mind but without trying to trace through all of their implications.

Suggestion I. Universities should provide students with a catalog of the modules of specialized knowings available and the teachers claiming competence to profess them. Speaking practically, this goal could be accomplished by adding two or three lines to each staff member's item in the faculty directory, listing in order of claimed competence that member's modules of specialization. Parenthetically, the numbers of courses being taught could be matched, along with an added index of the faculty by module titles. A very carefully worded faculty questionnaire designed to minimize the length and number of module claims and to standardize their format would have to be administered first. Such a catalog would enable students at all levels to seek intelligently for combinations of modules which they deem relevant to their own interests; to locate as program advisors those faculty members whose module specialization patterns most closely match their own developing interest pattern; and to more effectively mesh their desired module selections with departmental requirements. For the faculty, such a module breakdown would facilitate fuller utilization of available personnel in developing new interdisciplinary research and teaching activities. For the university administration, an explicit module description should make possible a better assessment of strengths and weaknesses in a university's sampling of "knowings about the universe," earlier awareness of potential new spheres of knowing, and a more sensitive matching of instructional supply to educational demand.

Suggestion II. Universities should maximize the number and variety of specialized courses at middle levels and minimize the number of introductory (at lowest levels) and survey (at highest levels) courses, with the specialized courses being available to both undergraduate and graduate students. Operating within the module system, students could put together their own "introductions" to a field, tailoring them to their own senses of relevance, from the offerings available at the middle levels. Existing introductory courses often either contain a great deal of prespecialization departmental material (designed to serve as a prerequisite for more advanced courses in that field) *or* degenerate into popularizations that may only pretend relevance and be deceptive as to later specializations in that field. Survey "proseminar" courses at the graduate level (usually required) bore some of the students all of the time and all of the students some of the time; if a graduate student is going to specialize within a departmental field, as all students must, then much of the same material will be gone over in greater detail later; if the material is not germane to the specialization, the student can do just as well reading a few well-selected books about it in preparation, for qualifying examinations.

A large variety of specialized middle-level courses makes it possible to adjust programs flexibly to changes in spheres of knowing. For example, linguistics in the 1940s was never considered by psychologists to be relevant for one who planned to teach and do research in the psychology of language—but no psycholinguist today would deny that this module is essential. As to opening specialized middle-level courses to undergraduate and graduate students indiscriminately, my own experience has been that equally motivated and intelligent students at the two levels are equally capable of handling the specialized modules that I profess—sometimes with some carefully selected background reading for the undergraduates. By the age of 18 or so, human beings have reached their asymptotes as far as *ability* to learn is concerned; the performance of junior fellows at Harvard and elsewhere certainly testifies to this conclusion.

Suggestion III. Universities should maximize lateral interdepartmental relationships among and within courses and minimize hierarchical interdependence of courses within departments. Students at all levels should have as much freedom as possible to put together their own integrated specializations from among the modules available in the university. The major inhibitors of such freedom are prerequisites for higher level courses and course requirements for departmental programs (for students minoring as well as majoring in a subject, and in terms of numbers as well as natures of courses). I realize that departmental fields of specialization operate under different pressures (often from ultimate employers) for guaranteeing particular competences in their graduates. But usually these competences are more in the nature of *skills* (which often can be acquired on the job) than in the nature of *understandings,* and I suspect that often the pressures are to maintain traditions and continue servicing the administrating and teaching habits of senior professors. Since most courses at undergraduate as well as graduate levels are presently concerned more with understanding than skill, prerequisites are minimal and could be met by selected background readings or early experience in the course itself. Lateral relationships among courses in different departments, as parts of specialized programs for small groups of or even individual students, can be facilitated both by cross-listing (where some permanence of the interrelationship is anticipated) and by increasing the number of extra departmental electives permissible in programs. Where new interdisciplinary trends are developing, courses can be jointly taught by people in different departmental faculties.

Suggestion IV. Universities should allow for more flexibility in the length of and credit for courses. The present system tends to standardize courses into lengths of one or (occasionally) two semesters, although the material to be taught might be more appropriately encapsuled into units of other sizes, ranging from a probable minimum of half a semester to a probable maximum of two semesters. The

modules of knowing to be professed do not come in neatly standardized chunks. Nor is credit for courses necessarily measured in contact hours (for example, a skill-producing laboratory versus a
theoretical issues seminar). In general, the shorter the professing time
for modules (with a minimum, say, of half a semester) and the smaller
the unit of credit (with a minimum, for convenience, of one unit), the
greater will be the number of modules a student can absorb and the
greater the student's freedom to generate uniquely relevant patterns
of modules for his or her own developing specialization. In this connection, the differences in undergraduate and graduate grading and
unit-counting might sensibly be eliminated. The kind of educational
process I envision would also fit better in a quarter system than in the
present semester system.

   *Suggestion V. Departments should organize their majors at both
graduate and undergraduate levels in terms of a wider variety of subprograms leading to degrees, such subprograms involving different*
(although often overlapping) *patterns of within-department and
between-department modules.* I think this recent trend is certainly
consistent with both the fluid recombining of modules of knowings
and the rapidly changing specializations needed by society. Degrees
offered in terms of "fields" (departments) are usually misleading.
Psychology provides a very good example of this: The graduate with a
Ph.D. may be reasonably expert in the measurement of sensory
thresholds, somewhat knowledgeable in perception and experimental
psychology generally, but may know little about group dynamics and
absolutely nothing about the diagnosis of disturbed human beings. A
graduate with a Ph.D. in electrical engineering may happen to know a
great deal about the human nervous system and biological systems
generally, yet his or her academic credentials will not explicitly show
that knowledge.

   When a university or a business corporation is hiring "a psychologist" or "an electrical engineer," to do so on the basis of these
degree labels could be disastrous. In practice, universities, corporations, and government agencies inquire into the modules of knowing
that the prospective employee has mastered—that is, what the graduate is actually competent to do or profess. I therefore suggest, as a cor-
ollary, *that both graduate and undergraduate degrees be awarded in
terms of subprogram rather than departmental labels,* thereby coming
closer to the module cluster the student has acquired, with departmental involvements indicated parenthetically (for example, Ph.D. in

psycholinguistics [psychology, linguistics, and philosophy], or Ph.D. in general systems theory [electrical engineering, mathematics, and psychology]).

Suggestion VI. Thesis committees for students should be selected so as to provide as close a match as possible to their actual module combinations. I have already suggested that a student's advisor(s) should be sought in terms of mutual correspondence between the professor's and the student's modules of knowing; this same principle should apply to the chairman of a student's thesis committee. This practice would imply that the thesis chairman might not necessarily be in the same department (in terms of the organizational structure of the university) as the student, although usually he or she would be. As I believe the system presently operates at the graduate level in most universities, a minimum of three members (including the chairman) must represent the student's major department and a minimum of one or two members must represent the student's minor (or minors).

Under the module system, the student's thesis committee would be selected jointly by the chairman and the student (with departmental and graduate college approval) so as to represent as faithfully as possible the unique combination of modules of knowing that the student claims to have integrated in his or her education, with no constraints in terms of departmental affiliations. Since the entire conception of minors would be dissolved into finer module units, no regulations concerning minors would be required. Thus a student obtaining a degree in general systems theory might have as chairman a professor in electrical engineering; the other members of the committee might include professors in mathematics, psychology, philosophy, and biology, all of whom have specializations bearing on the student's module cluster and (usually, but not necessarily) have been involved in the student's education.

As an adjunct to this suggestion, I propose *requiring a thesis* (or an equivalent) *from undergraduate seniors.* This system was active at Dartmouth when I was majoring in psychology, and my undergraduate thesis—a combination of experimental research on visual-auditory-verbal synesthesia with a search of anthropological field reports for evidence of synesthetic universals, along with a bit of theory in aesthetics and semantics—actually set a pattern for my work ever since. Particularly in the kind of module system I am proposing, the undergraduate scholar *also* needs an opportunity to demonstrate that he or she has, indeed, put together a viable cluster of knowings about the universe. I would suggest a thesis committee of three members, determined as above (with the chairman being closest in module matching), and a degree explicitly indicating the student's personal focus as well as the major departments involved in module integration—as was suggested for graduate student degrees.

CONCLUSION

I began this chapter with the propositions that "knowings" about the universe are necessarily limited and increasingly specialized for those who "profess" about them, and that the search for personal and social relevance, involving the individual creation of new integrations of "modules of knowing," is the primary business of those being "professed at" (the students) in a university. Since by the nature of human organizations, including universities, structures tend to become tightly pyramidal (and increasingly isolated at their departmental peaks) rather than loosely spherical (representing more accurately the overlapping regions where new foci of "knowing" develop), the problem for the future of higher education becomes one of maximizing the freedom of students at all levels to select and integrate their own "modules" while retaining the organizational advantages of departmental pyramids. My six suggestions were designed to maintain the integrity of specialized "modules of knowing" while expanding the freedom of new "professors-to-be" to recombine existing modules in terms of their own judgments as to personal and social relevance. If the human species is to reach even the year 2000—to say nothing of moving on beyond it—I think such radical changes in university structure are essential.

Communication and Development

Network Analysis of the Diffusion of Innovations: Family Planning in Korean Villages

EVERETT M. ROGERS

INTRODUCTION

My first personal contact with Wilbur Schramm and the Institute for Communication Research at Stanford University occurred at a 1961 conference on the two-step flow of communication. At that time a number of researches were underway on the interpersonal communication process that occurred after a message was delivered by a mass medium to an audience. In undertaking these investigations, communication scholars were much influenced by the two-step flow model (Lazarsfeld and others, 1944) and the concept of opinion leadership (Katz and Lazarsfeld, 1955). One field of active research on this topic, which I represented at the 1961 Stanford conference, investigated the diffusion of agricultural innovations among farmers.[1]

The conference concluded that although the concept of opinion leadership might be of much potential usefulness, the two-step model did not actually tell us very much and could not be adequately tested, because it was unfalsifiable. More generally, however, our 1961 meeting helped head communication scholars in the general direction of analyzing the interfaces of interpersonal and mass media communication.

Unfortunately, for most of the ensuing sixteen years we have lacked adequate analytical tools to fully explore this research problem. But now, network analysis allows us to probe the nature of communication flows among the members of a system. Obviously, such methodological tools must be accompanied by appropriate theoretical advances or the net result will be only sophisticated but raw empiricism.

The purpose of this chapter is to argue for the unique advantages that network analysis can provide to study the diffusion of innovations, and to illustrate certain of these intellectual benefits with data from a study of the diffusion of family-planning innovations among village women in Korea.[2] My general position is that most diffusion research in the past is characterized by a psychological bias in that the individual has been the unit of analysis, thus preventing adequate understanding of the relational nature of interpersonal communication. Network analysis provides a means to put structure back into diffusion research, and perhaps, even more broadly, into communication inquiry.

THE CLASSICAL DIFFUSION MODEL

The four main elements in any diffusion event are (1) the *innovation,* defined as an idea perceived as new by the potential adopting unit, (2) which is *communicated* through certain *channels,* (3) over *time,* (4) among the members of a *social system.* Because of the processual, over-time, interactive nature of diffusion, one might naturally expect diffusion scholars to investigate the social networks through which the innovation spreads from member to member of a system. Strangely, such network analysis has been almost entirely missing from the considerable body of social scientific inquiry on the diffusion of innovations. The reason can be traced, I believe, to the historical origins and the more recent development of the field centering around the fact that diffusion researchers are an invisible college structured around a once-revolutionary paradigm.

Although the origins of research on the diffusion of innovations trace from European beginnings, the revolutionary paradigm for diffusion occurred in the early 1940s when two sociologists, Bryce Ryan and Neal Gross (1943), published their study of the diffusion of the significance among Iowa farmers of planting hybrid seed corn. These investigators gathered data by personal interviews with all the Iowa farmers in two communities. The rate of adoption of the agricultural innovation followed an S-shaped, normal curve when plotted on a cumulative basis over time. The first farmers to adopt (the innovators) were more cosmopolite (indicated by traveling more frequently to Des Moines) and of higher socioeconomic status than later adopters. The typical Iowa farmer first heard about the innovation from a seed corn salesman, but interpersonal communication with peers was especially important in leading to persuasion. The innovation–decision process from awareness–knowledge to adoption averaged about nine years, indicating that considerable time was required for this process to occur.

One of the deficiencies of the hybrid corn study was its lack of attention to opinion leadership patterns in the interpersonal diffusion of the innovation within the two Iowa communities studied, although sociometric data about diffusion would have been easy to gather; all the farmers in the two systems were interviewed (Katz, 1960).[3] Only in much later diffusion studies did scholars begin to give proper attention to interpersonal communication flows, and such diffusion networks have still not received their just due by diffusion students.

RISE OF THE INVISIBLE COLLEGE

Research on the diffusion of innovations has, since the hybrid corn study created the "revolutionary paradigm," followed the rise-and-fall stages of "normal science" (Kuhn, 1962), although the final stage of demise has not yet occurred (Crane, 1972). The hybrid corn study set forth a new approach to the study of communication and human behavior change, soon to be followed up by an increasing number of scholars. Within ten years (by 1952), over 100 diffusion research publications had appeared; during the next decade (by 1962), another 450; and by 1977, another 2,450. Today more than 3,000 publications discuss the diffusion of innovations. Thus, the amount of scientific activity devoted to investigating the diffusion of innovations increased at an exponential rate (doubling almost every two years) since the revolutionary paradigm appeared thirty-three years ago, as Kuhn's (1962) theory of the growth of science would predict.

One advantage of the organization of most fields of scientific research (like the study of diffusion) as an invisible college around an intellectual paradigm is that the scientific consensus thus provided lends a great deal of stability and standardization to the field. For instance, comparisons across the 3,000 diffusion publications are greatly facilitated by the fact that they share a common paradigm, especially since the late 1960s, when Rogers with Shoemaker (1971, p. 47) concluded that diffusion research was emerging as "a single, integrated body of concepts and generalizations."

The fact that many diffusion studies look a great deal alike allows the results to be cumulated in an orderly manner. This slow, incremental progress by a scientific field is made possible by the stability provided through the invisible college that rests on the informal communication patterns among the scientists involved.[4]

The standardization of research approaches around the classical diffusion model has limited the contribution of diffusion research to furthering the scientific understanding of human behavior change. The Ryan and Gross (1943) study was so influential in affecting later studies of diffusion that Crane's (1972, p. 74) analysis (of rural sociologists investigating diffusion) found the hybrid corn study was responsible for fifteen of the eighteen most widely used "innovations" (defined as the first use of a dependent or independent variable in a research publication in the diffusion field), and accounted for 21 percent of all 201 innovations! "A significant proportion of the innovative work in the area had already been done by the time the field began to acquire a significant number of new members" (Crane, 1972, p. 67).

Most of the thirty-four years and the other 2,999 publications dealing with the diffusion of innovations have only followed up on the original leads provided by the hybrid corn study, exploring them in greater empirical detail but seldom breaking really new ground. In short, the study of innovation has not been very innovative.

THE PSYCHOLOGICAL BIAS THAT SHORTCHANGES STRUCTURE

The psychological bias in diffusion research stems from an overwhelming focus on the individual as the unit of analysis, and from these researchers' acceptance of how social problems are defined. As a result, the transactional and relational nature of human communication involved in the diffusion process tended to be overlooked, at least until fairly recently.[5]

The overwhelming focus on the *individual* as the unit of analysis in diffusion research (while largely ignoring the importance of communication *relationships* between sources and receivers) is often due to the assumption that if the individual is the unit of response, the individual must consequently be the unit of analysis (Coleman, 1958). This monadic view of human behavior determined that the "kinds of substantive problems on which such research focuses tended to be problems of 'aggregate psychology', that is, within-individual problems and never problems concerned with relations between people" (Coleman, 1958). The use of survey methods in diffusion research often "de-structured" such human behavior: "Using random sampling of individuals, the survey is a sociological meat-grinder, tearing the individual from his social context and guaranteeing that nobody in the study interacts with anyone else in it" (Barton, 1968).

Only recently and rarely has the main focus in diffusion research on the individual as the unit of analysis shifted to the dyad, clique, network, or system of individuals—to the communication relationships between individuals, rather than on the individuals themselves.[6] Encouraging attempts to overcome the psychological bias in communication research are provided by the coorientation model, by relational analysis,[7] by network analysis, and by the general systems approach (Rogers and Agarwala-Rogers, 1976; Richards, 1976).

These conceptual–methodological approaches suggest that even when the individual is the unit of response, the communication relationship can be the unit of analysis via some type of sociometric measurement. Sampling and data-analysis procedures for network analysis, and appropriate concepts and theories linking these concepts, are being worked out, but we still have a long way to go.

A second reason for the artificially "de-structured" psychological bias in diffusion research is the acceptance of a person–blame causal-attribution definition of the problems investigated. *Individual–blame* is the tendency to hold an individual responsible for his or her problems, rather than the system. Obviously, what is done about a social problem, including research, depends upon how the problem is defined.

Illustrations of individual–blame can be cited in various types of behavioral research; Caplan and Nelson (1973) find a high degree of individual–blame in psychological research on such social problems as highway safety and race relations. Person–blame rather than system-blame permeates most definitions of social problems; seldom are the definers able to change the system, so they accept it. Such acceptance encourages a focus on individual variables in social science research. Often, the problem definer's individual-level "cause" becomes the researcher's main variable.

Diffusion research was as guilty as other types of behavioral research in following an individual–blame approach: "Seldom is it implied in diffusion documents that the source or the channels may be at fault for not providing more adequate information, for promoting inadequate or inappropriate innovations, etc." (Rogers with Shoemaker, 1971, p. 79). This type of psychological bias in diffusion research began with the hybrid seed corn study, as we pointed out previously. Ryan and Gross (1943) did not gather sociometric data about the interpersonal diffusion of the innovation within their two Iowa communities of study even though they found that interpersonal communication from neighbors was essential in clinching adoption decisions, and that their sampling design of a complete census of farmers in the two communities was ideal for gathering relational data for network analysis purposes. The Ryan–Gross investigation was sponsored by the Iowa Agricultural Experiment Station and the Iowa Agricultural Extension Service at Iowa State University, the major research and development agency and the main change agency for hybrid seed, respectively. Not surprisingly, then, Ryan and Gross implicitly accepted a person–blame viewpoint of the diffusion problem they investigated; the researchers assumed that the Iowa farmers should adopt the obviously advantageous agricultural innovation.[8]

RESTORING SOCIAL STRUCTURE TO DIFFUSION RESEARCH WITH NETWORK ANALYSIS

The refocusing of diffusion researches had to wait until later investigations, when it became a common procedure for scholars to ask their respondents sociometric questions of the general form: "From whom in this system did you obtain information about this innovation?" The sociometric dyad represented by each answer to this question could consequently be punched on an IBM card (including data on the characteristics of the seeker and the "sought" in the information relationship), which then could become the unit of analysis.

The relational data thus obtained were utilized to provide deeper insight into the role of opinion leaders in the two-step flow of communication, a conceptualization that was originated prior to most diffusion research by Lazarsfeld and others (1944). Later research showed that the two-step flow hypothesis turned out mainly to be an oversimplification (as the flow of communication may have any number of steps), but the concept of opinion leadership[9] has much theoretical and practical utility. Diffusion researches were able to advance understandings of opinion leadership because of their unique capacity to focus on the flow of *innovations,* new messages (to the receivers) that seemed to leave deeper (and hence more recallable) scratches on their respondents' minds. The tracer quality of an innovation's diffusion pathways aids the investigation of the flow of communication messages, and especially aids the role of certain individuals like opinion leaders in this flow.

THE NETWORK ANALYSIS APPROACH TO DIFFUSION

Network analysis is a method of research for identifying the communication structure in a system in which sociometric data about communication flows or patterns are analyzed by using interpersonal relationships as the units of analysis. This tool promises to capitalize on the unique ability of diffusion inquiry to reconstruct specific message flows in a system and then to overlay the social structure of the system on these flows. The innovation's diffusion brings life to the otherwise static nature of the structural variables; network analysis permits understanding the social structure as it channels the process of diffusion.[10]

The essence of the diffusion of an innovation is the human interaction through which one individual communicates a new idea to one or more other individuals. Any given individual in a system is likely to contact certain other individuals and to avoid most others. As these interpersonal communication flows become regularized and patterned over time, a communication structure emerges which is predictive of human behavior. Basically, communication network analysis mathematically describes these linkages in an interpersonal communication structure.

The first, and very partial, attempts toward network analysis of the diffusion process simply identified opinion leaders in a system and determined their mass media and interpersonal communication behavior as distinctive from that of their followers. This approach was only a slight extension of the usual monadic analysis in the direction of a more relational type of analysis.

Next, diffusion scholars began to plot sequential-over-time sociograms of the diffusion of an innovation among the members of a system. Tentative steps were taken toward using communication relationships (such as sociometric dyads) as the units of analysis. This advance allowed data analysis of a "who-to-whom" communication matrix and facilitated inquiry into the indentification of cliques within the total system and how such structural subgroupings affected the diffusion of an innovation, and of specialized communication roles such as liaisons,[11] bridges,[12] and isolates, thus allowing communication research to proceed beyond the relatively simpler issue of studying correlates of opinion leadership as a variable. Now the *communication structure* of a system could be identified, quantified, and analyzed.

Further, the measurement of various communication structural indexes (like communication integration, connectedness,[13] and system openness[14]) for individuals, cliques, or entire systems (like villages or organizations) now became possible and could be related to the rate of diffusion or adoption occurring in these systems. General propositions began to emerge from such network analysis—for example, that the rate of adoption of an innovation in a system is positively related to the system's connectedness.

These network analyses necessitated a new kind of sampling, as well as a shift to relational units of analysis. Instead of random samples of scattered individuals in a large population, the network studies often gathered data from *all* of the eligible respondents in a system (like a village, for instance) or a sample of such systems (Table 5-1). *Usually the research designs for network analysis, as compared to monadic analysis, meant less emphasis on the ability to generalize the research results, which was traded off for a greater focus on understanding the role of social structures on diffusion flows.* If such research were to study social structure, it had to sample intact social structures, or at least the relevant parts of them.

TABLE 5-1. Comparison of Monadic and Network Analysis in Research on the Diffusion of Innovations

Characteristics of the Research Approach	Type of Diffusion Research Approach	
	Monadic Analysis	Network Analysis
Unit of analysis	The individual	The communication relationship between two (or more) individuals
Most frequent sample design	Random samples of scattered individuals in a large population (in order to maximize the generalizability of the research results)	Complete census of all eligible respondents in a system (like a village), or a sample of such intact systems
Types of data utilized	Personal and social characteristics of individuals, and their communication behavior	Same as for monadic analysis, plus sociometric data about communication relationships
Main type of data-analysis methods	Correlational analysis of cross-sectional survey data	Various types of network analysis of cross-sectional survey data
Main purpose of the research	To determine the variables (usually characteristic of individuals) related to innovativeness	To determine how social structural variables affect diffusion flows in a system

EFFECTS OF COMMUNICATION NETWORKS ON HUMAN BEHAVIOR

The term "network" is the communication analogue to the sociological concept of group, but network is distinct from group in that it refers to a number of individuals (or other units) who persistently interact with one another in accordance with established patterns. Networks can be measured sociometrically, but usually they are not visually obvious. Nevertheless, they are quite real, at least in their effects on human behavior.

The importance of networks in explaining behavior was recognized by Georg Simmel (1964, p. 140), writing about sixty years ago, who stated: "The groups [networks] with which the individual is affiliated constitute a system of coordinates, as it were, such that each new group with which he becomes affiliated circumscribes him more exactly and more unambiguously."

More recently, Granovetter (1974, p. 4) pointed out "the enormous, though often unnoticed, constraint placed on individuals by the social networks in which they find themselves." Further, Granovetter (1974, p. 98) noted: "Personal contacts are used simultaneously to gather information *and* screen out noise, and are, for many types of information, the most efficient device for so doing."

Overall, the various researches on communication networks suggest the general proposition that *the communication networks in which an individual is a member partly determine his or her attitudes and overt behavior.*

This statement is entirely plausible, and not of much value in itself for understanding human behavior, but represents a point of departure for communication network analysis in moving to specific tests of hypotheses about *how* networks may influence individuals' behavior at the individual, dyadic, clique, and systems levels. We seek to illustrate this potential of various types of network analysis later by our research findings on diffusion networks for family planning in Korean villages.

If Georg Simmel were one of the first to recognize the theoretical significance of networks in understanding behavior change, Jacob L. Moreno, the father of sociometry, provided the basic methodological tools to measure network variables (Moreno, 1934). Moreno's sociometric measurement techniques and the sociograms that resulted from his data analysis afforded the first graphic realization of Simmel's call for a "geometry of social relations." Moreno acknowledged Simmel's influence on his conceptualizations of communication networks.

In the years since Simmel and Moreno, communication network analysis has come a long way. The distance it has come, at least in amount of effort expended, is illustrated by a recent bibliography (Freeman, 1973) on social networks[15] that includes almost 1,000 publications. The distance that the field has yet to go can be illustrated by the lack of standardly defined concepts, and their appropriate empirical measures for understanding exactly how networks affect behavior. To date, communication network analysis has been more of an assumption, a philosophy, and a faith than theoretically sound approach to scientific research on human behavior change. But the potential exists.

SOME PROBLEMS IN COMMUNICATION NETWORK ANALYSIS

Several difficulties are involved in communication network analysis. One problem is that sometimes the dynamic process of communication relationships among the members of a system may be so fleeting that networks cannot be accurately charted; then the plotting of sociometric communication relationships within a system is but an evasive illusion. Imagine trying to capture, in quantified terms of "arrows" and numbers, the total human interaction that occurs in even a small system in one day! Impossible, you say. True. Sociometric data actually reflect only the grossest of communication behavior, the main lines of communication that are most frequently and heavily used. The "weak ties" that occur in systems, the lightly used flows, are seldom reported by respondents in sociometric researches, and hence are rarely analyzed in network studies: Granovetter (1973) argues that this problem is especially serious because these "weak ties" are different in nature from the "strong ties" (the regularized communication patterns that are usually reported by respondents and investigated in network analyses). For example, Granovetter shows that weak ties are more likely to be informationally rich.

In one sense, this measurement problem associated with network concepts centers on the validity of sociometric measure of communication flows. This validity question has no final solution, although a multimeasurement approach can help. For example, a triangulation of measurements (perhaps including observation and tracer analysis along with sociometric questions) might be utilized in studying the same respondents in a system. We agree with Webb and others (1966, p. 1): "No research method is without bias. Interviews and questionnaires must be supplemented by methods testing the same social science variables, but having different methodological weaknesses."

Multimeasurement implies that "each method can be strengthened by appealing to the unique qualities of the other methods" (Sieber, 1973). We chose the two Korean villages of study as an illustration in the present chapter because we have other data about them in addition to the sociometric information.

A further problem is that more than one set of communication networks may exist. A given individual may have a different set of communication partners for each of a myriad of topics; and each of these personal networks may be somewhat overlapping and can be superimposed on the others. For example, one of our Korean respondents may talk to Mrs. Moon about family planning, but to Mrs. Chung about her child's health problems. So network relationships are single-stranded as well as multistranded.

Communication networks are the "threads" that hold a system together; one reason they are so difficult to study is because they are so numerous. The threads can easily become a tangled ball to the investigator. One of the practical problems of communication network analysis is the immensity of the task. In a system of 100 members, each of the 100 individuals can talk to the 99 others, so that 9,900 communication relationships are possible. In a 200-member system, 39,800 communication dyads are possible, and in a system with 5,000 members, nearly 25 million are possible, which exceeds the processing capacity of most modern computers. One solution is to break the total communication system down into subsystems, or cliques; this technique makes the complexity of interpersonal communication more manageable.

Up to the present time, efforts aimed at studying communication networks have been hampered by the inability to manually handle and analyze the great amounts of data necessary to construct networks of relatively large-sized systems. Recent methodological advances in computerized network analysis now allow us to understand many added dimensions of interpersonal communication networks which were previously hidden.

The computer methods of network analysis illustrated shortly employ strict mathematical criteria for explicitly identifying cliques and communication roles in the network data (Richards, 1975). This formalization and utilization of precise criteria eliminates the major problem in using manual or visual methods: Different roles and cliques are often identified by different investigators when examining the *same* set of data. With the mathematization of computational rules executed by a standard computer program, such judgmental errors can be eliminated, and the capability of making inter- and cross-network comparisons is facilitated (Richards, 1976). We shall now illustrate these particular advantages of methodological procedures for network analysis.

NETWORK ANALYSIS OF FAMILY PLANNING DIFFUSION IN KOREA

In the remainder of this chapter, we proceed to illustrate the potential usefulness of network analysis of diffusion with data gathered via personal interviews with all the 1,052 fertile-aged, married women living in a sample of twenty-five Korean villages (Park and others, 1974). For the sake of simplifying our illustration of network analysis, we deal mainly with a comparison of two of these twenty-five villages; each has thirty-nine respondents. One (village A), has a relatively successful family-planning program with 57 percent of the eligible couples currently using a family-planning method, while in the other (Village B), only 26 percent are practicing a method. Both villages were about equally exposed prior to our data-gathering to a rather standardized national family-planning program which sought to diffuse such methods as the IUD, oral contraceptives, and sterilization.

During the personal interviews, the respondents were asked several sociometric questions, including the item on which our present illustration is mainly based: "With whom in this village have you discussed family-planning ideas most frequently?" The skilled interviewers were females, allowing same-sex homophily in the interviewing situation, which is important in facilitating communication about a somewhat taboo topic like family planning in Korea (Rogers, 1973). We believe that our sociometric data thus obtained are generally accurate and of high quality.

The sociometric data on family-planning diffusion were subjected to a particular type of cross-sectional network analysis developed by Richards (1975), in which:

Step 1. The sociometric data for the thirty-nine respondents in each village are arranged in a who-to-whom matrix with each row representing the choosers and each column representing the individuals chosen. Each entry in this incidence matrix is a reported communication relationship.[16]

Step 2. The units in the choice matrix are ordered into cliques by a gradual approximation process. A *clique* is a subsystem whose units communicate more with each other than with units outside of the subsystem. Clique identification is approached by iterating the ordering of the units into configurations that gradually become more clique-like. *Units* (respondents) *are placed in adjacent positions in the who-to-whom matrix on the basis of the similarity of the units with whom they interact.* [17] Ordering on the basis of this criterion is accomplished simply by computing the mean of the identification numbers of the individuals with whom a respondent interacts.[18] Then all of the respondents are placed in order of these mean scores, from low to high, along the "who" and "whom" dimensions of the matrix. This procedure (after several reorderings) tends to concentrate the respondents' communication relationships in our Korean villages toward the diagonal of the who-to-whom matrix, and thus is beginning to arrange the respondents in cliques.

In further iterations of this procedure, in which the respondents are given new identification numbers after each reordering, the clique structure becomes increasingly apparent. One might imagine each dyadic communication relationship as a rubber band that gradually pulls pairs of individuals more closely together into subsystems of individuals who interact mostly with each other (Richards, 1975).

We terminated the reordering process when less than 10 percent of the respondents changed their position on one dimension of the who-to-whom matrix from one iteration to the next. This point occurred in each of the two villages after six iterations.

The three criteria specified by Richards (1975)[19] for clique identification are: (1) Each clique must be comprised of at least three members (so, for instance, respondents 4 and 63 in Figure 5–1 are an isolated dyad, not a clique); (2) Each clique member must have at least 50 percent of her communication relationships within the clique; (3) All members of a clique must be directly or indirectly connected by a path lying entirely within the clique.

One of our villages of study (Village A, with the relatively successful family-planning program) has one large clique of twenty individuals (Clique I), plus two smaller cliques, an isolated dyad, and four isolates (Figure 5–1). The other village has two larger cliques of fifteen individuals each, plus a small clique, and four isolates (Figure 5–2).

Step 3. A sociogram can be constructed to visualize the sociometric data about interpersonal diffusion. The sociogram presents (in an easily recognizable form) the main features of the communication structure: (1) *cliques,* (2) *liaisons,* who link two or more cliques but are not members of them, (3) *bridges,* who belong to one clique but commu-

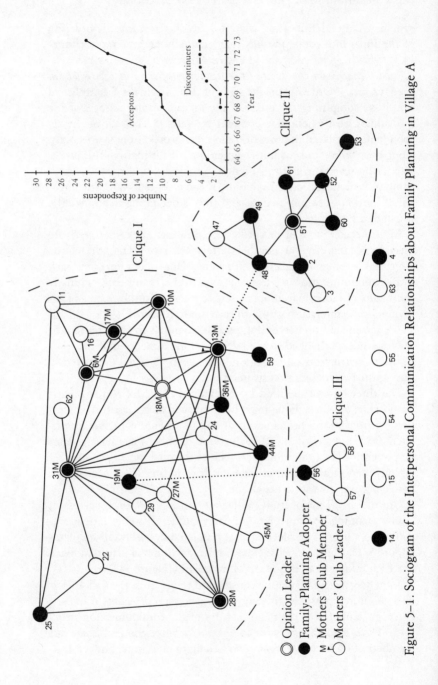

Figure 5–1. Sociogram of the Interpersonal Communication Relationships about Family Planning in Village A

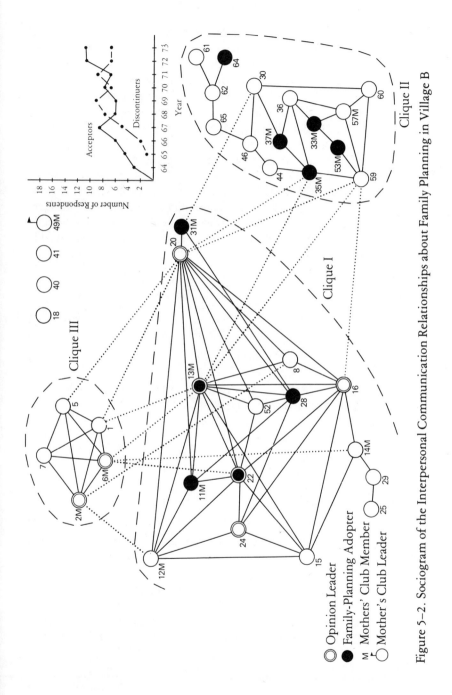

Figure 5–2. Sociogram of the Interpersonal Communication Relationships about Family Planning in Village B

nicate with individuals in another clique, and (4) isolates, individuals who do not communicate with anyone. We also identify the members of the family planning mothers' club (a voluntary association of mothers in each village to promote family planning and other community development activities)[20] and the club leader in each of the village sociograms, so as to enable contrasting the formal relationships (membership and leadership) of the mothers' club with the informal communication structure of family-planning diffusion.[21]

Step 4. Various indexes of communication structure can be constructed in order to describe the nature of the interpersonal communication structure at the individual, clique, or system level: connectedness, integration, dominance, differentiation, and openness. For example, we computed an index of system connectedness, defined as the degree to which the units (individuals) in a system are linked by communication flows by the formula

$$\text{System Connectedness} = \frac{\text{Number of actual communication relationships in a system}}{\text{Number of possible communication relationships in a system}}$$

The denominator is $\frac{N(N-1)}{2}$, or 741 in each of our two villages of thirty-nine individuals. The connectedness index for Village A is 86/741 or .116, and for Village B is 102/741 or .37. Thus Village B is somewhat more connected than Village A.

Connectedness can also be indexed at the clique level; for example, the clique connectedness index for Clique III in Village B (Figure 5-2) is 1.00, which is greater than the index of .37 for Clique I in Village B.

NETWORK VARIABLES IN EXPLAINING THE RELATIVE SUCCESS OF DIFFUSION ACTIVITIES

Now we focus on several sets of findings from our network analysis of family planning diffusion in the two Korean villages; first we consider various network reasons why Village A has a more successful family-planning program than does Village B.[22]

1. *Village A has a higher degree of overlap of the informal clique structure with the mothers' club membership than does Village B.*

In Village A, all of the mothers' club members are in the largest clique, while in Village B, the mothers' club members are scattered throughout the communication network of the village in various cliques (Figures 5–1 and 5–2).[23] This overlap of the formal organization with the informal clique structure is also shown by the tendency for mothers' club members to communicate mainly with each other in the more successful village, where the homophily index for mothers' club members is 0.73, as compared to .56 in Village B.[24]

2. *Involvement of pro-family planning opinion leaders in the mothers' club is greater in Village A than in Village B.*

In the successful village, 88 percent of the opinion leaders are mothers' club members, while in the less successful village, 43 percent of opinion leaders are mothers' club members. In the successful village, 88 percent of the opinion leaders are currently practicing family planning, but only 28 percent in the less successful village. Most of the remaining 72 percent of the opinion leaders in Village B have adopted, and later discontinued using, family-planning methods, while little discontinuance occurs in Village A.

3. *The mothers' club leader in Village A is located more centrally in the communication network than is the case in Village B.*

The mothers' club leader in Village A is an important informal opinion leader who maintains a direct communication relationship with eleven of the thirty-eight other eligible women in her village (Figure 5–1). She is also important in interpersonally linking the major cliques in her village. The mothers' club leader in Village A is at the center of the interpersonal communication network for family planning; moreover, she has been a family-planning adopter since prior to 1964. She was elected leader by the club members and is perceived as a local informal expert on medicine and health matters by the village women, as her brother is a medical doctor, and she is a very credible source of family-planning information.

In contrast, the club leader in Village B is completely isolated, without communication relationships to any other women in her village (Figure 5–2). She is not practicing family planning and is apathetic toward the mothers' club, as she was appointed to be the club leader by the village chief rather than elected by the members. She is illiterate and is also an older woman. The mothers' club in Village B seldom meets; when it does, the leader often does not attend.

The data in Figures 1 and 2 were gathered in our 1973 survey. When we returned to these two villages in 1975, the mothers' club in Village

B had officially disbanded due to its inept leadership and its lack of overlap with the informal communication structure of the village causing interclique rivalries within the mothers' club, and due to financial difficulties.

PERSONAL COMMUNICATION NETWORKS

Previously, we defined a *network* as the interconnected individuals who are linked by patterned communication flows. A *personal communication network* is the interconnected individuals who are linked by patterned communication flows to any given individual (Laumanm, 1973, p. 7). For the purposes of the present analysis, we find it convenient to anchor a network on an individual rather than a clique (Mitchell, 1969, p. 14). Each individual carries around with him or her a personal network of other individuals with whom he or she consistently interacts about a given topic. Thus each individual possesses his or her own small communication environment for a given topic or issue. This personal network partly explains the individual's behavior.[25]

How do our respondents' personal networks explain their decisions to adopt (and/or discontinue) the innovation of family planning over time? Figure 5-3 shows how an increasing percentage of Respondent 31's (in Village A) personal network adopted family planning from 1969 to when she herself adopted in 1972.

An individual is more likely to adopt family planning if a larger proportion of her personal network consists of individuals who have adopted previously. The percentage of the personal network made up of family-planning adopters was calculated for each eligible woman in our sample for each of the ten years covered by our survey data.[26] The personal networks for each year were adjusted to exclude women who were not yet married (and who were thus not usually in the village, nor likely to be regarded as adult peers by our respondents). The cumulative data are grouped by the percentage of the respondents' personal networks who have adopted family planning.

Among women who have personal networks with 10 percent adopters or less, only 10 percent adopt family planning themselves. A steady increase occurs in this percentage of women adopting as the proportion of their personal networks who have adopted rises, reaching a maximum of 69 percent among women who have personal networks with 71 to 80 percent adopters. This trend is stronger and more consistent in Village A than in Village B. We conclude that in general *an individual is more likely to adopt a family-planning innovation if more of the individuals in her personal network have adopted previously.*[27] This conclusion is hardly surprising, but it again suggests the potential of network variables in providing fuller understanding of the diffusion process (and in fact, a kind of understanding that is precluded unless one analyzes the data in network terms).

THE STRENGTH OF WEAK TIES

Out of the network analyses of interpersonal diffusion has grown a research issue called "the strength of weak ties" (Liu and Duff, 1972; Granovetter, 1973).[28] The general proposition summarizing this research is that: *The informational strength of dyadic communication relationships is inversely related to the degree of homophily (and the strength of the attraction) between the source and the receiver in each dyad.* In other words, an innovation is diffused to a larger number of individuals and transverses a greater social distance when passed through weak ties rather than stong (Granovetter, 1973).

Each individual operates in his or her particular communication environment for any given topic, consisting of a number of friends and acquaintances with whom the topic is discussed most frequently. These friends are usually highly homophilous (or similar) with the individual and with each other, and most of the individual's friends are friends of each other, thus constituting an "interlocking network" (Rogers, 1973; Laumann, 1973). This homophily and close attraction facilitates effective communication, but it acts as a barrier to prevent new ideas from entering the network. So not much informational strength exists in an interlocking network; some heterophilous ties are needed within the network to give it more openness. These "weak ties" enable innovations to flow from clique to clique via liaisons and bridges. In the total network an integrating and cohesive power is lent to the weak ties.

Network analysis of the diffusion of the IUD in the Philippines demonstrated this strength of weak ties: The innovation spread most easily within interlocking cliques among housewives of very similar social status (Liu and Duff, 1972). But heterophilous flows were necessary to link these cliques; usually these "weak ties" connected two women who were not close friends and enabled the innovation to travel from a higher-status to a somewhat lower-status housewife. So at least occasional heterophilous dyadic communication in a network was a structural prerequisite for effective diffusion.

We analyzed the sociometric data from our two Korean villages to

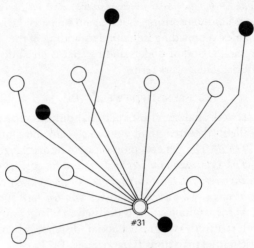

1969 Personal Network Adoption = $^4/_{12}$ = 33%.

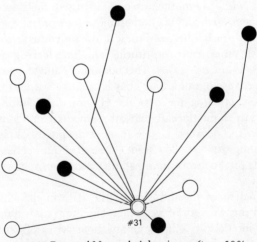

1970 Personal Network Adoption = $^6/_{12}$ = 50%.

Figure 5–3. An Illustration of Respondent # 31's Adoption of Family Planning as the Percentage of Adoption Increased in Her Personal Communication Network from 1969 to 1972

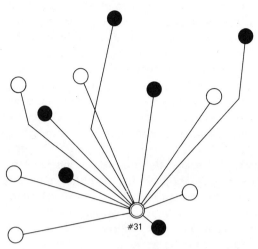

1971 Personal Network Adoption = $^6/_{12}$ = 50%.

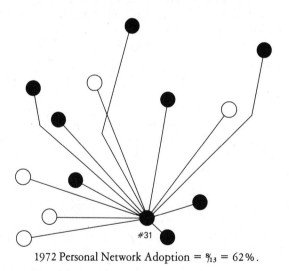

1972 Personal Network Adoption = $^8/_{13}$ = 62%.

● Adopter of Family Planning

○ Nonadopter of Family Planning

test the "strength of weak ties" hypothesis in the family-planning communication networks. This analysis explored the strength of communication ties in five specific hypotheses, each derived from the original Granovetter statement, relating such variables as linking ties, reciprocality,[29] homophily on mothers' club membership and adoption of family planning, and differences in planning knowledge between dyadic partners, all with the strength of ties. The unit of analysis in all cases is the dyadic communication *relationship* between two individuals about family planning. The strength of a sociometric tie between two dyadic partners is measured by the number of communication contacts which they share (this measure is the same one that we described previously as the basis for computing proximity in clique identification).[30] The degree to which two individuals share communication contacts (that is, the degree to which their personal communication networks overlap) is the best single measure, we believe, of the strength of their communication bond.

The major findings of this dyadic analysis of weak ties are:

1. *Tie strength and reciprocal ties.* Reciprocal ties are stronger in both villages than nonreciprocal ties. The seventeen reciprocal ties in Village A have a mean strength of 3.8, compared with an average strength of 2.6 for the fifty-two nonreciprocal ties. The mean strength of the eighteen reciprocal ties in Village B was 3.8, while the sixty-six nonreciprocal ties averaged 2.9. So reciprocal ties are stronger, as we would expect.

2. *Tie strength and linking ties.* The number of ties linking different communication cliques is rather small, but in both villages they are weaker than nonlinking ties. In Village A, the two linking ties had an average strength of 1.0, compared with 3.0 for the sixty-seven nonlinking ties. Village B has fourteen linking ties, averaging 2.4 in strength, and seventy nonlinking ties with a mean strength of 3.4. As hypothesized, the interclique linking relationships are weaker than ties within cliques.[31]

3. *Tie strength and heterophilous communication between mothers' club members and nonmembers.* In Village A, communication ties linking mothers' club members and nonmembers are weaker (than ties between members and between nonmembers). In Village B the reverse is true. Mean tie strength in the heterophilous (on club membership) relationship of club members and nonmembers is 2.5 in Village A, compared with a mean tie strength of 3.1 for the homophilous relationships of member/member and nonmember/nonmember.

In Village B, the mean strength of ties joining heterophilous members/nonmembers is 3.3, while the homophilous ties average 3.1. We had expected stronger ties in more homophilous relationships but did not find support for our hypothesis in Village B. Nevertheless, these data are consistent with our earlier finding that mothers' club membership conforms more closely to natural communication cliques in Village A than in Village B.

4. *Tie strength and heterophilous communication between adopters and nonadopters of family planning.* In Village A, the heterophilous ties between adopters and nonadopters are relatively weaker than the homophilous adopter/adopter and nonadopter/nonadopter ties. Nonadopters are not well integrated into the family-planning communication network of the village, whose norms generally are favorable to family planning. In Village B, ties between pairs of family-planning adopters are strong, as are ties between adopters and nonadopters, but the homophilous ties between nonadopters are relatively weak. Although our results are not completely consistent, again we see that homophilous ties are generally stronger than heterophilous ties.

5. *Tie strength and family-planning knowledge.* The women in our two Korean villages were each asked a set of ten "how-to" knowledge questions about family planning.[32] The difference in the number of correct responses by the two dyadic partners was calculated for each family-planning communication dyad. In Village A, no consistent relationship occurred between tie strength and family-planning knowledge differences. In Village B, mean tie strength increased from 2.9 to 3.7 as knowledge differentials rose from 0 to 3 or more. So contrary to our expectations, we found heterophily on family-planning knowledge to be related to tie strength in Village B.

Perhaps the general point is that by converting the knowledge variable, measured for each individual respondent, into a dyadic variable, we were able to include it in a relational hypothesis with tie strength. Hopefully communication research can move into relational-type thinking more easily as network analysis provides empirical measures of relational concepts.

IMPLICATIONS FOR FUTURE RESEARCH

The theme of this chapter is that various types of network analysis offer potential for diffusion research to break out of its past psychological bias, by stressing alternative uses of interpersonal communication relationships as units of analysis, and/or units of measurement.

We sought to illustrate this potential with examples from our network analysis of family-planning diffusion in Korea.

This work leads to the following implications for future research on diffusion networks.

1. A *content analysis* of the communication messages that flow through interpersonal patterns is needed, in order to improve the ability of the communication structure to predict diffusion and adoption. These messages may be negative rumors about the side effects of family-planning methods, personal testimonials from satisfied adopters, misinformation, and so on. Appropriate research designs and measurement techniques need to be developed in order to sample these interpersonal messages.[33] Measurement of the content of these flows should enrich our capacity to understand the effects of such network communication.

2. Network analysis should be incorporated in research on *system effects* in the diffusion of innovations. *System effects* are the influences of the structure and/or composition of a system on the behavior of the members of the system. An individual's behavior is influenced, in part, by the system of which he or she is a member.

In our twenty-five villages of study in Korea, we found much indirect evidence of the effect of the village on individual adoption of family-planning innovations. For instance, one of our villages has 51 percent adoption of the IUD and only one vasectomy adopter; another village has 23 percent adoption of vasectomy; yet another is a "pill village" (Park and others, 1974). These village-to-village differences in preference for specific family-planning methods are certainly not random and reflect the impact of communication networks in each village in "standardizing" a common behavior among the members of each village.

Studies of systems effects need to incorporate network variables (like connectedness) as possible intervening variables between the independent system-level variables (like the average level of mass media exposure in a village, or the strength of its mothers' club) and such dependent variables as the individual's adoption of family-planning innovations.[34] Thus, we might gain an improved understanding of the process of how system effects occur.

3. Improvements are needed in *sociometric measurements* of communication flows. For example, the "seeking" question on which the present analysis was mostly based ("With whom in this village have you discussed family-planning ideas most frequently?") might be con-

trasted, and perhaps supplemented, with data from another sociometric question (a "sought" type) asked in our Korea survey: "Which other women in this village have obtained information about family planning from you?" Perhaps a multimeasurement approach to the communication flow data would contribute to greater accuracy, especially if some nonsociometric measures (like observations) were also included. At present, one of the main weaknesses of communication network analysis is its complete dependence on sociometric measurement.

4. *Over-time measures* at t_2, t_3, and so forth, need to be made in order to contrast these data and results with the cross-sectional correlational analysis of one-shot survey data represented by the present analysis. Such over-time data about sociometric communication relationships are almost entirely missing in past research on networks. Essentially, we need to determine the reliability of sociometric data and their generalizability across time periods, as well as how network structures change over time.

Perhaps in closing we might stress the possibility of incorporating network analysis as one component in the typical survey research on the diffusion of innovations. For instance, personal communication networks can be measured in a random sample design by asking each respondent questions about his or her network partners (Laumann, 1973). Or, with appropriate changes in the sample design, data can be gathered from a sample of all the respondents in intact systems (like villages); the loss in generalizability may often be compensated for by the extra insight offered by the network analyses thus made possible. The research strategy of including network analysis as at least one component of survey researches on diffusion would allow use of alternative units of analysis, and units of measurement, than just the individual.

And thus the psychological bias of diffusion research might begin to be overcome.

NOTES

1. The role played by Wilbur Schramm in diffusion research is different than in such other fields as television's effects on children, instructional television, and others, where he engaged in this research and synthesized what was known. In the case of diffusion, Wilbur Schramm was instrumental in recognizing this field as essentially a special aspect of communication research. During the early 1960s, through conferences, his various books, and his influence on his students, he directly and indirectly brought the diffusion field into communication research, thus changing both.

2. This chapter reflects three years of research on communication networks in the diffusion of family-planning innovations in Korean villages. Collaborators in this work were Hyung Jong Park and Kyung-Kyoon Chung, School of Public Health, Seoul National University; Sea-Baick Lee, William S. Puppa, and Brenda A. Doe in the Department of Population Planning, University of Michigan; Noreene Janus and William D. Richards, Institute for Communication Research, Stanford University; and D. Lawrence Kincaid of the East-West Communication Institute. The 1973 survey in Korea was supported by the Asia Foundation.

3. Such census-type sampling designs in which a sample of intact groups like communities are selected have not been especially common in diffusion research since the Ryan and Gross (1943) study, as diffusion researchers have mainly pursued the objective of generalizability of results from random samples of individuals. In fact, not until the Coleman and others (1966) study of the diffusion of a new antibiotic among doctors in a medical community did the potential of sociometric analysis of diffusion actually begin to be realized. One exception is the work of Professor Herbert F. Lionberger, who has been engaged in such research since the early 1950s in Missouri communities.

4. For example, Crane's (1972) network analysis of the cliques among diffusion scholars in the rural sociology research tradition in the mid-1960s (when rural sociology was paramount in studying diffusion) showed that two main cliques, one of twenty-seven members and one of thirty-two members, dominate this invisible subcollege. Each clique was headed by an "opinion leader," often an individual who was relatively early on the scene of diffusion research and whose followers were former students whose dissertations he or she directed. These opinion leaders tended to be the high producers of scientific literature in the diffusion field. Opinion leadership was very concentrated in the invisible college; 6 percent of the 203 scientists in the rural sociology tradition received 58 percent of all the sociometric choices, indicating who informally influenced the scholar's research (Crane, 1972, p. 74).

5. This section of this chapter borrows directly from Rogers (1976) where, in addition to the psychological bias in diffusion research, the pro-innovation bias (an assumption that the innovations studied are "good" and should be adopted by everyone) and the lack of an over-time process orientation are also discussed.

6. A somewhat parallel plea for communication network analysis has been made by Sheingold (1973) for the field of voting research.

7. *Relational analysis* is a research approach in which the unit of analysis is a relationship between two or more individuals (Rogers and Bhowmik, 1971).

8. A similar assumption is made by many other research-oriented institutions, when they imply that the user system should utilize the innovations resulting from research (Rogers and others, 1976).

9. Opinion leadership was usually measured as the number of sociometric choices received by an individual; thus it is *measured* in relational terms but reduced to an individual characteristic of the respondent when the individual is the *unit of analysis,* as in most past research.

10. About the only other place in communication research where network analysis has been used to restore social structure to the communication process is in investigations of organizational communication (Rogers and Agarwala-Rogers, 1976).

11. Defined as an individual who links two or more cliques in a system but who is not a member of any clique.

12. Defined as an individual who links two or more cliques in a system from his or her position as a member of one of the cliques.

13. Defined as the degree to which the units in a system are interconnected through communication linkages.

14. Defined as the degree to which the units in a system exchange information across the system boundary with their environment.

15. We do not make much of a distinction in this report between "communication networks" and "social networks," although one might imagine a social network relationship, such as between a military general and a private, in which interpersonal communication rarely or never occurs.

16. We considered each communication relationship to be reciprocal, whether it was reported as such by the respondent or not, as each such interaction usually involves a certain degree of two-way information exchange.

17. In most previous attempts at clique identification, the criterion for grouping was to position individuals together *if they interacted with each other, rather than on the basis of the similarity of the units with whom they interacted.*

18. For example, in Figure 5-1, respondent 2 reports communication relationships with individuals 3, 48 and 51. These identification numbers are weighted by the number of shared links so as to accelerate the "cliquing" process by giving less weight to sociometric choices that probably go outside of the clique. The weighted mean of the identification numbers for respondent 2 is $\dfrac{2 + 3(1) + 48(2) + 51(2)}{1 + 1 + 2 + 2} = 33$, placing respondent 2 next to respondent 62 and respondent 48 in a reordered matrix (Rogers and others, 1977). The thirty-nine women in Figures 5-1 and 5-2 do not have consecutive identification numbers because certain households, numbered consecutively on the village map, did not contain an eligible female respondent (that is, married and in the reproductive age range).

19. A fourth criterion, somewhat more difficult to apply in some situations and one which we did not follow, is that if any one member were removed from the clique, it would remain intact.

20. Numerous investigations of mothers' clubs in Korea are available, for example, Kincaid and others (1974), Park and others (1974), and Park and others (1976).

21. We also identify the informal opinion leaders on the sociograms (Figures 5-1 and 5-2). These opinion leaders are those individuals sociometrically nominated by at least 10 percent of the other respondents in their village.

22. Such nonnetwork explanations for the relatively greater success of

family-planning diffusion activities in Village A as (1) home visiting by family-planning field workers, and (2) group meetings about family planning, are actually more frequently reported by respondents in Village B (Rogers and others, 1977). However, mass media exposure to family-planning messages is somewhat greater in Village A than in Village B.

23. Suggesting that the future potential diffusion of family planning in Village B may be greater than in Village A if the mothers' club could somehow become more effective. Also, Clique II in Village A (Figure 5-1) has 80 percent adoption of family planning and no mothers' club members, while Clique I has only 55 percent adoption. Clearly, other factors than just mothers' club membership explains the adoption of family planning in Village A.

24. *Homophily* is the degree to which pairs of individuals who interact are similar in certain attributes, such as beliefs, values, social status, and the like (Rogers with Shoemaker, 1971, p. 14). Our homophily index can measure, for example, the degree to which mothers' club members in a village interact with each other (as opposed to interacting with nonmembers). For example, the homophily index of .73 in Village A means that 73 percent of all communication relationships were from club member-to-member, or from nonmember-to-nonmember.

25. In the present section, the individual respondent is still the unit of analysis, but the independent variable of personal network behavior is *measured* as a relational variable, although the dependent variable of innovativeness is not.

26. The measure used is a simple percentage. Another possible measure is a weighted proportion, which assigns greater weight to strong ties than to weak ties. The index of the strength of a tie between two individuals who communicate with each other might be based on the degree to which their personal networks overlap (Granovetter, 1973).

27. Professor Mark Granovetter at Harvard University is presently constructing mathematical models of "collective action," in which each individual in a system is assumed to possess a somewhat different level of resistance (or inertia) toward an innovation, which must be overcome at a certain threshold level of adoption by the peers in one's personal network, thus producing the familiar S-curve of diffusion.

28. These two sets of authors independently discovered the diffusion strength of weak sociometric ties and published articles with identical names within a few months of each other in 1972–1973, although approaching the issue in somewhat different ways. Although Professors Liu, Duff, and Granovetter were well read in the diffusion literature, they had not previously published on this topic, and their articles show a relatively fresh approach to analyzing diffusion networks. Perhaps this relative newness in working with the classical diffusion model was one requisite for the originality of their contribution.

29. *Reciprocal ties* are communication relationships in which the partners both nominate each other; *nonreciprocal ties* are relationships in which only one partner has been nominated.

30. Each respondent was limited to a maximum of five nominations in

responding to the sociometric question, so our range in tie strength measures is restricted, compared to what we could have obtained by asking each respondent about the strength of his or her relationship with *each* other member in the system (as in a so-called roster study). However, the distortion introduced by this factor does not appear to be very severe in the present case.

31. In both villages, we find the liaisonness of communication ties is negatively related to their reciprocality. None of the linking ties in either village is reciprocal, while 25 percent of the nonlinking ties are reciprocal.

32. These questions asked how often it was necessary to take contraceptive pills, if men could use the loop, and so forth.

33. As an example, Robert Gillespie has utilized a small number of diary-keepers to record what they heard (and overheard) about family planning during a communication campaign in Esfahan Province, Iran; then he was able to content analyze their daily diaries.

34. Sea-Baick Lee is pursuing this research approach to studying system effects in his Ph.D. dissertation at the University of Michigan.

REFERENCES

Barton, Allen. "Bringing Society Back In: Survey Research and Macro-Methodology." *American Behavioral Scientist, 12,* 1–9, 1968.

Caplan, Nathan, and Stephen D. Nelson. "On Being Useful: The Nature and Consequences of Psychological Research on Social Problems." *American Psychologist, 28,* 199–211, 1973.

Coleman, James S. "Relational Analysis: A Study of Social Organization with Survey Methods." *Human Organization, 17,* 28–36, 1958.

Coleman, James S., and others. *Medical Innovation: A Diffusion Study.* New York: Bobbs-Merrill, 1966.

Crane, Diana. *Invisible Colleges: Diffusion of Knowledge in Scientific Communities.* Chicago: University of Chicago Press, 1972.

Freeman, Linton C. *A Bibliography of Social Networks.* Bethlehem, Penn.: Lehigh University, Department of Social Relations, Mimeo Report, 1973.

Granovetter, Mark S. "The Strength of Weak Ties." *American Journal of Sociology, 78,* 1360–1380, 1973.

_____. *Getting a Job: A Study of Contacts and Careers.* Cambridge, Mass.: Harvard University Press, 1974.

Katz, Elihu, and Paul F. Lazarsfeld. *Personal Influence.* New York: Free Press, 1955.

Katz, Elihu. "Communication Research and the Image of Society: Convergence of Two Traditions." *American Journal of Sociology, 65,* 435–440, 1960.

Kincaid, D. Lawrence, and others. *Mothers' Clubs and Family Planning in Rural Korea: The Case of Oryu Li.* Honolulu: East-West Communication Institute, Mimeo Report, 1974.

Kincaid, D. Lawrence, and June Ock Yum. "The Needle and the Ax: Communication and Development in a Korean Village." In Wilbur Schramm and Daniel Lerner, eds., *Communication and Change: The Last Ten Years—And the Next.* Honolulu: University Press of Hawaii, 1976.

Kuhn, Thomas S. *The Structure of Scientific Revolutions.* Chicago: University of Chicago Press, 1962.

Laumann, Edward O. *Bonds of Pluralism: The Form and Substance of Urban Social Networks.* New York: Wiley-Interscience, 1973.

Lazarsfeld, Paul F., and others. *The People's Choice.* New York: Duell, Sloan, and Pearce, 1944.

Liu, William T., and Robert W. Duff. "The Strength of Weak Ties." *Public Opinion Quarterly, 36,* 361–366, 1972.

Mitchell, J. Clyde. "The Concept and Use of Social Networks." In J. Clyde Mitchell, ed., *Social Networks in Urban Situations.* Manchester, England: Manchester University Press, 1969.

Moreno, Jacob L. *Who Shall Survive?* Washington, D.C.: Nervous and Mental Disease Monograph 58, 1934.

Park, Hyung Jong, and others. *Mothers' Clubs and Family Planning in Korea.* Seoul, Korea: Seoul National University, School of Public Health, 1974.

_____. "The Korean Mothers' Club Program." *Studies in Family Planning,* 7 (10), 275–283, 1976.

Richards, William D., Jr. *A Manual for Network Analysis (Using the NEGOPY Network Analysis Program).* Stanford, Calif.: Stanford University, Institute for Communication Research, Mimeo Report, 1975.

_____. *A Coherent Systems Methodology for the Analysis of Human Communication.* Ph.D. Thesis, Stanford, Calif.: Stanford University, 1976.

Rogers, Everett M., and Dilip K. Bhowmik. "Homophily-Heterophily: Relational Concepts for Communication Research." *Public Opinion Quarterly, 34,* 523–538, 1971.

Rogers, Everett M. *Communication Strategies for Family Planning.* New York: Free Press, 1973.

Rogers, Everett M., with F. Floyd Shoemaker. *Communication of Innovations: A Cross-Cultural Approach.* New York: Free Press, 1971.

Rogers, Everett M. and others. *Extending the Agricultural Extension Model.* Stanford, Calif.: Stanford University, Institute for Communication Research, Mimeo Report, 1976.

Rogers, Everett M. "Where We Are in Understanding the Diffusion of Innovations." In Wilbur Schramm and Daniel Lerner, eds., *Communication and Change: The Last Ten Years—And the Next.* Honolulu: University Press of Hawaii, 1976.

Rogers, Everett M., and Rekha Agarwala-Rogers. *Communication in Organizations.* New York: Free Press, 1976.

Rogers, Everett M., and others. *Network Analysis of the Diffusion of Family Planning Innovations Over Time in Korean Villages: The Role of Mothers' Clubs.* Stanford, Calif.: Stanford University, Institute for Communication Research, Mimeo Report, 1977.

Ryan, Bryce, and Neal C. Gross. "The Diffusion of Hybrid Seed Corn in Two Iowa Communities." *Rural Sociology, 8,* 15–24, 1943.

Sheingold, Carl A. "Social Networks and Voting: The Resurrection of a Research Agenda." *American Sociological Review, 38,* 712–720, 1973.

Sieber, Sam D. "The Integration of Fieldwork and Survey Methods." *American Journal of Sociology, 78,* 1335–1359, 1973.

Simmel, Georg. *The Web of Group Affiliations,* translated by Reinhard Bendix. New York: Free Press, 1964.

Webb, Eugene J., and others. *Unobtrusive Measure: Nonreactive Research in the Social Sciences.* Chicago: Rand McNally, 1966.

Communication and Development

DANIEL LERNER

"Development" as an international ideology began with a communication—the State of the Union message delivered to Congress by President Harry S. Truman in January, 1949. The fourth point of President Truman's message announced a "bold new program" of United States technical assistance and financial aid to poor countries around the world. This policy, which became known as "Point IV," was soon adopted by other rich countries, as well as by regional and international organizations. Thus came into operation the development paradigm —aid from richer to poorer countries—that has been a major factor in the world political process over the past quarter-century.

BACKGROUND

Development has been an integral part of the turn of history since World War II. The immediate postwar period was marked by three interrelated sequences: (1) decline of Europe as the world power center; (2) bipolarization and domination of the world by the two nuclear superpowers; and (3) emergence of the Third World. The passing of European imperialism entailed the emergence of new nations as former colonies became independent political entities. The end of tutelage required the start of training for self-management. In this sense, postwar decolonization was the source of development ideology and procedure.

The reasons for such development are clear. At independence, virtually none of the new nations was capable of adequate self-management in terms that would satisfy the newly independent peoples. The heady wine of independence led these people to expect a better life promptly. Now that the imperalist expropriators had been expropriated, the native peoples expected that they would enjoy the benefits of their own lands and their resources. But the available resources turned out to be rather meager. The emerging peoples of the postwar years were mainly rural and agricultural, uneducated and illiterate, isolated and "nonparticipant," and very poor.

The problem before them was how to move rapidly from poverty toward prosperity. The direction of movement of the social goals of development was clear: toward prosperity. The questions that proved perplexing had to do with tempo and technique. Tempo was important because these new nations were in a hurry. Technique was important because these nations had little—and needed much—that was productive of rapid economic growth.

Indeed, just this lack of appropriate technique had locked these peoples over centuries into the "vicious circle of poverty." Economists seemed agreed that these peoples were poor because they had no industry; they had no industry because they were poor. Plainly, the way out of this vicious circle seemed to be to provide these emerging peoples with the money and know-how (economic aid and technical assistance) needed to industrialize. Thus aid was the watchword of the first development decade, when some observers noted that "steel mills are becoming the cathedrals of the twentieth century."

However, the decade's experience with accelerating industrialization turned out to be quite disappointing. Western economists began to revise their views of the most appropriate technique for development. W. Arthur Lewis earlier had defined development as "rising output per head,"[1] in terms of the western neoclassic growth model. By the 1960s, however, economists were exploring alternate conceptions and techniques to accelerate development for Latin America. Raul Prebisch of the Economic Commission for Latin America (ECLA) of the United Nations was advocating the technique of "technical innovation" as a way of "leapfrogging" the western model of development and accelerating economic growth. For countries somewhat less developed than many of the Latin American countries, economists were talking about the less-demanding techniques of "import substitution."

Perhaps the prime example of the changing perspective on technique for accelerating economic growth was found in India. There, over the first decade or so of independence, the outstanding statistician Mahalanobis had insisted, following the Soviet model to which he gave preference over the western model, upon steel mills and all other appurtenances of industrialization. By the 1960s, however, forced industrialization in the Soviet manner was clearly not readily compatible with the democratic ideals proclaimed by the government of India. Moreover, economic studies made clear the fact that India was paying more to import food than its industrial production (little of it exportable for foreign exchange) was worth. A definite shift was made from industrialization to import substitution as a major technique of economic growth for India. The initial result of this shift, as demonstrated primarily in the Punjab, was the famous "green revolution." Yet, as this significant growth in agricultural production failed to spread rapidly into other regions of India, disenchantment overtook even this more modest technique of economic growth.

As the policies and techniques preached by economists failed to accelerate productivity ("rising output per head"), or even to increase total product in many sectors, frustration in many developing countries shifted the emphasis from production to consumption. By 1960 many economists were giving their attention to "rising income per head" as the end and means of economic growth. This shift of focus from production to consumption also eventuated in frustration, because income per head failed to accelerate in most poor countries, and consumption of many necessities (food and housing) even declined in some of them.

The outcome of the early development years was widespread frustration, with which we shall deal more fully below. In many developing countries which were not growing according to expectations, the spread of economic frustrations produced, mainly among "leftist" intellectuals and politicians, a revulsion against western "materialism." When we recall that most development efforts during these early years did not produce the goods specified by economists, the reason for this response becomes clear. That most of the poor countries had seized upon these economic proposals as salvation is irrelevant. The more relevant point is that, as economic policies and panaceas failed to improve the living conditions of the poor, the leaders of many less-developed countries turned against western materialism as "the god that failed."

Of special interest for the purposes of this chapter is the concomitant shift from economics to communication as a source of policy thinking about development. This shift was signaled by the turn of many development economists to "noneconomic factors" and of other social scientists to "human factors." As the late Max F. Millikan put it a decade ago: "Of all the technological changes which have been sweeping through the traditional societies of the underdeveloped world in the last decade . . . the most fundamental and pervasive in their effects on human society have been the changes in communication."[2]

We use the term "communication" in the broadest sense, to include the general process of attitude-formation and attitude-change by which a society is shaped. Indeed, the shaping of transitional societies—since the passing of traditional society and the partial rejection of the western model—is the central theme of this chapter.

ISSUES

Among the many and varied "human factors" that have bedeviled development effort over the past quarter-century, four sets of issues appear paramount. We label these concisely, and therefore too simply, as ideology, nationalism, adaptation, and "dynamic equilibrium." This section consists of a brief exegesis of the four sets of issues as human factors.

IDEOLOGY

The modernization of the more-developed countries (MDC) of Western Europe and North America was animated, over five centuries, as J. B. Bury and other scholars have shown, by the idea of "progress." The quest for modernization in the less-developed countries (LDC) over the past quarter-century has been animated by the idea of "development."

Both "progress" and "development," like all resonant key symbols, are full of ambiguity. One man's progress is another man's poison; one man's development is another man's disaster. These key symbols have been communciated in such ways as to promote widespread *ambivalence*—possibly the key symbol of what is happening in LDC today.

Ambivalence arises when a person simultaneously wants two values—two objects of desire—that are incompatible within a simultaneous time frame. The most usual form, in strictly economic terms, is that neither national nor personal incomes rise fast enough to permit simultaneous increases of investment and consumption. The household economy of a marginal farmer usually requires that he choose *either* better tools and seeds (investment) *or* better food and clothing (consumption). Similarly, the formulators of the national economy of an LDC usually must choose between increasing aggregate productivity or sharing the available product.

On a deeper level, in terms of human factors, ambivalence arises from the conflict of old and new values. A traditional father wishes to send his son to the time-honored religious school but faces a conflict when he perceives the benefits his son can derive from the new secular training school. Later on, in the same family, the traditional mother wishes to keep her postschool adolescent son living and working at home but also faces a conflict when she perceives that his newly acquired literacy and skills will earn him a better living—and thereby a better life—in a distant city.

Those parents and children who resolve their ambivalence in favor of the secular school and the urban job break the traditional ties and create a "transitional" family. When enough families choose to follow this same route, the society as a whole becomes transitional. With a critical mass of people committed to trying the new ways, the burden of ambivalence becomes less oppressive for the remainder. They can more easily choose the new ways because others they know and respect have already done so. Thus traditional values recede and institutions deteriorate, ceding pride of place to the new transitional (presumably "developmental") ways and means.

This process had been going on for fifteen years or more in most LDC before their intellectuals began to cry havoc. Dismayed by the accelerating rate at which psychocultural "transition" was outrunning socioeconomic "development," some of these intellectuals decided the time had come to stop this dangerous trend—possibly to reverse it. People of the LDC were to be recalled to traditional values and relationships. The galloping and apparently endless race toward "development western style" was to be slowed, stopped, and pointed into new "indigenous" paths.

The past decade or so has shown that this reversal was easier said than done. We must not fault the intellectuals of the LDC, who overreacted against a bill of goods that intellectuals of the MDC (presumably including myself) had been overselling them during the critical early years of development effort. The intellectuals of the LDC ran into the same set of "ideological" issues that intellectuals of the MDC had already perceived as insoluble in ideological acids.

Just as development economists had earlier recognized their limits and called for "human factors" research, so development humanists were recognizing that some economic parameters were invariant regardless of continent, creed, color, class, or condition of life. No "rising output per head" could occur without rising productivity, nor could "rising income per head" occur without a larger product. The optimum solution, for LDC as for MDC, is to bake bigger pies together rather than compete separately for larger shares of the same pie.

The economic parameters have been subjected to a large array of "human factors" that have been expressed on the world scene as "nationalism." Nationalism has been the chronic problem of the MDC for centuries—the principal source of its wars, the laurel of its victories, the solace of its defeats. That LDC adopted the dubious structure of nationalism as their own implicates them equally in the malfunctioning of development efforts to bake a bigger pie. The political results of structuring all peoples of the world into nations are so severe that we take nationalism as our second set of issues.

NATIONALISM

The adoption of the nation-state as a political structure has brought with it a complex array of problems for LDC. The nations of LDC come in a variety of shapes and sizes. Some appear to be too large to be viable under a single unified national government. India, for example, has gone through two major subdivisions—Pakistan and Bangladesh—since its formation as a nation in 1947. Other countries are too small to be viable as nation-states. Examples are the tiny island-nations, with populations numbered in thousands or even hundreds, that have been created around the Pacific Basin over the past decade. Most LDC simply are too poor to be viable nations on a long- term basis.

The national political structure is compromised even more seriously by the deep ethnocentrism which pervades many of the LDC. We use the term ethnocentrism in the large sense to include the strong conflicting components of culture, region, and language as well as race. The division of India and Pakistan surely was motivated as much by differences of religion as by the size of the subcontinent. The further division which produced Bangladesh was certainly motivated, at least in part, by the common ties of the Bengali language.

Where ethnocentrism has not yet produced secession, it has produced separatist movements that make stable government as a nation-state extremely difficult. Such is the case of Bougainville in Papua New Guinea. Such also is the case in Fiji, where the former Indian minority now actually outnumbers the indigenous Fijians. Even where the separatist movements have not yet compromised the existing political structure, they have created pervasive dissension that usually is counterproductive to national development efforts. A prime example of this dissension occurs in Malaysia, where the huge Chinese minority (approximately 37 percent) and the smaller Indian minority (about 11 percent) have been restrained by legislation explicitly favoring the indigenous Malay people. Since Malaysian development heretofore had been promoted largely by the Chinese and Indian minorities, clearly the racist element in legislation over the past decade is likely to impede national growth in the future.

Similar results appear to be inevitable in some countries where ethnocentrism has led to outright xenophobia. One need hardly look further than the beastly treatment of Indians in East Africa to see the dire effects of ethnocentrism rampant. In many parts of Southeast Asia, the "overseas Chinese" have been subjected to equally invidious, though less violent, policies.

A final set of problems emanating from the national structure of political life is the hampering effect on regional activity. Many development projects require regional action—that is, action involving both formal and informal cooperation among several nations—to be effective. Examples occur wherever international waters are involved in development planning. The Jordan Valley Authority, proposed a quarter-century ago, was never allowed to function owing to the Arab–Israeli conflict, although all nations involved would clearly have benefitted from such an authority. Similarly, the Mekong Delta Project, which would have brought substantial benefits to several nations in the former areas of Indochina, was never put into effective action.

Even where nations have created a regional structure, as in the Association of Southeast Asian Nations (ASEAN), its capacity for effective developmental action has been severely limited by nationalism. An example is the rediffusion television satellite to be placed over Indonesia in the near future. This satellite has the capacity to reach all four of the other ASEAN nations—the Philippines, Singapore, Malaysia, and Thailand. Yet, after long negotiations, not one of these nations has "bought into" the Indonesia satellite, which, accordingly, will operate strictly on a national basis.

Probably the strongest charge that can be brought against nationalism in an LDC is that it inhibits those personal and social transformations upon which the LDC depends for the economic development it seeks and needs.

TRANSFORMATIONS

Development invariably requires a transformation of lifeways and the institutions through which they are enacted. In the early years of development, planning, and research, people spoke of the "transfer of institutions." However, the notion of "transfer" clearly soon became too superficial. One may transfer a sum of money, or even a piece of technology, but the moment this money or technology comes into use, it requires a behavioral transformation in the receiving LDC. A communication satellite cannot become operative in Indonesia, nor can a steel plow in India, without transforming the behavior of its "users" in very deep ways. I described this situation earlier:

> The process whereby more developed societies influence less developed societies always involves some institutional "discontinuity" in the less developed societies (some "break" with the past).[3] This is so because traditional societies, while adaptive to internally generated problems, lack efficient mechanisms of consensual response to external challenge. The traditional code's available stock of responses typically provides no compelling behavioral directive for meeting an unprecedented new challenge. Some enthusiastically accept; others uncompromisingly reject. With such dissension, which calls into question the suddenly inadequate code of traditional lifeways, intrusion occurs and disruption begins.
> Note, however, that the controlling component of this sequence is *internal* to the traditional society. The initial intrusion comes, it is true, from the outside. But its impact depends upon the reaction of the indigenous people. An intrusion that is widely ignored or evaded or rejected has little or no impact. It is only an intrusion which is "internalized" by a significant fraction of the population that can have any lasting effect. The formation of dissent thus is the fulcrum of the attitudinal–behavioral sequence, which, on this analysis, presents itself primarily as a communication response.[4]

This fact has been made quite clear in the recent work by Everett Rogers and Alex Inkeles. In his work on the diffusion of innovations, Rogers has shown that adoption always involves adaptation. In every case where an innovation has come from the outside, its effective use in the new environment has required a transformation. The fundamental process whereby the transformation is accomplished we call "communication." Alex Inkeles has gone even further in his monumental study *Becoming Modern*, by documenting his proposal that no development occurs apart from the transformation of personal attitudes and behavior. Inkeles states:

A modern *nation* needs participating citizens, men and women who take an active interest in public affairs and who exercise their rights and perform their duties as members of a community larger than that of the kinship network and the immediate geographical locality. Modern *institutions* need individuals who can keep to fixed schedules, observe abstract rules, make judgments on the basis of objective evidence, and follow authorities legitimated not by traditional or religious sanctions but by technical competence. The complex production tasks of the *industrial order*, which are the basis of modern social systems, also make their demands. Workers must be able to accept both an elaborate division of labor and the need to coordinate their activities with a large number of others in the work force. Rewards based on technical competence and objective standards of performance, strict hierarchies of authority responsive to the imperatives of machine production, and the separation of product and producer, all are part of this milieu, and require particular personal properties of those who are to master its requirements.[5]

DYNAMIC EQUILIBRIUM

Some theorists have contended that "dynamic equilibrium" is a contradiction in terms because a social system cannot be both dynamic and at equilibrium simultaneously. If the concept is carried to extremes, this dichotomy is doubtless a problem. But conceived in relative terms—that is, as much dynamism as is compatible with equilibrium—it represents an important, possibly indispensable, goal for developing countries.

I have formulated the notion of "dynamic equilibrium" in terms of a Want:Get Ratio (WGR). This ratio stresses the individual and behavioral components of a stable social system; expressed as an equation, it would look like this:

$$\text{Stability} = \frac{\text{Gets}}{\text{Wants}}$$

In some ideal situation, the coefficients attached to each of these three terms would be identical, and the social system would be perfectly stable, because all participants in the system would be getting exactly what they wanted. In the real world, no such ideal system exists. The formula is therefore to be understood heuristically—that is, as a goal toward which social systems should tend. In LDC, this goal requires as much attention to public communication as to economic development.

Development efforts clearly are a major term of the equation. They determine how much "gets" will be available in the society. However, no amount of "gets" will maintain personal satisfaction and social stability unless they are in approximate balance with "wants." This balance is the business of communication, for communication shapes people's desires, aspirations, and expectations—in short, the bundle of human "wants." If these "wants" rise faster than the "gets," then even large increases in the available economic shares will not provide an adequate quantum of "gets." On the other hand, if communication is adequately integrated with development plans and programs, then it can help shape "wants" in such a manner as to maintain a reasonable, or at least tolerable, balance with the available supply of "gets."

Two factors weigh heavily upon LDC's efforts to maintain the sort of balance between growth and stability that represents "dynamic equilibrium." These factors are the acceleration of history, and mobilization of the periphery.

The acceleration of history is represented by Table 6-1. The right-hand column shows the acceleration rate at which communication revolutions have occurred. The modern west took approximately 400 years to incorporate the first revolution of print technology—four centuries passed between Gutenberg's invention of movable type and the incorporation around 1832 of a "penny press" into the daily lifeways of European peoples. All of this time was required for the west to develop a class of people large enough to support a penny press. This class of people included those who acquired enough literacy to read a newspaper with ease, earned an extra penny to spend, and were motivated to spend this penny on a newspaper rather than on cakes and ale. As the four successive communication revolutions occurred at an accelerating tempo during the past century, these European peoples were prepared to incorporate them by their long experience in handling information through print, particularly through the daily newspaper.

TABLE 6-1. Five Communication Revolutions

Technological Innovation	Communication Channel	Approximate Age in (years) 1975
Movable type	Print	500
Camera	Film	100
Vacuum tube	Radio	50
Picture tube	Television	20
Satellite	World network	10

The situation in LDC provided a stark contrast to the western historical picture. Most LDC became independent political units only within the past quarter-century. Most of them still have large majorities incapable of reading. Most peoples in LDC have few extra pennies to spend. Yet, in this brief quarter-century, they have been drawn into the dazzling new world of electronic communications. In these few years, countries like India and Indonesia, still afflicted with high illiteracy and poverty rates, have "leapfrogged" into the 1975 world of television satellites. Other LDC are preparing to follow them into this momentous acceleration of history.

Mobilization of the periphery is a major consequence of the acceleration of history that we have just sketched. Every communication revolution has greatly widened the circle of participants in public affairs. People who lived in rural isolation throughout their long history now are suddenly exposed to news of the world through film, radio, and television. Gamal Abdel Nasser foresaw some of the consequences twenty years ago when he said:

> It is true that most of our people are still illiterate. But politically that counts far less than it did twenty years ago. . . . Radio has changed everything. . . . Today people in the most remote villages hear of what is happening everywhere and form their opinions. Leaders cannot govern as they once did. We live in a new world.[6]

To cope with the acceleration of history and the consequent mobilization of the periphery, LDC have passed through three major phases of psychocultural transformation and sociopolitical organization in the past quarter-century.

PHASES

Scholars appear to agree that development patterns vary considerably from one LDC to another and that these "culture-specific" variations are essential to a full understanding of any particular LDC. Yet I believe that important "regularities" are common to all of development experience over the past quarter-century, regardless of cultural variations. These "regularities" are manifested in a sequence of three phases: (1) rising expectations, (2) rising frustrations, and (3) military takeover.

PHASE 1: RISING EXPECTATIONS

All of us are familiar with the "revolution of rising expectations," a phrase created by Harlan Cleveland and popularized by Eugene Staley.[7] At the start of the development decades, around 1950, "rising expectations" were almost universally regarded as a good thing—at least by western and westernizing development thinkers, planners, and activists. It was believed that as people's expectations rose their efforts to achieve (what David McClelland has called "need achievement") would increase accordingly.[8] This theory was a direct extrapolation from the western experience in which rising expectations had indeed stimulated rising efforts, rising innovations, and rising productivity. Such sociological concepts as Max Weber's "Protestant ethic" were developed to account for the almost universal association of effort with reward in the western mores.

Two decades later, most or us are aware that this western association of reward with effort—of personal achievement to satisfy personal expectations—has not become widely operative in LDC. Few of us believe that this hiatus occurred because the peoples of Asia failed to accept the virtues of Protestantism. Some of us have blamed "cultural imperialism" as the promoter of "consumerism."

Yet I believe that the desire for the material good things of life is natural and humane. Indeed, the "rising expectations" of LDC have gone far beyond material wants to embrace desires for a higher "quality of life"—for example, information for self-betterment, education for one's children. I therefore prefer the more subtle proposition that the LDC failure to associate reward with effort derives from the fact that the LDC was led—thanks to the counterproductive use of charisma and communication—to put the values of consumption *before* the values of production.

For, just as the LDC has reordered the western sequence of modernization, so has it reoriented the system of values that accompanied western development. People who were granted the franchise upon independence without being obliged to pass through the ordeals of a poll tax or a literacy test naturally expected many of the good things of modernity to come their way without effort. Peoples of LDC have been more sharply oriented toward consumption than production by their recent experience—and particularly, as we shall see later, by their communication experience. This pattern is a direct reversal of the western sequence, in which many centuries of rising productivity elapsed *before* the "idols of production" began to yield pride of place to the "idols of consumption."

PHASE 2: RISING FRUSTRATIONS

Because their achievement—particularly in economic development—has lagged so far behind their expectations, many peoples of LDC have moved from rising expectations into a second phase of rising frustrations. People simply have not been getting what they had been led to want by their charismatic leaders through a faulty "mass media" strategy. As a result, the WGR has become seriously imbalanced, and the peoples of LDC have suffered continuing and deepening frustration.

Nasser put his thoughts about radio, which we cited above, into action on a very large scale. He allocated a significant portion of Egypt's resources to the expansion of Egyptian State Broadcasting as well as its international propaganda channel, "Voice of the Arabs." He distributed free community receivers to villages throughout Egypt and other Arab lands. By the use of radio and its associated change-agents (following the 1902 Leninist concept of "agitprop"), Nasser sought to build the Revolutionary People's Rally and transform the Egyptian polity on short notice.

But Nasser's high expectations suffered severe setbacks. In very many villages the community receiver was attached to the mosque, and its operation was controlled by the *imam* (the leader of the Moslem community). A usual practice was to turn on the radio for the daily Koran readings and traditional Arab songs—and then to turn it off again when these programs were over. The political change-agents reported back that the radio was giving them little or no help in creating the new participant polity. The Revolutionary People's Rally promptly came under the influence of the local *oomdahs,* the traditional village autocrats. In his autobiography, Nasser acknowledged his many setbacks.[9] In the last years of his short life, he avowed defeat of his political expectations. He died a frustrated man.

Another charismatic leader, Sukarno of Indonesia, explained rising frustrations not in terms of the failure of his own communication policy, but rather by projecting the blame onto foreign communications. While in Hollywood, he accused the movie moguls of being "revolutionaries." Naturally, they were greatly surprised by this epithet. They were used to being called many bad names (such as "box-office bandits" and "dream factories"), but never had they been called revolutionaries.

Surkarno explained that they were "unconscious revolutionaries" because in nearly all of their films somewhere or other a refrigerator appeared. Indonesian moviegoers were naturally curious about these big white boxes and found out what purpose they served. They were delighted with the idea of boxes that would keep foods cool and, quite naturally, wanted them for themselves. Sukarno concluded that, in a hot country like Indonesia, a refrigerator is a revolutionary symbol. In two hours any of these films can stimulate desires for more refrigerators than Indonesia can produce in twenty years.[10]

PHASE 3: MILITARY TAKEOVER

The second phase of frustration thus led, as the Yale psychologists have never tired of telling us, to both regression and aggression, both of which are highly counterproductive to development. Regression entails a great waste of scarce resources. An example is the continuous series of failed literacy campaigns which UNESCO politely calls "dysfunctional literacy."[11] In plain language, this term means that people cannot read, and the resources expended on bringing them literacy have been wasted.

Aggression, the other reaction to frustration, is an even more serious obstacle to development in recent experience in LDC. Aggression not only wastes scare resources but often willfully destroys them. I need hardly emphasize the impact of the great eruption of aggressive action, in MDC as well as LDC, over the past decade. The aggressive reaction to frustration has been misguided because it displaces acceptable economic wants into the form of ineffectual political demands.

What people want usually must be produced by the economic sector of any society. The political sector is not itself a substantial producer of goods and services. At best, even where a large "public sector" exists, government shapes production mainly by its control over the allocation of resources. However, the governments of most LDC have been too poor in resources to be able to exert very significant influence upon productive operations. The political regimes of LDC have been undermined because their economic sectors have failed to produce enough to satisfy the wants generated largely by the regimes' own misuse of the mass media.

Thus aggression, expressed in the "politics of the street," has led to the third phase of recent history in LDC—military takeover. This phase is indeed a "regularity." As all of us are aware, most of Asia, like most of Africa and Latin America, is today under some form of military regime or martial law.

Many of us probably decry and even despise military regimes. Yet we need not despair. Historical experience, of both East and West, indicates that military regimes are transitory. Coercion as a method of governance is inherently unstable. No coercive military regime has been able to repress the aspirations of its people over a very long period of time. Since the military are no better equipped than the politicos to boost production rapidly, they rely on repression rather than satisfaction of popular wants—on coercion rather than charisma. When the repression becomes unbearable, one military junta replaces another. As an instance, Syria had twenty-seven such takeovers in its first decade of independence. More than 200 such takeovers occurred in the second development decade.

Eventually the population organizes and acts to get at least some of what it wants. Gabriel Almond has referred to this process as "interest articulation" and "interest aggregation."[12] The process operates by the recognition and "articulation" of common group interests, and by the cumulation and "aggregation" of these interest groups into instruments of political action—for example, a labor union, a social "movement," or a political party.

In recent history of LDC, such political aggregations often have been organized and led by an innovative coalition of intellectuals (including journalists and students), junior officer cadres, and the new urban industrial workers (including the unemployed). In this process, communication has played an important role—a role which is certain to increase over the years ahead.

COMMUNICATION NEXUS

Communication has played an important role in shaping and misshaping development patterns over the past quarter-century. Especially important, as illustrated by Nasser's reliance on radio for revolutionary "modernization of the periphery," have been the mass media created by electronic technology. Wilbur Schramm has put the matter in a sentence: "In the developing countries the last ten years have been the Decade of the Transistor."[13] Schramm further suggests that the next ten years may well become the "Decade of the Satellite." Communication satellites are bound to produce a "multiplier effect" upon the world diffusion of mass media, telecommunications and data transmission (for example, computerized data management systems). It is therefore worthwhile to project their probable increase in the next decade in order to foresee their impact upon social change around the world.

An American television satellite (ATS-6) developed by the National Aeronautics and Space Administration (NASA) leads directly into the next decade because it is already stationed over India for a challenging series of educational experiments (both educational television and instructional television). For several years I was a consultant to the director of this Indian experiment—the late Dr. Vikram Sarabhai. Under his direction, unfortunately cut short by his premature death four years ago, the Indian experiment was a brilliant example of the "leapfrogging" process which communication technology makes possible. Given the problems raised by India's "acceleration of history" and its instant "mobilization of the periphery" (for example, the universal suffrage declared in 1947), this type of "leapfrogging" over the long western experience is what India needs most.

What is now scheduled to happen in India is also likely to occur in many other developing countries during the next decade. Brazil has already expressed great interest in acquiring a similar educational satellite for its own use. Every populous nation spread over a large land mass or archipelago is likely to want—and many are likely to get—such satellites. Educational satellites are particularly valuable for "leapfrogging" in countries which have not yet made a large investment in the traditional modes of schooling that require costly buildings, equipment, supplies, and a vast corps of trained teachers. As I mentioned, Indonesia has ordered a Hughes rediffusion satellite to begin operating in the near future. Such countries as Iran, China, Thailand, and the Philippines are obvious candidates for satellite development in the years ahead.

At the present time, American activity in communication satellites appears to be decelerating. An ATS-7 is on the drawing boards at NASA, but when, or even whether, this latest model will be produced is not clear. However, other MDC are entering the satellite field more actively. Canada, Western Europe, the USSR, Japan, and others will doubtless be producing satellites during the next decade.

Beyond the satellites are the "spinoff" communication technologies that appear each year in ever-increasing profusion. While all MDC are deeply involved in electronic innovation, Japan has emerged as probably the most proficient producer of new communciation equipment in the past decade. For example, Sony has produced a jeep-mounted, transistor-powered television receiver that can be used in the most remote villages without electrical power supply. This unit is capable of displaying live television, kinescopes, videotapes, cassettes—virtually the full range of audiovisual innovations that have become widely available in the last ten years.

This equipment's range indicates that future developments will not be confined to education, important as that is. The concern with rural development will surely foster interest in the Sony unit and similar innovations. Doubtless governments and communicators will seek to bring the new technologies and techniques to bear upon the alleviation of rural poverty by the improvement of agricultural practices in the years ahead.

Another great area of innovation is arising by linking the satellite with the computer. In Hawaii, the PEACESAT satellite network (ATS-1) has been linked with the local ALOHA computer program. Many other data-management systems have been linked with satellites elsewhere in the United States. The satellite–computer linkage opens a vast field of innovation which Simon Ramo, an active pioneer and forward thinker in this field, has called "intellectronics." Data management of this type can be applied to almost every sphere of activity in a society, and can be used on a worldwide basis. Its effects are already becoming visible in such fields as transportation, government administration, banking, business administration, and scientific research of all types. Its use will surely spread widely to include everything from hospital administration and medical care through high-rise construction and household chores. We foresee these technological developments of the next decade. What will these developments mean to us and to the societies in which we live?

PERSPECTIVES

We have seen that the communication developments of the past decade have not been an unqualified blessing. In some cases, they have disrupted personal lives by creating expectations that could not be satisfied. Rising frustrations thus engendered have, in some cases, so severely imbalanced the Want:Get Ratio as to promote military takeover, subvert political regimes, and impede economic development.

We have every reason to be wary in appraising the popular impact of new technologies in the coming decade. While we have no reason for cynicism, every reason exists for informed realism—perhaps with a dash of skepticism. This means that we should not expect the technologies that will be *created* in the next ten years to be efficiently and equitably *absorbed* into all social systems during the next ten years. The individual capacity to invent always outruns the societal capacity to absorb. The LDC will have to develop efficient ways of evaluating the costs and benefits of each available technology in their own national contexts. Among the short-term costs (which may become long-term benefits) are the societal "transformations" that each adoption of a technological innovation will require.

Doubtless disparities and frustrations will continue and disequilibria and disruptions will result from the accelerated tempo of technological innovations. However, if we keep our expectations relatively modest for the short run and keep the longer run in perspective, then we may be reasonably confident that the new technologies will eventually provide improvements in the quality of life. Such a perspective was revealed over the past quarter-century by the Israeli decision to postpone television for some fifteen years after the technology was readily available. A similar perspective was shown in the past decade by the American decision to postpone production of supersonic transport (SST) for civil use, even though the technology was readily available. By such policy decisions, we are likely to bring rational policies to bear upon the heedless pace of technological innovation.

The great question for the decade ahead is whether the new world communication network will contribute significantly to world cooperation. A realistic perspective will be tinged with some skepticism. We began to talk of a world communication network centuries before it came into being. Just so, we have been talking about world unification for decades without moving significantly toward it in our actual political life. Ten years ago, Marshall McLuhan talked blithely about the "global village," but we know that it has not yet come into existence. Nor is it likely to do so over the next decade.

Consider the issue of direct satellite broadcasting. On this very issue, the United States was handed its most stunning defeat at both the United Nations and UNESCO. A discussion of the pros and cons of the American position on this matter is not appropriate in this context (although I will confess that I found more demerits than merits in it). The relevant point is that 101 nations lined up against the United States to express their distrust—and even their fear—of direct satellite broadcasting by any power with the technological capability of doing it. When anxiety is so widespread, much more than technology will be required to make world communication contribute to world unification.

The "much more" that is needed must be produced by development scholars like ourselves as well as by those who make and operate the public policies that shape MDC–LDC relations around the world. Our past record leaves us all with much to be modest about, but modesty does not imply despair. Important "success stories" have been recorded throughout LDC over the last ten years. In shaping the next ten years, communication specialists in development have a particularly important role in integrating our capacity to absorb the new technologies. Let us hope that we shall play this role well.

NOTES

1. W. Arthur Lewis. *The Theory of Economic Growth*. Homewood, Illinois: R. D. Irwin, p. 3, 1955.
2. Max F. Millikan. In D. Lerner and W. Schramm, eds., *Communication and Change in the Developing Countries*. Honolulu: East-West Center Press, p. 3, 1967.
3. Note the comment on this discussion by J. J. Spengler: "Suppose we are in advanced country A and wish to transfer to underdeveloped country U a given institution I. I is imbedded in a loosely or a tightly integrated culture complex Ca, and there performs a set of functions Fa. If the culture complex Cu in country U is not very different from Ca and the objective is the performance of the same kind of function Fu (~ Fa), we can speak of transfer. But as we depart from these conditions, because Ca differs from Cu or because the set of functions Fu differs somewhat from Fa (because some are otherwise performed), we have more than a transfer problem. We have a transformation indicated. It is essential, therefore, to contrast Ca and Cu and Fa and Fu and determine when it is transfer that suffices and when it is more."
4. Daniel Lerner. "The Transformation of Institutions." In William B. Hamilton, ed., *The Transfer of Institutions*. Durham, N.C.: Duke University Press, p. 9, 1964.
5. Alex Inkeles and David H. Smith. *Becoming Modern*. Cambridge, Mass.: Harvard University Press, p. 4, 1974.
6. Quoted in Daniel Lerner, *The Passing of Traditional Society*. New York: Free Press paperback, 1964.
7. Eugene Staley. *The Future of the Underdeveloped Countries*. N.Y.: Harper, 1954.
8. David C. McClelland. *The Achieving Society*. Princeton: Van Nostrand, 1961.
9. Gamal Abdel Nasser. *Egypt's Liberation: The Philosophy of the Revolution*. Washington: Public Affairs Press, 1955.
10. Quoted in Marshall McLuhan, *The Medium is the Message*. N.Y.: Bantam Books, 1967. Recall as well Professor Hidetoshi Kato's report on the watching of American movies in the early 1950s by Japanese, who paid more attention to the dishwashers than to Frank Sinatra.
11. Cf. S. C. Dube's reference to "functional deafness" in radio-listening, in W. Schramm and D. Lerner, eds., *Communication and Change: The Last Ten Years—and the Next*. Honolulu: University Press of Hawaii, 1976.
12. Gabriel A. Almond and James S. Coleman. *The Politics of the Developing Areas*. Princeton: Princeton University Press, 1960.
13. In W. Schramm and D. Lerner, eds., *op. cit.*

Communication Policy and Planning for Development: Some Notes on Research

FREDERICK T. C. YU

The need to study communication policy and planning has acquired a new importance in the 1970s—not only in developing countries but also in developed countries. "Communications policy research" has emerged as a field of study.[1] "Development Support Communication" (DSC to its practitioners) has become a new speciality in communications studies. Public inquiries and serious debates on telecommunications and media policies are conducted in many countries. Efforts such as the Prospective Planning Project, which the National Iranian Radio and Television started in 1974, have attracted increasingly wide attention.[2] Calling the 1970s "the communication decade," UNESCO has sponsored a variety of publications, conferences, and activities "to help Member States in the formulation of their mass communication policies."[3]

This surge of global interest in the study of communication policy and planning portends both promise and trial for the fast-growing but underdeveloped field of development communication research. The interest could be an uplifting or upsetting experience. It could inspire some long-needed research into some of the lingering, stubborn, and unyielding questions about communication and development. It could involve another flurry of debates around the same old quarrels and simply deepen the frustration of those students of communication and development who feel that the field is already in a rut. Quite clearly, it presents a challenge. For convergence of political, social, economic, and technological developments compels developing countries—and developed countries, too—to come to grips with the question of communication policy and planning after years of tinkering. Pool states the problem in two sentences: "Perhaps the most extensive communications policy studies around the world have been on communication and development,"[4] and "The role of communications in development is perhaps the policy issue most urgently in need of study."[5]

We may ask: Why is the study of communication policy and planning in developing countries so uncommonly difficult? What are the problems we face? What can we do about some of these problems? What research is pressing, promising, or pertinent?

Obviously, the difficulties rest deep in the nature and process of development, the breadth and complexity of communication, and the culture and conditions of a developing country. But, equally obviously, such an observation serves no useful purpose unless we say something pertinent about the roots of these difficulties. To do so, we must view the whole field of communication and development.

In the early days of development communication research in the 1950s, the concept of development was for all practical purposes synonymous with economic growth. In his *Mass Media and National Development,* Schramm uses the language of the United Nations to define a "developing" or an "underdeveloped" country as "one in which the annual per capita income is $300 or less" and adds: "That is all we mean when we speak of an 'underdeveloped' country."[6] Then the concept was broadened to include certain noneconomic—mostly cultural and social—aspects. In a report of the Secretary-General of the United Nations in 1962, for instance, development is defined as "growth and change;" change, "in turn, is social and cultural as well as economic, and qualitative as well as quantitative."[7] In recent years, the concept of development has become even broader, and the emphasis has shifted from what is called "development of things" to "development of man." What has come to be known as "The Cocoyoc Declaration," a document prepared by a group of development specialists and UN officials who met at Cocoyoc near Mexico City in 1974 at a UN-sponsored symposium, "Patterns of Resource Use, Environment, and Development Strategies," reflects such a view:

> Our first concern is to redefine the whole purpose of development. This should not be to develop things but to develop man. Human beings have basic needs: food, shelter, clothing, health, education. Any pro-

cess of growth that does not lead to their fulfillment—or, even worse, disrupts them—is a travesty of the idea of development . . . . We believe that thirty years of experience with the hope that rapid economic growth benefiting the few will "trickle down" to the mass of the people has proved to be illusory. We therefore reject the idea of "growth first, justice in the distribution of benefits later."

Development should not be limited to the satisfaction of basic needs. There are other needs, other goals, and other values. Development includes freedom of expression and impression, the right to give and to receive ideas and stimulus. There is a deep social need to participate in shaping the basis of one's own existence, and to make some contribution to the fashioning of the world's future. Above all, development includes the right to work, by which we mean not simply having a job but finding self-realization in work, the right not to be alienated through production processes that use human beings simply as tools.[8]

This broadened concept of development has almost acquired the status of a new religion in the world of developing countries. But what is the impact of this new developmental dogma on development planning and communication policies? No clear consensus has yet been formed on the question.

In the literature of development studies, we find much to suggest that the excitement over the shift from "development of things" to "development of man" has inspired more debate among politicians and pundits than research by development specialists and communications scholars. Myrdal, for instance, states the case quite bluntly:

In presenting their concepts, models and theories, economists are regularly prepared to make the most generous reservations and qualifications—indeed, to emphasize that in the last instance development is a "human problem" and that planning means "changing men." Having thus made their bow to what they have become accustomed to call "the non-economic" factors, they thereafter commonly proceed as if those factors did not exist.

Most economists do this without offering any apology. Some excuse themselves by stressing that they do not feel competent to deal with these "non-economic" factors. In either case they commonly fail to explain what the neglect of these factors implies for the validity of their research.[9]

Recent development communication literature contains an abundance of discussion on the use of communication for developmental purposes but a glaring absence of a serious and systematic attempt to achieve some conceptual clarity of this core notion of development. Seemingly, students of development communication, particularly practitioners of the new speciality of Development Support Communication (DSC), either believe that they have all the conceptual clarity they need about development or have decided not to waste any more time on abstract concepts but to get on with the real business of development communication. One can easily irk some of these DSC specialists simply by asking them to define development.

A common complaint of communication researchers and practitioners is that communication policies and plans are too often in the hands of those who do not know enough about communication to set up or contribute to the communication systems that best serve the development needs of their countries. Halloran, for instance, says:

> The mass media and mass communication are matters of vital significance and public concern, yet decisions about the media which impinge on the lives of millions of people are being taken, and policies formulated, by those who have little knowledge about the nature of the communication process and who, apart from their own vested interests, do not normally think in terms of the capacities, the potential, or the social consequences of even their own communication systems.[10]

The anxiety is justified and the problem is real. But one can turn around and ask the community of development communication whether it possesses as much knowledge about the nature of the development process as it should and whether it can afford to be fuzzy, ambiguous, or just plain arbitrary about development. We all know that "research on communication and development," as Frey tells us, "suffers from the vagueness and conflict which surround the latter term."[11] But how much longer can this old question be dodged?

This question should not be dismissed lightly as frivolous fiddling with words; it should be regarded as a symbol and sign of our time. Consider the attitude of the community of development communication. One specialist in the field writes:

> If I were pressed for a definition of development communication, I would say that it is the art and science of human communication applied to the speedy transformation of a country and the mass of its people from poverty to a dynamic state of economic growth that makes possible greater social equality and the larger fulfillment of the human potential.
> Development is no transplant. Given our definition, it can only be a Third World phenomenon. So that, accept it or not, it is our responsibility to explore its dimensions, cultivate it and, above all, use it.
> The purpose of Development Communication is to advance development. Development requires that a mass of people with a low rate of

literacy and income, and the socio-economic attributes that go with it,
first of all be informed about and motivated to accept and use a sizable
body of hitherto unfamiliar ideas and skills in very much less time than
the process would normally take. Stated in these terms, the job of
development communication is the process of development itself.[12]

At the annual meeting of the International Broadcast Institute at
Cologne in 1975, a report of the Working Committee on Communication in Support of Development has these definitions of the key terms:

Development: The improvement of the well being of the individual
and the betterment of the quality of his or her life.
Communication: The transfer of information between individuals or
groups of individuals by human or technical means.
Development Support Communication: The systematic use of communication in the planning and implementation of development.[13]

Some years ago, Jacques Barzun was so troubled by the misuse or
abuse of the word "education" that he wrote:

The whole mass of recrimination, disappointment, and dissatisfaction
which this country is now suffering about its schools comes from using
the ritual word "education" so loosely and so frequently. It covers
abysses of emptiness. Everybody cheats by using it, cheats others and
cheats himself. The idea abets false ambitions.[14]

"Development" is, in some ways, an even more troublesome ritual
word than "education." It is a halo word—and a loaded one, too. It
stands for all that is needed and desired in a developing country, but it
leaves out of account much that is unpleasant and undesirable in the
country. It has been accepted for so long as an answer to so many problems that one forgets the nature of the question.

Development policies, until very recently, were regarded as "catch
up policies," which were "intended to overcome opportunity lag on
the part of countries that lacked a science-based technology."[15] This
concept is no longer accepted or even tolerated in Third World countries. The above-mentioned "Cocoyoc Declaration," for instance,
puts it this way:

We reject the unilinear view which sees development essentially and inevitably as effort to imitate the historical model of the countries that for
various reasons happen to be rich today. For this reason, we reject the
concept of "gaps" in development. The goal is not to "catch up," but
to ensure the quality of life for all with a productive base compatible
with the needs of future generations.[16]

Moreover, development policies are no longer defined in domestic or national terms but are regarded as issues which require global solutions. Increasingly, the issue of development is linked with a new agenda of global or crossnational welfare issues and policy problems: energy, ecology, food, health, housing, population, poverty, resource depletion, income disparity, space interrelationship, respect and preservation of mankind's cultural diversity and alternative style, and autonomous capacity of a nation to develop.

This linkage of problems is a reflection of a basic change now taking place in the international system as a whole. The international system, as Brzezinski describes it, "is changing from a system designed to promote interstate peace to a system also designed to promote intrastate progress; from a system designed to make possible greater global economic productivity to a system also designed to enhance greater economic equity."[17]

These changes are of truly major dimensions. They raise fundamental questions about man and society, about national goals, and about existing arrangements and future relations in the world. They introduce difficult dilemmas for individuals and nations. They have already set in motion confrontations of clashing interests and conflicting demands, and the outlook seems to hold little but more cycles of conflicts and confrontations.

It is all very easy—and fashionable these days, too—to say that we live in an intimately interdependent world, that formulation of communication policies should go beyond the traditional rather piecemeal approach to individual communication systems, and that we should get global perspectives in communications plans and policies. It is difficult enough to get students of development and communication in any country to reach a consensus on the nature and extent of global interdependence, a notion which is still regarded with considerable suspicion in the Third World. But to ask them not only to sort out the "interdependence" problems but also to work them into development plans and communication policies is perhaps to expect too much. The task would be ridiculous if it were not also imperative.

For this task to be completed, we need no less than a major conceptual breakthrough in our thinking about communication and development, and about the "interdependence"—at national, regional, and global levels—between communication systems and political, economic, cultural, and social systems. Unless we have this conceptual breakthrough, to talk sensibly about new strategies or future directions of research on communication policy and planning for development would be difficult. As things stand now, we seem to have difficulty even in organizing our confusions and conflicts about the role of communication in development.

The art of the possible in this situation is to start thinking about communication policies and planning in developing countries *realistically, relationally,* and—this factor may be difficult for some countries—*publicly.*

First, thinking *realistically* means to understand, or at least to recognize seriously, that every nation has the communication system it has earned; that to exaggerate the role of communication in development is easy and common; that communication researchers and practitioners tend to charge themselves—or think they are charged—with responsibilities that they are unable to discharge; and that the so-called development communication operates in a very narrow gap created by what is politically acceptable, economically feasible, socially desirable, and technologically available.

A common assumption of students of communication is that "in a developing country one often needs to plan the installing of a new communication system almost from scratch."[18] An equally common but sharply different view is the following one suggested by Lester B. Pearson:

> We should never forget, in short, that the developing peoples do not start from scratch in a new world but have to change and grow and develop within a context unfavorable to them, because in the past their position has been largely determined by the interests of other nations. If we forget this historical context, we will not understand the problems that now exist; nor will development cooperation to solve them be likely to succeed.[19]

A more neutral and perhaps more useful assumption would be that every developing country has to start with its inherited communication system and develop it as it goes along, that the structure of a communication system is dictated by politics and economics and is, to a certain extent, shaped by geographical, linguistic, and cultural forces, and that as many communication systems exist as do countries. A convenient way for developing countries to start thinking realistically about communication policy and planning is to try to have a clear idea of what these communication systems are and to see what changes in policy and planning are within their means and what are not. These communication systems can be viewed along three dimensions: (1) function, (2) control, and (3) degree of technological sophistication and diffusion.[20]

Individualistic versus collectivistic needs. We do well to agree with Lasswell that "the basic emphasis of the policy approach, therefore, is upon the fundamental problem of man in society, rather than upon the topical issues of the moment."[21] What goes on and comes out of a communication system reflects what basic beliefs a country holds about the nature of man, the nature of society, and the relation of man to society and the state.

We could classify all social systems in the world on the basis of the fundamental problem of man in society by placing them on an individualism–collectivism continuum. At one end of this continuum are countries which preach the faith of individualism, placing the individual above the group. At the other end of the continuum are countries which profess the doctrine of collectivism, placing the group above the individual. At the individualism end are all the major western countries plus Japan, with the United States as the extreme case. At the collectivism end are the Communist countries, with China as the extreme case. In between are the developing countries.

The American concept of individualism sees human beings as individuals and as ends in themselves. It maximizes individual choices and allows men and women to rise and fall by their own efforts. It considers the preservation and enhancing of the dignity of the individual as the goal of society. It regards the assent of the individual as the standard of political legitimacy. It accepts society as it is and people as they are. Fundamental to this model is the idea that people have the ability to reason and to recognize self-interest, that people must have maximum opportunity to exercise reason and pursue self-interest in a free society, and that no society can be free without free flow of information and ideas.

The Maoist model of communism does not see man as an individual. It vows to eradicate all conceivable forms of individualism and to concentrate on common good and collective goals. It views man as a member of collectivities at various levels of comprehensiveness and consciousness—the classes, the masses, the people, and so forth. It does not accept society as it is and people as they are. It opposes conditions as they exist. It insists on the creation of a new socialist man as the prerequisite for the building of a new socialist state. It judges the worth of a person in terms of his or her ability to restrain selfishness and of service to the people. Fundamental to this model is the idea that revolutionary development is not just a complete change of the structure of social institutions but also a total transformation of the cultural ethos that shapes the inner spirit of man. It requires constant and massive uses of persuasive and coercive communications to alter the attitudes and thought patterns of human beings, to mobilize and manipulate the energy and enthusiasm of the masses, and, to use a familiar Chinese Communist slogan, "to destroy selfishness and establish collectivism" *(po ssu li kung)*.

The American model of individualism, in short, is built on belief in personal sovereignty; its commercial and private-enterprise communication system serves a people who can do pretty much what they will. The Chinese Communist system of communication is designed strictly to serve an ideology to produce what Benjamin Schwartz calls "the emphasis on the individual's total self-abnegation and total immersion in the collectivities as ultimate goods."[22]

Maximum versus minimum government control. We could use another continuum to classify all communication systems in the world on the basis of government control. At one end of this continuum are all Communist countries—with China again the extreme case—where the communication systems are under strict government control. At the other end of this continuum are western industrialized countries plus Japan—with the United States again as the extreme case—where the communication systems are under predominantly private control. In between are all other countries—all the developing countries included—where the communication systems are under mixed governments and public and private ownership and control.

No communication system in the world is completely free of government control. In broadcasting, government licensing is required in every country, for example. But, in terms of ownership and control, no broadcasting system in the world is as private and commercial as the American system.

While strict control of public media is required in all Communist countries, considerable variation occurs among them. What has somehow set China apart is the Chinese Communist Party's massive and vigorous use of a propaganda machine which includes not only all mass media but every means or method of "struggle, criticism and reform," indeed every channel of influencing attitude and behavior.

As far as developing countries are concerned, the pertinent questions to ask are: (1) What parts of the communication system are under government, public, private, or mixed ownership? (2) How is the communication system controlled by the government? (3) To what extent or in what way is any part of the communication system under foreign control or influence?

The matter of foreign control or influence has generated a good deal of discussion among communication researchers and development specialists, and the role of multinational corporations (MNC) in communications in developing countries has become a major issue. Much has been written about the MNC's control over communications as a source of their power in developing countries. Barnet and Muller, for instance, have observed that "the three essential power structures in underdeveloped societies are typically in the hands of global corporations: the control of technology, the control of finance capital, and the control of marketing and the dissemination of ideas."[23] A group of Third World journalists urgently ask Third World corporations to fight against "near monopoly of international communications—including those among Third World countries—by TNCs (transnational corporations) linked to their dominance of many and influence in almost all Third World country media."[24]

One hears a good deal of talk these days about the problem of "communications ecology" of the world, which is defined as: "in particular, the one-way flow of international and cultural material, from the industrialized world to the developing world."[25] Christopher Nascimento, minister of state in the office of the Prime Minister of Guyana, states the problem this way:

> It is the presence and the power of foreign-owned multinational mass media empires in developing nations that poses one of the greatest threats to independent development.
> The problem which has been, and is still, facing many a developing nation, however, is that they inherited public communications systems, press, broadcasting and external telecommunications, which are foreign owned and controlled: systems which have been developed and are still managed with little commitment to national needs and little thought for indigenous cultural demands; systems which are motivated by and programmed for profit.
> In the broadcasting media, many a developing nation has been tempted into sophisticated systems, notably television, for no better reason than "everyone else has it." Media empires have been quick to take advantage of this lack of understanding to introduce management contracted broadcasting systems to governments; which glitter with the coat of "national interest sugar" but which leave the metropolitan media companies with a handsome profit and the host countries with a handsome headache.[26]

Degree of technological sophistication. Communication researchers have observed that "historically, government action has accounted for comparatively little in the development of communication policy in America," and that "to a much greater extent, economic, social, and technological forces lying outside government have spurred media growth and guided their direction."[27] The same can be said about developing countries. Schramm has reported impressive media growth in developing countries in Asia, Africa, and Latin America during what he calls "the decade of the transistor" from 1963 to 1973. For instance, the number of radio receivers in Africa went from 6,020,000 in 1963 to 14,038,000 in 1973; in Asia from 17,059,000 to 74,931,000; and in Latin America from 22,482,000 to 50,306,000. The figures for television receivers: 329,000 to 1,510,000 in Africa; 868,000 to 6,969,999 in Asia; and 4,756,000 to 18,896,000 in Latin America. The number of copies of daily newspapers during this period went from 3,319,000 to 4,387,000 in Africa; 14,028,000 to 24,896,000 in Asia; and 15,730,000 to 23,551,000 in Latin America.[28]

These statistics indicate, very clearly, that developing countries have come a long way in media development. But these same figures suggest, equally clearly, that these countries still have a very long way to go. These two-thirds of the world's people have no more than one-fifth of the world's radios, about one-fifth of the world's newspaper circulation, and less than one-tenth of the world's television receivers. The United States has about twice as many radio receivers as do all the developing countries together. Japan alone has a daily newspaper circulation of 57,820,000, in comparison to 63,000,000 for two-thirds of the world's population.[29]

To compare these figures with those for the United States and Japan is perhaps unwise and unfair. A much fairer and far more important question would be: How many developing countries have attained that minimum goal which UNESCO set in 1961: "Every country should aim to provide for every 100 of its inhabitants at least ten copies of daily newspapers, five radio receivers, two cinema seats, and two television receivers."[30]

The purpose of this essay is not to propose some fancy formula that would arrange all countries in the world neatly on the three continua and assign each country a numerical value with some degree of precision. But in order to think *realistically* about communication policy and planning in a developing country, it is important at least to examine the communication system first along these three dimensions—function, control, and media technology—to decide where the system stands and to have some idea about what the country should, could, and would do.

Developing countries have hard decisions to make about the function, control, and media technology of a communication system; harsh realities exist that are difficult to get around. For a developing country to talk about the development of its people while standing clear from the fundamental question of the human and society makes little sense. A developing country cannot just be laudatory about the need to respect the wisdom and wishes of the masses if the elite or the leadership is not only ignorant of the masses but remains remote or arrogant, if the masses have little interest or faith in the leadership, and if the communication system does not serve the expressive needs of the people. Importing some of the Maoist styles or practices of development does a developing country no good if it has neither the taste nor the stomach for class struggle and revolution.

Control of communication has become an increasingly crucial and controversial issue in developing countries. The following opinion of an official in Guyana seems to be a common sentiment of government officials, if not the common people, of developing countries:

> Two things occur, however, when an independent government of a small third world nation seeks to challenge the presence of a foreign owned multi-nationals seeking to maintain a dominant hold on the media. First, a storm is raised that "freedom of the press" is being threatened. Second, the multi-national warns of the potential it has for destroying the nation's international image, especially with regard to foreign private investment.
>
> The alternative for many a poor developing nation is going to have to be, at least for a time, government ownership of the mass media. This does not rest easy in the mind of the libertarian of the Western world, but let him remember that when his country was at a similar stage of development, the diversified channels of public communication, which are available to the people today, did not exist and the accepted communications ethic was that there should be no publishing which would not be in the interest of the state and its citizens.[31]

The view is understandable, and much of it is not easily refutable. But the pertinent question to be raised is whether this way of thinking about communication policy and planning is realistic. New developing nations have a perfectly natural concern with independence, sovereignty, and noninterference; they have a right to be nervous about all conceivable forms of "cultural imperialism," "information imbalance," and "communication ecology"—to cite just a few popular phrases of Third World countries' dialogues.

But, as Brzezinski states: "It is also these nations that are especially insistent that the international system increasingly shift the focus of its concern from a preoccupation with the preservation of peace to a greater concern with the promotion of global development, especially in order to obviate the existing inequalities in the material conditions of humanity." Brzezinski adds: "To accomplish that objective, closer cooperation among nations and a measure of interference in the internal affairs of some by others, will almost be inevitable."[32]

To say that developing countries should learn to respond creatively to the challenges of new technology in this era of revolution in communication has become trite. But, realistically, how far can this creativeness of the developing countries go?

Schramm has written about developing countries going from "the decade of the transistor" (1963–1973) to "the decade of the satellite" (1973–1983). This technology means a quick and great step forward in creating a modern communication system in a developing country. And a number of developing countries—India, Indonesia, Iran, and Brazil among them—have been experimenting with plans to take advantage of this new technology. But satellite communication has become controversial in international politics, and some developing countries seem to be more interested in talking about the need to resist "satellite penetration" than ways to make creative use of this flourishing technology.

We cannot yet predict what shape this "decade of the satellite" will take. Developing countries should—and probably would— exert some influence in the shaping of some sensible international policy for satellite communication. But, to be realistic, because of the economics and complexity of the technology, satellites are likely to continue to be controlled and managed by investors in industrialized or developed countries rather than residents of the "global village"—at least for awhile. Such an observation implies neither doom nor gloom. It simply states a problem of satellite communication which developing countries should learn to understand and handle.

If such a view is hard for developing countries to accept, the following may be more helpful:

> When a new technology emerges, it emerges in the context of the culture of its creators or adaptors. Hence an existing technology is not value neutral; it is freighted with the aims and priorities of its creators,

owners, controllers or adaptors. Cable and satellite (like radio, television, computers and other technological creations) serve the cultural values and aspirations of whatever society employs them. Consequently an assessment of ultimate use of application cannot be made (or ought not be made) without reference to the social–cultural context in which it emerges.[33]

Second, thinking *relationally* means understanding a great variety of relation questions: between communication systems and political, economic, social, and technological systems: between the process of development and the process of communication; between or among various actors in communication policy and planning; between researchers and their clients; between planners and users of research; between political intent and developmental goals; between knowledge questions and value questions; between basic and applied research.

The study of these questions would be helpful in our search for a frame of reference to relate the various aspects of communication policy research; to avoid the mistake of throwing policy, empirical value, and scientific questions arbitrarily together in an investigation; to make sense of research studies which tend to construct entire systems of explanation around single factors or issues (for example, family planning); and to work out a coherent taxonomy to lead to a systematic body of knowledge rather than a collection of confusing and contradictory assumptions, data, and insights.

One researcher has focussed on three sets of interrelated policy-making: (1) the industry and technology for likely developments and social and political consequences; (2) the government—to determine how to get desired public actions; and (3) the people—to find the basic values, goals, and priorities for action.[34]

Pool has suggested the need for research on research between and among several types of actors in communication policy and planning in developing countries. He sees five domestic actors:[35]

1. Populace
   a. rural
   b. urban
2. Intelligentsia
3. Government
4. Field Workers
5. Communication Institutions

and two foreign actors:

6. Foreign Sources of Information

7. Foreign Sources of Technology

Figure 7–1 shows, for instance, how communication institutions in a developing country relate to other actors, both foreign and domestic:

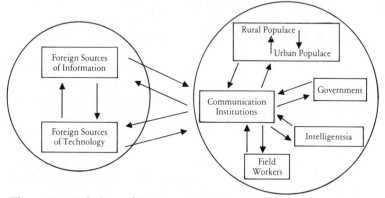

Figure 7–1. Relations of Communication Institutions in a Developing Country

One way to think relationally about some of the major aspects of the problem is to try to answer twice a question like the following: first, about development and, second, about communication:

WHO plans, decides, administers?
WHAT?
FOR WHOM?
AT WHAT AND WHOSE COST?
WITH WHAT RESPONSE?
AND RESULTS?
AND WHY?

The WHO includes individuals, groups, and institutions as planners, decision-makers, administrators, practitioners, and others involved in the policy-making or planning process. Under the WHAT are policies, plans, programs, or projects. To ask the question FOR WHOM? is to understand whose interests or needs are served—both in name and in fact. Two assumptions lie behind the question: AT WHAT AND WHOSE COST? One assumption is that every policy or plan has a price; the other is that policies are, almost always, choices of action which benefit some at the expense of others. The "response" includes of course support, opposition, and feedback in general. To study the "results" is to examine the consequences, both intended and unintended, and to raise the question, "What comes next?" The importance of the final WHY? question is obvious.

Third, the case for thinking *publicly* is stated very clearly by Professor Horst Ehmke, West German Federal Minister for Research and Technology and for Posts and Telecommunications: "Politically feasible solutions for the development of our communications system can be found and developed only in public discussion, not within circles of civil servants, technicians or market planners meeting behind closed doors."[36] Professor Ehmke was talking about the problem of developing information technologies. He considered it necessary to ask the citizens which possibilities from the wide spectrum of what is technically feasible they regard as expedient and desirable, and which as superfluous or dangerous. He also asked politicians and planners to "lay open their aims," and social groups—including newspaper publishers—"to disclose their interests." And he prescribed "frankness" as the prerequisite. His reason:

> It is unlikely that any other field of technological progress will influence the quality of life—or, better, the discussion on what qualities of life we consider worth striving for—in the same way, during the next few decades, as the new communication technologies.[37]

This advice is sound. Most developing countries could easily accept this principle, even applaud it, but not necessarily apply it. Much of what has passed as development communication research deals mainly with would-be persuaders—mainly government and action groups—to get people to do what they think is best for the people. Development specialists and communication practitioners are interested in ways to reach more people—particularly the right people—to get the message across and to get the desired action achieved. The following definition of development support communication, suggested by one who is identified as a "development communication specialist," reflects this view:

> Development communication is the systematic application of appropriate knowledge, sensitively designed and strategically presented to the concerned components of change-agent-systems and project-community-systems for the purpose of inducing intelligent action to achieve pre-determined development goals.[38]

For those who believe these goals to be the concern of development communication, the problem of research is relatively simple. And, presumably, they should have plenty to learn from both market researchers on Madison Avenue and propaganda-agitation practitioners in Communist countries. But the problem is quite a different one for those who cannot and will not settle for anything less than the development of the human being.

We need not dwell on the difficulty of getting developing countries to think publicly about policy and planning in communication and development. Much of the difficulty is political. For instance, political leaders or power-holders naturally want to support those developmental goals that would strengthen their own positions; they wish to discourage those who see them as barriers to development. And a good deal of the difficulty is cultural. The elites, for instance, have a hold on the masses in these countries. Members of the elites—whether political, financial, intellectual, military, or mixed—probably find it much easier to work or even to die for the masses, than to live or even to work with the masses. Even in Communist countries such as China where the policy of "mass line" is deemed sacred, a constant concern of the Party is that its cadres do not always appreciate or practice the principle that "policies must always come from the masses and go back to the masses."

But communication researchers must at least recognize the need for developing countries to think publicly about communication policy and planning. Such a recognition is not going to be easy because not all communication researchers are accustomed to thinking this way themselves. Perhaps because of the background of propaganda studies during and after World War II, and the experience in agricultural extension work—both played an important role in the development of the field of communication research in the early days—communication researchers still speak of people often as "targets" rather than participants in policy-making or planning.

Another explanation has to do with the relationship between communication research and its client. The line of distinction between policy research and policy advocacy is very thin indeed. Even the so-called scientific, empirical, value-free research conducted for one client—for instance, a family planning agency—is more likely to be guided by the interest of the client, or at least by what the client has perceived as interests of the people, rather than by what a communication researcher has found to be interests of the people.

The decision on value questions if often taken out of the hands of researchers before they enter a project in policy or planning studies. The work researchers are left to do is often in the area of public acceptance of policy decision, and they are usually guided by principles such as the following one stated by MacRae: "No matter how technically correct a social or political decision may be, it will be supported more readily if those affected have taken some part in it or been consulted about it."[39]

But the question before us is not merely one of public acceptance of policy decision. It is one of involving the public in the formulation of policies and decisions on communication and development. It means finding ways to generate discussion of communication policy and planning by the public, to improve and increase means of a communication system to serve expressive needs of the people, and to ensure improved information flows to the decision-making centers.

We see still another responsibility of communication policy—that is, to serve as a "third voice" between decision-makers or planners and the public by exerting itself more to probe and report on the adequacy of the flows of information that enter into policy-making as well as the functioning of the policy processes at various stages. The function of a disinterested critic is to appraise or evaluate communication planning studies conducted by self-serving institutions. While this role may seem to be a far-out responsibility for communication research, it is a function which is needed by the public and which cannot be left to the government. The press is often entrusted with this function but, for understandable reasons, the performance of the press has not been completely satisfactory.

The purpose of this chapter is not to propose a strategy or a list of priorities for research. To talk about a research strategy for some hundred or more developing countries is dangerously misleading. A research strategy is, after all, something which each developing country should work out to fit its own needs and local environment. But we may be able to indicate possible objectives of any strategy and suggest a few pertinent and promising areas of inquiry, in addition to those already indicated or implied.

1. A familiar claim of developing countries is that they are searching for alternative political, economic, and social systems between capitalism and communism. What they need is a "Third System" or a "Third Way." Just what kind of alternative communication systems are needed to promote, propel, or perfect such a "Third System" or "Third Way" is by no means clear. But a safe guess is that developing countries cannot hope to make much headway with the "Third

System" or "Third Way" unless they come to terms with the basic question of the human being and society.

2. The theoretical starting point for study of communication policy and planning ought not to be the would-be persuaders (government, for instance) but individual and social needs. Important reasons exist for letting "the people" become the initiators, the planners, and the beneficiaries of development and communication policies instead of mere "targets" of some development projects or communication messages.

3. No serious communication policy research can afford to continue to concentrate on mass media while ignoring traditional folk media and other channels of popular culture. Students of development and communication have for some years been hammering hard on the theme that "the mass media play a major role in creating a climate for modernization among villages but are less important in diffusing technological innovation . . . although their potential of doing so is high; that mass media channels are more effective when combined with interpersonal media as in media forums; and that the traditional media such as village theater and traveling storytellers have an important potential for development purposes, especially when they are combined with the modern electronic and print media."[40] In Africa, for instance, "communications in the villages are mediated through the marketplace of ideas as found in traditional religion, observances, divination, mythology, witchcraft, cult societies, age-grades, the chief's courts, the elders' square, secret and title societies, the village market square, the village gong-man, history, skills, socialization, education, affiliations, indeed the total experiences of the villager as a result of the village environment."[41] But traditional and folk media have yet to be illuminated by much serious or even visible scholarship.

4. Another neglected area of communication research has to do with certain institutions and facilities of delivery and distribution of information. Such institutions as post offices and labor unions and such facilities as telephone and telegraph come to mind. They are beginning to be studied in the emerging field of communication policy research.[42] They deserve far more serious attention than they have so far received.

5. Problems of development which are widely recognized and obviously important remain unexplored. Corruption is one such problem. Coercion is another.

Friedrich calls corruption "a major obstacle to economic and other development."[43] Myrdal states: "The prevalence of corruption provides strong inhibitions and obstacles to development."[44] The *Economist* (June 15, 1957) raises the question of corruption as toxic or tonic in development. Horowitz complains that "the relationship of deviance to development has remained largely unexplored at the more prosaic and, I dare say, more significant levels. Particularly important in the connection is the relationship of development to corruption and bribery."[45]

But what do we know about corruption in communication systems? Students of development and communication are seemingly too concerned with the hygienic model of development to want to be bothered with such problems of deviance.

6. If the above suggestions seem to be too "far out" for conventional communication research, let us consider a few specific research tasks proposed at an international conference on communication policy and planning by two respected and reflective men in communication research.

Daniel Lerner said that he would give top priority to understanding the roles that communication—local, national, regional, international—plays in integrated development. He asked: How does communication enter into the *formulation* of development policies and plans? How does it enter into their *implementation?* To answer these questions, Lerner proposed to begin with a systematic comparative analysis of "success stories" in recent development programs—for example, the Comilla project in Bangladesh, the Amul Dairy Cooperative in Gujerat, the "green revolution" in the Punjab, the family-planning program in Taiwan, the multilingual program in Singapore.

Lerner also saw the need for a parallel comparative analysis to be made of recent development "failures" and "mixed" cases. These case studies, he added, should be made with a uniform checklist of hypotheses (or at least indicators) that would produce comparable findings. The purpose is to determine the *common* and *variant* communication factors in all these cases. Such empirical generalizations may not be conclusive, but hopefully they will help systematize our present diversity of hunches in ways that will lead to theoretically based research on propositions that can be tested in future development programs.

Pool proposed two specific studies: (1) a really well-done study of television flow, taking account of trends and needs for regional cooperation by small countries; (2) a systematic review of the actual restrictions imposed by various less-developed countries on flow of information (that is, nonamusement communication). The purpose of the second would be to ascertain what motivates these restrictions and how far they inhibit technical progress, promote such progress, or are indeterminate in that respect.

7. Finally, many questions proposed by communication scholars in the past have not been attacked, and a variety of promising areas of inquiry have not been followed up. Frey, for instance, outlines a number of these questions and areas in his work on communication and development.[46] He asks, for instance, how types of personality and types of communications might be linked; whether "different communication systems and their distinctive roles demand certain types of personalities, or at least certain limits in the range of acceptable personalities"; what to do with the largely unexplored territory of the psychic products of development and their relation to communication and to political change; why it is important to have systematic, comparative, and comprehensive analysis of the relationships between international communications and the process of development; why it would be useful to have at least "a good descriptive inventory of the external communication contacts of a single developing society over time to place alongside its domestic developmental chronicle"; what is involved in a communication strategy and a planning capacity to integrate mass media more closely with the educational system, transportational planning, informal communications networks, mass organizations, and other institutions of the developing society—among many other questions.

More recently, a number of communication researchers have made another attempt to structure the field of mass communication research and to identify major issues and future directions.[47] Lerner thinks that "for future communication research on the contemporary international area, no set of problems appears more urgent than the putative 'revolution of rising frustration' in the less developed countries." He asks, for instance:

Can we determine an optimum "dosage" of expectations for a sick society (as a physician does for an individual patient)? By what indices can any such dosages be objectified and generalized (as by the medical indices of age, weight, pulse, blood pressure)? How shall such an index as illiteracy be factored into the system of equations needed to deal contextually with the "organized complexity" presented to the researcher by any social organization?[48]

NOTES

1. Ithiel de Sola Pool. "The Rise of Communication Policy Research." *Journal of Communication*, 24:2, pp. 31–42, Spring, 1974.
2. Eddie Ploman. "Report on Iran." *InterMedia*, 3, No. 2, p. 16, October, 1975.
3. John A. R. Lee. *Towards Realistic Communication Policies: Recent Trends and Ideas Compiled and Analysed*. UNESCO, Reports and Papers on Mass Communication, No. 76, 1976. Earlier UNESCO reports on the subject: *Mass Media in Society: The Need of Research*, No. 59, 1970; *Proposals for an International Programme of Communication Research*, COM/MD/20, 1971; *Report of the Meeting of Experts on Communication Policies and Planning*, COM/MD/24, 1972.
4. Pool. *Op. cit.*, p. 34.
5. *Ibid.* p. 39.
6. Wilbur Schramm. *Mass Media and National Development*. Stanford, Calif.: Stanford University Press, and Paris: UNESCO, pp. 9–10, 1964.
7. *The United Nations Development Decade: Proposals for Action* (Report of the Secretary-General). New York, pp. 2–3, 1962.
8. "The Cocoyoc Declaration." *Development Dialogue*, No. 2, p. 91, 1974.
9. Gunnar Myrdal. "Cleansing the Approach from Biases in the Study of Underdeveloped Countries." *Social Science Information*, VIII, No. 3, p. 13, June, 1969.
10. James D. Halloran. "The Problems We Face," *Journal of Communication*, 25:1, p. 15, Winter, 1975.
11. Frederick C. Frey. "Communication and Development." In Ithiel de Sola Pool, Wilbur Schramm, *et al.*, eds., *Handbook of Communication*. Chicago: Rand McNally College Publishing Company, p. 340, 1973.
12. Nora C. Quebral. "What Do We Mean by Development Communication?" *International Development Review*, 1973/2; Vol. XV, No. 2, p. 25. See also Nora C. Quebral, "Development Communication," in Juan F. Jamias, ed., *Readings in Development Communication*. Laguna, Philippines: University of the Philippines at Los Banos, pp. 1–11.
13. Report of Working Committee I: Communication in Support of Development, IBI Annual Meeting, 1975 (mimeographed). See also "Working Committee I: Development Support Communication." *Intermedia* (International Broadcast Institute), 3, No. 2, p. 5, October, 1975.
14. Jacques Barzun. *Teacher in America*. Boston: Little, Brown and Company, p. 8, 1945.
15. Harold D. Lasswell. "The Future of World Politics and Society." In Wilbur Schramm and Daniel Lerner, eds., *Communication and Change: The Last Ten Years—and the Next*. Honolulu: University Press of Hawaii, 1976.
16. "The Cocoyoc Declaration." *Op. cit.*, p. 91.

17. Zbigniew Brzezinski. "The Changing International System, and America's Role." *The Sunday New York Times,* Section IV, p. 15, October 5, 1975.
18. Ithiel de Sola Pool. *Op. cit.,* p. 34.
19. Lester B. Pearson. *The Crisis of Development.* New York: Praeger, p. 17, 1970.
20. For a discussion on contrasting communication systems in the world, see W. Phillips Davison, James Boylan, and Frederick T. C. Yu, *Mass Media: Systems and Effects.* New York: Praeger, 1976.
21. Harold D. Lasswell. "The Policy Orientation." In Daniel Lerner and Harold D. Lasswell, eds., *The Policy Sciences.* Stanford: Stanford University Press, p. 8, 1951.
22. Benjamin Schwartz. "Modernization and the Maoist Vision." *China Quarterly,* No. 21, p. 11, January-March, 1965.
23. Richard Barnet and Ronald Muller. "Global Reach." *New Yorker,* December 2, 1974.
24. "Towards Third World Communication" (extracts from the 1975 Dag Hammarskjold Report on Development and International Cooperation). *Communicator* (India), p. 19, October, 1975.
25. "Freedom of Speech in a Media-Bound World." *InterMedia* (International Broadcast Institute), No. 3, p. 1, 1973.
26. "The Media—and the Question of Monopolies." *InterMedia,* No. 3, pp. 6–7, 1973.
27. Davison, Boylan, and Yu. *Op. cit.,* p. 207.
28. Wilbur Schramm. "Ten Years of Communication Development in Developing Regions," a paper delivered at East-West Communication Institute Conference on Communication and Change in Honolulu, January 1975 and published in Wilbur Schramm and Daniel Lerner, eds., *Communication and Change: The Last Ten Years—and the Next* (Honolulu: University Press of Hawaii, 1976); Professor Schramm reports that 1973 figures are from unpublished UNESCO survey data, obtained through the kindness of E. Lloyd Sommerlad, Director of Mass Communication Planning and Research for UNESCO, Paris; 1963 figures are from *UNESCO Statistical Yearbook.*
29. *The Japanese Press, 1975,* published by Nihon Shinbun Kuokai (The Japanese Newspaper Publishers and Editors Association), Tokyo, Japan.
30. UNESCO, Mass Media in the Developing Countries. A UNESCO Report to the United Nations, Reports and Papers on Mass Communication, No. 35, 1961.
31. "The Communications Ecology." *InterMedia,* No. 3, p. 7, 1973.
32. Brzezinski. *Op. cit.*
33. Charles A. Wedemeyer. "Satellites, Cable and Education, Looking Beyond the Classroom." *Public Telecommunications Review, 3,* No. 4, p. 15, July/August, 1975.
34. Susan Krieger. "Prospects for Communication Policy." *Policy Sciences: An International Journal, 2,* No. 3, pp. 305–319, Summer, 1971.
35. Discussed at the International Conference on Communication Policy and

Planning for Development, East-West Center, Honolulu, Hawaii, April 5-10, 1976.

36. "West German Takes a Look at the Future of Information Services." *InterMedia,* No. 5, p. 6, 1974.

37. *Ibid.* p. 8.

38. H. A. Anvari and G. K. Rezai. "Communication for Development—The National Iranian Development Communication System." *Seminar on Motivation, Information and Communication for Development in African and Asian Countries,* sponsored by International Broadcast Institute (London), p. 38, 1975.

39. D. MacRae, Jr., "Some Political Choices in the Development of Communications Technology," in *The Information Utility and Social Choice,* H. Sackman and N. Nie, eds. Montvale, N.J.: AFIPS Press, p. 208, 1970.

40. Everett M. Rogers, "Communication and Development," *The Annals of the American Academy of Political and Social Science, 412,* pp. 44-54, March, 1974.

41. F. O. Ugboajah, "Mass Communication in African Traditional Societies." International Broadcast Institute, *Seminar on Motivation, Information and Communication for Development in African and Asian Countries.* London, p. 44, 1975.

42. Pool, "Communications Policy Research," *op. cit.*

43. Carl J. Friedrich, *The Pathology of Politics.* New York: Harpers, p. 318, 1972.

44. Arnold J. Heidenheimer, ed. *Political Corruption.* New York: Rinehart and Winston, p. 474, 1970.

45. Irving Louis Horowitz, "Research Priorities for the Second Development Decade." *Studies in Comparative International Development,* Rutgers University, 7, No. 2, p. 185, June, 1972.

46. Frederick W. Frey, "Communication and Development," in Ithiel de Sola Pool, Wilbur Schramm and others, eds., *Handbook of Communication.* Chicago: Rand McNally College Publishing Co., pp. 337-432, 1973.

47. W. Phillips Davison and Frederick T. C. Yu, eds. *Mass Communication Research: Major Issues and Future Directions.* New York: Praeger, 1974.

48. *Ibid.,* pp. 91-92.

Communication Issues

Public Television:
Too Much Ambition
and Overcommitment?

JACK LYLE

Today most communities of the United States have available something called "public television." Its form, if not its existence, owes much to the work of the Carnegie Commission on Educational Television, which submitted its report early in 1967.[1] Riding on impetus created by the commission's report, proponents of public television were able to get passed and signed into law the Public Broadcasting Act of 1967.[2]

The report and the subsequent enabling legislation called for provision of federal funding. They also gave tacit approval to a transition from "educational" or "instructional television" to "public television." Certainly within the context of the most widespread and widely used mass medium in history, the existence of something called "public television" is appropriate.

But what is "public television"? What does the "public" in its title really imply?

The Corporation for Public Broadcasting came into existence in 1968. The Public Broadcasting Service (PBS) began operation in 1970. But a survey putting those questions to the viewing public—or to the members of Congress—would no doubt reveal at best a hazy image full of contradictions and inaccuracies. By the standards of audience awareness and use, "public television" appears to be a misnomer.

But are public awareness and use the standards by which public television is to be judged? What standards or criteria are appropriate?

This question touches at the heart of the most fundamental problem faced by public television at the time of the passing of the Public Broadcasting Act—a problem which it faces today and which it will face in the future. To date, no agreed-upon standards have been established against which to make judgment. Such a situation may make · it impossible for critics to pin explicit "failure" upon the system, but it also makes it impossible for the system to prove "success."

Some qualification is appropriate. The Public Broadcasting Act does stipulate technical goals for the system. Having clear-cut goals, the technical and engineering staffs of the system have been able to move ahead in orderly, purposeful manner. And they can point to objective results. Public television is now available to the vast majority of the American public; an efficiently operating interconnection distributes programming to most of the stations; a decision has been made to move toward a satellite system which will expand both the reach and the capacity of the interconnection in a highly cost-effective manner. Despite the handicaps of ultra-high frequency (UHF) allocations and a backlog of inadequate or insufficient equipment at some stations, public television is today a technical success.

But what about the content of the system—the programs? That question immediately provokes an embarrassing confusion of response. And the confusions can be traced to both the Public Broadcasting Act and the Carnegie Commission Report.

A historical note is appropriate, for public television did not spring full-blown from these two documents. The basic cadre of the system today called "public television" preexisted them. That cadre consists of the "educational stations" that had been licensed to utilize channels reserved for noncommercial educational use within their locality. By the start of the 1960s, enough "educational stations" had been telecasting for a sufficient period of time to make an assessment both possible and appropriate. The most thorough assessment was provided by *The People Look at Educational Television*,[3] a book which appeared in 1963. Wilbur Schramm was the senior author, working with Ithiel de Sola Pool and me. But "education" and "educational" are themselves rather slippery words. They are words we frequently use to veil activities to give them an appearance of respectability—to slip them in by the side door.

Schramm, Pool, and I observed (in 1963) that the evening non-school programming of educational television was primarily reaching an elite audience: those with above-average education and above-

average occupational and social status, those most likely to be concerned with civic issues and public affairs. What interested these people,
what attracted them to "educational television," was largely programming which fell into the categories of "culture" or intellectual
stimulation. We made the point that, if those responsible for educational television were operating on the premise that they were providing educational opportunity for the educationally disadvantaged,
they were not achieving their goal. Perhaps, we implied, they should
reconsider the allocation of their resources among options open to
them and provide more emphasis on intellectual or quality cultural
programming.

This line of thought had already developed among some persons
within educational television. Thus the "public television" recommendations of the Carnegie Commission Report were not new. Rather
they reflected thinking which had been going on for some time among
people involved and interested in educational television.

Several operational philosophies were evolving. Some people remained committed to the concept of educational television and were
primarily concerned with finding new resources to the end of trying to
do a more effective job of educating via television. Others were more
intrigued with the prospect of building for the United States an
equivalent of what the British Broadcasting Corporation (BBC) is to
Great Britain, or at least what they thought the BBC to be. Actually
their perception of the BBC was (and is) highly selective and perhaps
bore little resemblance to the totality of that admirable and venerable
institution.

By the time the Carnegie Commission came into being, no consensus had been achieved. Within the several approaches, the thinking
had not been as systematic as one would desire.

Unfortunately, the Carnegie Commission Report did not really provide the systematic approach which was badly needed. It is highly
significant that despite its fulsome rhetorical appeal to the American
public in support of the concept of a public television system, the
Commission's report did not consider the critical questions of who will
watch public television and why.

John Macy makes a telling point in his retrospective book[4] concerning the foundation of the Corporation for Public Broadcasting (CPB),
which he served as its first president. Macy states that the support of
President Lyndon B. Johnson was a crucial factor in facilitating the
rapid legislative response to the Commission's recommendation. Macy

points out that Johnson began his career as a school teacher. The president's support was largely based on the arguments put forth concerning television's potential to improve the quality and scope of educational opportunity which could be provided to the American public.

Since the language of the Public Broadcasting Act concerning programs is vague, it has provided ample opportunity for persons of different points of view to impose different criteria for evaluating the system. Two concepts were strongly stressed in both the Commission Report and the enabling legislation: the concept of "alternative programming" and the concept of bedrock localism. The power structure of public broadcasting, particularly the board of CPB, stresses that the system does not and should not operate in competition with the commercial stations. Rather it provides alternatives to the programming televised by the commercial stations. Inevitably perhaps, the concept of "alternative programming" becomes equated with "minority interest programming." This minority interest may be based on race, political philosophy, cultural tastes—or almost anything.

Similarly, great emphasis is based upon the fine old American tradition of "home rule." PBS is not called a network, but rather an interconnection. As CPB Chairman-emeritus James Killian has frequently described it, the interconnection should be something of a cafeteria line from which the individual local stations pick and choose from programs offered, and from which they then can arrange their own menu or schedule of programs for local transmission. In addition great emphasis has been placed on the potential for the public stations to fill a vacuum created by the fact that most commercial stations have abdicated their responsibilities to do local programming.

Both these concepts are strongly stressed in the Carnegie Commission Report; significantly, Killian was not only a charter member of the CPB board but also chaired the Carnegie Commission.

The public broadcasting legislation came at the height of a cycle of concern for civil rights and equal opportunities. Proponents of the bill were able to rally additional support for the concept of public television by bringing in those who represented groups which felt that they had less than adequate access to or unfair treatment from the dominant, commercial television structure. But for such support, the officers and members of such groups obviously expected a quid pro quo. This expectation became institutionalized when CPB created an Advisory Council of National Organizations (ACNO). Ostensibly convened to provide advice and guidance on programming decisions, AC-

NO has also been seen by CPB officers as a means of rallying pressure groups for support during Congressional hearings.

Rightly or wrongly, the Congress did not follow the recommendations of the Carnegie Commission regarding how the federal government should provide for financial input into the system. The form which was decided upon, appropriation by Congress, unfortunately meant that the support provided was the least likely to provide direct contact between the individual citizen and the system. Such contact might have been provided by either a set fee similar to that used to support Britain's BBC or Japan's Nippon Hoso Kyokai (NHK) or by a tax on purchase of new sets. Instead, the Congress became the financial intermediary, so to speak, between the citizen and the receiving system. This arrangement had several unfortunate consequences.

It heightened the probability that the system would continue indefinitely to operate under political scrutiny.

It deprived the system of a means of rapidly creating public awareness and a sense of participation to the system. To be candid, one might fairly question the extent to which those operating the system really wanted such a sense of participation, for this also implies a relationship of direct accountability.

The system which did emerge is one which combines several sources of financial support and requires operational compromises. Most stations are highly dependent upon heavy inputs from the local and state educational systems, from foundations, from commercial underwriting, and from direct viewer contributions. The federal input constitutes only about one-fourth of what is required. While that fourth is absolutely crucial to the national system and to many stations individually, it comes with many strings attached.

To obtain an idea of the complicated operational structure which results from this edifice of compromises, one should read Natan Katzman's monograph on how programming decisions are made in public broadcasting.[5] His tortured charts attempting to illustrate the operational relationship of components of the system emphasize the handicaps under which the system operates. But readers will have difficulty finding this advice, for only a few copies of this monograph were distributed. Officials of CPB ordered the bulk of the 2,500-copy press run destroyed, claiming the work contained inaccuracies and that the tone was not favorable to CPB. This destruction occurred after Katzman had spent over a year checking his manuscript with appropriate sources throughout the system. The long delay in publication and the subsequent suppression of the edition underline the general feeling of discouraged wonderment that the system operates at all![6]

The great tragedy is that the question of a public television system was not dealt with as a total integral concept in 1952, when the channels were reserved for noncommercial use. At that moment, the creation of an efficient and coherent system would have been feasible. But while such a system was technically and organizationally feasible, it was not politically acceptable, and so the moment passed. Instead, pieces of a potential system came into being with individual, independent, and perhaps incompatible goals and vested interests. By 1967, creation of a coherent system would have required wiping the slate clean and starting anew. That action would have been bitterly fought by the already existing institutions. Any system created in 1967 would have had to deal with the divergent pieces already in existence.

In the nine years since the passing of the act, much of the energy of the system has been devoted to trying to reconcile these differences. This effort has been made at the expense of improving the content of the system's programs. Technical requirements of the system are relatively (but not totally) devoid of opportunities for conflict, so the previously noted remarkable progress has been made on the technical front. But in terms of programming, in terms of creating a real relationship with the American public, the results are much more discouraging.

In trying to explain the lack of public impact of the system's programming, technical weaknesses have frequently been invoked. In particular, much has been made of the acknowledged competitive disadvantage which goes with UHF channel allocations. However, this argument has always been attenuated by the fact that in markets where commercial UHF stations operate, some of these stations have achieved much greater audiences than public stations—in some instances even when the public station is on a VHF assignment. These situations raise doubt concerning the extent to which the "UHF handicap" explains the small audiences. Some station and program managers have suggested that poor programming and inadequate promotion may be more important factors, but such suggestions are uncomfortable for many in the system, particularly those making decisions on programming.

Public television has not been without its "successes." "The Incredible Machine," a high-quality program produced in cooperation with the National Geographic Society and lavishly promoted thanks to underwriting from the Gulf Oil Corporation, for the first time attract-ed a larger audience for PBS than the audiences achieved by some of the commercial networks in the same time period. In other, less spec-tacular, instances, PBS programs have achieved quite respectable au-diences in terms of numbers. Such "successes" underline that the basic problem today lies not with the technical aspects of the system but rather with the programming aspects.

These successes are a further embarrassment because they underline the system's failure to evolve a clear criterion of success—a sure indica-tion of a more basic failure, the failure to define clearly program goals. In these instances of "success," the criterion used is that of the com-mercial networks—absolute numbers of viewing households. Yet dur-ing the years when numbers have been small—as indeed they still are for most programs—the system's managers have argued (with con-siderable cogency) that this criterion is certainly not sufficient, even if appropriate, for a system whose charge is to produce "alternative" programs, to fill the void left by the content of the commercial sta-tions.

A fact more often admitted privately than publicly by those involved in and sympathetic to public television is that most of the programs are bad. They are bad by the criterion that they are dull. Too often strong grounds also exist for suspecting that the programs do not achieve their announced intentions even for those who do watch. All too often the badness of programs has been excused by the fact that they are well-intentioned. Yet entirely too few of these programs, while claiming specific behavioral or attitudinal goals, have been put to empirical tests. Their apologists assume that if the programs are watched, they are effective. And that assumption is naive, perhaps dishonest.

This suggestion of intellectual dishonesty is further strengthened by the addition of the comment that the programming had to be done on a shoestring budget and hence really did not have a fair chance.

This attitude brings to mind comments by Paul Klein, who gained considerable expertise as a top executive in programming at NBC. For some years, Klein has had what might be called a frustrated affair with public television. Through the help of the Ford Foundation, his advice has been made available to, but little used by, the programming peo-ple of public television. This situation appears to have been improved in the 1975–1976 season. The appointment of a former NBC col-league, Lawrence Grossman, as president of PBS, may further change the situation. Klein has long argued that too much concern has been given to filling the schedule for the sake of filling the schedule. A better approach, he has suggested, would be to concentrate on fewer but better-quality programs, repeating them a number of times for maximum impact. Such repetition is an opportunity unique to public television. And, indeed, it may be necessary if "alternative" programs are to have a chance to achieve their actual potential.

The point is that "alternative" programs must attract their viewers in a competitive situation. Members of the intended audience for whom the alternative is designed, while perhaps members of distinctive subgroups, are also members of the general public. As such, they are likely to be strongly attracted by the popular programs of the commercial networks. Thus if the "alternative" is shown only once, at least some portion of viewers who might be interested is likely not to watch, because the program conflicts with a more highly valued commercial program. But if the program is repeated in another time slot, conditions might be more favorable to their viewing it. Analyses of Nielsen ratings in past years have shown a trend for public television programs to achieve larger "shares" of audience during the summer months when the commercial network schedules consist largely of repeated programs from the previous season.

An invidious comment frequently heard is that the best programs on America's public television are those it imports from Britain. "The Forsyte Saga," "Upstairs Downstairs," and "Jennie" have been superior program series. But we must remember that these series are *selected,* not only from the BBC but also from the commercial television service of Great Britain. They do not reflect the average quality of television programming in England, as the tone of this criticism implies. This implication makes the criticism unfair to the commercial networks as well as to public television.

As Klein has suggested, part of the problem is that public television has rushed to fill an ambitious network schedule with insufficient production resources. To date, few series intended as "purposeful alternatives" have had anything approaching adequate production funding.

"Feeling Good" is perhaps the only series which set out to do a specific job with specific segments of the population in mind and had adequate resources both for production and for developmental research in support of the production. Unfortunately the series was not a success in either its first attempt or its second, with a revised format. Because the program was unique in its specificity of the "alternative" it wished to provide and in its adequacy of resources, too much has been made of its "failure." Another factor was that the series was the first attempt by Children's Television Workshop (CTW) to move into adult programming. The great success of CTW with "Sesame Street" and "The Electric Company"—and in raising money for production—has generated both admiration and envy among other public television production units. Perhaps too much was expected above and beyond the specific goals CTW set for the program.

Each season, many series with more resources and easier goals fail on the commercial networks. That failure is an anticipated fact of life. Public television's problem has been that it has had too few eggs to put in its basket; thus when one program is found to be bad, the loss is much more obvious.

In the 1975–1976 season, public television has seen a marked increase in financial resources for production, and several ambitious American-produced series have been introduced; several others are in preparation. This situation is encouraging but not without some worrisome points.

Is public television teetering at the brink of a slope down which commercial television has already gone, the slide to emphasis on national programming at the expense of local programming? The Carnegie Commission Report, the Public Broadcasting Act, and much of the rhetoric of the system itself has emphasized public television's special obligation at the local level. Traditionally this obligation has been translated as a call for locally produced programs, particularly programs focussing on local issues and public affairs. With pride, interest has been directed to programs such as "51st State" in New York, "Newsroom" in San Francisco and Dallas, "Feedback" in Jacksonville, "Hawaii Now" in Honolulu, and series in a number of states providing unique coverage of state legislatures.

Today discussions concerning localism contain the suggestion of a subtle shift to emphasize control of the program schedule rather than production. Control of content is shifted from local production to the democratic voting of stations on which programs they will jointly fund for national availability. Public television has not gone down that slope as yet, and just how close it is to the brink is debatable. But the pressures which would move it closer are undeniable. Local production has not increased commensurately with the provision of funds from CPB.[7]

Not the least of those pressures is the substantial growth in the amount of corporate underwriting the system has received in the last two years. This increase in underwriting is largely—but not solely—responsible for the stronger production budgets mentioned earlier.

This situation holds a certain exquisite irony, which sees "noncommercial" public television being rescued, if you will, by the commercial sector. Under the existing regulations of the Federal Communication Commission, the public stations are forbidden to carry commercial messages. However, they can give acknowledgment of contributions toward production funding at the start and close of a program. This acknowledgment can give only the name—visually or orally, or both—of the contributor. Corporate slogans or symbols cannot be used. The practice is all very low key; the viewer has little to object to.

Under the authorization bill which was passed and signed in 1976, the amount of money which the system receives from the government is tied to the amount of money it can raise from other sources. The government will provide one dollar for each two and one-half dollars raised from other sources, up to a maximum amount.[8] Corporate underwriting plays an important role in helping the system raise "matching funds."

The complete underwriting picture is considerably more complex than the short credit at the beginning and end of the program. Underwriting grants provide certain tax benefits to the corporations. They also constitute corporate "good deeds," so to speak. Corporations, like individuals, rather like to get credit for their good deeds. The five-second mentions are a little less than totally satisfying, perhaps, as recognition. Increasingly, tie-in promotion for underwritten programs appears in other media. Thus the underwriter may make additional funds available to the system or to individual stations to place ads in newspapers. Or the underwriting corporation itself may develop an extensive promotional campaign in newspapers and magazines. In such ads, no restrictions are placed on "tooting the corporate horn."

This type of promotion leaves the program itself unspoiled by commercials. It also provides immensely valuable visibility for both the individual program and for public television generally—visibility which is desperately needed. As noted at the outset, one of the major problems which has faced the system has been a lack of public awareness—a problem resulting in part from poor or low visibility. As noted earlier, much of the success of "The Incredible Machine" must be attributed to the fact that the Gulf Oil Corporation, the underwriter, also mounted a quite elaborate program of national advertising for that single program. Gulf spent more money on this promotion than most public television series have available for production during the entire year. From the standpoint of increased visibility, this tie-in advertising is a definite plus for the system. Some grumbling may be heard from the commercial networks who see this promotion and underwriting expenditure as money which might be diverted from them but, for now anyway, this concern is probably not worrisome.

But two other aspects of underwriting and tie-in advertising are perhaps worth a pause. In discussing the "successes" of the 1975–1976 season, the point was made that "success" was stipulated in terms of the criteria of the commercial network—the number of viewers.

Corporate underwriting may be a part of corporate "good deeds," but the people who handle the underwriting are usually those who handle the corporation's promotion and advertising. They are accustomed to dealing with the tools of the commercial broadcasting industry—Nielsen ratings, cost-per-thousand-viewers, and so forth.

They are also accustomed to dealing with network situations, where programs are shown according to a standard time pattern across the country. One can easily sympathize with the puzzled frustration they feel when trying to promote a program they have underwritten for distribution over PBS. To spend a great deal of money for four-color full-page ads in a national magazine and have to say "check your local paper for program time" is less than satisfying. To promote specific program time, the underwriters must resort to a campaign using local newspapers, a procedure which, for a big corporation, is very costly and less satisfying than a glossy national magazine approach. Perhaps the most effective promotion is to buy ads on commercial television. But again the variable schedules of public television mean arrangements must be made at the local station as well as or instead of at the network level if program air time is to be given.

One result has been a trend for underwriters to concentrate their tie-in promotion budgets in the top ten markets. In this way they can minimize the newspapers or local commercial stations which must be used and still reach a large proportion of the nation's potential viewers. But this strategy provokes considerable grumbling among the public stations in other markets who are very sensitive to what they consider "second-class citizen" treatment at the hands of the big city stations. Using a bicentennial-type analogy, public television is somewhat in the situation of the original thirteen states trying to operate under the Articles of Confederation rather than the Constitution. The smaller units feel they should be equal to the larger ones.

The promotion problem does provide a handy point which those who advocate a "network" operation can use to apply pressure on the individual stations. If the stations will carry the program at the time it "comes down the line" on PBS, opportunity is created for a coordinated national promotion campaign from which they, not just the big city stations, can benefit. After all, they may decide to schedule in coordinated national fashion, so they still have "local control." This subtle point is frequently argued in not-very-subtle fashion.

The fact that underwriting is generally handled by people accustomed to dealing with commercial television presents another aspect. Possibly some stockholder may not be satisfied with the tax benefits or the abstract "good deeds" aspect of underwriting. If management can make the additional point that millions of people actually watched the program, the stockholder is likely to be mollified. Not surprisingly, the big underwriting money has strongly tended to go for programs which among the program mix of public television have the best chance of attracting the most viewers. Programs for children, drama, music and dance, history, science provide opportunity for large numbers and little controversy.

It requires more courage than perhaps should be expected of corporate doers of good deeds to make funds available for minority programming, programs on issues which indeed may provoke hostility as well as criticism. Such courage has not been totally lacking, but is relatively rare.

Yet programs of that type certainly are included in the "alternatives" which the rhetoric of public television pours forth to justify both its existence and the input of federal funds. And the programmatic nature of the benefits of increased corporate underwriters have not gone without bitter attacks from minority spokesmen.

An argument which can be and is made to rebut these attacks goes as follows. The corporate underwriting picks up the tab for the system's "elite" programs. Thus the system can put more of its own money into the development of programs for minority interest, programs dealing with public issues. This response can be received with some skepticism. The largest grants to CPB for development of new programs are for drama, music, and dance.

At the local station level, the performance is not much better. The Station Program Cooperative (SPC) is the mechanism through which the individual stations can use the federal funds channeled to them through CPB to exercise control over a considerable portion of the programs to be distributed by PBS. To date, the stations have not shown much in the way of either imagination or initiative in putting their money down for programs of minority interest or possible controversial nature.

The stations, like the underwriters, have developed an appreciation of audience numbers. They continue to express a commitment to minority programming, but the elitist nature which has dominated the evening audience since the days of educational television is appreciated for some very practical reasons (and when appropriate, is pointed out with pride to underwriters).

Direct viewer support is an important source of station income. In recent years, heavy pressure has been exerted from both within and without the system to increase this support. Such support is functional in providing a practical testimony of public support as well as the dollars themselves. "Pledge nights" and "pledge weeks" proliferate through the system, culminating in public television's version of a programming extravaganza—the "Station Independence Program" (SIP). The SIP is a package of programs provided in a concentrated period in the spring together with coordinated assistance for staging an intensive campaign to obtain viewer pledges or "memberships." The SIP is not unlike the "hyped" schedule of specials the commercial networks develop for the key Neilsen measurement periods. Indeed, it is carefully scheduled so as not to conflict with those periods.

As pledge appeals have expanded, some observers have been sufficiently concerned with this phenomenon to take out their stop watches. Disconcerting reports have been made of noncommercial stations spending more time in membership appeals than the commercial stations devoted to advertisements. Concern over this situation within the system is somewhat assuaged by studies which continue to show that most viewers understand the need for these appeals and are tolerant of them. But unquestionably the practice does weaken one of the unique aspects which public television can claim in contrast to commercial television.

Perhaps more worrisome is another aspect of the pledge or membership campaigns, an aspect related to program choice. Considerable experience has now been documented and analyzed in this sphere. Useful guidelines on various aspects of operational strategy have been developed by Statistical Research, Inc. under the joint CPB/PBS/Ford Foundation Station Independence Program. The programs which are most likely to generate the greatest viewer response in pledges or memberships are very similar to those which are also most desirable to the corporate underwriters. Broadly speaking, they are the cultural programs. This fact should not be surprising. These programs are the most likely to achieve large audiences. They also are the most likely to attract the upper middle class of professional families whose discretionary income makes it easier for them to contribute as compared to minority families.

Program directors and station managers do strive from a mix of programs through which they can attempt to satisfy the diverse obligations that they have assumed or had thrust upon them. However, given all these factors, they are understandably tempted—a tendency against which they must keep up their guard—to put on more of the types of programs which have proven successful in producing viewer contributions and in obtaining corporate underwriting.

Back in 1963, the evening audience of educational television was called elitist, both from the standpoint of socioeconomic indicators and from the standpoint of being an audience which was purposefully selective in its television viewing.

In the second half of the 1970s, public television says it is striving to eliminate the socioeconomic elitism, albeit not very successfully to date except with its daytime children's programs. However, the fact that it adheres to a philosophy of "alternative" programming means that it must deal with an "elite" audience from another standpoint: Its viewers must come to it on a purposeful, selective basis. Again and again the goal of public television is stated to be to provide programs for different groups at different times, not to try to get the largest possible audience all of the time as is the case with commercial television. But the implication is also that over time because these different groups are attracted, public television has served most of the total public.

Service of the total public is the true sense of "alternative programming," and is certainly a worthy goal. But the nagging question keeps rising: Is it really feasible, given the nature of television habits which are deeply established in the American public? The professional middle class is the "easy" audience for public television. Its members are the most likely to be "selective" viewers, the least likely to be satisfied with the programs of commercial television, although the differences between socioeconomic groups appear to have diminished since the early 1960s.[9] Less affluent viewers and minority viewers, on the other hand, are the heaviest users of television, and one might argue that commercial television is catering to their desires. Those who respond that commercial television does not provide for the "needs" of these people may really be saying that it does not provide for the needs which the social critics perceive for these people, rather that the needs the people themselves feel. One of the more discouraging facts of public television life is that its black programs have not attracted a large proportion of black viewers, nor have its programs for women attracted a large proportion of women. Program quality and problems of scheduling and promotion may contribute to this fact. But the stronger suspicion is that in the television marketplace the programs are not competitive for their "target audience" with those on the commercial stations. Discouragingly, in the afternoons when "Sesame Street" is programmed against cartoon shows on the commercial stations, it loses its "competitive" edge.

Public television presents a classic case of poor policy planning, of piece-meal funding which has now reached a considerable total but which has produced an incoherent program. The confused and redundant structure of the system has only been touched on in this chapter. While it contributes to the incoherence, it is not the base cause of it.

Public television stations have accepted millions of dollars from the federal government in support of the concept of educational programs. If John Macy is to be believed, educational expectations actually made the critical difference in getting the Public Broadcasting Act passed and signed. Equipment grants administered by the Department of Health, Education and Welfare have played a significant role in building or expanding the plants of public stations all over the country. Can public television justify this public investment on the basis of their daytime programming for school use? The CPB board has indicated otherwise, signifying a commitment to broader educational goals.

In support of their request for appropriations under the Public Broadcasting Act, the system invariably seeks the support of minority interest groups. CPB has organized ACNO for this purpose. Such actions engender expectations among the spokesmen and activists of such organizations which may or may not be realistic within the context of firmly established viewing preferences and patterns among the groups they claim to represent.

Understandably, with all these problems, one sometimes hears the rueful comment that maybe the federal money is more headache than benefit. But realistically, the system could not have been built as quickly as has been the case if that money had not been provided.

Public television officials state that their goal is to provide "alternative" programs and, through diversity of alternatives, reach all the public. Have they perhaps promised too much to too many in the frantic attempt to obtain funding to build and operate a system?

Considering all the rather sobering factors, we can easily understand and perhaps sympathize with the drift toward the "fourth network" concept, including its implications of an emphasis on "elitist" programs of culture and intellectual stimulation. After all, the concept of subsidization of the fine arts is gaining acceptance. Corporate as well as individual gifts play a substantial part in keeping afloat the museums, symphony orchestras, and repertory theaters of the nation.

Perhaps open broadcasting is not the best or most appropriate way to seek to achieve some of the goals or responsibilities which public broadcasting now carries. Perhaps the millennium of "television of plenty" which the cable people keep promising would solve the problem. But like many millennia, it stays on the horizon.

While we wait for it to arrive, public broadcasters and the Congress may appropriately reexamine the situation. Surely the promises made or implied and the expectations against which the system is held accountable are too diverse. Perhaps the time has come to reconsider and restructure them into a more modest but realistic program.

NOTES

1. Carnegie Commission on Educational Television. *Public Television: A Program for Action.* New York: Bantam Books, 1967.
2. U.S. Congress, Senate. *The Public Broadcasting Act of 1967.* Pub. L. 90–129, 90th Congress, First Session.
3. Schramm, Wilbur, with Ithiel de Sola Pool and Jack Lyle. *The People Look at Educational Television.* Stanford: Stanford University Press, 1963.
4. Macy, John, Jr. *To Irrigate a Wasteland.* Berkeley: University of California Press, 1974.

5. Katzman, Natan. *Program Decisions in Public Television.* Washington: Corporation for Public Broadcasting, 1976.

6. At this writing, plans for publication of the manuscript are being discussed by the National Association of Educational Broadcasters and the National Center for Educational Statistics of the U.S. Office of Education. The latter organization was a joint funder of Katzman's work with CPB and the Aspen Institute Program on Communication and Society.

7. Katzman, Natan. *Public Television Program Content: 1974.* Washington: National Center for Educational Statistics, Corporation for Public Broadcasting, 1975.

8. As of mid-1976, the amount of this maximum is still being debated.

9. Lyle, Jack. *The People Look at Public Television. 1974.* Washington: Corporation for Public Broadcasting, 1975.

Mass Media Effects:
New Research Perspectives

STEVEN H. CHAFFEE

The great mass media industries of today developed as part of the industrial revolution of the nineteenth century and the continuing technological revolution of the twentieth.[1] The United States mass press of the 1830s served the expanding population of a nation of businessmen, in which questions about the social value of a commercial enterprise scarcely had any place. The innovative muckraking magazines and the aggressive metropolitan newspapers that flowered in the 1890s were themselves instruments of reform, attacking "big business" enthusiastically enough to obscure the fact that they were part of it. Film and radio grew up in the self-indulgent era of commercialism that followed World War I, under the control of public-be-damned autocrats. But television has, almost from the beginning of its mass diffusion in the 1950s, found itself beset by a proliferating tangle of demands for public accountability. To an extent, these pressures have spilled over onto the earlier mass-communication industries, disturbing the complacency of once-remote media barons.

This recent historical shift toward media accountability is usually attributed to two major factors: the fact that broadcast media must be publicly regulated at least to the extent of allocating radio frequencies and television channels to particular local stations; and the widespread disenchantment with the massive institutions of American society that grew out of the extended depression of the 1930s.[2] A careful student of the current media-reform movement might well conclude that a third factor should be added to this brief list—the development of social research on the effects of mass communication. The tools of media-effects research are employed on all sides: by pressure groups to document their special cases, by public agencies interested in propagating their campaigns via mass channels, and by the media themselves to improve the potency of their product. Those social scientists who offer the conceptual and methodological skills for investigating the social impact of mass communication find themselves in a seller's market. They also find that their study of that impact is increasingly used to modify the very thing they are investigating.

VARIETIES OF MEDIA EFFECTS

Even a cursory examination of the empirical research literature reveals many concepts of possible effects—and indicators of "effectiveness"—of the mass media. A few simple distinctions will indicate the multiplicity of approaches. First, we can separate effects that can be attributed to a medium because of its physical properties and the sheer time a person devotes to it from effects that are traced to specific content it transmits. Next a traditional division is made among the reception of information, the modification of behavior, and changes in feelings, opinions, and intentions to act; these divisions are generally labeled the cognitive, behavioral, and attitudinal (or affective) categories of media effects. A third set of distinctions concerns the unit of observation; an effect may manifest itself in the individual member of the audience, in the interpersonal interaction between two (or a few) audience members, or in the corporate activity of a larger social system such as a community, a formal organization, or a nation. This simple list, which includes one dichotomy (physical versus content-specific effects) and two trichotomies (cognitive–behavioral–attitudinal and individual–interpersonal–system) produces an eighteen-cell matrix ($2 \times 3 \times 3 = 18$). And, as shall be seen, several quite different kinds of effects may be considered in some of those eighteen cells.

An examination of a random collection of studies of media effects, or even of most summaries of that literature, would not give the impression of nearly as much variety as the preceeding paragraph suggests. A definite plurality, and quite probably a solid majority, of all studies to date would fall into the one cell representing individual-level content-specific attitudinal effects. The first major program of studies, initiated during World War II by Carl Hovland, was almost entirely built in this single model.[3] These studies were so well designed and executed that they encouraged imitation and spin-offs. Not uncommonly today one may find citations of Hovland's work of several decades ago as the point of origin for current research, for example in such areas as source credibility, persuasibility, and the duration of effects.[4] But as the title of this paper implies, new research perspectives are being developed and pursued in the effects field. To a considerable extent they consist of explorations of some of the seventeen other cells in our 2 × 3 × 3 matrix.

EFFECTS OF THE MEDIA AS PHYSICAL AND TIME-CONSUMING ENTITIES

The production of mass media is a large and growing sector of the economy in the United States[5] and throughout most of the postindustrial world. Publication of daily newspapers rivals even the giant United States automobile industry in the value of industrial production.[6] The total payroll for the creation, fabrication, and distribution of newspapers, magazines, radio, hi-fi, television, and film represents a significant portion of the nation's work force. As with all mass-production industries, environmental costs arise. For instance, the newsprint for the thick newspapers that most Americans receive each day consumes a great deal of wood pulp from shrinking forests, and paper production is a major river-polluting industry. (Also, newsprint has been in chronic shortage worldwide for some years.) Another familiar example is the home television receiver, which draws a significant amount of electrical power some five hours each day in the typical household. The economic and environmental impact of the mass media on society has been little studied until very recently, and indeed has not ordinarily been considered part of "media effects" research at all—although it would seem to belong in any comprehensive cost-benefit analysis.

A second physical aspect is that the mass media introduce socially visible objects into people's immediate living environment. One's television set is a piece of furniture in the home; magazines are artfully arranged on coffee tables and books on shelves. These artifacts of mass communication need not be "consumed" for their content in order to serve socially expressive purposes. A person's perceived social status can be manipulated by conspicuous consumption of fashionable or approved media items—or by nonconsumption, as in the case of the self-styled intellectual who "wouldn't have a television set in the house." Many writers have made passing mention of this symbolic use of media consumption, but such usage has received little research attention.[7]

Time spent with mass media, on the other hand, has been a standard research topic. Surveys routinely include self-reported estimates of the hours a child spends watching television or the minutes an adult devotes to the newspaper in an average day. Somewhat curiously, these measures are usually treated as "cause" rather than "effect" variables. Watching television, to be sure, exposes the viewer to material that may have certain content-specific effects (see below). But the act of spending hours viewing is itself manifestly an effect of the existence of television. The key "effect" regards what the person has *not* been doing while watching television. In their comparison of "Teletown" and "Radiotown," two neighboring communities that differed mainly in that the second did not receive a television signal, Schramm, Lyle, and Parker addressed this very question; they were able to give fairly precise estimates of the reduction in play, sleep, reading, film attendance, and so forth, attributable to television.[8] Unfortunately the example set by this study has been followed more by direct replication than by extension into novel areas. Clues abound. When a football game is shown on television, attendance at the game is decreased; so, it appears, is the incidence of burglaries, at least when the telecast occurs at night. Water levels in community reservoirs reportedly drop suddenly during television's commercial breaks, due apparently to the simultaneous flushing of many toilets. City streets seem practically deserted during the telecasts of important football games. From such examples one gets the sense of a great deal of rescheduling of peoples' lives as a consequence of mass media. While this shifting of times to accommodate media schedules may seem trivial from the individual's viewpoint, thoughtful research might demonstrate that some of it is important for the functioning of the system as a whole.

A fourth general class of effects that are not content-specific has to do with the *dissipation* of feelings that lead a person to the media. Lyle and Hoffman[9] asked a sample of children and adolescents which of several activities (reading a book, watching television, listening to music, among others) they were likely to do under various psychological conditions (when you feel alone, when you are tired, when you are angry, and so on). While media use is presumably one effect of being, say, lonely or angry, the data imply also that the alleviation of this condition is the anticipated effect of the media activity. Also implicit is the assumption that the specific content encountered in the medium does not matter much; the responses indicate that each medium is sought under differing conditions *as a medium* rather than in search of a particular program or song or story. The "gratifications" served by the mass media as general entities have been commingled with those served by specific types of content in much research.[10] In the area of public-affairs information and news, recent data indicate that the effect that is sought is content-specific but not medium-specific.[11] A precise accounting of those effects that are sought in medium-specific fashion (without regard to content) has yet to be undertaken.

Another general effects question is that of feelings toward the media themselves. Many studies have been made of the relative credibility of different media and of the general evaluations of the media and of people who work in media industries. For instance, surveys have shown that newspaper reporters rank a bit below undertakers in job prestige norms; that most people say they get most of their news from television and would believe a television news report if it differed from one in a newspaper; and that parents and children are very eager to get television before it comes to a community—and very thankful for it once it arrives.[12] The origins of these and other attitudes about the media have not been studied in any detail, except for some data on demographic correlates.[13] Some of the causes of these attitudes toward the media will undoubtedly turn out to be content-specific, but others will not. For example, one reason parents welcome television is that it gets children out from underfoot, functioning in effect as a cheap babysitter. Institutionalized persons appreciate the sheer availability of media because in many cases they would otherwise have nothing to occupy their time. Negative feelings toward media are often expressed too, for various reasons. We have the conceptual and methodological tools to investigate these matters much more thoroughly.

CONTENT-SPECIFIC EFFECTS OF THE MEDIA

When people refer to "media effect," they ordinarily have in mind some particular type of content that is delivered via mass media, rather than general effects of "the media" as physical and time-consuming entities. Commonly, a distinction is made between content provided by our presentday media that would have been delivered by other means in their absence, and content that would not reach people *at all* but for the existence of media channels. But this division is more often a distinction than an important difference. Usually at stake is content that gets propagated in greater or lesser amounts, or to larger or smaller numbers of persons, because of the kind of media systems we have. For example, violent and pornographic scenes in drama date back to antiquity, although they seem to be employed with astonishing frequency by today's film and television writers. News about governmental activities, even though it may not be covered much more extensively than a few generations ago, reaches a wider citizenry now due to the dissemination capabilities of news magazines, wire services, newspapers, and television.

Changes in the methodology of media-effects research reflect the idea that media systems control the amount, rather than the kind, of communication in society. The early experimental model of Hovland lent itself to categorical statements about the effects of *presentation versus withholding* of a particular item of media content.[14] Today, one finds many studies of the effects attributable to *heavy versus light* exposure to a particular type of content; so many channels offer so many kinds of material that the concept of an experiment "control group" is practically impossible to operationalize for some of the most interesting categories of content.[15] Historically, we have shifted from the experiment to the field survey as the more widely applied method for hypothesis testing, although experimental tests are still preferred in content areas where they are feasible. Such a shift would seem to be retrogressive—it does indeed seem so to many—without new methods for drawing causal inferences from nonexperimental data.[16]

Information gain is obviously one criterion for the assessment of media effectiveness; for the most part, this criterion has seemed too obvious to be very interesting to most investigators. Knowledge has traditionally been treated as a less consequential outcome than either "attitudes" or "behavior" in weighing the impact of mass communication on society. And yet propagation of information is the way most media professionals, when asked, characterize what they are trying to accomplish. And, interestingly, informational outcomes are often cited by media audiences as their reason for spending time even with what appears on its face to be purely entertainment programming.[17] To the extent that these expressed motivations are valid indicators, they should lead to more attention to broadly informational media effects.[18]

Something of a recession, on the other hand, seems to be underway in the area of affective outcomes of mass communication. Attitudinal effects were once assumed to represent an intermediate in a fixed psychological process that led from the intake of raw information to the exhibition of corresponding overt behavior.[19] The current perspective is instead one in which behavior and information are often treated as important specific indicators of media effectiveness, without assuming that they derive their social meaning from a presumed connection with attitudes.

Behind this shift has been the gradual accumulation of evidence that the direction of causation linking attitudes to knowledge and behavior is ambiguous. Experiments have demonstrated that a change in a broad social attitude (racial prejudice) can produce *subsequent* changes in expressed information.[20] Cognitive dissonance theory proved to be a good predictor of attitude changes that *followed* forced compliance with a new behavioral standard.[21] Careful examinations of studies in which both attitudinal and behavioral changes have been induced show low correlations between the two, and remarkably few examples of directly parallel effects.[22]

This ambiguity does not necessarily indicate that attitudinal effects have been declared irrelevant and are no longer thought worth assessing. Rather, they have been put in their conceptual place. When favorable opinions themselves are desired, as in the case of an oil company's institutional advertising or of a one-issue candidate's antiabortion or antiracism campaign, affective reactions may well be more important criteria of effectiveness than is any knowledge gained, or concrete behavior. On the other hand, when one's goal is to sell soap or purchase automobiles, the overt behavior of product supersedes attitudes; a corporation does not especially care if its brand is more loved than others so long as it is purchased. Many informational campaigns are tied to longer range attitudinal or behavioral goals, so much so that Hyman and Sheatsley in their classic explanation of "why information campaigns fail" defined failure almost exclusively in affective-behavioral rather than in informational terms.[23] More recent investigators have set forth conditons under which information campaigns might succeed, but these hinge to a considerable extent on holding to information transmission as one's superordinate goal.[24]

A fair amount of information, sometimes called "mobilizing information," conveyed via mass media has direct implications for one's behavior without necessarily activating any intermediating affective response. For example, the television and theater logs in the daily newspaper are basically informational and are usually consulted by a person whose general behavioral intention has already been determined; only a bit of shaping is required to get the person to the right place at the right time. Other examples include the media weather report, which may control your decision to plan a picnic or to plant a garden on a particular day; the end paragraph of a news story, which tells you where and when a political event that you might otherwise have missed is to be held; or the obituary notice that informs you of the funeral arrangements for a long-time friend.

Two classes of behavior relevant to the question of media effects can be distinguished. First, things which people have always done one way or another are modified on the basis of media inputs. The other category consists of those activities in which one would not have engaged at all had it not been for the propagation of a new message that could only be brought via mass communication. The first of these groups of behavior is doubtless the more common, but the second is in many ways more intriguing to the student of media and society.

Most of the major behavioral outcomes which are thought to be modified by media content existed before our present media resources came into being. If a quantity of pornographic or violent material occurs on the screen, and even if it can be linked empirically to increase in sexual offenses or aggressive acts, the obvious fact remains that pre-electronic society experienced approximately the same range of problems with sex and violence as we do today. Television has brought presidential addresses "live," and the gore of distant wars only slightly delayed on film or tape, into our living rooms; but previous generations learned what their presidents had said and had vivid images of their wars, albeit the transmission took a bit longer, reached fewer people, and was probably subject to more distortion in the process.

An individual finds it difficult to conceive of new activities he or she engages in as made possible only by modern media. But studies that examine the behavior of many persons simultaneously and in concert have noted numerous examples of effects for which mass communication is a necessary, not just a sufficient, condition. One of the most vivid was the group hysteria in certain neighborhoods that was created by the Orson Welles "War of the Worlds" broadcast in 1938.[25] Most sociologists agree with the statement that it is not inconsequential that we are all able to laugh at the same joke at the same time.[26] Political scientists often view mass communication as a means of holding the society together while it undergoes change rather than as an activating agent for change in itself.[27] Unquestionably our present-day capacity for organized social action is greatly enhance by the means of communication open to us.

Students in introductory classes in mass communication are sometimes given a chance to compare their lives with and without media by being assigned to "abstain" from any media inputs for a period of several days. While hardly scientific, these exercises are often illuminating. The students report that they find some media inputs impossible to avoid, as in the case of billboards and Muzak: that they find others ingrained in necessary activities, such as radio music while driving, or magazines while waiting for a doctor's appointment; and that some media activities are essential to their present form of existence, such as studying textbooks for their classes. Occasionally a student even reports suffering "withdrawal symptoms" such as craving candy after several days without the habitual mass media.

Of all the activities that mass media make possible, perhaps the most important is the immediate broadcasting of information about an impending crisis or a current disaster situation. Schramm has commented that the national experience of grief and readjustment following the assassination of President John Kennedy in 1963 was eased greatly because it could be widely shared via the mass media.[28] Coleman has analyzed the "crisis" role of the media in terms of a series of phases in the development and resolution of a community conflict.[29] When a local issue such as fluoridation or school busing arises, the news media are sometimes slow in detecting and explaining it. As many parties take strongly opposed stands, outrageous statements are often made; much of this debate is communicated via informal discussion channels, where rumor and slander can flow unchecked. The media cannot expand their coverage beyond their relatively fixed capacity—only so many column inches of newspaper or minutes of newscast per day; and they have their rules about what is appropriate to publish, which may exclude unverified, libelous, or obscene statements. Coleman sees a community conflict as approaching resolution once it is brought under the control of media coverage, in which an attempt is made to separate truth from falsehood and to check hyperbolic statements against one another.

The role of the mass media in handling more chronic sources of community conflict has been addressed in a series of empirical studies by Tichenor, Donohue, and Olien.[30] They find newspaper editors in small towns working to avoid the appearance of conflict while, in metropolitan areas, prestige and power go instead to those editors who are able to identify points of conflict in the community and bring them to the public consciousness.[31] The effectiveness of the mass media in handling intense social conflict is potentially a much more important one than the modest research literature on it to date would suggest. After all, when a social system is threatened from outside (for example, by disaster) or internally strained (as by a divisive political issue), the performance of its communication system is most critical.

This conflict-centered approach to the social effects of mass communication contrasts sharply with the earlier emphasis on attitude-management research in this field. The modification of one's feelings toward a class of objects has usually been studied in controlled situations where the target individual could be assumed to be invulnerable to outside influences. The Hovland group found what may be the optimal "field laboratory" in the Army's boot camp, where the soldier's daily life was extremely well controlled and practically identical from day to day and from one recruit to the next.[32] (Even so, some findings, such as the anomalous "sleeper effect," might be attributable to informal social organization within the barracks based on educational differences among the recruits.[33])

But even laying aside the methodological shift from controlled experimentation to the crisis- and conflict-management field studies that are proliferating today, an important conceptual change is apparent in the notion of "effective" communication. Hovland and his imitators began with an assumption that change of attitude (or behavior) in a certain direction was the desirable outcome. For instance, the Army needed to prepare its recruits psychoemotionally for combat; an effective orientation film would render them more enthusiastic about going to war alongside United States allies and against the Axis powers.[34] Similarly, in political research, an "effective" message persuades someone to vote for the candidate advocated. In marketing, the job of most advertisements is obviously to sell the advertised brand to consumers. Public relations speeches and releases are designed to build a favorable "image" or "climate of opinion" for the organization, agency, or firm that produces them. Messages that fail to accomplish these directional goals are deemed "ineffective."

This assumption is not made in crisis-management and conflict-resolution studies of media effects. Instead, "success" is inferred if the system survived the crisis without breaking apart. An effective resolution of a community conflict is indicated by a number of attibutes: the absence of bloodshed or the exercise of raw power; the speed and ease with which an outcome was reached; or the degree to which the various parties to the resolution are satisfied with it and with the process through which it was achieved. We might expect to see in communication-effects studies of the future more criteria of effectiveness with this nondirectional flavor.

Much of the day-to-day work of the news media does not deal with dramatic crises. "Slow news days" occur, and much routine coverage is made of the progress of bills through legislatures, of the campaigns of hopeful candidates for higher offices, and of distant events that have no clear connection to the immediate concerns of the bulk of the media audience. Are the media "ineffective" in their efforts to perform these humdrum tasks well, simply because they a) are not influencing attitudes in a particular direction and b) are not resolving any societal crises? One would like to be able to say, "No, of course these activities of the media are important, too." But present modes of research in effect define the nonpersuasive and noncrisis efforts of the mass media as ineffective by default.

Two current theoretical themes that involve content-specific psychological effects are interesting in that they do not presuppose any bias or directionality in media content. They find the "cause" in the simple variable of either mentioning or not mentioning a particular item in the media, even if it is mentioned in what seems to be a "neutral" fashion. The earlier of these themes in terms of research is the effect of "mere exposure" to a communicated item on one's attitudinal responses to it. The other is the concept of "agenda-setting" effects of the media, an idea that was around for many decades before its time for empirical test arrived.

The most thorough study of "mere exposure" is that of Zajonc.[35] He experimentally varied the frequency with which audience members saw particular photographs (of faces) during a series of presentations; a subsequent tendency arose to assign more favorable evaluations to those which had been seen most often. Becker and Doolittle applied this principle to the mass media, in an experiment using brief radio advertisements for political candidates.[36] Their finds were curvilinear; more frequent exposure to a candidate's name resulted in more favorable ratings up to a point—after which continued repetition produces a decline in evaluations. In a world where public figures vie for the spotlight and hire publicity agents to secure media exposure, that so little is known about the attitudinal impact of exposure per se is remarkable.

The agenda-setting hypothesis focuses on an effect that lies short of attitudinal persuasion, although the effect is essential to the persuasion. As the proposition has been put, the media may not be especially powerful in telling people what to think, but they can be quite successful in determining what people will think *about*.[37] McCombs and his colleagues have consistently found correlations between the rankings people make regarding the importance of various social "problems" and the frequency with which local mass media mention those problems.[38] McLeod and Becker have used a comparative design in which they examine the problem rankings of groups exposed to media that contain different content emphases; the rankings given by these different audiences resemble those of their respective media.[39] Despite these convergent results, however, the finding is apprently limited to certain groups of persons, such as those who are seeking guidance on political questions.[40]

The current wave of interest in agenda-setting is centered in schools of journalism and is derived partly from ethical concerns within the news industry. The journalist's standard of objectivity has traditionally been considered satisfied where no directional bias could be demonstrated in content analysis of one's news. But direct persuasion is no longer deemed the only effect of importance. The issues a person considers important provide the cognitive background against which that person's specific opinions will be developed and tested. Agenda- setting has societal-level implications, too. The issues on which most problem-solving effort is likely to be expended are those that people consider most important; to the extent that the news industry controls which problems will be addressed, it also determines which will get ignored.

One final topic that has attracted considerable research attention in the past few years is the concept of a "knowledge gap" in society. The hypothesis is that the informational mass media are attended primarily by people who are already relatively well informed. Thus the gap is widened between the knowledgeable and the uninformed sectors of society, which in turn may make more difficult the functioning of the society as a total system.[41] While several studies, particularly in agrarian settings, have found a widening knowledge gap that can be attributed to media influence, some studies are also showing the reverse—that media inputs can bring the less-informed sector up to parity.[42] The conditions under which each of these patterns can be expected to occur pose an important research problem.

INTERVENING PROCESSES IN MEDIA EFFECTS

Many researchers, in writing their reports of studies in which some sort of effect of mas communication has been demonstrated, have betrayed a deep sense of unease about the inadequacy of their understanding of the phenomenon they have isolated. The two-variable

model consists of a measure or manipulation of variation in exposure
to media content (independent variable) and an observation of change
in some aspect of thought or behavior (dependent variable) that is empirically linked in a systematic statistical fashion to the independent
variable. Enough fairly impressive cause–effect research of this type has
accumulated to assure us that the mass media do indeed have a variety
of effects on individual behavior.

What has been lacking, although it too is beginning to accumulate,
is three-variable research in which the psychological processes that intervene between media exposure and its effects are studied. If a boy is
shown a filmed fight and subsequently acts more aggressively than
before, we might conclude that the film has created an effect. But we
may not understand what the intervening process has been and, lacking that knowledge, we may not have much idea how counselors or
parents might themselves intervene to control the process after the
media exposure has occurred. About as many different theories exist
regarding these processes as there are theorists, and only slightly more
active researchers.

In the example of the fight film, for instance, one interpretation
might be that the boy is simply imitating the behavior he has been
shown; perhaps that behavior was not included in his total repertoire
of acts before, and now it is.[43] Or perhaps a process of "identification"
is involved; he wants to behave like a grown, strong man, and what he
has seen indicates to him that fighting is an appropriate mode of
behavior for the type of person he is striving to become.[44] Still another
account might be that the fight film aroused him to the point where
he felt like doing *something* physically active; any form of activity
would have sufficed, and his subsequent aggressive behavior was only
one of many possible outlets for this generalized arousal.[45] All three of
these hypothesized intervening processes have some empirical support, and perhaps all of the processes described occur in some viewers.
The research problem is to determine the conditions under which one
or another process becomes activated. The theoretical problem is more
imposing, in a way, because it involves sorting out the relationships
among the intervening processes which may interact with one another
in various complicated combinations.[46]

Intervening processes have fascinated psychologists of media effects
for years. Hovland and his associates set a model for careful experimental testing of alternative hypotheses based on different
scenarios of intervening psychological events.[47] The new stimulus to

better understand such processes is not simply an academic one. Some effects of mass media are considered undesirable outcomes (for example, aggression activated by media violence), and others are socially positive bits of socialization (for example, imitation of altruistic media models). Educators and social counselors would, as a rule, like to work from the presumed effects of media as a starting place; their programs would thus have to be tailored to minimize antisocial effects and to maximize desirable ones. This tailoring calls for a degree of fine tuning of social intervention programs that simply cannot be done with our present primitive state of knowledge about the processes at work in the production of media effects.

As an example, consider the concept of "perceived reality" of violent presentations. One set of experiments indicates that young people respond more aggressively to media violence when they are told it is real ("news clips"), and less so when they are told it is fictional ("just actors").[48] Correlational studies appeared to corroborate this finding.[49] But an attempt to teach grade school children how television shows make scenes look real, when they are not, failed to reduce the violence-aggression link.[50] A number of reasons might be advanced to explain this nonfinding. Perhaps the intervention program should have focussed on the unreality of plot lines rather than of dramatic production; perhaps a program of only a few weeks' duration is insufficient to counteract a lifetime of socialization; perhaps the experiments on perceived reality are not generalizable.[51] The point is that one is at a loss to pinpoint and pursue any one of these very different possible flaws; as things are, our understanding of the role of perceived reality as an intervening element in socialization through media is very limited. Even so, the role of perceived reality is one of the few intervening factors that has been investigated in any systematic or sustained way; we understand far less about most other suspected processes.

NEW METHODOLOGICAL PERSPECTIVES

As mentioned, recent media-effects research has made something of a shift toward the field study and, correlatively, away from laboratory experimentation. Hovland, to be sure, had the best of both worlds in his Army studies, where he took advantage of a highly controllable field situation in which his experimental manipulations would scarcely be noticed.[52] Upon returning to academe, though, he was forced to choose between the opportunities for control in the laboratory and the ring of generalizability that a field study lends to a finding.[53] In a well-known essay, he outlined the relative merits of the two methods and a number of reasons why one should expect media effects to be easier to demonstrate in the laboratory experiment than in the field survey.[54] Field studies have typically dealt with socially more momentous (and thus less modifiable) effects than have experiments; field studies are typically much more slipshod about such matters as precision of measurement or exact specification of either the causal variable(s) or the hypotheses at stake. Worse, they provide evidence that is at best more equivocal than that yielded by the controlled experiment. Each type of study is capable of showing a statistical correlation between media exposure and a suspected consequent behavior. The experiment is superior in its capacity to specify the time-order involved in this relationship; it guarantees that the cause precedes the effect, whereas in survey analysis, time-order must be inferred. Third variables that might influence (or account for) the observed correlation are handled differently in the two methods. In surveys, suspected third variables must be explicitly identified and measured; then they are partialed out statistically; those that escape the imagination of the investigator are not controlled at all. In the experiment, third variables (including those that fail to occur to the investigator) are controlled in two ways. Those variables that vary within individuals are controlled by random assignment of subjects to conditions; those that vary from one situation to another are controlled by force—that is, by standardizing the situation and not allowing it to vary. Thus one reviewer who has found a set of experiments at variance with his own findings has been prompted to complain that "they smell of the laboratory."[55]

A major shift in thinking about media-effects research in recent years has been the growing realization that *these methodological traditions are not necessarily in conflict*. They are different ways of bringing evidence to bear on the same questions. One should not feel obliged to choose one body of research to believe, and at the same time choose to ignore a second. If theoretical propositions are stated properly, both experimental and survey evidence should be relevant to them. Each camp has been fond of pointing to flaws in the other's methodology. Where the two approaches yield different conclusions, this criticism might make some sense, but the principal flaw lies in the fuzzy language in which hypotheses have been stated and generalizations drawn therefrom. Where the two methods yield similar conclusions, their respective shortcomings are of little consequence, because they do not share the same flaws. The prime case in point has been television violence research, where experimentalists and survey researchers found themselves quite in accord—and in both cases much more comfortable with their "tentative" conclusions once they saw the corroborating evidence derived from the alternative method.[56]

Still, the greatest boost for field-survey studies has come not from corroborating evidence from the laboratory nor from any theoretical innovations regarding media effects. Instead, advances in correlational methodology in general have in recent years provided an empirical rationale for inferring time-order relationships from nonexperimental data. Whereas experimenters employ *design* features such as random assignment and control groups to isolate relationships over time, survey researchers have had to turn to new modes of *data analysis* to accomplish this isolation. The approximation to an experiment's power to infer time-order is still distant; untested assumptions and equivocal interpretations remain in these developing forms of survey analysis. But one can no longer acceptably assert that "you can't say anything about causation from correlational data, because you have no evidence about time-order."

Two modes of analysis need to be distinguished. The more popular mode is path analysis.[57] Synchronous (single-wave) survey measures of a number of variables are organized according to a hypothesized sequence of causal events. The correlations among these variables are then analyzed as a single set; the result is an empirical model that indicates what the strength of each hypothesized "path" linking a set of variables would be if the total hypothesized causal model is valid. A complicated multivariate model with a number of time sequences can be tested; events that hypothetically occur near one another in time should be more strongly related than those the model assumes to be separated by greater time gaps and intervening events. Paths that turn out to be nonsignificant when partialed can be discarded and a simplified ("trimmed") version of the model accepted; or, if the data fit poorly with the model, the model can be discarded entirely and another hypothesized in its place. This method is hypothetico-deductive, not a theory-free inductive search for the single "best fit" model. To run an infinite series of such tests for all possible model linking a large set of variables is neither scientifically sound nor, often, feasible. Like experimentation, a path analysis begins with a set of integrated theoretical propositions about the relationships among some variables; these propositions are then tested as a set with empirical data. The fact that the investigator might accept a path model because it fits well with the data does not rule out the possibility that other theoretical models linking the same variables might also accord well with empirical findings. (The same is true of experimentation, with the major procedural difference being that the experimenter would have to devise an entirely different experiment to test a second hypothesis.) Examples of path-analytic hypothesis testing in communication effects research include those of McCrone and Cnudde, Bishop, and Jackson-Beeck and Chaffee.[58]

The second mode of analysis that has helped revive field-survey studies of media effects is cross-lagged panel correlation. Unlike path analysis, this method makes some special demands on design as well as on analysis, since it requires repeated measurement of both media exposure and the hypothesized effect at several points in time. This mode is also more limited in terms of the number of variables that may be involved in the hypothesis to be tested. Still, development of the Rozell-Campbell baseline[59] and other data-analytic models has helped to stimulate a surge of longitudinal panel studies in the communication-effects area. Nearly ten years elapsed between the suggestion by Schramm et al.[60] that this mode would be the optimal way to study the impact of media on developing children and the first reports of empirical findings in this area based on panel data; these early reports included the Lefkowitz et al. ten-year study of television violence and the acquisition of aggressive behavior,[61] and both short- and long-term contributions of media inputs to political socialization.[62] Unfortunately, the studies to date have involved only two time points; to have measures of both variables at three points in time is essential to assess reliability separately from the measurement of real change in either variable over time.[63]

A different kind of methodological formulation evident in recent media-effects research is based on the theoretical concept of *contingent causation*. That the mass media do not influence all persons in the same fashion has long been recognized; indeed, many persons are not affected in any perceptible way by many media inputs. This knowledge has led to a search for, and to some extent a discovery of, the contingent conditions that govern media effects. For instance, experimental exposure to filmed violence does not produce heightened aggression in all youngsters; this effect seems to be limited to those who are somewhat aggressive at the outset.[64] The agenda-setting power of the mass media does not extend to all citizens, only to those who for various reasons are seeking guidance in interpreting current events in their role as voters.[65] Nomothetic linear models such as path analysis and cross-lagged panel correlation, which assume that a hypothesized effect should hold for all persons, are inappropriate when one's hypothesis is instead that only under certain contingent conditions will any effect occur.

A procedure has been developed, and explicitly recognized as essential by a minority of investigators, in which a broad population sample is first separated into subgroups on the basis of the hypothesized contingent orientations that govern media effects; linear tests of the supposed effect are then run separately on each subgroup.[66] To the extent that this procedure is adopted, it can serve to render much more explicit the theories that are developed regarding media influence. A simple correlational analysis might conclude that a particular media campaign had a 10 percent effect; one's feeling about that result would be rather different if, instead of suggesting a change of 10 percent among all persons, the change could be shown to represent a 100 percent change specific to a group that comprised only 10 percent of the sample. Physically partitioning samples on the basis of contingent orientations that are necessary for a media effect to operate is likely to become more common in future research; this trend is a sign both that we understand quite a bit about the total influence process and that we are going to be able to learn more.

TWO MODEST PROPOSALS

Rather than try to summarize the ganglion of trends reviewed above, this chapter concludes with two suggestions for new directions in media-effects research that would build on several of these trends. Neither is limited to content-specific effects, nor to research with attitudinal persuasion, nor to individuals as such.

TELEVISION AND FAMILY CONFLICT

Schramm, Lyle, and Parker, in their seminal studies of television and children, found a great deal of evidence that those children who spent many hours with television were also the ones who reported considerable conflict with their parents over life goals and aspirations.[67] This correlation the researchers interpreted to mean that the family conflict led the child to seek escape into the "fantasy-oriented" world of television. But direction of causation is equivocal when one is working with purely correlational evidence; the thesis could be the reverse: the heavy use of television causes conflict to build within the home.

Several reasons lead us to suspect that this latter proposition might be true. Television offers competing programs at the same time on different channels, and these programs are designed to appeal to different audiences. A significant amount of conflict might well arise between parents and children over which program to watch at a particular hour. We have evidence that children do not see the same kinds of programs when they are viewing television in the company of their parents as when only children are watching.[68] Specifically, youngsters are considerably more likely to watch violent programs with their parents than they are when viewing alone or with other children. This shift in viewing behavior may often involve some strain in the parent-child relationship. (The fact that the shift is followed immediately, in many cases, by exposure to television's stylized aggressive solutions to interpersonal conflicts is all the more disquieting.)

As Schramm has noted, time spent with television is considered by many to be a violation of the "work ethic" that permeates American society.[69] Whereas reading can be justified as "improving the mind," television is far less likely to be characterized that way. Since most children spend three to five hours a day with television, and since this viewing to some extent has cut into the time that might be devoted to more socially admired activities, we might hazard the guess that television viewing is a cause—rather than simply the effect—of parent-child conflict over the youngsters' long-range life ambitions.

A traditional topic of parent-child disagreement is that of bedtime. The general tendency is for children to attempt to stay up well after the time established by their parents as appropriate for them to go to their bedrooms. (In the age of television, it would not be totally facetious to define a "child" empirically as a person who goes to sleep when evening prime-time programming ends and the late-evening news comes on.) Daily viewing logs show that a majority of children in fact stay up until the news, a type of program that rather few of them care to watch.[70] In the United States, this news program typically occurs at 11 P.M. (10 P.M. Central Time); if the parents have set any earlier bedtime, battles will occur.

The standard sources of family conflict are thought to be sex and money, and one would be hard put to maintain that television might turn out to be a rival to either of these factors. But to some extent, television exacerbates problems in parent-child relations arising from both other factors.

Television has become increasingly permeated with broad sexual references, including both comedies and dramas built around prostitution, homosexuality, rape, and such less weighty matters as promiscuity, propositioning, and adultery. However clever or well done these entertainments are, they raise problems within the family. Parents differ enormously in the extent to which they care to discuss sexual matters with their children and in their plans for the proper timing of discussions of those topics they do intend to take up eventually. Television threatens to upset those plans, bringing into the home intergenerational tensions that would not otherwise have existed —or at least would not be so obvious. The traditional "birds and bees" talk between parent and child may not easily be deferred until the child reaches some point of passage in the life cycle such as the end of grammar school or the onset of puberty; terms such as "gay" and "hooker" occur commonly enough on United States television today that a certain number of children are bound to inquire as to what they mean. Some parents, themselves scarcely comfortable with street language, surely find this usage a source of unease; at best, the situation seems unlikely to render parent–child communication any smoother.

Money is the root of almost all commercial television, an industry that thrives by delivering sponsors' products to the eyes of potential consumers. One important target group is the children, who are exposed to many messages designed to instill a desire for various dolls, toys, games, and so forth. Although research on "consumer socialization" has not yet proceeded very far, a valid distinction seems possible between the orientations to the marketplace held by young children and more mature viewers. While adults see advertisements as rival claims in a competition for their limited financial resources, children interpret them more in terms of a "want-get" situation. That is, they have learned that to some extent they can get what they want; they do not have much money—indeed, few families could afford to buy their children all of the products that television advertisements induce them to desire—so their method of getting is to pressure their parents into buying things for them. The transaction becomes one of interpersonal affection rather than a commercial one; the child whose demands are indulged presumably is to feel more loved, while the deprived youngster draws an opposite inference. Ward and Wackman have opened up the study of the "family communication about consumption," to use their very neutral term, which is stimulated by television ads.[71] We might hypothesize that a good deal of this communication is rather tense and irascible.

The list above is based mainly on inferences from findings that previous researchers have not interpreted as indicators of family-conflict effects of television. Such a hypothesis is likely to arise only in a time when media effects on social units, rather than on isolated individuals, are coming to be considered.

DIVERSITY AND CONSTRAINT IN PUBLIC OPINION

A final suggested direction for new effects research is offered in the spirit of the Bicentennial of the American nation. The premise of our grand 1776–1976 pseudoevent was that we should reexamine the principles put forth by the Founding Fathers and consider how they can be renewed and extended today. In the area of mass communication, the most basic constitutional principle is that of freedom of the press. As Schramm has noted, Madison and Jefferson were concerned with "freedom from," while in the twentieth-century's preoccupation with social responsibilities of the media the stress is more upon "freedom for."[72] This attitude is more than an addition to the original intent; it is to a great extent a substitution. Freedom of the press *from* governmental constraints had, in principle, no particular goal other than to maximize the probability that a diversity of viewpoints would be able to vie in a "marketplace of ideas." A more content-specific view is taken today, in which the media are maintained as free institutions *for* the transmission of a variety of opinions; if some sides to a question lack access to the media, and thus to the public, current policy holds that access should be provided. In addition to obvious examples such as the "equal time" rule and the "fairness doctrine" in broadcast policy, many instances of efforts to maintain a competitive media system might be cited; competition, which is prized because it maximizes the chance for diversity, is thought to be thwarted by such phenomena as cross-media ownership, the one-newspaper city, media chains and networks, and other forms of consolidation and standardization.[73] The industry's plea in the face of complaints about these trends is generally that the news media's economic health, which is strengthened by business consolidations, is essential if they are to provide "common carrier" channels for diverse viewpoints—as they are expected to do under the "freedom for" approach.

The argument is an eternal one, resting in part upon untested assumptions about media effects. The criterion variable at stake is not any particular type of outcome but rather the total diversity of public opinion. The first premise, rather obscured in the financial and political debates in this age of Big Media, was that a wide range of viewpoints should find their way into public expression and thus be taken into account in the formulation of public opinion. This premise implies that the appropriate criterion for assessing the "effectiveness" of a media system would be the diversity—not the specific content—of viewpoints that are available to a wide audience via mass media and cognized and held by citizens. If the "fewness and bigness" which, Schramm notes, characterize today's news media exercise constraints over public opinion, these structural effects should manifest themselves in less diversity of media content and of public opinion.

Research on public opinion typically finds that a particular individual is rather consistent in political judgments across time, but considerable variation may be found from one individual to another on a topic at any given time. Given this finding, and the general value accorded to diversity of viewpoints in traditional democratic theory, to assess the "effectiveness" of the mass media solely by the extent to which they produce change within the same individual across time seems neither reasonable nor productive. Instead, we should expect to find assessments based on variation across individuals—that is, on diversity within the system as a whole.

A versatile measure of diversity has been available to communication researchers for several decades, in Shannon's definition of "entropy."[74] The uses of this tool for the study of human communication have been outlined by Weaver and have been considered explicitly for mass communication research by Schramm.[75] Shannon's measure of entropy (H) has several properties that make it potentially quite useful for assessment of system diversity. First, it is nondirectional; it can be applied to a set of nominal categories that are not themselves ordered in any evaluative way. Second, it yields a single summary estimate of diversity for each system at each point in time, and such estimates can be compared directly with one another. The computation of H for this purpose would require a set of mutually exclusive categories of public opinion that are as a group exhaustive of the total body of opinions possessed by the members of a system. While no such "perfect" opinion-content coding scheme has been devised, we have some reasonable approximations to it—close enough to permit some exploratory research at least.

The degree of entropy as measured by H is a function of two parameters of a set of categories: Entropy increases as the total number of categories increases; and entropy is greatest when as equal number of events falls into each of the several categories—decreasing to the extent that the number in one category exceeds that of another. These mathematical properties seem intuitively satisfying for an assessment of public opinion in terms of diversity. Greater diversity arises when the range of opinions is wider (more categories); less diversity is apparent when one or a few viewpoints dominate the scene (inequality of categories).

For example, in a highly popular war, little opposition is usually expressed, even via a "free" press. Only the one policy of fighting on to victory is to be found in people's opinions; diversity is zero. When the wisdom of a war policy is questioned, however, the range of alternatives may expand at least to two; one may approve the war or disapprove it. In the case of a limited war, such as the United States efforts in Korea and Vietnam, two "anti" positions are available: One may argue instead for all-out war or for complete withdrawal from hostilities. Opinion diversity, as measured by H, would be greater when three different positions are advocated by different citizens than if only two were advocated. And diversity would be greater the more nearly equable the numerical strengths of the different positions. If three positions were possible but one was accepted by no one, then from an empirical standpoint no more diversity would exist than if only two positions existed; use of the statistic H would reflect this empirical reality, since it takes no account of categories that are theoretically conceivable but that do not in fact occur with any frequency. A "far out" position held by only a very few people would not appreciably increase H as a measure of diversity.

The concept of a "community" need not be limited to the idea of a group of persons who reside in one locale. The mass media create their separate communities; for example, those who read newspapers (fewer than three of every four adult Americans) effectively constitute a separate community from those who rely mainly on television for their news. We might expect media subcommunities to differ from one another in terms of diversity of public opinion. For example, agenda-setting research has shown some differences between those who read one or another newspaper within the same city.[76] Use of H as a criterion variable shows some interesting effects of "media richness" on "agenda" measures in which the person is asked to identify the nation's (or state's) most important problem. A greater degree of entropy exists in communities that are served by *more than one* daily newspaper; in preliminary analysis of two large-scale surveys, this finding held up when the total population of the community was statistically controlled.[77] (Less difference in entropy occurs between one-newspaper towns and those with no daily, which suggests that this measure is indeed getting close to the issue of diversity itself.)

Questions about the nation's most important problem do not provide the optimal instrument for assessing diversity through the measurement of entropy, to be sure. Further, one cannot be certain that Shannon's H measure is sensitive enough to detect the subtle shadings of difference in the quality of public opinion that are at stake in the debate over the proper role of the press in a free society. The statistic has, however, proven itself capable of isolating differences in various kinds of media content, and its extension to the analysis of public opinion would enable researchers to address new hypotheses in the media-effects field.[78]

It would be possible to compare communities (or nations) that vary in their degree of control over media, or to examine much more thoroughly their media resources. Hypothetically, opinion entropy should be greater not only in media-rich locales but also where the press has greater freedom to present diverse viewpoints. Economic constraints could be assessed in the same fashion as legal and political constraints. The underlying "effects" proposition that some equivalence exists between media content and audience cognitions would also lead investigators to measure entropy in content, comparing locales with different politico-economic environments for their media. In all these cases, entropy should be stressed as an attribute of the community as a system; it need not extend to the level of the individual citizen, nor even to individual media, within that community. The collective diversity, across the many persons and media within a system, is at stake.

OVERVIEW

As is clear from both the review of recent trends and the speculation about future directions, this paper is grounded in the conviction that the mass media are indeed influential societal institutions. Historically, this original viewpoint was severely eroded in the 1940s and 1950s, when a belief that media effects are severely limited replaced the early fear of media domination.[79] Both conceptual broadening of the effects hypothesis and methodological advances that have refined our capacity for testing effects have contributed to a swing back. Noelle-Neumann has characterized this swing as a return to the image of "powerful media."[80] While no one should be so naive as to assume that whatever occurs in the mass media will immediately and thereafter color everyone's thinking, the limited-effects model provides an equally oversimplified image. Easy answers to the social questions raised by the growth of mass media cannot be arrived at from uncritical extensions of limited findings. They require the hard work of careful empirical analysis.[81]

NOTES

1. For a sociological analysis of the diffusion of mass media, see Melvin DeFleur, *Theories of Mass Communication.* New York: David McKay, 1966.
2. Consult Theodore Peterson, "The Social Responsibility Theory," in Fred S. Siebert, Theodore Peterson, and Wilbur Schramm, *Four Theories of the Press.* Urbana: University of Illinois Press, 1963.
3. Carl I. Hovland,   Arthur A. Lumsdaine,   and   Fred D. Sheffield, *Experiments on Mass Communication.* Princeton, N.J.: Princeton University Press,   1949;   Carl I. Hovland,   Irving L. Janis,   and Harold H. Kelley. *Communication and Persuasion.* New Haven: Yale University Press, 1953.
4. As examples: On credibility, Jack McLeod and Garrett O'Keefe, "The Socialization Perspective and Communication Behavior," in F. Gerald Kline and Phillip J. Tichenor, eds., *Current Perspectives in Mass Communication Research.* (Beverly Hills: Sage Publications, 1972; on persuasibility, Vernon A. Stone and James L. Hoyt, "The Emergence of Source-message Orientation as a Communication Variable," *Communication Research 1:* 89–109, 1974; on duration of effects, Steven H. Chaffee, "The Interpersonal Context of Mass Communication," in Kline and Tichenor, *op. cit.*
5. Fritz Machlup, *The Production and Distribution of Knowledge in the United States.* Princeton, N.J.: Princeton University Press, 1962.
6. Jon G. Udell, *The Growth of the American Daily Newspaper.* Madison, Wisc.: Bureau of Business Research and Service, University of Wisconsin, 1965. Newspaper production accounted for about 1.5 percent of manufactures, automobiles for 1.8 percent; meat products, drugs and medicines, lumber and many other industries ranked lower. Recent United States Department of Commerce figures show newspapers as the country's third largest source of employment, following the steel and auto industries (*U.S. Industrial Outlook,* January, 1976).
7. For a thoughtful discussion, see Wilbur Schramm, *Responsibility in Mass Communication.* New York: Harper & Bros., Ch. 9, 1957.
8. Wilbur Schramm, Jack Lyle, and Edwin B. Parker, *Television in the Lives of Our Children.* Stanford, Calif.: Stanford University Press, 1961.
9. Jack Lyle and Heidi Hoffman, "Children's Use of Television and Other Media." In Eli Rubinstein, George Comstock, and John Murray, *Televi-*

sion and Social Behavior, Volume IV. Television in Day-to-Day Life: Patterns of Use. Washington, D.C.: U.S. Government Printing Office, 1972.

10. For a comprehensive survey of current work in this area, see Jay G. Blumler and Elihu Katz, eds., The Uses of Mass Communications. Beverly Hills: Sage Publications, 1974.

11. Steven H. Chaffee and Fausto Izcaray, "Mass Communication Functions in a Media-rich Developing Society," Communication Research, 2: 367–395, 1975; Lee B. Becker, Jack M. McLeod, and Dean A. Ziemke. "Correlates of Media Gratifications," supplemental paper presented at roundtable discussion at American Association for Public Opinion Research convention, Asheville, N.C., 1976.

12. Paul K. Hatt and C. C. North, "Jobs and Occupations: A Popular Evaluation." In Reinhard Bendix and Seymour Martin Lipset, Class Status and Power. Glencoe: Free Press, 1953; Richard F. Carter and Bradley S. Greenberg. "Newspapers or Television: Which Do You Believe?", Journalism Quarterly, 42: 29–34, 1965; Schramm, Lyle, and Parker, op. cit.

13. An example is Bruce H. Westley and Werner Severin, "Some Correlates of Mass Media Credibility," Journalism Quarterly, 41: 325–335, 1964.

14. Hovland, Lumsdaine, and Sheffield, op.cit.

15. Heavy versus light exposure of children to televised violence, for example, was the basis for positive effects inferences in several studies reported in George Comstock and Eli Rubinstein, eds., Television and Social Behavior, Volume III. Television and Adolescent Aggressiveness. Washington, D.C.: U.S. Government Printing Office, 1972. Some success in predicting from heavy versus light viewing of television in general to stereotyped perceptions of society has been reported in George Gerbner and Larry P. Gross, "Living with Television: The Violence Profile," Journal of Communication, 26: 172–199, 1976.

16. Such nonexperimental methods as path analysis and cross-lagged panel correlation are discussed later in this paper. Consult Hubert M. Blalock, ed., Causal Models in the Social Sciences, Chicago: Aldine-Atherton, 1971, for a diverse set of perspectives.

17. A striking emphasis on informational uses of television is reported in Brenda Dervin and Bradley S. Greenberg, "The Communication Environment of the Urban Poor," in Kline and Tichenor, op. cit. See also Blumler and Katz, op. cit.

18. It has been pointed out that the study of media "uses and gratifications" through self-report and in a utilitarian framework probably biases both the results and their interpretation in the direction of overstating informational motivations. See James W. Carey and Albert L. Kreiling, "Popular Culture and Uses and Gratifications: Notes toward an Accommodation," in Blumler and Katz, op. cit.

19. An explicit learning model along these lines is presented as the conceptual basis for the studies reported in Hovland, Janis, and Kelley, op. cit.

20. Milton J. Rosenberg, "An Analysis of Affective-cognitive Consistency," in Rosenberg, Hovland, William J. McGuire, Robert P. Abelson, and

Jack W. Brehm, eds., *Attitude Organization and Change*, New Haven: Yale University Press, 1960. The appearance of this volume—based on models of cognitive inconsistency—in Hovland's Yale studies demonstrates that a sound research program can produce novel conceptual formulation.

21. Leon Festinger, *A Theory of Cognitive Dissonance*, Stanford, Calif.: Stanford University Press, 1957, especially chapters 4 and 5.
22. The discrepancy between these two types of effects is probably attributable to loose conceptualization of theoretical links between them and common causes in independent "variables" that are presented in the form of complex messages. See David R. Seibold, "Communication Research and the Attitude-verbal Report-overt Behavior Relationship: A Critique and Theoretic Reformulation," *Human Communication Research, 2:* 3–32, 1975; Steven J. Gross and C. Michael Niman, "Attitude-behavior Consistency: A review," *Public Opinion Quarterly, 39:* 358–368, 1975.
23. Herbert Hyman and Paul B. Sheatsley, "Some Reasons Why Information Campaigns Fail," *Public Opinion Quarterly, 11:* 412–423, 1947.
24. Harold Mendelsohn, "Some Reasons Why Information Campaigns Can Succeed," *Public Opinion Quarterly, 37:* 50–61, 1973; Dorothy F. Douglas, Bruce H. Westley, and Steven H. Chaffee, "An Information Campaign that Changed Community Attitudes," *Journalism Quarterly, 47:* 479–487, 492, 1970.
25. Hadley Cantril, Hazel Gaudet, and Herta Herzog, *The Invasion from Mars*, Princeton, N.J.: Princeton University Press, 1940.
26. The relationship between entertainment and other types of media content in preparing a society for organized social action is discussed in Charles R. Wright, "Functional Analysis and Mass Communications," *Public Opinion Quarterly, 24:* 605–620, 1960.
27. Donald J. McCrone and Charles F. Cnudde, "Toward a Communications Theory of Democratic Political Development: A Causal Model," *American Political Science Review, 61:* 72–79, 1967.
28. Wilbur Schramm, "Communications in Crisis," in Bradley S. Greenberg and Edwin B. Parker, eds., *The Kennedy Assassination and the American Public*, Stanford, Calif.: Stanford University Press, 1965.
29. James S. Coleman, *Community Conflict*, New York: Free Press, 1957.
30. George A. Donohue, Phillip J. Tichenor, and Clarice N. Olien, "Gatekeeping: Mass Media Systems and Information Control," in Kline and Tichenor, *op. cit.;* Tichenor, Jane M. Rodenkirchen, Olien, and Donohue, "Community Issues, Conflict, and Public Affairs Knowledge," in Peter Clarke, ed., *New Models for Mass Communication Research*, Beverly Hills: Sage Publications, 1973; Tichenor, Donohue, Olien, and J. K. Bowers, "Environment and Public Opinion," *Journal of Environmental Education, 2:* 38–42, 1971.
31. Olien, Donohue, and Tichenor, "The Community Editor's Power and the Reporting of Conflict," *Journalism Quarterly, 45,* 243–252, 1968. Conflict-avoidance in "shopper" newspapers that service local districts

within metropolitan areas is also stressed in Morris Janowitz, *The Community Press in an Urban Setting*, New York: Free Press, 1952.

32. Hovland, Lumsdaine, and Sheffield, *op. cit.*

33. This hypothesis is outlined in Chaffee, "Interpersonal Context," *op. cit.*

34. This global goal of the films was in fact not achieved, according to the findings of Hovland, Lumsdaine, and Sheffield; each film was rather successful in getting across its specific points and in modifying general attitudes toward the various peoples involved in the war, but the films had little or no effect on the individual soldier's eagerness to enter combat.

35. Robert B. Zajonc, "Attitudinal Effects of Mere Exposure," *Journal of Personality and Social Psychology, Monograph Supplement, 9*, 1–27, 1968. For similar findings using words as the objects of evaluation, see Steven H. Chaffee, "Salience and Pertinence as Sources of Value Change," *Journal of Communication, 17*, 25–38, 1967. The literature is reviewed in Michael L. Ray and Alan G. Sawyer, "Repetition in Media Models: a Laboratory Technique," *Journal of Marketing Research, 8*, 20–39, 1971.

36. Lee B. Becker and John C. Doolittle, "How Repetition Affects Evaluations of and Information Seeking about Candidates," *Journalism Quarterly, 52*, 611–617, 1975.

37. This statement is paraphrased from what is usually cited as the first appearance of the agenda-setting hypothesis, Bernard C. Cohen, *The Press and Foreign Policy*, Princeton, N.J.: Princeton University Press, 1963.

38. Maxwell E. McCombs and Donald L. Shaw, "The Agenda-setting Function of the Media," *Public Opinion Quarterly, 36*, 176–187, 1972; David Weaver, Maxwell E. McCombs, and Charles Spellman, "Watergate and the Media: A Case Study in Agenda-setting," *American Politics Quarterly, 3*, 458–472, 1975; Lee B. Becker, Maxwell E. McCombs, and Jack M. McLeod, "The Development of Political Cognitions," in Steven H. Chaffee, ed., *Political Communication*, Beverly Hills: Sage Publications, 1975.

39. Jack M. McLeod, Lee B. Becker, and James E. Byrnes, "Another Look at the Agenda-setting Function of the Press," *Communication Research, 1*, 131–166, 1974. For a comparison of the McCombs and McLeod approaches, see Becker, McCombs, and McLeod, *op. cit.*

40. Weaver, McCombs, and Spellman, *op. cit.*; McLeod and Becker, "Testing the Validity of Gratification Measures through Political Effects Analysis," in Blumler and Katz, *op. cit.*; Chaffee and Izcaray, *op. cit.*

41. Phillip J. Tichenor, George Donohue, and Clarice Olien, "Mass Media and Differential Growth in Knowledge," *Public Opinion Quarterly, 34*, 158–170; John T. McNelly and Julio Molina R., "Communication, Stratification and International Affairs Information in a Developing Urban Society," *Journalism Quarterly, 49*, 316–326, 339, 1972.

42. Examples include Tichenor, Rodenkirchen, Olien, and Donohue, *op. cit.*, and Douglas, Westley, and Chaffee, *op. cit.*

43. Albert Bandura, Dorothea Ross, and Sheila A. Ross, "Imitation of

Film-mediated Aggressive Models," *Journal of Abnormal and Social Psychology, 66,* 3–11, 1963.

44. Albert Bandura, "Social-learning Theory of Identificatory Processes," in D. A. Goslin, ed., *Handbook of Socialization Theory and Research,* Chicago: Rand McNally, 1969; Jack M. McLeod, Charles K. Atkin, and Steven H. Chaffee, "Adolescents, Parents and Television Use," in Comstock and Rubinstein, *op. cit.*

45. Percy H. Tannenbaum and Dolf Zillmann, "Emotional Arousal in the Facilitation of Aggression through Communication," in Leonard Berkowitz, ed., *Advances in Experimental Social Psychology, Vol. VIII,* New York: Academic Press, 1975; Zillmann, James L. Hoyt, and Kenneth D. Day, "Strength and Duration of the Effect of Aggressive, Violent, and Erotic Communications on Subsequent Aggressive Behavior," *Communication Research, 1,* 286–306, 1974.

46. An attempt to organize the major variables in social learning from television into a single theoretical scheme is presented in Chaffee and Albert Tims, "The Psychology behind the Effect," a chapter in George Comstock *et al., The Fifth Season: How Television Influences Human Behavior* (in preparation, Rand Corporation).

47. Perhaps the best example of the use of this model is Rosenberg *et al., op. cit.*

48. Seymour Feshbach, "Reality and Fantasy in Filmed Violence," in John Murray, Eli Rubinstein, and George Comstock, eds., *Television and Social Behavior, Vol. II. Television and Social Learning,* Washington, D.C.: U.S. Government Printing Office, 1972.

49. McLeod, Atkin, and Chaffee, *op. cit.;* John M. Neale and Robert M. Liebert, *Science and Behavior,* Englewood Cliffs, N.J.: Prentice-Hall, 1973, pp. 110–112.

50. John C. Doolittle, "Immunizing Children against the Possible Antisocial Effects of Viewing Television Violence: A School Intervention Curriculum," Ph.D. dissertation, Univerity of Wisconsin, 1975.

51. An attempt to manipulate perceived reality as a means of heightening sex-role learning has been reported by Suzanne Pinegree in "The Effects of Non-sexist Television Commercials and Perceptions of Reality on Children's Attitudes toward Women," a paper presented to International Communication Association convention, Portland, Oregon, 1976.

52. Hovland, Lumsdaine, and Sheffield, *op.cit.*

53. Hovland, Janis, and Kelley, *op. cit.;* Hovland, ed., *The Order of Presentation in Persuasion,* New Haven: Yale University Press, 1957; Hovland and Janis, eds., *Personality and Persuasibility,* New Haven: Yale University Press, 1959; Rosenberg *et al., op. cit.* The typical "laboratory" in these studies was a high school or (more often) college classroom, where different experimental conditions could easily be created in self-administered protocols.

54. Hovland, "Reconciling Conflicting Results Derived from Experimental and Survey Studies of Attitude Change," *American Psychologists, 14,* 8–17, 1959.

55. Jerome L. Singer, ed., *The Control of Aggression and Violence:*

Cognitive and Physiological Factors, New York: Academic Press, 1971, Chapter 2.

56. See, for example, Liebert, "Television and Social Learning: Some Relationships between Viewing Violence and Behaving Aggressively (Overview)," in Murray, Rubinstein, and Comstock, *op. cit.;* Chaffee, "Television and Adolescent Aggressiveness (Overview)," in Comstock and Rubinstein, *op. cit.*

57. This method can be traced back to Sewall Wright, "The method of Path Coefficients," *Annals of Mathematical Statistics, 5,* 161–215, 1934; its current ascendance in sociology began with Hubert M. Blalock, *Causal Inferences in Nonexperimental Research,* Chapel Hill: University of North Carolina Press, 1964.

58. McCrone and Cnudde, *op. cit.;* Michael E. Bishop, "Media Use and Democratic Political Orientation in Lima, Peru," *Journalism Quarterly, 50,* 60–67, 101, 1973; Marilyn Jackson-Beeck and Chaffee, "Family Communication, Mass Communication, and Differential Political Socialization," paper presented to International Communication Association convention, Chicago, 1975. The latter results are summarized in Chaffee *et al.,* "Mass Communication in Political Socialization," in Stanley Renshon, ed., *Handbook of Political Communication,* New York: Academic Press, forthcoming 1977.

59. R. M. Rozelle and Donald T. Campbell, "More Plausible Rival Hypotheses in the Cross-lagged Panel Correlation Technique," *Psychological Bulletin, 71,* 74–80, 1969. See also David R. Heise, "Causal Inference from Panel Data," in Edgar F. Borgatta and George W. Bohrnstedt, eds., *Sociological Methodology 1970,* San Francisco: Jossey-Bass, 1970.

60. Schramm, Lyle, and Parker, *op. cit.*

61. Monroe M. Lefkowitz, Leonard D. Eron, Leopold O. Walder, and L. Rowell Ruesmann, "Television Violence and Child Aggression: A Followup Study," in Comstock and Rubinstein, *op. cit.*

62. Chaffee, L. Scott Ward, and Leonard P. Tipton, "Mass Communication and Political Socialization," *Journalism Quarterly, 47,* 647–659, 666, 1970.

63. In path-analytic terms, a two-time cross-lagged model is "underidentified," because it lacks sufficient information to test the causal path represented by the coefficient between the Time 1 independent variable and the Time 2 dependent variable. See Otis Dudley Duncan, "Some Linear Models for Two-wave, Two-variable Panel Analysis, With One-way Causation and Measurement Error," in Blalock, *op. cit., 1971.*

64. Leonard Berkowitz, *Aggression: A Social Psychological Analysis,* New York: McGraw-Hill, 1962.

65. Weaver, McCombs, and Spellman, *op. cit.;* McLeod and Becker, *op. cit.*

66. Peter Clarke and F. Gerald Kline, "Media Effects Reconsidered: Some New Strategies for Communication Research," *Communication Research, 1,* 224–240, 1974; Kline, Peter V. Miller, and Andrew J. Morrison, "Adolescents and Family Planning Information: An Exploration of Audience Needs and Media Effects," in Blumler and Katz, *op. cit.;*

Chaffee, "Contingent Orientations and the Effects of Political Communication," paper presented to Speech Communication Association convention, New York, 1973. A slightly different approach is to assess the person's degree of involvement with different topics and then to predict differential experimental effects for differing involvement orientations. For examples, see Michael L. Rothschild and Michael L. Ray, "Involvement and Political Advertising Effect: An Exploratory Experiment," *Communication Research, 1,* 264–285, 1974; Lawrence Bowen and Chaffee, "Product Involvement and Pertinent Advertising Appeals," *Journalism Quarterly, 51,* 613–621, 1974.

67. Schramm, Lyle, and Parker, *op. cit.*
68. Bradley S. Greenberg, Philip M. Ericson, and Mantha Vlahos, "Children's Television Behaviors as Perceived by Mother and Child," in Rubinstein, Comstock, and Murray, *op. cit.*
69. Schramm, Lyle, and Parker, *op. cit.*
70. Lyle and Hoffman, *op. cit.*
71. Scott Ward and Daniel Wackman, "Family and Media Influences on Adolescent Consumer Learning," *American Behavioral Scientist, 14,* 415–427, 1971.
72. Schramm, *Responsibility, op. cit.*
73. Since early in this century, the number of daily newspapers in the United States has declined steadily; a corresponding increase has occurred in the number of one-newspaper cities; in addition, historical trends point toward single business operations for competing papers, consolidation of independent newspapers into chains, and ownership of newspapers by businesses that also own other media outlets in the same markets. These trends have given rise to attempts to assess the impact of competitive factors on press content, but to date this effort has not been extended to effects analysis. For examples, see Raymond B. Nixon and Robert L. Jones, "The Content of Non-competitive vs. Competitive Newspapers," *Journalism Quarterly, 33,* 299–314, 1956; Guido Stempel III, "Effects on Performance of a Cross-Media Monopoly," *Journalism Monographs,* No. 21, 1973; David H. Weaver and L. E. Mullins, "Content and Format Characteristics of Competing Daily Newspapers," *Journalism Quarterly, 52,* 257–264, 1975.
74. Claude E. Shannon and Warren Weaver, *The Mathematical Theory of Communication,* Urbana: University of Illinois Press, 1949.
75. Shannon and Weaver, *op. cit.;* Schramm, "Information Theory and Mass Communication," *Journalism Quarterly, 32,* 131–146, 1955.
76. McLeod, Becker, and Byrnes, *op. cit.*
77. Steven H. Chaffee and Donna Wilson, "Media Rich, Media Poor: Two Studies of Diversity in Agenda-holding," paper presented to Association for Education in Journalism convention, College Park, Maryland, 1976.
78. A recent example is James H. Watt and Robert Krull, "An Information Theory Measure for Television Programming," *Communication Research, 1,* 44–68, 1974.
79. Joseph T. Klapper, *The Effects of Mass Communication,* New York: Free Press, 1960.

80. Elisabeth Noelle-Neumann, "Return to the Concept of the Powerful Mass Media," in H. Equchi and K. Sata, eds., *Studies of Broadcasting,* 9: 67–112 (1973). For a thorough rejection of the limited-effects position in the area of political communication, see Sidney Kraus and Dennis Davis, *The Effects of Mass Communication on Political Behavior,* State College, Pa.: Pennsylvania State University Press, 1976.
81. Preparation of this paper was partially supported by a grant from the Wisconsin Alumni Research Foundation, through the Graduate School of the University of Wisconsin. The author thanks John T. McNelly for his helpful comments on an earlier draft.

Popular Culture

HIDETOSHI KATO

WHY "POPULAR CULTURE"?

"Popular culture" is an ambiguous term because every "culture"—defined by anthropologists as a "way of life" or "design for living"—is a system of a people's shared experience which, by definition, must be "popular." Therefore, "popular culture" sounds tautological. Just as culture is with us and inside us, so is "popular culture." I feel that "popular culture" is essentially synonymous with "culture," and that "popular culture research" should be placed as a branch of cultural anthropology. Indeed, the *subject matter* which so-called popular culturalists deal with is the elements of a culture which can be easily identified and located, for instance, in the index of the Human Relations Area File (HRAF) compiled by G. Murdock. Indeed, in the past, whenever I wrote papers and essays on culture, including "popular culture," I used to consult with the HRAF for resource materials. Theoretically, as well as practically, I see no reason why "popular culture" cannot be treated simply as "culture."

However, for several historical reasons, "popular culture" and its research had to be distinguished, though vaguely, from "culture" and its research. In the first place, anthropological tradition in the past century defined itself as a discipline devoted *solely* to preliterate, tribal cultures, such as those of Native Americans or those in Oceania, Africa, and so forth. Anthropologists concentrated their efforts on studies of kin relationships, rituals, artifacts, languages, and many other aspects of "primitive" cultures; they consciously avoided work on "complex" societies. A few adventurous anthropologists (Ruth Benedict, Margaret Mead, Rhoda Metraux, Geoffrey Gorer, and others) were brave enough to conduct research on complex societies, especially in the 1940s, but they remained a marginal minority. A cynic may tend to wonder if "civilized" cultures were a taboo for anthropology. But for many good reasons, anthropologists avoided dealing with highly complex societies such as industrial societies. An anthropologist who specialized in the material culture of a tribe in central Africa once told me that the number of artifacts made and used in that particular culture was about thirty to fifty (simple clothing, ornaments, weapons, utensils, and so on). He added that in a department store in Tokyo, some 500,000 kinds of merchandise were coded in their computer. The implication was that the study of material culture in an industrialized, civilized, and highly complex society like Japan, using the methods of traditional anthropology, was almost impossible. Indeed, an anthropologist (or folklorist) will not find much difficulty in accumulating, classifying, and analyzing fifty oral traditions found in a preliterate tribal society, but he or she will feel quite desperate to work on millions of folk tales (such as movies, television programs, detective stories, and so forth) produced and distributed in a highly industrialized and commercialized society. Thus, anthropologists' avoidance of complex societies was probably wise. The study of cultures of contemporary civilized society thus came to be relegated by anthropologists to sociologists.

Modern sociology, however, also showed little interest in the cultural aspects of complex societies because, by tradition and definition, sociology has been concerned primarily with social relations and social structures. "Popular culture," which was implicitly defined as the culture of complex participant societies, did not attract much attention from sociologists. Sociologists who stressed the arrival of "mass society" did become aware of the importance of "mass culture." Such sociologists as Ortega y Gasset, David Riesman, Leo Lowenthal, and others paid much attention to "popular culture" or "mass culture," but the majority of sociologists did not follow such leads. As a result, "popular culture" as a *social phenomena* and a *problem area* was neglected by modern anthropology as well as by sociology.

Then, a group of scholars and intellectuals became interested in filling this vacuum. They were, as far as the American scene was concerned, scholars in literature and arts. These people were perceptive enough to investigate the significance of new literary and artistic genres appreciated by the millions, genres whose characteristics were fundamentally different from "pure" arts or "highbrow" literature. They thought that a study of Mickey Spillane detective stories was as important as a study of James Joyce, and a critical treatise of Coca-Cola advertisements had a social significance equivalent to one on Da Vinci. So, they went on to study Walt Disney, science fiction, *Playboy* magazine, Beatles comic books, Woolworth merchandise, and any other new art form with popular appeal. Their approaches to the *problem area* have been so liberal and provocative that they demonstrated its importance, though some social scientists have criticized their lack of proper methodology and their tendency to become subjective and impressionistic, sometimes even dogmatic.

A tragedy in past popular-culture research is that social scientists did not have much contact with people in art and literature, and vice versa. Indeed, "popular culture" is the *problem area* which should be approached by interdisciplinary or (transdisciplinary) efforts involving such disciplines as anthropology, sociology, social psychology, history, and folklore, as well as the arts and literature. *Popular-culture-oriented* sociologists, art historians, literary critics, economists, architects, and so forth, may be at work, but for me to see a person self-defined as a pure "popular culturist" is rather difficult. A "popular culturist" cannot lack his or her own "home discipline." Popular culture is a *social phenomenon* and a *problem area* to which inter-disciplinary efforts have to be applied. As suggested in the preceding paragraphs, I hesitate to look at "popular-culture research" as an independent discipline, and to label anyone as a *pure* "popular culturist." The only exception I might admit are professionals whose major interest is the study of cultures—that is, anthropologists of a special breed. Even they probably would not like to be called "popular culturists" but would rather be known as cultural anthropologists whose interest is in complex societies.

COMMUNICATION RESEARCH AND POPULAR CULTURE

Among other disciplines involved in popular-culture research, a group of scholars has specialized in communication research. Since culture (including popular culture) is a shared experience of the majority of a people, and since the only means by which an experience is shared is communication in its broadest sense, communication research had to play an important and indispensable role in the studies of cultures. As a matter of fact, such scholars as Gregory Bateson and Jurgen Ruesch argued that a culture *is* a set of communication processes. For example, in America, as well as in many industrial societies, certain television programs are watched by millions of people. The messages carried by the program may be the reflection of the value system of the society; at the same time, such messages may contribute to the shaping or reinforcement of such a value system. Indeed, communication *organizes* and *maintains* a culture and the values characteristic of that culture. The media employed in the processes of communication may be divergent. They involve both verbal and nonverbal, discursive and presentational symbols. But a series of communication is what makes a culture possible. The communication between parents and children, teachers and students, among peer group members and community members is the means by which values are transmitted and a culture is integrated. *Communication* makes a culture possible.

The term *communication* must be used broadly enough to include all forms of human interaction—from proxemics to highly sophisticated uses of symbols, from tribal oral tradition to satellite broadcasting. Only by expanding the definition and scope of communication can communication research contribute adequately to the study of cultures. Those engaged in the study of cultures, including popular culture, are in need of more such input from communication research. Actually, modern communication research, from its beginning, paid attention to popular-culture phenomena either explicitly or implicity.

For instance, in his classic work *Radio and the Printed Page* (1940), Paul Lazarsfeld tried to see what kind of radio *program* reached what kind of *audience* for what *reasons* and with what *effects*. His primary concern was to examine the possible use of radio as a new medium of education and learning, but he found that people were much more interested in listening to entertainment programs such as serial drama or quiz programs. Indeed, according to his survey, American people at that time spent some five hours listening to daily serials and less than thirty minutes listening to educational programs (home economics, religious, and so on) per week on the average, and ironically, those who belonged to lower income brackets, for whom education was most needed, did not attend to "serious" programs. Apparently, the daily serials, quiz shows, and other forms of new entertainment brought about by radio were a part of the new popular culture. The heroes and heroines of popular daily drama became a common concern of the mass audience. Indeed, the *Radio Research* series edited by Lazarsfeld and Stanton and published in the 1940s can be seen as an effort to investigate *why* people like entertainment programs rather than educational or instructional ones; out of these efforts came such insightful studies as Herta Herzog's "Motivation and Gratification of Daily Serial Listeners."

Wilbur Schramm also has been very attentive to popular-culture phenomena and never forgot the popular-culture aspect in communication research. He included the best media studies with popular-culture orientation—such as Herzog's radio research, Katherine Wolfe and Marjorie Fiske's comic study, and the readership study by Douglas Waples and others—in his *Process and Effects of Mass Communication* under the heading of "The Primary Effect" subtitled "Why They Attend to Mass Communication." Though he did not use the terms "popular culture" or "mass culture" often, he wanted to observe and analyze *why* people like entertainment transmitted by mass media. He has been aware of the fact that mass communicators tended to "adopt what has been called 'lowest common denominator' approach" and thus created a communication environment where "a very large proportion of attention to the mass media is to material which indexes itself as entertainment, or to picture and other spectacular material which offers relatively easy going and high levels of excitement."

Apparently mass media, especially electronic media, had great impact upon the nature and structure of cultures everywhere in the world. Many research reports revealed that, ever since the introduction of radio and television, the behavior pattern, assumptions, and views of the world and the whole life-style of many peoples have changed drastically. Daniel Lerner, for example, discovered tremendous sociocultural changes which took place in the village life of the Middle East after radio was introduced. The villagers became more attentive to urban information and showed less interest, if not less trust, in traditional authorities such as the village chief; thus they acquired what Lerner called "psychic mobility." His brilliant book *The Passing of Traditional Society* actually dealt with a series of cultural *revolutions* rather than mere *changes* brought about by new communication and transportation devices. A new communication technology makes a new communication system which makes a new perspective for a culture. The printing machine invented by Gutenberg in 1450 contributed, as many scholars have shown, to the shaping of a society and culture where exploration of inner self, such as the Protestant ethic, was encouraged. Electronically processed sight and sound, such as movies and television, are now building a new era in communication as well as in the outlook of cultures affected, if not dominated, by such new media.

At this point, we must face another semantic problem in reference to the usage of the term "popular culture" as distinct from "culture" at large. In conventional usage, "popular culture" seems to denote mainly the entertainment aspect of media. Education is an element of any culture, but most of us would not include education as a part of "popular culture." Popular culture is, in our perception, something entertaining, amusing, fun, exciting, and sensational. Best-selling detective stories are popular culture, but government publications are not. "Bonanza," "Hawaii Five-O," and many other programs being broadcast in prime time by commercial stations are popular culture, but instructional programs of educational televison channels are not. "Disneyland" is popular culture, but physical education given at schools is not. Science fiction is popular culture, but textbooks on chemistry are not. The distinction between the two culture elements in contemporary society, therefore, seems to be in the fact (or the assumption) that popular culture is full of fun while non-popular culture lacks the fun element.

The very fact that new electronic media is heavily loaded by the fun element involved contemporary communication research in popular-culture research. As a matter of fact, many studies published under the label of popular culture are essentially media studies with special emphasis on the fun element. Since media became so familiar to us all, and since most of us became captives of what Martha Wolfenstein once called "fun morality," media study in terms of popular culture itself became very popular not only among communication researchers but also among literary and artistic critics.

Popular culture is a problem area where many disciplines can meet; such interdisciplinary ventures can be most stimulating and promising. For example, the impact of television has been one of the most urgent and serious topics in communication research in the past two decades. During the course of survey and research in this field, researchers felt that more intensive and extensive collaborations with educators, critics, psychologists, and broadcasters were needed. A reader glancing at any bibliography on this subject will be struck by the variety of approaches and disciplines represented. Television, technically speaking, is simply a new means of mass communication. But its sociocultural implication is so broad and profound that it requires vast intellectual cooperation, and such collaborative efforts are still in their beginning.

PROBLEMS OF VALUES

Popular-culture research as an interdisciplinary venture is extremely inviting and promising, but at the same time it holds many traps and dangers. First, discussions of popular-culture phenomena are heavily loaded with value judgments, and even within my limited knowledge, many people are emotionally involved in the values of popular culture. Popular culture, like other problem areas of social sciences, is a social fact about which a series of objective and value-free investigations is needed, but many people talk about popular culture in terms of "pro and con." Certain groups of intellectuals like to see themselves as a new breed of quasi-populists. In their minds, popular culture is unconditionally good because it entertains the mass of people, who are unconditionally good. They defend sex, violence, commercialism, new fads and fashions, and whatever is problematic on the basis that, after all, these topics are the people's choice—and the people are always right. On the other extreme of the continuum, another group of intellectuals attack popular culture by saying that its materials are so bad in their artistic taste that they would not only degenerate but also endanger the public. This group of intellectuals are also the people who see a crisis in "high culture." Sometimes, they tend to try to show their viewpoint by, for instance, what Reuel Denney once called "conspicuous nonownership of TV."

In my personal observation, however, both groups share two characteristics in common—that is, elitism and snobbery. For those who attack popular culture, no explanation may be necessary, because they are the explicit defenders of "highbrow"culture. The quasi-populists are somewhat complicated. They are often the people who are simply against traditional elitism, and therefore they may be "anti-snob-snob." After all, in either case, those who have been disputing over popular-culture phenomena are intellectuals; they have thus excluded themselves from those who are actually involved in popular culture solely as audience or spectators. Either pro or con, the people who speak about popular culture are not a part of it. They are outsiders. The only difference between the two groups is a matter of taste. Unfortunately, many intellectual endeavors were wasted in pro-or-con, good-or-bad assumptions. Popular culture is a problem area where deep prejudices are confronting each other with more or less emotional tones.

Second, in the study of popular culture, we do not have much methodological consensus nor is much effort being made to establish such consensus. In the United States, scholars in literature and arts discovered and tried to fill the intellectual vacuum. Their approaches to popular-culture phenomena, which were essentially descriptive and often subjective, cannot persuade social scientists who are looking for data which can be objectively verified. At the same time, social scientists, including communication researchers, suffer difficulties in finding appropriate analytical methods and techniques in certain areas of investigation. For instance, the content analysis of television programs is extremely difficult because of the nature of the medium. In traditional content analysis, dealing with verbal symbols—counting frequencies of key words, sentences, or themes—was a common practice. But a television program is audiovisual and nondiscursive, with color and sound; how can a researcher identify the meaningful "unit"? Even such classification or categorization as "educational" program can be disputable, especially in a country where broadcasting is a commercial business and where broadcasters use the term "educational" to defend themselves.

Furthermore, "effect" study of popular culture, or media at large, is extremely complicated. In a "media-saturated" society like the United States or Japan, one cannot isolate a single message to see its effect on the people in an experimental situation. People are exposed to various media messages, and we cannot make any definitive cause-and-effect statement vis-à-vis, for instance, a particular television program and juvenile delinquency. In Japanese juvenile court, youths who committed crimes tended to attribute their conduct to television; that is, youths often said that a certain television program had *motivated* them to commit crimes. But such statements often are doubtful, because these young people may be using violence and other criminal models depicted in television programs as scapegoats to justify their innocence. Certain meaningful correlations, with many intermediate variables, may be detected between a program and the behavioral characteristics of its audience. But we cannot say that the program was a *cause* and the behavior of a certain segment of the audience was its *effect*.

In the study of dissemination of a particular news item, such as President Kennedy's assassination, a researcher can trace the flow of information by asking people how and when they learned the news.

By doing so, a study in communication process can be established. But the contents of the entertainment programs broadcast at prime time are so diffuse and ambiguous that even to identify their messages is difficult. In terms of methodology, we must admit that popular-culture research is still somewhat chaotic, and the disciplines involved in this field, including communication research, are sometimes conflicting rather than cooperating.

Third, especially in the American context, certain ethical values, such as puritanical values, are another source which prevents objective and proper study of entertainment-loaded media. From the viewpoint of puritanical work ethics, entertainments usually have negative value; therefore, American researchers experience, either consciously or unconsciously, moral or ethical constraints in spite of the prevailing "fun morality." Again, value judgments precede, or preoccupy, the studies in entertainment aspects of mass media. Indeed, very often, the term "popular culture" is itself a value terminology. One can stay calm and neutral with the use of terms such as "nuclear physics" or even "voting behavior," but we tend to be more or less emotionally involved whenever somebody uses the term "popular culture." So-called popular culturists often accelerate such emotional involvement by their writings.

Finally, a danger has existed that when we discuss popular culture, many of us neglect *people orientation.* An art critic may develop his or her thinking out of meanings grasped almost intuitively from popular-culture materials, for instance, "Superman." In other words, a critic is often contented to explore only what popular culture *means to him or her,* and does not try to see what it means *to people.* The critic can make inferences, but very often such inferences are not based on empirical efforts. The *people* play the most important role in popular-culture issues—how *people* react, perceive, and use certain popular culture materials is *the problem.* But "popular culturists" have tendencies not to be much interested in people who are actually the *users.* Many value statements made about popular-culture phenomena do not represent the interests and values of the people. They are, very often, value statements by individual critics.

TOWARD A COMPARATIVE APPROACH

Popular-culture research as it stands now holds numerous pitfalls and even dangers. However, we should not stop inquiries into this problem area. What we need now is a new perspective and a new approach to popular-culture phenomena.

At the outset of this article, I stressed that, theoretically speaking, no distinction need be made between "culture" and "popular culture," and further suggested that the latter might be a subcategory of the former, and that the core of popular-culture research should be cultural anthropology combined with communication research and other disciplines. Personally, I would like to see more inputs from anthropology into this particular area of intellectual inquiry.

Indeed, seen from the anthropological viewpoint, popular culture is as old as the history of mankind. For example, according to some of the historical (even archaeological) findings, graffiti were left in ancient shrines by artisans who worked on the construction. All of us are familiar with graffiti in the subways, the school cafeterias, and the washrooms of contemporary societies, but graffiti as a strange form of self-expression has at least several thousands years of history. The cave painting of the neolithic age had, as archaeologists tell us, a magical function but, at the same time, these paintings might have held an embryo of the play element. Peoples of the world have been very inventive and imaginative in creating their own cultures. They designed their own houses with certain decorative motifs, composed their own music and songs, created ornamental artifacts, and systematized their fantasies into mythology and folk tales which were transmitted from generation to generation through oral tradition. All these acts were "popular culture," too.

In my opinion, the assumption that "popular culture" is exclusively a product of modern industrial society is misleading. Wherever and whenever people have lived, they have created a popular culture of their own. Folktales and legends told by the village chief to the children of a tribal community are different in many respects from cartoon programs on television watched by millions of children of our society, but as far as the socializing of fantasies is concerned, these two forms of communication are fundamentally the same. Children's popular culture in the tribal society and in the United States today are *comparable*.

Many rural communities in Asia, Africa, and elsewhere have theater performances. The theater buildings may be very primitive, and the performances may seem very naive. But the emotional involvement of the audience can be comparable with that of the Broadway musical theater. I would like to encourage a series of such analogies for comparative research on popular culture in the future.

One may argue that popular culture in its narrowest sense is peculiar to advanced societies where mass media dominate and that such communication as oral tradition belongs to "folk culture" which is basically different from electronic media. But probably more similarities than differences exist, more continuities than discontinuities occur. From 1974 to 1976, I was privileged to conduct an annual "comparative popular-culture seminar" at the East-West Communication Institute under the directorship of Wilbur Schramm and Jack Lyle. During these sessions, I shared a firm belief with many participants from Asia, the Pacific, and North America that common people in each culture are alike in their inventiveness in shaping and using a popular culture of their own. As a matter of fact, newer electronic media in many developing countries today were found to be merely new technologies to transmit messages and values indigenous in each culture. We cannot assume that, because of the introduction of universal new media, popular culture all over the world is becoming a monoculture, creating what Marshall McLuhan called the "global village."

Frankly speaking, American "popular culturists" have tended to see popular culture as essentially an American phenomena and to neglect the fact that each society has its own popular culture with which American popular culture can be compared. For instance, in a comparative study of communication and sociability, the Iranian coffee shop, the Malaysian community hall, the American cocktail party, the Japanese tea ceremony, Fijian kava drinking, and many other institutionalized gatherings in many diverse societies were shown to have similar functions, in spite of their apparent differences.

As many anthropologists have suggested, the comparative approach is the method through which a culture is best understood. The characteristics of Japanese culture, for instance, can best be revealed when some aspects of the culture are compared with those of other cultures, whether they are Chinese, American, Indonesian, or British. The same principle must be applicable to the studies of popular cultures. In order to understand the popular culture of a country, one should look for comparable data in other cultures. Popular culture as a social phenomenon is *not* so peculiar to particular societies as one might be tempted to imagine. Any society has its own popular culture, and popular cultures of the world, despite differences in the stages of economic development and in social system, are comparable. We will be struck, if we take that comparative approach, by both diversities and regularities in the lives of all peoples. Such discoveries are a most encouraging source of intellectual joy, which leads us to a deep trust in humanity.

The term "popular culture" is itself frequently an emotional bomb. But if we become aware of the existence (or coexistence) of popular cultures throughout the world—and if we can appreciate the wisdom of the peoples crystallized in each of their popular cultures—then we shall be able to look at popular culture with less prejudice and more understanding.

Communication and Policy

Communication Research and Its Applications: A Postscript

PAUL F. LAZARSFELD

Paul F. Lazarsfeld responded enthusiastically to our invitation to contribute to this book. He had just written a paper for *An Introduction to Applied Sociology* (1975), in which he had devoted several pages to a resume of an important proposal by Wilbur Schramm to the newly created Ford Foundation. He wrote us describing his plans to write of the exegesis of this Schramm report and its consequences.

Paul Lazarsfeld died in 1976 before he could complete his considered tribute to Schramm. With all of the scholarly world, we mourn the passing of this creative man, who did so much to shape the half-century of communication research appraised in this book. We are gratified to have even this brief postscript from "PFL." We trust that the guidelines he provides will help improve the future contributions of communication research to society.—*The Editors.*

At which points do there characteristically arise obstacles to the utilization of research in the formation of policy? For which kinds of practical problems is the use of applied social science presently pointless, and for which kinds is it extremely useful, if not indispensable? Does the role of research practitioner differ when he is part of a research staff attached to an operating organization and when he is in a research agency independent of the client organization? How does the researcher come to reformulate the practical problems of the policymaker so that an investigation appropriate to the problem can be designed?

The fact is that we are only now beginning to learn something of the actual, rather than the supposed or ideal, relations between basic and applied social research. These would be clarified by training seminars centered on reports of actual cases of research applied to policy by practitioners who took part in the research. They would present a compact factual memorandum on the case including materials on the research organization, its formal and informal relations with the policy-makers in question, the form in which the policy problem was originally put, and the apparent expectations of the client regarding the nature of the research and the uses to which it might be put. The student members of the seminar, working as teams of two or three, prepare a research brief bearing on the case. The seminar meetings themselves represent a kind of clinical session, where the practitioner indicates, serially and piecemeal, what he did in fact do, comparing this with the suggestions set forth in the briefs of the students. Students come progressively to see that policy-oriented research involves a sequence of choices among alternative research decisions which might have been taken. They learn something of the way in which practice differs from theory, not in the ignorant sense of that phrase (which implies that theory is somehow inferior to practicality), but in the significant sense that considerations other than those expressed in an abstract theory need to be taken into account when research is oriented toward questions of policy.

. . .The newly created Ford Foundation had a Division 5 (now defunct) which was dedicated to the behavioral sciences—a term created by the planning committee for that division. Its director, Bernard Berelson, was aware that the planning committee had urged the Foundation to sponsor "immediate studies of the current application of the knowledge of human behavior and of feasible means for extending such applications." He commissioned Wilbur Schramm to write an appropriate proposal. Schramm, one of the pioneers in communications research, was at the time directing a communications department at Stanford and had wide practical experience in public service and private consultation. He chose an advisory committee; among its members were a staff member of Rand, a representative of the Michigan Group Dynamics Center, and the president of a major advertising agency. One of the two sociologists on the committee was Donald Young, who, as the director of the Russell Sage Foundation, represented their traditional interest in application and who had also been chairman of the study group which had sponsored the Lyons

Report . . . .It was Schramm's intention to advise the Foundation about modes of advancing the complex activities of applying science to problems of human behavior. The term "utilization process" reappears throughout the memorandum. It contains a chapter on past accomplishments, but contrary to the usual cliché, Schramm stresses that a decreasing rate of success is to be expected as applications are made in fields of increasing complexity. An interesting section lists 21 rules that might help to advance utilization; rules 10 to 18 deal especially with the interplay between research and user. The document reports interviews with participants on both sides. Especially valuable are pages 19–27, which reproduce a speech by Samuel Stouffer not published elsewhere.

The final 25 pages contain the recommendations to the Ford Foundation. Cleverly, the author first discusses five reasons why they might not enter the field: the problem is not urgent; there is no solution in sight anyhow; other sources of financing are available; it is too expensive for the results obtainable; and finally, it could get the Foundation into public-relations problems.

After refuting these arguments, preliminary proposals are made, always stressing that only slow progress can be expected and that, therefore, no large expenditures are recommended. Two general objectives are envisioned:

1. More effective relationships between the custodians of behavioral science knowledge and the individuals and groups responsible for its application in society.

2. Better understanding of the social problem and process of applying scholarship to action—its mechanisms and methods, uses and needs, and conditions which limit its effectiveness.

A great variety of concrete tasks which deserve support are listed. Training is, of course, one, including analysis of "cases," the collection of which might be especially commissioned. Interestingly, very high priority is given to the "identification and classification of action problems in behavioral fields," the lack of which is felt by many authors, including ourselves. Schramm proposes machinery to attain this goal. It is imaginative but quite complicated, which might explain why no single author has yet succeeded (pp. 88–90). The culminating need is "research on utilization as a process in society." The mood of the Schramm report and its affinity to the war experience is best represented by this passage:

The Foundation may be able in the future to specify and commission experimental research, but it is far more likely to have to wait for a promising situation and proposal, and then back a man. In time it should be possible to support a program of research on the utilization process as sophisticated as Hovland's program on persuasive communication at Yale, but there is now no Hovland interested in doing such a program. And it may well be that the time is not ripe. Preliminary case studies, statement of rough propositions, training of middleman—all will help to prepare the way.

The Schramm document was never published in full. Parts of it are reproduced in Part III of the Reuss Committee report but without the recommendations to the Ford Foundation. It also does not contain the statements by experts, which is understandable, because this committee itself collected expert opinion. The reprinted parts, however, contain Schramm's 21 rules and are therefore still valuable.

Shortly after this memo was submitted, the Ford Foundation dissolved its behavioral science division. We hope that the files on this decision will some day be made available. Action on social problems was turned over to subject-matter divisions which undoubtedly commissioned studies relevant to their missions. But the chance to make "applications" a topic of research in its own right was again lost. While an increasing number of writers expressed the need for such a move, it certainly was not the subject of popular demand among sociologists, as can be seen from the final episode in this historical account.

Technology and Policy in the Information Age

ITHIEL DE SOLA POOL

In this chapter, I shall discuss the "modernization" of the communication systems in advanced industrial societies. Communication and modernization of underdeveloped countries has interested scholars for the past quarter-century. Much of Wilbur Schramm's work has addressed such questions as how to provide the means for dissemination of education and technical information and how to build effective mass media in societies that have been beset by poverty, illiteracy, and inexperience. In this chapter I shall not deal with communications issues that face the less-developed countries (LDC), but rather with questions arising in the most advanced.

For social scientists concerned with the study of communications, a relationship is clear between the topic of this chapter and the topics taken up in relation to the LDCs. In this chapter, as in studies of communications and development, the characters of the communications institutions themselves are taken as variables.

The character of an institution in the process of change is treated as problematic. When institutions remain substantially as they were when their inhabitants grew up within them, policy discussions may take place about what the institutions should do, but the nature of the institutions themselves will be taken for granted.

In the developing world, the communication systems have been changing with fantastic speed as they imitated technologies and practices that had been developed over long periods in the west. Thus contrary to a common stereotype, change has been rapid in the less-developed countries and slow in the advanced countries. In the last few decades, however, the technology of communication has been changing so rapidly in the west that the system can no longer be taken for granted. The system itself becomes the object of policy debates.

ASPECTS OF COMMUNICATION TECHNOLOGY

Four aspects of the technologies of communication are likely to change advanced industrialized societies in the last quarter of the twentieth century as much as broadcasting did in the first half, or as printing did five centuries earlier. Those four characteristics of present communication developments are: (1) the emergence of an information society, (2) convergence of modes, (3) distance insensitivity of costs, and (4) both scarcity and abundance of bandwidth.

THE INFORMATION SOCIETY

The significance of an "information society" has been expounded most effectively by Jean Gottman, Marc Porat, Edwin Parker, and Ronald Abler.[1] Dividing the United States labor force between an information sector and all other sectors, Porat and Parker found that the information sector employed only 10 percent of the United States labor force in 1900, 27 percent in 1960, and 48 percent in 1970, and would employ a predicted 51 percent by 1980. The growth in the decade of the sixties was extraordinary and, while the rate has flattened since then, more people in this country now earn their living by manipulating symbols than by making or handling goods.

For a million years of human history, only a tiny minority of mankind engaged professionally in intellective activities; these activities are now, at least in the United States, the normal activity of the majority. That fact has enormous social implications.

One implication which Parker is fond of stressing is that an increased portion of our national product consists of what economists call "public goods." Most goods are appropriable by individuals; when they have been appropriated they are no longer available to other individuals. The person who appropriates the good can properly be charged for its cost. A public good, however, is still available for use by others after someone has used it. When one person walks through a park, so can another; what should each pay? When one person uses some knowledge, so can another. Against whom should the cost of the knowledge be assessed? The fact that these questions do not have simple answers underlies the difficulties the Congress is having with the notion of copyright. Consider, for example, the difficulty of assessing what a cable television viewer or cablecaster should pay for enjoying the use of a television broadcast.

A second possible implication of the information explosion is the fostering of a new form of social inequality or elitism. The argument is put forward, for example by Natan Katzman,[2] that while everybody will get more information as the information flow in society grows, the greatest proportion of increase will go to those who already have the most information. They have the resources of money, education, and skill to absorb more of the new flow. Thus the gap between the information rich and the information poor grows.

Quite frankly, I wonder whether that theory is true. It can represent a danger against which policy must fend. Certainly forces are tending in that way; those who have information are in the best position to assess new information. Yet countervailing factors exist as well. It is hard to believe that a society in which half of the age cohort start a higher education will have a wider spread between the information rich and the information poor than one where higher education was a rare privilege.

A third and also controversial assertion about an information society is that it suffers inherent malaise and instability. Large numbers of young people, and indeed virtually all young people who come from the information-processing classes, are obliged to go to school for many years beyond their biological maturity and are virtually obliged to accept the emotional discipline of paper-pushing jobs. One might argue that the information society makes demands on a substantial proportion of humanity, both as to intelligence and temperament, that are not congenial. In some way, those who find themselves in this bind are likely to protest and dissent.

While reactions of that sort undoubtedly do occur in some instances, one may legitimately question how statistically major this problem is in the information society. It may be a major problem; we simply do not know yet—the evidence is not all in.

Thus while good reasons exist to be uncertain as to what the effects of the information society will actually be, clearly we seem to be headed toward that kind of society; for better or worse, we will soon find out what sort of society it is. That society will certainly need as good and efficient a job of education in childhood and reeducation in adulthood as we can provide so that as many people as possible have the tools and interests to operate in that society. The mass media as well as the schools have a role to play in that process. Broadcasting, publishing, and the press will play a critical role in setting the quality of life in an information society.

CONVERGENCE OF MODES

Whenever more than one mode of communication is operative, the competition between modes becomes an important dynamic in the communication process. At the time of the Reformation, the character of society in different parts of Europe was in part shaped by whether the dominant religion allowed its teachings to be transmitted through printed copies of the Bible in the vernacular or only through the word-of-mouth teachings of a specialized priesthood. When the telegraph was inventeded, it represented a challenge to the post offices, which in most countries took it over and thus controlled the relative rates and allocation of traffic between the modes. When the telephone was later invented in 1876, it represented a major blow to telegraphy, virtually killing for decades the switched teletype system which was just beginning to emerge. Western Union tried to get hold of the telphone business with the inventions of Elisha Grey and Thomas Edison but lost out in the patent contest. Later in 1901 when long-distance wireless telegraphy was invented, and more particularly in 1907 with the invention of the vacuum tube, the cable network of the telphone system was threatened by competition. American Telephone and Telegraph (ATT) in the early 1920s tried to become the chosen monopoly for broadcasting as well as for the wired voice network, but ended up signing an agreement with Radio Corporation of America (RCA) to stay out of broadcasting in return for its landlines being used for interconnecting radio stations into networks. Through one of its subsidiaries, ATT also got into the business of sound movies. When ATT established Bell Labs in 1925, it gave that organization a very broad charter of research in order to acquire strong patent positions in all the areas tangential and therefore potentially competitive with telephony. The invention of the transistor, with its significance for broadcasting, is one fruit of that broadminded and dynamic policy.

Thus competition between modes of communication is nothing new. We could carry the story further by noting Paul Lazarsfeld's studies in the mid-1930s of the impact on the newspaper of the introduction of radio news.[3] Still more recently, general magazines, such as *Life,* were driven out by the greater cost-effectiveness of television as an advertising medium for campaigns addressed to the entire mass audience. We could certainly find many more historical examples if we wished. Yet, in very significant ways the barriers between modes were much greater in the past than they are today or than they will be in the future. The examples of competition between modes that we have just given were to some degree exceptional events. The normal situation in the past has been one in which the technology of each mode was sufficiently inflexible and sufficiently different, so that each mode settled down to being used in a distinctive way for purposes for which it had a competitive advantage. The mails were used for carrying pieces of paper between persons; telegraphy for sending written messages fast; telephony for voice conversations between pairs of persons; radio for broadcasting; movies for theater presentations of entertainment. Such alternative possibilities as, for example, home movies, telephone conferences, mailing of voice recording, and the like, remained marginal. To a large extent, each mode stayed off each other's turf.

The neat divisions between different modes that existed for the past three-quarters of a century no longer hold. The explanation for that change lies in the magic of modern electronics. Through computer logic, large and enormously complicated electronic bit patterns can be manipulated. These patterns can be stored in electronic memories, converted in format, and transmitted instantaneously to remote destinations. Thus all sorts of communications processes—be they in text, voice, or picture—that were handled in the past in unique, cumbersome, nonelectronic ways, can now be mimicked in an astonishing variety of new electronic ways. The basic limits are rarely technical. Electronically, one can do virtually anything one wants to do. The limits are what regulation will allow and what is economic. Limits are set by the availability of resources—for example, spectrum and money. To provide services economically may require complex social and political organization. The appropriate organization may be very different from that of the media in the preelectronic era. These earlier communications organizations are often endangered by new ways of delivering the same services. The consumer may consider it a blessing if twenty years from now letters no longer have to be hand-delivered by a postman perhaps three days after mailing, but arrive instead by instantaneous electronic means to be read off a television screen or, if desired, printed out on a typewriter terminal. Consumers may also be pleased to watch motion pictures on a video player at a time of their choice, either by buying a videodisc at a store or by taping the show from a phone line or cable system while they sleep. But what consumers see as augmented choices constitute competitive threats and dilemmas to industry and regulators.

The United States government, motivated by an antitrust philosophy, has up to now followed the policy of keeping each industry under its purview as separate as possible. For example, it has adopted rules to prevent theaters and television and cable stations from offering the same movies at the same time. More important, ATT and Western Union, which once fought for each other's turf, have been rigidly separated. Bell carries voice; Western Union carries telegrams. Bell was compelled to sell its TWX system to Western Union's Telex. But both Bell and Western Union now carry computer data on their lines. And the arrival of all-digital transmission will even abolish the difference between voice and data transmission. On advanced digital transmission systems to which phone systems are moving, voice is no longer carried as an analogue signal but is sampled several thousand times a second, translated into digital bits, and transmitted in a flow that is physically indistinguishable from data. That fact has many implications, including the possibility of storing the spoken message in a computer for later retransmission. Thus the voice telegram will become a possibility. Why should the sender of a telegram from Cambridge to New York phone New Jersey, as he does today, to read his text to a clerk who phones it to the New York addressee or transcribes it into the Western Union office to be mailed by post? The whole system is now an anachronism and will become more so as it becomes technically possible for the sender either to typewrite a message or to talk it over identical phone lines for temporary storage in a computer for retransmission to the receiver when convenient. If Western Union is threatened by that development, so is the postal system. What will happen to the already troubled postal service, designated by the Constitution itself as a federal function, when its services collide with telegraphy and telephony? A Canadian Post Office study has estimated that 45 percent of first class mail already starts in a computer (bills and the like) and 20 percent ends up in a computer. To print out that data onto paper for handling by clerks is becoming much too expensive. So we are moving into an era where the separate existence of three major institutions is in question: the public institution of the postal service; the nation's largest private company, ATT; and specialized private carriers such as Western Union. What will be their future form?

Convergence of modes is also observed in mass communication. In

Britain, the post office, BBC, and ITV are experimenting with a system (know by BBC as Cefax and by the post office as Viewdata) for providing a written news display over the air to the television screen, as cablecasters in the United States are doing over extra channels. Vendors of drama for pay are experimenting with CATV, cassettes, video discs, and over-the-air pay television. These alternatives are all feasible. A number of now-operating technologies make it feasible to receive and deliver individually addressed pictures, text, or voice over the same basic delivery system. In addition to computers which control the data representations and flows and the memories which store the information for shorter or longer periods, channels must be developed with adequate bandwidth to carry copious information to an audience. Coaxial cables used for CATV or glass optical fibers, which in the coming decade will be an alternative to copper wires and coaxial cable, provide such broadband channels. This growth of available bandwidth is another major policy-relevant change taking place in communications technology.

BANDWIDTH

If communications in print can be measured by or are constrained by the column inches or pages transmitted, so the volume of electronic communication can be measured by the bandwidth of frequencies used. The prospective exhaustion of one natural resource—the broadcast spectrum—has been an impetus for the development of new technologies for transmitting broadband signals.

Many analogies to the energy situation exist. Both in regard to spectrum and in regard to oil, profligate use of a finite resource threatens exhaustion soon. But the date of exhaustion keeps being postponed by the discovery of better technologies for drawing on the reserve. As a result, Cassandras tend often to be dismissed as alarmist. Yet clearly technology has only bought reprieves; the day of reckoning remains. In consequence, scientists seek to find substitutes for the scarce resource. These substitutes are, indeed, being found, but each has its price and its special problems. For communications, the resource that is being depleted is the usable spectrum. In the United States, by law, the spectrum is a free good for which no price is charged. It is allocated by license to citizens who ask for it. By now, more than a million transmitters use citizen band, including about a quarter million amateurs and the radios in ships, airplanes, taxis, trucks, and police cars. Microwave phone circuits and transmissions relay to and from satellites. These uses of the spectrum are in addition to broadcasting. In addition, about half the spectrum has been preempted by the government, mostly for national security use. In the absence of any market, how can anyone judge the relative value of alternative uses? How can one choose between applicants who are all staking claim for the same resource? The government as an applicant argues the primacy of national defense. The mobile service users argue that theirs is the only service which cannot string wires as a substitute way of carrying signals. The broadcasters claim that the whole public, not just special interests, is served by them.

The exhaustion of spectrum by these conflicting claims on a free good has been postponed, partly because science has learned how to squeeze more stations into the same space without interference. (Note the Office of Tele-Communications Policy's [OTP] recent proposal to squeeze 200 more VHF stations onto the American air, the so-called "VHF drop-in"). More important, however, we have learned to use shorter and shorter waves. For example, radio broadcasting originally came in the 300- to 3000-kilocycle medium wave band. In the thirties, FM radio and television were assigned to the 30- to 300-milocycle VHF band. Additional television was later provided in the 300- to 3000-milocycle UHF band along with microwave, developed during the war. By now, most telephone long-line circuits are carried by microwave rather than cable.

Satellite transmissions are among the new uses for which spectrum is needed today. A satellite floating 22,300 miles above the equator may send its signals toward earth, covering one-third of the earth's surface or, if the beam is narrowed, an area still perhaps 1,300 miles across. It must use a wave length that is not in use in terrestrial transmissions in the reception area. Especially for transmission of television to small low-cost receivers, the signal must be strong with much bandwidth. The only place where such spectrum can be found is above the presently heavily used spectrum, for example, 14 and 16 gigahertz. (Thus direct transmission to present television sets is not possible; they are not built for those frequencies.) While new technologies may allow the use of higher and higher frequencies, a limit will be reached, particularly as the higher frequencies are less and less efficient and economical. The process is like that of drilling for oil supplies in poorer and poorer oil fields. So, sooner or later, some users have to be pushed off the free air waves onto the more expensive transmission medium of coaxial cables or some other alternative.

Moving off the airwaves offers a remarkable advantage, along with the disadvantage of having to pay. With coaxial cable, and in the future, even more, with optical fibers, a volume of information (that is, bandwidth) that no one ever had available over the air can be transmitted. Transmission of thirty-five television channels over a single cable is practical, for example. Instead of being limited to, say, four television stations in an average city, an unlimited number becomes technically possible—what the Sloan Commission called the television of abundance.

Possibly, however, cable may fail to become a universal transmission medium in the United States. (About 14 per cent of television sets in the United States are now on cable, and the number grows only a point or two a year.) The reason why CATV may never be as universal as over-the-air television is in part unfriendly regulation, in part the reluctance of citizens to pay a few dollars a month to upgrade what they can get free over the air, and also, in part, the prospective competition of optical fibers. That new technology may turn out to do everything coaxial cable can do and do it better. But do we have to wait for a new technology, or can we start gaining the advantages of cable now? If cable does grow, as hopefully it may in the next decade, then how will the next transition beyond coaxial cable be made in the next decade after?

The idea of using optical fibers for communication began to be developed in England around 1968. Telephone companies are already starting to experiment with fibers for trunking between switching centers; the hairlike filaments carry substantially more bandwidth than a heavy coaxial cable. However, their use still presents substantial unresolved problems. For instance, we do not yet know how to build efficient switches for transmission channels contained in the beam of light running down the glass filament. Thus it will be a few years before we know how far optical fibers will replace copper wire and coaxial cable.

Clearly, however, whether by optical fibers, coaxial cable, microwave, or by some combination of these, the American home or office of the 1990s will be reached not by just a telephone wire capable of carrying a voice signal plus a television set or two but by a wide electronic highway capable of carrying many two-way signals simultaneously—be they monitors, voice, television, facsimile, or data.

Below we turn to some public-policy implications of this development. We shall not expand on them yet, but before leaving the subject we should at least flag what some of the major policy issues will be. One thing at issue is the pace at which to change. The Federal Communications Commission and the existing media tend to protect the large investments in present communication systems against sudden obsolescence by new technologies. The $70-billion phone company plans some of its investments for a forty-year life. Should those plans be scrapped?

If America chooses to progress gradually, however, not every country will do the same. The United States has been until now at the forefront in telecommunications. Whether this lead will continue to be the case in all respects is not clear. Countries without America's great sunk investment in communications plant may leapfrog it. Japan is moving ahead faster on direct satellite broadcasting, for example. Canada is way ahead on CATV. Iran is thinking about having *two* domestic satellites to optimize its phone and broadcast services.

DISTANCE INSENSITIVITY OF COSTS

By that phrase we refer to a situation in which it costs no more to send a message a long way than a short way. At night, to call California from New York now costs little more than to call Chicago—one-third the distance.

Various technological reasons explain why declining costs in communication have been mostly in long-haul transmission. One is the geometry of satellite transmission. A message sent by satellite from point A to point B on the earth's surface travels 22,300 miles up and 22,300 miles down. Whether the two points on the surface of the earth are 500 or 5,000 miles apart makes virtually no difference, as long as they are in the footprint of the same satellite. Thus distance ceases to be a factor in calculating the cost of such a communication.

The same trend toward reduced long-distance-transmission costs are also observable in terrestrial communication. Advances have been made in coaxial cables and the even more dramatic prospects of such devices as optical waveguides. Transmission costs are also falling in microwave transmission and in undersea cables. Thus even without the advent of the satellite, long-distance transmission costs are becoming a minor part of the total bill.

That fact has enormous implications both for human interaction and for information systems. Until now, virtually all human interactions were heavily influenced by propinquity. For almost any human interaction, one could plot the frequency of interaction by distance, and the result would be a dish-shaped declining curve. Such data as place of origin of spouse, the store one shopped in, the destination of letters or phone calls, the areas of business dealings or scientific consultation would all follow that pattern. Today that pattern no longer holds for many interactions. New York and Los Angeles are far closer socially than are Peoria and Santa Fe, or than New York is to either. The invisible colleges among professionals today form almost in disregard of distance.

As information systems become computer-based, distance again ceases to be an important fact. Time-sharing systems, such as General Electric's Mark III, are spread as far as possible in latitude—for example, from Japan through the United States to Europe. The objective is to spread the customers over many time zones so that the peak hours in one place will fall during slow hours in other places. Load leveling on the systems computer is much more important for the economics of the system than the relatively modest communications costs. The same consideration, plus the greater efficiency of large computers, accounts for the fact that the main data base vendors—Lockheed, SDC, and the National Library of Medicine—offer their services nationally from a central computer. To absorb the communication costs of access from the far coast of the country is more economic than to load the data base in the memory of regional machines.

In the case of dynamic data bases that change constantly, an additional reason for keeping the base in one place is to avoid the problems of keeping the various copies synchronously updated. Even data bases that are only added to, but do not otherwise change, may be natural monopolies in that the main cost is creating the data base. Once one organization has compiled the physics literature of the last decade, for example, for anyone else to go through the same work all over again makes very little sense.

Thus we can look forward to a world in which a great many information activities will be carried on over large distances in total disregard of national boundaries. The principle of the free flow of information will become more important than it has ever been before. In the past it was a moral principle of the highest merit as an expression of the basic rights of the human being and a proper restriction on the authority of governments. In the future it will remain that, but in addition it will be an economic principle that can be violated only at a great cost in efficiency. Just as trade in goods has been beneficial and mercantilism has been bad for the wealth of nations, so in the flow of information, freedom will mean economic progress and productivity, and restriction on free flow will mean waste and backwardness.

POLICY CONSEQUENCES

Numerous policy issues stem from the four characteristics of emerging communications technologies that I have just described. Technology is in the driver's seat.

A great physicist once said to me, after going through the arithmetic of the number of stars and planets contained in the universe, that at least several hundred of them must hold life. The mystery, he said, is not whether life exists elsewhere in the universe but, given that it must, why no civilization has communicated with us, since among the hundred, by any statistical process of chance, several would be at least several millenia more advanced in evolution than man. Perhaps, I replied jokingly, they are sufficiently advanced not to want to communicate with us. No, he replied indignantly, progress depends so critically on communication that for such a species to win in the struggle for survival without maximizing its development of communication is inconceivable.

Without trying to resolve this cosmic issue, I would like to take my physicist friend's viewpoint at least to the point of arguing that what the new communications technologies make possible will in fact be done. The competitive advantages of having abundant information and of abolishing the barriers of distance are so great that societies that fail to take full advantage of them will wane, and those that use them will survive. In the end, then, the new technologies will be with us.

If technology is in the driver's seat and we are going to enter an information society in which broadband electronic communication brings us the services now delivered by a variety of modes, and does so without respect for boundaries and distance, what are the policy consequences that we can forsee? To try to answer this question, I recently went through a short brainstorming exercise at Massachusetts Institute of Technology. For three-quarters of an hour, a group of us tried to list the important communications policy issues of the present and near future. We did not apply any selectivity. The list is simply one intuitive set of judgments. Anyone else's list would differ somewhat, but would, I am convinced, overlap to a considerable degree. We came up with fifty-two issues. The next step was to group these into related clusters and then to group the clusters. Let me review the main themes around which these issues clustered.

In the broadest aggregation, one set of issues concerns the social impact of the new communications technologies. Another set of issues deals with how to promote culture, public awareness, and free discussion. A third set of issues concerns how to maintain progress and innovation in communications facilities. Finally, a number of issues concern the organization of the industry to serve the public.

SOCIAL EFFECTS

Among the many social effects of modern communications, one may note some profound changes in the urban and regional distribution of activities. One issue is how to make investment in communications contribute to a desirable territorial plan. To illustrate the point, we may look at the history of the telephone. Before the telephone, businesses of each kind would locate in a neighborhood, side-by-side with each other, so that when one needed information or to do business one could simply walk down the block or drop in at the corner coffeehouse. Rents in desirable neighborhoods were high. With the arrival of the telephone, a business could move to cheaper quarters further up or further out. Thus the telephone contributed both to the skyscraper and to urban sprawl. It made skyscrapers practical not only by enabling someone on the twentieth floor to remain in easy touch with the world, but also during construction, by enabling the construction manager to stay in contact with workers on the scaffolding. It made suburbanization practical by enabling commuters to stay in touch with their homes and by keeping branches in touch with their headquarters. Thus a strange dual process contributed to the mid-twentieth-century urban pattern of a dense downtown and remote urban suburbs with a ring of desolation in between. Continued improvement of telecommunications today may be contributing to the erosion of the downtown. On-line computing, facsimile, and improved telephony are making a downtown location less and less important in such fields as banking and finance. Policy on communication rates and services can affect the speed with which such changes occur.

In some countries, such as France and England, communications policy is being used to facilitate the moving of people and activities out of the primate central city into the provinces and new towns. In the United States, ambivalence obscures the goal. Some experts advocate the new rural society; others advocate keeping downtowns intact.

In many countries the issue between localism and national centralization of communications is a political one. The United States broadcasting system is predicated upon the desirability of localism. For this principle, we pay a considerable price in spectrum, in the number of stations available to the average viewer, and in the inability to meet the desires of geographically distributed minorities. Yet the principle of localism is important in providing a base for the civic culture by strengthening communities. Other countries have made the reverse choice. In many developing countries, the central government feels so vulnerable to regional separatism that no broadcasting is allowed except from the national capital. Those countries pay for that choice by the atrophy of local government.

A parallelism exists between these issues of localism versus centralization and some international issues. On a global scale, the issue is control within the sovereign unit or openness to inputs from outside it. That issue appears in a number of controversies, including those about direct satellite broadcasting, international computer networks, satellite parking spaces, and cable in border areas. Those countries who would close their borders talk about cultural imperialism, data sanctuaries, and foreign ownership of important national media. Those who wish to communicate freely point to the inefficiencies that result from autarchic telecommunications manufacturing, to the opportunities for technical cooperation via telecommunications, and to the human right to know and to communicate. Those issues come to a head around satellites and spectrum.

MAINTAINING CULTURE AND FREE SPEECH

The second large family of issues concerns the support of culture and of freedom of discourse. A critical issue in every country is how to pay for material of cultural merit. Neither advertisers nor the mass audience will provide the funds that make possible works of great merit. In some form or other a combination of government and affluent customers does that almost everywhere. Pay television allows cultivated customers to express their taste. Government support is also needed. In the United States that issue in regard to public broadcasting has reached a provisional resolution recently with the adoption by the Congress of a more-or-less stable plan for long-range funding of public broadcasting. Similar issues are being raised, however, by those who wish to have satellite service available for education. They argue that the market for educational material exists, but that it cannot be aggregated without public action.

Copyright, another device for supporting culture, will become an increasingly thorny issue. No legislation that the Congress enacts will solve the issue, for the very nature of the converging technologies of modern communication is at stake. The basic idea of copyright rested upon certain aspects of printing technology. In the Gutenberg era, the obvious locus for control over communication was the printing press. Censors operated on that fulcrum. So did the copyright system, designed to compensate authors. No one tried to collect a royalty from the resale of books through thousands of book stalls; to do so would have been impossible. No one tried to impose a royalty on reading out loud from a book or lending it to a friend or assigning it in a school. The royalty was imposed at the one point at which easy control and a fairly reliable count of the numbers could be exercised. For the same reason, copyright was not applied until the last few years to speech or singing or acting. The basic law of copyright in the Anglo-American tradition required, for the sanction to be applicable, the production of a physical legible text.[4] Modern technology is eliminating the point of control. Xerography results in the distributed production of individual copies. Computer storage permits retrieval onto Cathode Ray Tubes (CRTs) or onto other computer memories or onto hard copy at any terminal location, and not only in the form of an exact copy but also in the form of modified and manipulated transformations of the material.

I am only raising issues; I am not arguing for any particular conclusion. Clearly, to reward those who create intellectual products is important. Some scheme for encouraging them has to be found. But it is naive to believe that it can be simply done by extending a scheme that grew out of one technology and mechanically applying it to others.

Closely related are the issues of freedom of speech and of privacy. In this country we have a curiously trifurcated regime. Under the terms of the Constitution, our system of print media is more or less unregulated. Our system of broadcasting is closely regulated—partly, in fact, to assure diversity of views and controversy. Finally, we have a system of regulated common carriers. Convergence among these historically separate forms of industry means that few communications firms will remain in the unregulated domain long and that services in the regulated and unregulated domains will be competing with each other. If our forefathers were correct in believing that government regulation would in the end endanger a free press, then these developments are quite ominous. Are we going to find ourselves in a situation in which no major firms in the communications industry are unregulated?

Alternatives are available. The Whitehead Cable report was an attempt to return to the print model in the electronic domain. In a realm where spectrum shortage is not a problem, this return is in principle possible. But that this tendency is in fact the direction of movement in national policy at the present time is far from clear. On the contrary, to protect broadcasting institutions we have government regulations which tell cablecasters who use no scarce medium and who therefore presumably have the full protection of the First Amendment that they may not play movies made between two and ten years ago or import programs from particular locations. Is it conceivable that if a political movement wished to put out its message in the form of a five-year-old movie, or wished to carry a rally from a distant city to its followers elsewhere, the Supreme Court could find it within the right of the government to interfere in any way? I personally find it hard to reconcile such regulations with the United States Constitution; yet they exist and they prevail, at least for the moment.

Other strong pressures point toward increased government controls of content. Concern exists about the effect of violent television on children, about the broadside way in which leaked government confidences are published, and about intrusions on individual privacy by media pandering to sensation. The eternal conflict between protection of the freedom of the communicator and protection of other values continues, and always will.

A widespread view that computer technology has made privacy particularly vulnerable has some validity. Manual files are much more easily violated than computerized ones; on the other hand, when computerized files are searched, the results are apt to be more complete and accurate. In short, violations of privacy in the computer age are apt to be less common but more threatening than those in the past. How to control those violations without infringing the freedom of inquiry of the investigator is a great dilemma.

MANAGEMENT OF INNOVATION

We have noted a third group of policy issues—those concerning progress in communications innovation. With massive investments at stake, strong vested interests mobilize to prevent rapid obsolescence by innovation. Broadcasters mobilize to block CATV or pay television. Post offices illegalize mailbox services on time-sharing systems.

The government regulators become part of the protective system. They do not wish to preside over the destruction of the industries they were set up to regulate. If they acted differently, they could indeed be blamed for the losses that investors and publics would suffer as established systems gave way to new ones.

Yet government also has the responsibility of promoting progress. It is the instrument that is supposed to prevent monopolies from standing in the way of change. It also provides much of the research and development of the new, in both the defense and space programs.

Real difficulties are presented in knowing how to organize research and development for communications, and also how to make the resulting technical information available to political decision makers. The structure of research and development varies greatly in different parts of the communications industry. The telephone monopoly has a superb laboratory. The postal monopoly does no significant research and becomes more and more technologically obsolete. The competitive broadcasting and publishing industries do modest amounts of serious research, but on the whole can be described as technologically backward. The competitive computer industry is a hotbed of technological change. None of these areas, at least in the United States, has a social science counterpart to Bell Labs. In Japan, the phone company does support a Research Institute for Telecommunications and Economics. In short, the situation varies greatly and in ways that cannot be explained by one sentence slogans.

Within government, decisions must be made in Congress, in regulatory bodies, and in operating bodies. These decisions need to rest upon an understanding of the new communication technologies, yet the decisions must normally be made by individuals who have a very limited grasp of the technology. In some other countries where the communications organizations are relatively self-contained bureaucracies, the engineers and specialists may be at the top. The problem in those countries is to provide the general public with access so that its complaints and desires may be heard. In the United States the situation is generally the reverse. The adversary process allows political and economic interests to be heard but provides no input for independent expert analysis. Neither extreme is satisfactory, but to wed those two approaches is not easy.

Who, for example is going to do the difficult trade-off analysis between a system of high-powered satellites which would allow the use of
many low-cost ground stations but would require more spacing on the
orbit, and low-powered satellites which serve to distribute signals only
among expensive national or regional ground stations? The quantitative trade-offs in such an analysis will not be well developed in an
adversary proceeding.

So as we move into an era in which fiber optics, high-powered satellites, cassettes or video disks, information retrieval, electronic mail,
and electronic funds transfer are the order of the day, we are going to
have to find a way to get better technological evaluations into the
hands of users in education, medicine, and social service, and into the
hands of government policy-makers.

THE STRUCTURE OF THE INDUSTRY

Finally, we must note a very large set of recurrent issues about the
structure of the communication industry. Should it be monopolistic or
competitive, public or private? How can the regulators avoid becoming the captives of the regulated, or if not captive, how can they be
prevented from making regulation an end in itself? What should be
the structure of the regulatory institutions? How should it be related
to the legislative and executive branches, the users, the industry?
Issues arise with regard to vertical integration and horizontal integration of the industry. Questions remain about pricing. Should it be by
value of service or cost? What about cream skimming and cross-sub-
sidization? What methods of accounting and allocation of joint costs
and of amortization are appropriate?

A related set of issues concerns control of the flow of communication. In many countries labor unions are trying to exercise a voice on
what the media say and how they operate in the society. Editors fight
with publishers for control of the content. Where cross-ownership or
chains exist, the various federated units struggle for their autonomy.
Where the medium is a carrier for messages produced by others, a
struggle arises between the customer trying to keep the carrier in a passive common carrier role and the carrier sometimes trying to use its
leverage as a monopoly to extend its activities. Abroad, a number of
Post Telephone and Telegraphs (PTTs) have moved into computing
services. The issue of the right to interconnect attachments with the
network is an expression of this problem.

Another related set of issues concerns methods of payment. Who should pay—government? advertisers? customers? Where payment is linked to services received, what objective function may be used to measure the value of information? What is the value of one use of the spectrum rather than another? How does one compare demands for fixed services, mobile services, broadcasting? Finally, what are the social utilities of having communication? How important is it for society to link the last remote rural resident? What is the social value of time devoted to public affairs? How much time should be given to public affairs, and how can one answer such a question anyhow?

In the coming decades, the most dynamic sector of our economy is likely to be communications services. While the growth of other sectors is limited by resource constraints, the flow of symbols can continue to add to the improvement of human life. Some resource constraints effect communication, too, such as diminishing supplies of newsprint and copper, but technological solutions will permit increasing processing of information at relatively low resource use. In the information society into which we are moving, knowledge and communication are among the few commodities that citizens of the whole world can be given more of without running afoul of the terrible resource constraints of growing population and rising expectations.

NOTES

1. Jean Gottman, *Megalopolis,* Cambridge, Mass.: MIT Press, pp. 576–580, 1961; Edwin B. Parker and Marc Porat, *Social Implications of Computer Telecommunications Systems,* OECD Conference Paper, February 4–5, 1975; Ronald Abler, *The Telephone and the Evolution of the American Metropolitan System,* Research Program on Communications Policy, Massachusetts Institute of Technology, 1976.
2. "The Impact of Communication Technology: Promises and Prospects," *Journal of Communication,* pp. 47–58, Autumn, 1974.
3. *Radio and the Printed Page,* New York: Diell, Sloan and Pearce, 1940.
4. *White Smith v. Apollo,* 209 U.S. 1(1908).

Building as Political Communication: The Signature of Power on Environment

HAROLD D. LASSWELL

The literature of politics, law, and government of the last few decades has given more attention than before to political communication. Among scholars, much of this emphasis is attributed to Wilbur Schramm. Some dimensions of the communicative process, however, have received rather casual mention. The aim of this essay is to suggest how this neglect may be overcome in one significant area, which is the planned and unplanned use of building as a channel of political communication.[1]

Writers have occasionally called attention to the fact that collective perceptions and behaviors may be modified by the physical environment which itself has been altered by intended or unintended initiatives. A well-known instance is the influence of the layout of the Houses of Commons on the continuity of the two-party system; or the effect of the hemisphere plan on the fragmentation or total unification of political parties in France or Italy.

When we examine the literature of architecture or of city and regional planning or of ecology, we discover a similar state of comparative neglect. Beyond emphasizing monumentality or the role of barriers in separating social groups from one another, the examination of edifices as a form of communication is rarely worked out in detail. It is exceptional to find an interpretation of political communication such as Wolfgang Braunfels proposes for the propaganda of the French and Spanish monarchies at their height.[2] The center of Versailles was "ex-

clusively occupied by the bedchamber, in which the king arose and
retired like the sun,'' and the chapel was placed to one side. In The
Escorial on the contrary, the royal apartments were arranged around
the chancel. The architecture communicated the message that "power, to be legitimate, requires piety and orthodoxy.''

Literature of general and special communication has underempha-
sized the channels, such as buildings, that while utilizing substantial
resources to constitute the signs, transmit a limited set of messages.
The principal focus of scientific attention has been on such parsimo-
nious conveyors of multiple messages as newsprint and electronic
waves.

In advanced industrial societies, contemporary human beings are
achieving a new level of awareness of what they do to the physical and
biological environment, and what the environment does to them. The
emphasis is on the destructive impact of the human race on water, air,
minerals, plants, and animals. Unmistakable as these destructive
consequences are, they are far from summing up the significance of
mankind for the natural environment or the answering impact of
physical surroundings on the quality of life. We are *transformers* as
well as destroyers. Living forms, especially human beings, add a distinctive frame of reference to the characteristic impact of physical
energies and particles on one another.

The novelty lies in the *symbolic* use that we make of our surroundings and the symbolic complexity of the way we interpret an altered
environment. Winds erode the rocks and disperse the sand. The
human distinction is that we are able to harness the wind to a mill,
and the mill becomes a pivot around which fixed habitations cluster
and new forms of sedentary life evolve. A transformed habitat changes
experience and behavior. The wind *moves;* human beings *act.*

When use is made of the environment, every person, in common
with all living forms, seeks to maximize such preferred events as the
accumulation of wealth and power. Our present concern is with political power, understood as the giving and receiving of support for decisions that significantly affect values in the whole community. Some
decisions are made in a "civil" arena that must be protected from external interference. The "civil" or internal arenas are distinguishable
from "military" arenas, in which the expectation of violence is the
fundamental characteristic. The demand to protect a civil arena may
give rise to the the building of walls and other fortifications; and the
walls perform a communicative as well as a physically restraining or

protective function. The walls convey messages of confidence to those who are behind the ramparts and messages of defiance and discouragement to possible enemies.

The deliberate changes in the environment that interest us have much in common with "architecture," if the conception of architecture is defined in a sufficiently inclusive manner. "Cultural materials" is the term that designates the materials (or energies) in a resource environment after they have been modified by human effort. Buildings obviously come in the category of cultural materials. "Technology" refers to the operations by which a group manipulates its culture materials for any purpose whatever. "Engineering" technology when applied (in an irrigation system, for example) does not necessarily imply communication. The overlap with our interest occurs when architecture masters engineering technology for purposes of political communication (in a fortification or palace, for instance).

Architecture can be conveniently distinguished from other skills, such as "sculpture," which are also specialized to the manipulation of resources for communication. We think of an architect as a specialist on the enclosure of living forms who employs enclosures to convey messages. *Our working definition of architecture is the handling of the material environment to achieve a degree of enclosure in fact, while simultaneously forming a symbol of enclosure. Obviously the symbol may or may not refer to political power.*[3] Sculpture is typically experienced from the outside looking in.[4] Architectural enclosures affect the perspective of the insider who is looking around or outside.

As will all working definitions that relate to some feature of social process, the conceptions of engineering, architecture, and sculpture provide a frame of reference and are not to be interpreted as hard-and-fast boundaries. The definitions are designed to serve the *functional* purposes of the scientific observer rather than to conform to the *conventional* usages of a particular culture or subculture. That phenomena overlap is to be taken for granted.[5] For instance, did those who were responsible for the Eiffel Tower think that they were engaged in engineering, sculpture, or architecture? How have successive audiences perceived the tower? If the designers thought of themselves as engineers, obviously the parsimony of engineering was also used to transmit a deliberate or unpremediated message of modernity, determination, and self-confidence to those for whom the image of France had been tarnished by military defeat. The enclosing function is as incidental to the Eiffel Tower as it is to the Washington Monument. The perspective is basically sculptural.

Buildings are instruments of political communication when they are constructed, modified, or destroyed for political purposes. The present discussion outlines the range of political outcomes and provides suggestive examples of how edifices may be involved in the process.

MILITARY AND CIVIL ARENAS:
SEPARATION AND INTERPENETRATION

The arena of world politics contains a power-balancing process in which the expectation of violence is a dominant characteristic. Perhaps the most elementary protection against assault is provided by a wall barrier. Such a walled enclosure is the fundamental pattern of a fortification. The wall blossoms into such elaborate structures as the barriers constructed by the Romans to shut the barbarians of North Britain out of the Empire, or those erected by the Chinese to exclude desert nomads. For those on the inside, the message is security. For those outside, the message is discouragement.

Enduring relations of hostility among peoples who occupy fixed territories produce characteristic alignments in the environment. Bodies politic cut down their vulnerability by constructing towers, walls, and garrisons and by exploiting natural barriers (mountains, deserts, marshes, and waters). The Maginot Line was ample testimony to the state of Franco-German relations. All the effective boundaries of a nation give symbolic as well as material indications of their enclosing, hence excluding, function.

The formation of national states is a double process: the overriding of subnational identities; the splitting of more inclusive previous loyalties. During the phase of active consolidation of a nation-state or empire, the most conspicuous architectural effect is to accentuate the primacy of the capital city. The positive side of nation building is the construction of new or the modification of old edifices and the organization of a network of subcenters at intervals from the hub to the periphery of the national domain. Negatively, nation building may result in the demolition of subordinate installations, especially those identified with rival centers of decision.

Revolutionary changes in the internal structure of particular political units typically innovate architectural changes, though on a less sweeping scale than in the French or the Russian world revolutions. To the extent that the new elite of a body politic sees itself as distinctive, whether in reference to its predecessors or contemporaries, structural changes occur. Hence the elite of a nation-state that has seceded from a larger unit tries to create symbols capable of setting it apart from older symbols of authority (which tend to reinstate the former submissive self) and to emphasize the existence of a brave new identity that enjoys excellent prospects for its values and institutions. In the United States, older forms in England were partially rejected in favor of new styles in the architecture of public buildings. The "new" in this case was a selection of motifs from the classical revival in Europe, since these motifs were especially congenial to Jefferson and other founding fathers.[6]

Military arenas grade insensibly into civil arenas, and a civil arena may be slowly or suddenly transformed into a military arena in which the expectation of violence is the primary fact that influences the orientation of public buildings. When civil consensus breaks down, the internal arena begins to approximate a full-scale military context. The transition is characterized by the segregation of like-minded persons who tend to group themselves together for congeniality and mutual support (including defense). The segregating response may align the "workers' quarters" of a city against its "better residential districts." A "front line" of police stations, barriers, and "checkpoints" may release a continuing barrage of messages that divide "us" from "them," and imply hostile motive and action.

MILITARY AND CIVIL ARENAS: THE VERTICAL AND THE HORIZONTAL

That *physical distance and position are likely to be internalized as psychic space* has long been recognized. The ruler who is "remote" and "above" modifies his self-image accordingly, and perceives himself as superior to other men. Similarly, anyone who is "close" and "below" is likely to adopt an image in which he perceives himself as much like those to whom he is close and who are inferior to those above.

Buildings are appropriate means of furthering "the strategy of awe." The traditional autocracies known to history have had time to execute the strategy of awe and to conform their physical surroundings to the requirements of a system in which the decision process is in the hands of a few. The Forbidden City in Peking is a grandiose example of aloofness achieved by exploiting the possibilities of vast horizontal planes with approaches arranged to constitute a gigantic maze. The Kremlin fully expresses autocracy; and it is noteworthy that after more than fifty years the Soviet regime has not seen fit to raze the Kremlin walls.

The sharpest contrast to despotism and autocracy is a well-established popular government. Officials meet citizens on a common level with minimal physical barriers separating them from their fellows. The White House in Washington expresses the basic relationship implied in a "strategy of fraternity."

Regimes in which power is narrowly held may rely on the "strategy of admiration" to play down the threat associated with the awe-inspiring. The "strategy of admiration" aims at the seduction of hostile elements. The object is not to overwhelm with majestic displays of power but to attract by putting up a fine show. To the "breed and circusses" strategy of ancient Roman leaders must be attributed the impetus that gave abiding form to the Colosseum, the circus, the bath, and the theater.

THE PHASES OF DECISIONS: DIFFERENTIATION AND DEMARCATION

Our model of the decision-making process distinguishes seven phases: intelligence (including planning), promotion, prescription, invocation, application, termination, and appraisal. Buildings tend to be physically differentiated in ways that facilitate the performance of a function (or of particular tasks within a function). The edifices may or may not be recognized as distinctively related to the function by persons who are familiar with the common usages of the culture in question. *External differentiation and demarcation* taken together imply that a viewer who is outside a building can identify the peculiarities of material or design that correctly indicate the decision phase to which the structure is adapted. *Internal differentiation and demarcation* imply that parts of a structure physically specialized to a function can be perceived as distinctive by an observer within the edifice. We refer to *nondifferentiation* and *nondemarcation* when these conditions are not met. An edifice may be devoted to the performance of more than one function and may be perceived as multifunctional.

INTELLIGENCE

We begin with the phase of decision specialized to the gathering, processing, and dissemination of knowledge. The watchtower is an edifice that evolved to meet the need to scrutinize the threats and opportunities in the immediate environment. The surveillance operations of a body politic with far-flung boundaries generate an elaborate system of direct observers, routes, centers, and subcenters of transmission and interpretation. The forms assumed by these installations are conspicuously affected by the technology of engineering current at a given time. Contemporary radar technology, for example, has led to the building of a belt of stations equipped to focus on flying objects and to include trained teams of observers to interpret shadows ("blips") on radar screens. The forms initially taken by these structures are dictated by the engineering requirements of the task. Other objectives—often taken into consideration by architects—are typically left to one side until the side effects of early experience stimulate support for multiple objectives pertinent to community planning.

In many early civilizations, the most direct revelation of human destiny was believed to be the stars. Observatories became a distinctive expression of the quest for clues to the future by scrutinizing the heavens. In one form or another a platform, a telescope, and a model of the night sky (a dome) were essential tools of inquiry, providing the king's astrologers with the data which they used to predict the success or failure of the monarch's public and private projects.[7]

Man also sought knowledge of cosmic forces by looking inside himself rather than at the stars above. The path of meditation, intoxication, and trance can be pursued in solitude or intermittently in company with others. When the culture pursues the way of solitude the impact on architecture is usually profound. Communion with the higher powers and the disclosure of coming things are perceived as requiring a "strategy of exclusion," the erection of barriers against interruption. The inner sanction often becomes a sacred palace; therefore walls and gates are set up along the route to the final mystery.

PROMOTION

Promotional activities are concerned with the mobilization of support. The opportunity to mobilize the whole tribe was built into the campsites and later into the permanent installations of the Arabs. The first step at every *hirah* set up in the course of their conquest was to mark out the area of the mosque, with a central place of assembly for the people. At the beginning of the thirteenth century A.D., the first Muslim Dynasty established itself at Delhi. When Qutb-ud-din captured the Hindu stronghold on that site, he dismantled a large temple at the center of the citadel and utilitized the stone remnants of twenty-seven temples to build the Qutb Mosque. An original feature was the great screen of masonry to separate the sanctuary from the courtyard, through the openings of which the congregation could view the Iman conducting the prayer.[8]

During the oligarchic phase of government in Great Britain, the meeting place of the "factions" was a place of assembly suitable to the "gentlemen" who participated in the "great game" of politics. Some of the seventeenth-century clubs were identified with revolutionary views. The Rota was founded by James Harrington in 1659, and among its members were some who were executed for their supposed subversive activities. Clubs usually met at taverns or coffeehouses; and private clubs sometimes emerged from such beginnings. The club-house began to appear as a recognizable city structure.

Perhaps the most distinctive contribution of Nazi Germany to architecture is to be found in the designs that were adapted to the ceremonial purposes of the Movement. The impressive colonnade at the back of the reviewing stands at Nüremburg provided an imposing backdrop for the 100,000 people who participated in the great parades. This architecture of ritualized affirmation is wholly inappropriate for the looser organization of the units in a genuine party system.[9]

PRESCRIPTION

To prescribe is to make articulate the fundamental goals and instrumental norms of a body politic. Despite infinite diversity of detail, the prescribers can be classified in a small number of recurring patterns: a chief executive and his advisors; a council of equals; a legislature; an assembly.

Since ancient Greek cities provided the facilities for large councils, Greek builders acquired experience in adapting materials and designs to the mutual convenience of speakers and large audiences. At Miletus the Council hall was nearly square, with seats rising in stages on three sides. At Megapolis (late fourth century B.C.), the *Thersilion* was a hall for a large government council. The roof (200' × 172') was supported on columns that were placed behind one another in radiating lines to afford an unobstructed view of the center of the hall where the speaker stood.

The most distinctive public building that arose in a Europe that was gradually removing itself from the constraints of feudal society was the city or town hall. The town hall appeared in the twelfth century, emphasizing both the individuality of the city and the requirements of either oligarchical or popular rule. A leading feature was the belfry, which provided a means of arousing and signalling the entire population.

The rise of representative government in the nineteenth century brought into being a distinctive, monumental edifice intended to arouse and confirm the self-confidence of the broader layers of society who were being drawn into more active and regular participation in public life. The national legislatures began to stand out on the horizon of the capital (and subcapital).

In France and the United States, the image of national legislative architecture crystallized. The old *Palais de Bourbon* was modified for the use of the Chamber of Deputies in 1807. Its twelve-column pediment front confirmed the classical style, as did the United States Capitol. The idea of an amphitheater was widely used to provide distinctive recognition to the speaker's rostrum, the well of the house, and the spectators—the three most conspicuous elements.

Confronted by the complex problems of contemporary life, legislative bodies have evolved a number of specialized organs. Deliberations on the floor are supplemented by committee hearings and debate and by expanded administrative staffs. In Washington, these changes are reflected in the multiplication of committee rooms and large offices for the Senate and the House.

INVOCATION

The invoking phase of decision covers initiatives taken to characterize concrete situations *provisionally* in prescriptive terms. Invocation also includes the initial arrangements made to put prescriptions into effect. Perhaps the most obvious specializations of the invoking function involve the security services, the police. These agents are usually authorized to characterize acts (provisionally) as violations and to detain alleged offenders. Facilities are needed to hold a suspected offender. These agents are also empowered to act on complaints.

The quarters of the prosecuting attorney, the grand jury, and the lower courts are adapted in many ways to the roles of those agents in the invoking process. In industrial countries like the United States, the direction of change in considering an alleged offender in criminal cases has been away from the threatening, intensely deprivational approach. The trend has also been to use less "legislative" methods of dealing with disputes "at the grass-roots level." We have been moving away from the big courtroom to the judges' chambers for the hearing of family controversies and the disposition of juvenile offenders. The newer buildings deemphasize the courtroom and create multiple rooms where people can meet "around the table" in an atmosphere conducive to "integrative solutions." Barriers between parties and judges are reduced, and everyone meets on a common level. The adversarial system is weakened by excluding certain third parties (including counsel) from the proceedings in many cases, at least during the exploratory stages.

A significant trend is the *solicitation* of complaints, which goes much beyond mere willingness to listen. Already, this openness to petition is reflected in such proposals as a number of "little city halls" distributed throughout the metropolis. The popularity of the "people's petitioner" (the ombudsman) is increasing, and may be expected to influence the arrangement of access to official ears.

APPLICATION

The applying phase is the *final* characterization and shaping of concrete circumstances in terms of prescription. Hence it covers the eventual decisions of a Supreme Court, a top regulating commission, or a chief executive. No sharp dividing line distinguishes the applying from the invoking phase; only when problems concern the later stages in the completion of a task is the application unambiguously involved.

The demarcation of a building at the application phase usually depends upon the use of distinctive designs by an edifice devoted to a specific task. For some time, a building specialized to punitive purposes has been easily identified. Prisons are designed to keep people *in* as well as to keep confederates *out;* and this attitude produces a fortress which, in effect, faces both ways. Historically, prisons have been conceived as communicating the idea that "crime does not pay." The heavy security prison is symbolized by the dungeon, essentially an artificial cave—sunless, airless, fecal, and full of instruments of torture—cut off from the world of man and nature. Prisons "scowl" with blank, thick, dull walls, surmounted by spikes and guards.

We have been describing the architecture of awe and intimidation, cruelty and retribution, as employed in penal administration. In democratic societies, a new vernacular is arising in the field of "correctional" architecture. Rehabilitation camps and farms, for instance, are transforming the penal image.

When we examine the increasingly complex network of modern administration, it is evident that specialized edifices have for some time been splitting off from an earlier and more general matrix. A distinctive courthouse took form in the later Middle Ages with the emergence in various cities of a *palais de justice.* The separation of judging from legislating, or from general administration, has been emphasized in English-speaking lands, notably the United States, where courthouses have given character to the skyline of a continent, expressing the demand for local autonomy against the States and Nation.

In various settings, external differentiation and demarcation have characterized treasuries, customs houses, embassies, and other task-oriented structures.

TERMINATION

When prescriptions are repealed and adjustments are made to cope with expectations of advantage that grew up when prescriptions were in effect, we are dealing with the terminating phase of decision. The most distinctive buildings having to do with termination are those that provide accommodations for previously powerful elements in society. In many cases the edifice continues to be occupied despite the changed role of the group in decision making, as when the power of a monarchy or a landholding class is reduced without interfering with the occupancy of a palace or a "House of Lords." In some instances, enhanced elegance offers partial compensation for diminished authority. The message is a denial of weakness or loss of power.

More commonly, perhaps, the visible consequences of termination policy have deprivational impacts, as when buildings formerly associated with the power elite are allowed to deteriorate. With the rise of Republican China and the reaction against the straitjacket of traditional Confucianism, the imperial palace in Peking and many Confucian temples and monasteries were first allowed to decay and then eventually revitalized.

Despite the importance of termination in a changing society, awareness of the importance of the function has been emerging rather slowly. The key questions are often dealt with incidentally in connection with other phases of decision. The rearrangement of pension claims and of claims to congenial residential facilities are becoming more common as the years pass. Undoubtedly, distinctive symbolic changes will occur in reference to officials who are authorized to terminate housing and various other arrangements.

APPRAISAL

The appraisal phase of a decision process is concerned with estimating the degree to which the goals of public policy have been reached and in assessing the causal factors involved. The first question that arises in an appraisal activity is what policy objectives are to be considered in evaluating the situation. In folk societies, the memory of the elders is the repository of goal or of instrumental prescriptions. With the advent of urban civilization and of literacy, written records became the primary source, and archives were developed. The *tabularium* stood conspicuously on the slope of the Capitoline Hill in Rome; and even if less favorably sited, national archives are an established part of the complex of edifices serving capitals.

The Roman Empire conducted systematic surveys of the accessible globe and devoted a building to a map of the empire. The enormous statistical requirements of modern appraisal call for buildings devoted to the census. The appraisal function is closely related to forward-looking or intelligence (planning) which has been referred to above.

THE INTERPLAY OF VALUES AND INSTITUTIONS

The value institutions that are relatively specialized to power interact with other value institutions in society. One value is "enlightenment," or the giving and receiving of knowledge. In what distinctive situations is knowledge obtained and exchanged? We think of scientific laboratories, university classrooms, editorial headquarters, and broadcasting operations. "Wealth" covers the giving and receiving of claims to the use of resources and includes production for the market. "Well-being" is the giving and receiving of opportunities for mental and physical safety, health, and comfort. "Skill" is the giving and receiving of opportunities to acquire excellence in occupations, professions, and the arts. Schools and professional associations are distinctly involved in the transmission of skill at all levels. "Affection" is the giving and receiving of love among individuals and the direction of loyalty toward group symbols (homes, memorials). "Respect" is the term for acts of recognition, such as the erection of an exclusive club, and the differentiation of social classes from one another. "Rectitude" refers to ethical and religious standards and evaluations and includes such organized activities as are connected with temples and churches.

The *relative position of power in a given setting is reflected in environmental emphasis on power*. A partial indicator is verticality, or the height of building (site included). *Silhouette analysis* may show that a single value has highest priority. Some capital cities, although not entirely devoted to government, posses an official building that dominates all others. The principal edifices of a university town are probably specialized to enlightenment. In many modern cities, businesses construct the tallest buildings. In some places, the principal feature is a hospital or recreational facility. The arts may dominate; or high-rise residential apartments. Cemeteries, monuments, and other respect installations may occupy the principal sites. For centuries, many European communities have taken for granted that a cathedral, a monastery, or some other edifice specialized to rectitude would command the skyline.

Significant trends and distributions become apparent when we compare silhouettes from one period to the next (as well as from place to place at the same time). Everyone would concede that the phenomenal rise of business in the nineteenth and twentieth centuries created a distinctive sky-view. Some of the evidence presently available suggests that government is today staging a comeback. The evidence is found not only in totalitarian states; renewed concern with "city centers" is apparent in liberal societies. The tremendous emphasis on communication (enlightenment) is best dramatized by the towers thrown skyward for radar and television purposes.

In some circumstances, we can recognize *the impact of power considerations on the location and style of buildings whose characteristic goal is some value other than power.* This impact is most apparent in times of military crisis—for example: enlightenment (underground laboratories); wealth (camouflaged factories); well-being (highly visible hospitals, if assumed to be ineligible targets); skill (schools in caves); affection (houses in barracks); respect (classless cemeteries); rectitude (garrison churches).

The imprint of past political communication is written on the face of a divided and militant globe, and on the living and working arrangements of a world where tendencies toward segregation of the self override self-integrating tendencies.

The physical environment conveys yesterday's message: "Your fundamental identity—your crisis identity—is with a nation-state; your range of common interests—as against special interests—is with the nation-state; your effective demands—in critical situations—are the demands that you make with your nation-state *on* other nation-states; and these dimensions are effective because your nation-state can mobilize your help in threatening and applying the coercion necessary to get results."

The physical environment also conveys another message from yesterday's wisdom and practice: "Granting that you must identify yourself in international crises with other members of your nation-state, it is not implied that you must identify equally with everyone. You are justified in separating yourself from persons who lack your superior qualities."

When the two messages are cojoined, they appear to support *"vertical" segregation, modified by crisis demands that reflect the security requirements of the territorial ("horizontal") nation-states*. The messages "get through" by controlling the focus of attention and by fostering net value gratifications for those who interpret the messages in acceptable ways.

The policy questions that arise in this context relate to the choice of goals and strategies appropriate to the arenas of politics at every level.[10] Buildings are part of the vast communicative process whose aggregate effect is to strengthen or weaken the impact of aspirations toward the realization of human dignity in theory and practice.[11]

NOTES

1. The late Robert Michels was an exceptional explorer of the interplay between politics and the arts. Among his essays: *Der Patriotimus, Prolegomena zu seiner sociologischen analyse,* Munich and Leipzig, 1912. Among contemporaries, see André Malraux, *The Psychology of Art,* tr. by Stuart Gilbert, 3 vols., New York: Pantheon Books, Inc., 1949–1950.

2. Wolfgang Braunfels, *Monasteries of Western Europe,* Princeton: Princeton University Press, p. 200, 1972.

3. Susanne K. Langer has developed the symbolic significance of art in *Feeling and Form: A Theory of Art Developed from Philosophy in a New Key,* New York: Charles Scribner's Sons, 1953. She advances the interpretation that "the primary illusion of plastic art, *visual space* appears in architecture as envisagement of an ethnic domain" (p. 100). This view is more penetrating than the formation in Bruno Zevi's *Architecture as Space: How to Look at Architecture,* New York: Horizon Press, 1957; or N. Plevsner, *An Outline of European Architecture,* New York: Pantheon, 5th. ed., 1957, at p. 23: "Nearly everything that encloses space on a scale sufficient for a human being to move is a building; the term architecture applies only to buildings designed with a view to aesthetic appeal." The degree to which communication is fully deliberate varies from the sophisticated, questioning planner to the unreflective conformist.

4. Henry Moore's remarks on the practice of sculpture are of particular interest in this connection. The sculptor, he writes, "gets a solid shape, as it were inside his head—he thinks of it, whatever its size, as if he were holding it completely in the hollow of his hand. He mentally visualizes a complex form *from all around itself;* he knows while he looks at one side what the other side is like; he identifies with its center of gravity, its mass, its weight, he realizes its volume as the space that shape displaces in the

air." In R. L. Herbert, ed., *Modern Artists on Art,* New York: Prentice-Hall, p. 142, 1964.

5. That political considerations have entered into the professional approach of architects is well understood in classical treatises in the field. That this approach includes the use of buildings for purposes of political communication is amply indicated by Vitruvius who describes how after the war against Persia the architects of public buildings in Greece designed statues of the women of Caryae as a means of shaming the memory of a Greek city that sided with the Persians. *Vitruvius: The Ten Books on Architecture,* tr. by Morris Hicky Morgan (New York: Dover Publications, pp. 6–7, 1960). Vitruvius also recommended that a shrine for Mars should be located outside the walls, and "citizens will never take up arms against each other, and he will defend the city from its enemies and save if from danger in war" (*op. cit.,* p. 32). See the recent commentary by Paul Goldsberger on the completion of the Albany Mall: "Buildings communicate messages, and it is hard to look at the [Legislative Office Building] and not think of a government obssessed with power and monumentality, but utterly lacking in any imagination or ideas" (*New York Times,* July 2, 1976).

6. Jefferson was impressed by the Maison Carré at Nimes, the best preserved of Roman temples. American classicism was especially successful in state capitols and buildings under federal auspices. Consult: *Thomas Jefferson and the National Capital, 1783–1818,* edited by Saul K. Padover, preface by Harold L. Ickes, Washington, D.C.: Government Printing Office, 1946; Talbot Hamlin, *Greek Revival Architecture in America: Being an Account of Important Trends in American Architecture and American Life Prior to the War Between the States,* New York: Oxford University Press, 1944.

7. In Chinese practice, the ming-t'ang was a magic building symbolizing and giving power in the universe. Ancient monarchs were supposed to have had one, and Confucian classics give some instructions about building a "Hall of Light." The T'ang dynasty decided to build one and eventually erected a colossal building over 300 feet high at the eastern capital, Lo-yang. The old texts, however, agreed that the ming-t'ang should be a modest thatched building.

8. Percy Brown, *Indian Architecture (Islamic Period),* Bombay: Taraporevala Sons and Co., p. 10, 1964.

9. Barbara Miller Lane, *Architecture and Politics in Germany, 1918–1945,* Cambridge: Harvard University Press, 1968.

10. Representative of Wilbur Schramm's policy-oriented contribution is *Mass Media and National Development: The Role of Information in Developing Countries,* Paris: UNESCO, 1964.

11. This essay is drawn from a more intensive treatment of the subject in an unpublished manuscript.

II
A LIFE IN COMMUNICATION RESEARCH

The Early Years

ELIZABETH SCHRAMM

Wilbur Schramm was born in the pretty, historic river town of Marietta in southeastern Ohio into the milieu of pompadours, sweeping
skirts, and parasols, of straw hats, suspenders, and gold watch chains.

His parents were musical. As they courted, his mother played the
piano to his father's violin. One day a young tornado forced Arch
Schramm to drop his fiddle in order to hold the door against the evil
forces outside, while the Tiffany lamp swayed a wind-tossed benedic-
tion. Arch was of German origin (Wilbur has since said: "It wasn't
easy, in 1914 through 1918, to have a German-sounding name").
Music was an old-country part of both Arch's and Louise's daily life;
this interest passed to Wilbur, who played as a flutist in later years in
the Boston Civic Symphony.

Since this book is about communication and social change, let us
recall that homemade music was an important part of evening life in
the America of 1907—which had no television, no movies, not even
radio. And if you wanted to know what was going on outside of Marietta, you had to learn how to read. Thus grew the tradition of the
three R's in small-town America.

A few generations back, some Schramms had left the Schramms-
burg area in southern Germany and settled in the fertile hill country of
southern Ohio. A large farm and a successful mill on the Ohio River
provided generously for the families which preceded the twelve-child
brood of which Arch was the youngest member.

Arch was a talented and vigorous young man. At 17, he was teaching in the local one-room schoolhouse, controlling the bullies who were older than he was and at the same time gently tutoring the little boys and girls. He soon moved to town—to Marietta—and began to read law in the office of a practicing attorney (the accepted way to learn the law before law schools were established). In time, he became a well-known lawyer, judge of the Children's Court, and prominent in civic affairs.

The ancestors of Louise Lang, whom he married, also came from the Bavarian region of southern Germany, where the Lang family starred in the Oberammergau Passion Play. And another family name—Bachman—points back to musical forebears.

Wilbur and his beloved little sister grew up as first grandchildren in a large family. He has pleasant memories of visiting his Uncle Fred's farm and running among the sheep, his red cap bobbing above the woolly white backs, to the consternation of aunts, uncles, and parents; of sliding down the steep sides of the Indian mound around which Revolutionary War heroes were buried, and later gathering arrowheads there. Wilbur's father carried him outside to see Haley's Comet; in new red rubber boots, Wilbur went with him to see the Ohio and Muskingum rivers overflow their banks.

He wasn't more than 9 or 10 when he ran away to war—World War I. At almost noontime, he put down his small bundle of worldly possessions and sat on the curbstone to ease feet shod in high-laced shoes and contemplate the pangs of hunger which were beginning to conflict with his patriotic intentions. "Where are you going, son?" There stood his father, on his way home to the midday meal with a fat white bag in his hand. "To war. Watchagot in the bag?" "Some fresh, warm buns from Pfaff's bakery—with icing, too. You had better come back and share these with the family. You can go to war later." Which he did—some twenty-five and thirty-five years later.

As he grew Wilbur escaped to the wide elm-shaded streets where cars were such a rarity that he and his friends could safely play "Kick the Can" and "Run Sheep Run." The clop-clop of the horse drawing the ice wagon punctuated hot summer mornings and drowsy afternoons. Hitching a ride on the back of an ice wagon brought the added bonus of a hard, cold chunk of ice to suck on—more refreshing in retrospect than today's ice cubes rattling in a glass.

First swimming lessons consisted in being tossed into the Muskingum River; graduation was a churn across the Ohio. Being accepted into sandlot baseball depended upon one's ability to provide a home-made ball and bat. Staying in the ranks meant that one speedily became expert in hitting, running, pitching, and catching. Wilbur stayed.

In time he became an enthusiastic and letter-winning member of all the athletic teams that high school and college could offer him. After graduation from Marietta College, he considered but refused an offer to play professional baseball. He also turned down offers to become a professional journalist and a musician, though he participated in each of these activities as the years passed.

Marietta was a musical community. Wilbur was introduced to simple tunes at home, to the glories of German baroque music in the Lutheran church he attended, to actual performance by private piano and flute teachers and by high school and college orchestras. Instead of delivering an oration or valedictorian at his college commencement, he played the *Londonderry Air* on his flute.

In those days of home-baked bread and family-created music, the possession of a phonograph and its "canned" music was a status symbol. Young Wilbur cranked up the Schramms' new acquisition, turned it to top volume, and strolled down the street to learn how far the one-and-only Caruso's voice could be heard. Not very many years later, he was painstakingly building a radio receiver and hearing through its heavy earset the faint fairy music from Station KDKA. From that day on, he was never without one or more of those instruments which are now known as the tools of mass media.

At the University of Iowa in Iowa City in the early 1930s, Wilbur stood before the first television picture ever to be broadcast—a postcard-sized picture in a four-foot-high cabinet. It showed a man talking, a university professor teaching his subject, foreshadowing educational television, which later evolved into public television. In 1974–1975, Wilbur participated in satellite programs across the entire Pacific region. Between these two events were all those communication projects and researches which you will be reading about in the remainder of this book.

Harvard Graduate School and a flute scholarship at the New England Conservatory enticed him to the East Coast after he had earned his bachelor's degree in political science at Marietta College. In Cambridge, he burned the candle at both ends, studying literature and philosophy with some of Harvard's great teachers, taking flute lessons and playing in the Boston Civic Symphony Orchestra, helping the graduate school's basketball team defeat the undergraduates, waiting tables, and working as a newspaper reporter and correspondent as he had done since his high school days.

One of his mentors advised him to drop "all zees foolishnesses" and concentrate on his music. So he dropped everything but his Harvard classes and thus began a career in the scholarly life. The choice of that road, in the words of his friend Robert Frost, "made all the difference—and way led on to way."

After a master's degree at Harvard, he earned a doctorate in American Literature under Norman Foerster at the University of Iowa and stayed at Iowa to teach English and to become the first head of the Iowa Creative Writing Program. Historic tree-shaded Iowa City, set in Grant Wood country, was a pleasant place to live during those Great Depression years. He married there, and his two children were born.

Iowa City was called by many "The Athens of the Midwest." It was a setting for well-known artists, actors, and writers and for others who stopped briefly to lecture or longer to visit and participate in the fine arts renaissance of the day. Robert Frost, Stephen Benét, Archibald MacLeish, Robert Penn Warren, Wallace Stegner, Josephine Johnson, Grant Wood, and Thomas Benton were only a few of the great ones who lent a sparkle to that academic scene.

From 1937 to 1947, Wilbur wrote quite a lot of fiction; one of his short stories won the O. Henry Award. Until Hawaii in the early seventies again gave him the time and inspiration to write poetry, his energies were enlisted in administrative duties, in communication research, and in scholarly professional prose, about which the other chapters in this book will have much to say.

The Iowa term was interrupted by a two-year stay in Washington, D.C., during World War II. He returned to Iowa in 1943 to become head of the School of Journalism. Next he went to the University of Illinois, where he became the first dean of communications and founded the Institute of Communications Research. In 1955 Wilbur moved to Stanford University for an eighteen-year stint as director of the Institute for Communication Research, which he created. Upon his "retirement" from Stanford, he took on the task of organizing the Communication Institute at the East-West Center. Today, happily relieved of all administrative responsibilities, he is writing poetry and prose once again, drawing on ideas that have intrigued him most of his life.

Friends have frequently commented on the number of different careers Wilbur has carried on consecutively and even concurrently, and wondered where he found the vitality. He drew it from many directions—athletics, nutrition, aspiration, inspiration, and, of course, his ancestry.

Once when we were visiting his parents during one of those hot Ohio summers, I observed Wilbur's mother rushing around her kitchen with skirts swirling, hair flying, face prettily flushed. The clothesline outside was laden, the washing machine was churning in the basement, preserves were bubbling on the stove, and other pots were steaming away in preparation for noontime dinner. When I marveled at her accomplishments, she replied, "Oh, I just get a lot of things started and then I have to take care of them." Her son, too, has started a lot of things in his life, and they all had to be kept going. For, as his old friend, the novelist Dorothy James Roberts, has described him, Wilbur is "one of those who has the habit of excellence."

The Literary Years

JAMES M. REID

In the summer of 1941, Wil Schramm appeared at the New York offices of Harcourt Brace and Company. He came for a two-month stint as guest editor in our trade department. Wil was among the first of several such visitors from academe to the world of book publishing. He came that summer from the University of Iowa, where he had founded the creative writing program with the aid, comfort, and advice of Norman Foerster, head of the English department, a great teacher of American literature. I had just persuaded Dr. Foerster to join our crew of teachers and editors on the early 1940s revision of our great high school series, *Adventures in Literature*. Dr. Foerster had agreed to write the literary history for *Adventures in American Literature,* the eleventh-grade book in the series; I always suspected that he involved Wil Schramm in the preparation of his fine contribution to the series.

In any case I was quickly attracted to Wil for, as editor-in-chief of Harcourt Brace's textbook department, I was constantly on the lookout for ways and means of involving top creative writers as authors of our textbooks, particularly our high school English books. And Wil, at that time, was reaching the height of his short story writing career. The *Atlantic Monthly* had just printed his great story, "Windwagon Smith." Other stories were on the way to publication. The only precedent for Wil's marvelous meld of historical fact and pure breathtaking fantasy was Stephen Vincent Benét's "The Devil and Daniel Webster."

I probably sought Wil out in his temporary office, but it could easily have been the other way. For Wil made the editorial rounds at Harcourt Brace, sitting beside one's desk and asking intelligent questions.

We were both mildly athletic, Wil more authentically so than I. He was a versatile athlete, with third base at the summit of his skill. At one point he admitted that he had rather seriously considered becoming a professional ball player. I was glad he hadn't for we might have lost a first-class writer. But he retained that limber third-base agility for years and years. And we shared deep interests in creative writing—I as editor and he as practitioner. We had the whole great world of literature, books, and ideas to explore together.

Through the years I was constantly amazed by the wide versatility of Wil's writing talent and the apparent but probably deceptive ease with which he wrote. I say "probably deceptive" because good writing is never easy; it takes hard work and hard self-discipline. After I had managed to sign him up, Wil always came through with his manuscripts for me—on time and in need of mighty little editing.

In 1942, I signed Wil Schramm to take over the literary history in *Adventures in American Literature* from Norman Foerster. I can safely say that Wil's literary history for "A.Lit.," which appeared in both the 1947 and the 1952 editions, has been read (and studied) by more readers than anything else he has written. This history ran to about 40,000 words, from the Pilgrim Fathers and Cotton Mather to William Faulkner, Thornton Wilder, Robert Frost, and Carl Sandburg in the 1940s. "A. Lit." was always the bestseller of the six-book *Adventures* series; in the forties, it sold at least 100,000 copies a year. Thus, more than a million copies of Wil's history were placed in the schools— assuming that each copy was used by at least five students, you have five million readers, Wil's largest audience. His story of American literature was not just read once over lightly but was studied intensively, discussed in class and enjoyed. Just as important from my point of view, it gave Harcourt Brace a genuine sales advantage over our arch rivals, Scott Foresman and Ginn! In the late forties, we in the textbook department persuaded Wil to produce an anthology of short stories for high schools. It was remarkable not mainly for its selections but for Wil's foreword, in which he gave his account, in full detail, of the creative process involved in writing a short story—a most illuminating, unique, and teachable feature.

In all the *Atlantic* and the *Saturday Evening Post* published fourteen of Wil's short stories, or "yarns" as he preferred to call them, in the six years from 1941 through 1947. In 1942 he won the O. Henry Award for short stories. All this while he was busy in the war effort in Washington or working in the Office of Strategic Services or the State Department. This production of fourteen stories in six years was normal procedure for Wil, as a glance at his books and articles and papers after his "literary period" surely testifies. My own theory is that he never slept!

Wil's short stories were a pride and joy. The impressive list included "Windwagon Smith," published in the *Atlantic Monthly* in 1941; and thirteen others published in the *Saturday Evening Post* between 1942 and 1947. Many of the stories were published by Harcourt in 1947 in a collection titled *Windwagon Smith and Other Yarns.*

But I was not satisfied; I wanted Wil to write a novel, which might well bring him the national attention that I felt his talent deserved. We discussed this proposed novel many times and at length, especially, I remember, when he drove with me for a weekend at my farm at Wallingford, Vermont. But pressures of various kinds always seemed to prevent his getting the requisite prolonged serenity he would require for a major work of fiction. Eventually even the writing of short stories stopped, and he turned out a vast series of professional books and valuable reports for the government and various foundations. Finally, in his sixties, he began to write poetry. Perhaps that's what Wil's talent really is—a poetic talent.

The Iowa Years

WALLACE E. STEGNER

In a way, to write the obituary of a dead friend would be easier than to record one's recollections of a living one. A dead friend isn't going to read what is written about him. He isn't going to correct facts, repudiate flattery, or in any other way threaten the record as the memorialist wants to establish it. A living friend is less submissive. Glad as one is to have him still alive, he is a challenge, even a sort of antagonist. He imposes constraints. He inhibits creativity.

So when I remember Wilbur Schramm as I knew him at the State University of Iowa in the early 1930s, I want to remember carefully, lest I be corrected by my betters. Wilbur has taught me enough already without having to teach me historical accuracy.

We arrived in Iowa City at the same time—in September 1930—I as an incomparably green and ill-prepared first-year graduate student from the wild west, Wilbur as a transfer from the Harvard Graduate School, where he had already completed the M.A. He had been well trained to begin with and had been seasoned for a year in the intellectual life in the place that called itself headquarters. I didn't even know what or where the intellectual life was.

Our rooms were next door to one another in the Quadrangle, an old brick barracks that would have struck me as dreary except that I was away from home for the first time and learning so fast that I didn't have time to notice. But one thing I did notice. True to my role as a wild westerner, I had decorated my dresser with a .38 in a gunfighter's holster and cartridge belt. Wilbur had adorned his with his flute, which he played in the university symphony, and with two photographs, one of the first flutist in the Boston Symphony and one of Bliss Perry. I had never before seen anybody hang up pictures of his *teachers*.

Within the tiny solar system of a graduate department, in the limited universe of a fairly small provincial school, acquaintance is all but instantaneous and friendship almost as sudden. A dozen or more of us graduate students in English lived in the Quad, ate at the same cafeteria, walked every morning across the river bridge to the same classes, hunted the same books in the same corners of the stacks, developed the same gripes and the same anxieties, faced the same crises at examination and term-paper time. Our lives were incredibly uniform and limited, considering that we were launched on the adventure of filling our heads with the best that has been thought and said in the world. Within weeks we knew one another as prisoners in a chain gang must know one another, and had begun to form into the pairs and clusters of preference, liking, repulsion, and friendship.

One of the pairings that began early and lasted was the Schramm–Stegner combine. Before long, the friendship got so close that we were writing paired papers for Norman Foerster's course in literary criticism, and Foerster had begun referring to us as Simon and Schuster. But in terms of what each of us gave and each of us got, it was not a friendship of equals. We were more like a younger and an older brother. Wilbur had little or nothing to learn from me; he seemed simply to like me. I not only liked him, I learned from him every time he opened his mouth. He was constantly being astonished, amused, or appalled at the deficiencies in my background and education. Not officiously, but simply out of generosity and friendship, he undertook to civilize me. His job was made easier when, sometime around midyear, my assigned roommate developed alarming inclinations to pat and want to kiss me. He had to be outmaneuvered, since he couldn't be moved out. Good-naturedly, Wilbur joined me in a plot to throw our adjoining rooms together into a suite, with a living room where we could all study and a three-bed bedroom where a man could feel safe. After the amorous roomy moved out in disgust, Wilbur and I roomed together through that year and the next, and he had full opportunity to civilize me properly.

Take music, as one example. When he found that at the age of 21 I had literally never heard a symphony orchestra and that my notion of a highbrow classical piece was *Liebestraum,* he began directing my radio listening and dragging me off to concerts, including those in which he played his flute. Out of thin air, at odd moments, he produced mini-lectures on the sonata form, on the structure of the popular song, or on the lives of the composers. With somewhat recalcitrant material, he didn't get far, but he got farther than anyone else ever did except my wife—to whom, naturally, he introduced me.

As with music, so with languages. I had some Latin, no Greek, and no modern languages except a little Spanish that was held to be academically unworthy. Before long, under Wilbur's tutelage, I was reciting poems of Goethe, singing *Lieder,* and being told (Wilbur had picked up a letter I had addressed to *Herr* Somebody) that when one addressed somebody in German one used the dative *Herrn.* For quite a while, a half dozen of us gathered late in the afternoon in a seminar room for a crash course in introductory Greek taught by our learned and generous friend. Like a doll stuck full of pins, my brains still retain little Greek poems about "the beautiful parsley" and little aphorisms like "big book, big evil," which for overworked graduate students didn't seem a bad motto.

Travel, too, by Wilbur's premises, had to be broadening. We hitch-hiked around together during vacations, and before the beginning of our second year in Iowa City we met in Chicago, the farthest east I had ever been, where we divided our time between Wrigley Field and the Art Institute. *Mens sana in corpore sano.* Similarly, when we once hitchhiked to visit relatives of mine in northern Iowa and Minnesota, we covered all the bases. I think it was at my suggestion that we went to hear Cab Calloway kick the gong around in Minneapolis. I know it was at Wilbur's that we went over to the University of Minnesota and sat in on a class of Franz Klaeber's. Klaeber had edited the *Beowulf* text we were using, and we got his autograph on our copies. Whose idea it was to carry our *Beowulf* texts on a hitchhiking vacation I don't know, but I can guess.

Early in our second year, the Depression came down on us hard. All the banks were closed, and money virtually disappeared. As an economy measure, we began cooking meals in our room, which was against the rules but which was not likely to be protested in the circumstances. With milk at two cents a quart and eggs around a nickel a dozen, we broke records for economy, using the window ledge for a refrigerator and a borrowed hotplate for a stove. The practice had certain pleasant consequences. One was a house mouse who moved in to take care of our crumbs. He lived in Wilbur's superheterodyne radio and did a hotfoot dance when the tubes warmed up. Another was the game we developed with potcovers.

On one of our hitchhiking expeditions to my grandfather's farm near Lake Mills, Iowa, my Uncle George had taught us to throw screwballs and sliders with a corncob. Adapting the technique to potcovers, we found that at fifteen-foot range we could throw hooks that would break three feet. I like to think that we were on the verge of inventing the frisbee. On Sunday mornings we used to stand at opposite sides of the room and throw breaking pitches at each other, keeping track of the balls and strikes, until the people below began pounding on the ceiling with a broom handle. Then we would go back, refreshed, to "The Fight at Finnsburg" or the folktale analogues of the tale of the Prioresse or Aristotle's *Poetics* or Longinus on the Sublime.

That life sounds frivolous, even childish. Actually it was therapeutic and essential. I, at least, couldn't have survived without those playful breaks, and without the few minutes after a cafeteria lunch when we rolled up paper napkins and shot baskets in the water glasses. A kind of desperation that invaded our studies and the times needed periodic, perhaps systematic, relief. Potcovers and rolled-up paper napkins and a kind of competitive playfulness are adequate recreational equipment if you accept them as such.

"*Freut euch des Lebens,*" Wilbur used to tell me, out of William Ellery Leonard's poem *Two Lives*. "Take ye joy of life!" He had that way of combining a little rudimentary language instruction along with his expressions of attitude and belief. But in the pinch he could offer much more than his prevailing geniality and charm and shrewdness. He was with me the night a telegram came announcing my brother's death back in Salt Lake City. Wilbur loaned me the money for a ticket and put me on the train, he put his overcoat on my back because I didn't own one, and he explained to me, some time during those bad hours, the etymology of the word "sympathy," which means "suffering with." And he did suffer with, just as in better hours he played with, or studied with, or thought with. Among his many gifts—intellectual, literary, social, athletic, and all the rest—was and is a most extraordinary gift for friendship.

The friendships of youth and early manhood, however close, cannot remain unchanged. Especially in the academic life, which in its early years is notably peripatetic (and expecially during the Depression, when you took any job you could get, no matter where), it is easy to

draw away from and lose track of friends. One can be guilty, too, of
becoming too absorbed in a career, and careers have a way of diverging
into new places and new associations. Circumstances have a way of
warping intentions and inclinations. My own circumstances bent me
first to Berkeley, then back to Iowa City briefly, then to a temporary
job at Augustana College in Rock Island, then back to Iowa City for a
summer session, then to Salt Lake City for three years, then to the
University of Wisconsin, then to Harvard, then to Stanford.

Wilbur's circumstances kept him at an ascending series of posts at
Iowa—first as director of the writing program and editor of *American
Prefaces,* then as head of journalism—before taking him off to the
University of Illinois as assistant to President George Stoddard and
director of the Press. Eventually his stars brought him to Stanford. By
that time our careers had diverged widely, for I stayed "literary" and
he went out into mass communications and public opinion research,
so that we saw less of one another than either of us wanted. We had
wives, families, preoccupations; we lived in different towns and taught
in different departments; we both traveled a good deal and were away
for extended periods.

And yet the closeness remains. It remained through all the years
when we rarely saw one another, and, as I sit down to recollect it, I see
that Wilbur had an extraordinary and continuing effect on my life. He
introduced me to my future wife, to whom he had already built me up
as somebody she ought to know. He published one of my first stories
in his *American Prefaces* magazine. He put something of mine in his
first anthology of short stories. When he had developed the writing
program at Iowa, he invited me to lecture. As if wheels had ground
around to some starting point, he was there to come to the lecture
platform to halt the questioning after my talk and tell me that word
had just come of my father's death. He didn't need, this time, to lend
me train fare or an overcoat, but he showed me all over again the
meaning of sympathy.

Out of nowhere, as years passed, he reached out and did me favors,
and by those favors affected my future. Teaching one summer at the
Breadloaf English School, he learned that a staff member for the
Breadloaf Writers Conference had fallen ill and had to be replaced
fast. By some hours of hard talking, he persuaded Theodore Morrison,
the director, that Wallace Stegner, who had then published one small
book and a few stories, would be an adequate substitute, and he came
down to Yaddo, where I was working, to tell me of his success. Out of

that Breadloaf fortnight, for which Wilbur was entirely responsible, came a later invitation to teach at Harvard, and out of the Harvard years much that I could not have anticipated, including the kind of enriching associations that Wilbur himself had commemorated in the photographs on his Quadrangle wall. Still later, when he was at Illinois and I was at Stanford, he offered me a job so tempting that it humbled me, for the offer demonstrated that neither his liking nor his confidence had wavered in the slightest in more than twenty years.

As I began by saying, he taught me much about all sorts of things, not least the meaning of friendship. I still don't know as much about that as he does, but I have been learning, ever since I was a gawk from Utah trying to master "Dream a Little Lullaby" on the banjo uke while Wilbur sat in his corner translating Catullus's love poems for relaxation. Because Wilbur has been a good teacher, I won't have to start with Cicero's "De Amicitia." I can simply go on remembering Wilbur's example.

The Illinois Years

ROBERT B. HUDSON

That George Stoddard and Wilbur Schramm were colleagues at Iowa was a stroke of good fortune for both men—Stoddard the senior, Schramm the junior. The friendship and mutual admiration developed at Iowa has held fast over the years. Margaret Stoddard, in writing about that relationship, says, "We had known Wil at Iowa, of course, and admired him and Betty so much. As dean of the Graduate College, George had much contact, happy, stimulating contact. And I remember back there George's saying, 'The more I look at the faculty the more I realize the quality lacking in many of them is *imagination,* and that is what makes Wil so interesting, so alert, so inspired.' So it was a natural thing to bring Wil to Illinois when we came from the Albany posts [New York State Commissioner of Education] back to the Middle West. Wil stopped by to see us many times when he was on government projects during the war and we found him always the same stimulating mind and person."

As soon as Schramm rejoined George Stoddard at Illinois in 1947, he became a member of the inner cabinet—the "let's-get-the-University-moving-again" group—and was a part of that wonderful, yeasty, innovative, dynamic period of growth which occasionally grips educational institutions (and nations) for short periods of time when dreams appear to be realizable and dissent is muted.

Schramm's first major thrust at Illinois was the creation of the Institute of Communications Research. Stoddard recalls that "the Institute . . . was for research on the problems of press, radio, films, and other forms of mass communication. Members of the Institute were drawn from the social sciences, journalism, radio, and publishing. By studying the basic problems of the present media and such forthcoming media as television and facsimile, by giving consulting service and offering graduate courses, they hoped to contribute to the more effective use of mass communication in society and to the better training of future communications men. A few specially qualified candidates were admitted each year to an interdepartmental program of study under the supervision of the Institute and leading to the degree of Doctor of Philosophy in Communications.''

The mark of an effective communicator is that he can persuade others to see merit in a conception and to join in implementing a course of action. Selling a joint program cutting across all the social sciences and getting it accepted by the Graduate College was no mean feat, but Wilbur Schramm is persuasive, and he was not without compensating inducements. The institute became a reality and enlisted the participation of some of the abler men in the social science disciplines. As soon as the program was announced, it began to attract bright young men and women, and within a few years it gained an international reputation, not only for the concept and faculty but most of all for the quality of its graduates.

To what extent the idea was original with Schramm and Stoddard is hard to say—ideas whose time have come have a way of emerging—but its implementation was unique. In 1950, the graduate school bulletin described the program in these terms:

> The University of Illinois admits each year a few qualified students to a program of graduate study in mass communications leading to the degree of Doctor of Philosophy. This doctoral program is administered by an interdepartmental committee, and the program itself is designed interdepartmentally to apply the methods and disciplines of the social sciences (supported where necessary by the arts and natural sciences) to the basic problems of human communication.
>
> The program is intended for students whose academic and professional experience qualifies them to study mass communications, and whose plans for careers are such as to make this interdepartmental degree more desirable than a degree in one of the social sciences. Among such careers may be the teaching of journalism, radio, or other communication subjects, research in the fields of public opinion or audience study, and executive jobs in the communication industries requiring breadth, perspective, and a scientific background.
>
> Prerequisites to admission to this program are at least one course in each of the following subjects: psychology, sociology, political science, economics, and statistics. . . .''

At the outset of the program, the faculty assembled the relevant literature from scattered sources for use by students, which led to one of the early compendiums in the field. *Mass Communications* was compiled and edited by Schramm and published in 1949. Its authors, in addition to Schramm, included such distinguished scholars as Harold D. Lasswell, Margaret Mead, Hadley Cantril, Gordon Allport, Frank Luther Mott, Rudolf Flesch, Paul Lazarsfeld, Walter Lippman, Robert K. Merton, Bernard Berelson, John Dollard, Louis Werth, Wendell Johnson, Daniel Katz, and others. That edition was later revised and updated, and a score of other readers in mass communications have since come on the market.

Once the institute was in place and the doctoral program approved, Schramm and Fred Siebert, director of the School of Journalism, moved to change the name of the school to School of Journalism and Communications in order to better reflect the scope of work now offered and to provide an administrative home for the doctoral program. The Illinois communication degree program has been emulated by many institutions in this country and abroad.

Soon after he landed in Urbana, the reports of the Hutchins Commission on a Free and Responsible Press began to make their appearance, and Schramm, together with Siebert, organized a series of seminars within the faculty to consider their implications. The series was a forward-looking intellectual exercise for a staff heavily oriented to traditional ways of viewing the press. One byproduct of this exercise took the form of a book, *Four Theories of the Press,* in which Schramm, Siebert, and Ted Peterson examined the authoritarian theory, the libertarian theory, the social responsibility theory, and the Soviet Communist theory of the press.

In a major reorganization move, Stoddard and Schramm next devised a seemingly radical restructuring of basic communication programs and services within the university and won approval for it. The restructuring created a Division of Communications, headed by Schramm as dean. The division took under a single administrative umbrella such diverse teaching and service units as the School of Journalism and Communications, the Speech Department, the Library School, University Libraries, University Extension, University Broadcasting, the alumni office, university publicity, athletic department publicity, agricultural information, the Allerton House conference center, and perhaps others. This grouping made some strange and unhappy bedfellows. (Table talk at the Faculty Club suggested that, since the central purpose of a university is communication, why not subsume the whole university under the new division?) But the restructuring was successful, and with some effective planning, sorting out, and elimination of duplication, a more coordinated effort and new initiatives took place. That the administrative arrangement worked was due in large measure to Schramm's tact, his appreciation of the views of colleagues, and, perhaps most of all, to a genuine friendliness on his part that helped in resolving many points of potential conflict and resistance.

As we have seen, at Illinois Schramm was a planner, an innovator, and an administrator. But all the while Schramm the scholar and teacher was in evidence. He had left behind his more carefree days as a creative writer when he had turned out such imaginative and delightful stories as "The Horse That Played Third Base for Brooklyn" and "Windwagon Smith." Trained as a writer/journalist *and* as a psychologist, he found psychology coming into ascendancy, and Schramm looked to complete the communication cycle—to be concerned with the decoder as well as with the encoder of messages.

Thus, in the teaching area, the Illinois years were a period of growth and consolidation for Schramm. A little like John Dewey, whose lectures were essentially conversations with himself, Schramm developed and honed his theory of the communication process in the presence of bright students. They followed him as he argued his points and would occasionally challenge an assumption until it was clarified. Together with them, he polished the rationale and firmed up his own thinking about how communication among humans takes place. The theories he developed at Illinois have been tested and verified in scores of research projects in the two decades that followed and are reflected in the millions of words that have flowed from his "magic typewriter" since then.

Electronic communication devices held strong attraction for Wilbur Schramm from the early days of radio, and his experiences with the Office of War Information (OWI) during the war clinched that interest and fired his imagination with their potential. He once even considered joining CBS but decided that corporate life and its goals were not entirely to his liking. Indeed, his inclinations ran toward noncommercial broadcasting. He had followed with interest the operation of the university radio station at Iowa; on arriving at Illinois, he determined to give the electronic medium his attention, on both the local and the national levels.

While awaiting a propitious time to make adjustments in the university broadcasting operation, he persuaded John Marshall of the Rockefeller Foundation to fund a two-week seminar for educational radio station managers to examine the state-of-the-art and to lift their horizons regarding the potential of their medium. The group—a score of managers and a half-dozen resource people—assembled at the University's Allerton House conference center in the summer of 1949 and ignited a movement that eventually claimed television channel reservations for education and laid the foundation for both instructional and public television. Initially, the group launched a radio tape "bicycle" network (now National Public Radio [NPR]) and drew up plans for a permanent staff and headquarters for the National Association of Educational Broadcasters (NAEB).

Schramm had a special role in the latter effort. He helped to design and carried to the Kellogg Foundation the NAEB's proposal for funding and, subsequently, was instrumental in making a home at Illinois for both the executive offices and the tape network. In recognition of this and many other contributions to educational communications, the NAEB in 1973 bestowed on Wilbur Lang Schramm its Distinguished Service Award.

Also in 1949, Schramm and Stoddard created the position of director of University Broadcasting and invited me to accept that office on a joint appointment with the School of Journalism and Communications. Author/newsman Quincy Howe was soon brought in to beef up broadcast news analysis (and to offer a journalism course in contemporary affairs), but innovation in radio was scarcely underway when most staff energies were suddenly turned toward the activation of a television station by the university. Both President Stoddard and Dean Schramm were highly supportive of this effort, and Stoddard led the bloody fight for it through the budget committees of the state legislature. Schramm's interest was to shore up the case for educational television (ETV) in terms of its educational impact; at this point, he began a systematic examination of the literature to discover how and to what extent learning takes place in the presence of television. At the point where the literature was exhausted, he began to devise new research and (now it can be told) he was destined to follow that trail for the rest of his life, seeking always the Holy Grail of the perfect communication cycle measuring a variety of input signals received in a wide range of viewing environments and cultural settings.

One day in 1950, Schramm came into my office in Gregory Hall and asked if I could take a speaking engagement for him in Houston. The reason: "I am flying to Korea on Thursday morning!" (In the shrunken world of the seventies, this plan may not sound strange, but then it seemed totally incongruous.) Since then, Wil Schramm has flown off to somewhere about every morning of the week. His search and mission has taken him to the developing nations of Asia, Africa, and Latin America, and among the educators of the Third World he is probably the best known and most respected private American. Former students and disciples await him at every stop, and the requests for his guidance and counsel are endless. Illinois launched him on this international odyssey.

In Urbana, the Schramms occupied a commodious and architecturally pleasing house on Douglas Place which Betty converted into a charming home. Daughter Mary was a star student at University High, and young Mike spent his spare time editing a neighborhood newspaper and constructing radio receivers. Wil, had he chosen another calling, would have been closing out a career as shortstop for the Cleveland Indians. As it was, in the flatlands of Illinois, before the Palo Alto pool or the Pacific Ocean off Ala Moana, Wil was reduced to a basketball and a hoop above his garage door for energy release and maintenance of muscle tone. His exercise attracted small boys in the neighborhood, including young Robin Hudson, and Wil always was generous in sharing the territory and giving ground in one-on-one matchups. He taught the boys the rudiments of the game and set them a fine example.

Teaching, after all, is the touchstone of the Schramm mystique— Wilbur is always the *teacher*. With students, he was one of the best, and colleagues grew through exposure to his mind. Through seminars and conferences, he has left his imprint on communication scholars around the world. But perhaps his teaching skills are most evident in his writing style, a style that involves the reader as though he were following the steps of a master. No wonder his typewriter is called "magic." It is played upon by a Pied Piper.

The Stanford Years

Lyle M. Nelson

Most scholars agree that Wilbur Schramm did not invent the typewriter. But a considerable body of thought holds that the typewriter was invented *for* Wilbur Schramm.

At Stanford, Wilbur and the electric typewriter discovered each other. Some five million words and four typewriters later (he literally wore the keys off two of them), Wilbur had become unquestionably the world's leading authority in the field of communication research.

What he began at Iowa and gave substance and form to at Illinois came into full bloom after he arrived at Stanford in 1955. The Institute for Communication Research became the wellspring from which flowed the newest, most innovative, and most far-reaching ideas and theories in a rapidly expanding field. In words, in applications of new strategies to communication problems in every corner of the world, and in the growing influence of a coterie of well-trained disciples, Wilbur Schramm more than any other one person launched what has now been called "The Age of Communication."

His productivity was awesome. He often wrote a book while colleagues were struggling through single journal articles. His twenty-five books or other major works totalled some 10,720 pages, together with what seemed a constant flow of journal articles, reports, and major speeches such as the Japan Prize Lecture and the Missouri Solomon Lecture. Moreover, many of these works were translated into at least a dozen foreign languages, ranging from French and Spanish to Korean, Japanese, and Arabic.

While some of Wilbur's major works were those he edited, he almost always contributed the key chapter or chapters. Likewise, some books were done in collaboration with colleagues, but invariably they were mostly pure Schramm in concept, in the reach of the scholarship, and in the dynamic impact of the words on paper.

"Writing a book or a report with Wilbur," one coauthor ruefully remarked, "is about like the old story of hamburgers made up of half rabbit and half horse. The net result is that the half Wilbur contributes is more like 90 percent."

Wilbur's "Stanford books" essentially fall into four broad categories, providing an indication of the tremendous range of his mind and interests. The categories include (1) those works which deal with the ethics and responsibility of the media, (2) those which help to define and advance the theory and methodology of the emerging field of communication research, (3) those which deal with the social impact of new media, chiefly television, and (4) those which relate communication to national development goals in other parts of the world. All of them are listed in the bibliography published in this volume; I will comment on but a few.

In the first category, *Four Theories of the Press* was published shortly after Schramm came to Stanford from Illinois. Written in collaboration with Fred Siebert and Theodore Peterson, the book was in manuscript form before Wilbur heeded Horace Greeley's advice (and the urgings of Stanford President Wally Sterling) to go west. Twenty years later, it remains one of the most widely quoted books in journalism courses dealing with the history, ethics, and structure of the world press.

In 1957, *Responsibility in Mass Communication* brought together and synthesized various theories of the role of communication in society. It quickly became the textbook and basic resource document for a new group of courses variously labeled in most university catologs as "Mass Communication and Society," "Responsibility of the Mass Media," "Mass Media and Public Policy," and the like.

In this category, too, appeared *One Day in the World's Press: Fourteen Great Newspapers on a Day of Crisis,* published by the Stanford University Press in 1959. This book examined treatment by newspapers throughout the world of the events of November 2, 1956, when

Egypt was under attack by British, French, and Israeli forces and when Soviet tanks entered Budapest after the Hungarian uprising. For this book, Wilbur received from Long Island University a special George Polk Memorial award for journalistic achievement.

Schramm's best-known and most widely quoted book probably still is *Mass Communication,* first published in 1954, before the "Stanford era," but revised in 1960 by popular demand. It is virtually impossible to walk into the communication section of any library in the world without finding a copy of this basic volume.

While all of Schramm's books have represented major contributions to the theory and methodology of communication—the objective he constantly held up to his Ph.D. students as the only real basis of scholarship—his *Science of Human Communication,* published by Basic Books in 1963, and the Paris-Stanford *Studies in Communication,* published by the Institute for Communication Research in 1962, most specifically dealt with the application of scientific disciplines to the study of communication. Wilbur always believed *Studies in Communication* should have received more attention than some of his more widely recognized works.

During this time, Wilbur's "magic typewriter" (some said that, like the famous tractor in one of his short stories, it could "fly" by itself) also turned out six books dealing with the impact of the rapidly developing field of television on the lives of Americans of all ages. These included *The Impact of Educational Television* and *New Teaching Aids for the American Classroom* in 1960, *Television in the Lives of Our Children* (with Jack Lyle and Ed Parker) in 1961, *Educational Television, The Next Ten Years* in 1962, *The People Look at Educational Television* (with Jack Lyle and Ithiel Pool) in 1963, and *Learning from Television: What The Research Says* (with Godwin Chu) in 1967.

Always an activist in terms of seeking ways to put communication to work to improve the lives of people, Wilbur made the Institute for Communication Research at Stanford the focal point for those concerned with harnessing the power of communication to the service of national development. In 1962 he was appointed the Janet Peck Professor of International Communication, the first such distinguished chair to be created in the Department of Communication at Stanford.

Seven of Wilbur's publications issued during this period helped to extend the Institute's reputation throughout the world. These works included *Mass Media and National Development* in 1964, *Communication and Change in the Developing Countries* (with Dan Lerner) in 1967, two UNESCO series also published in 1967—*New Educational Media in Action: Case Studies for Planners* and *The New Media: Memo to Educational Planners* (both with Phil Coombs, Friedrich Kahnert, and Jack Lyle), *Communication Satellites for Education and Development: The Case for India* (with Lyle Nelson) in 1968, and *Big Media, Little Media* in 1973.

As if his major areas of interests were not sufficient to occupy all of his energies, Schramm during his Stanford career also produced two lesser-known books dealing with totally different subjects: *Little House: A Study of Senior Citizens,* in 1961, and *Classroom Out-of-Doors: Education Through School Camping,* in 1969. He was fond of telling friends that he enjoyed writing the latter perhaps more than some of his "more serious" volumes.

Concluding the publications during Wilbur's Stanford years were the monumental *Handbook of Communication,* which he edited with Ithiel Pool and which was three years in preparation before its publication in 1973, and *Men, Messages and Media: A Look at Human Communication,* written in Hawaii while on a sabbatical at the East-West Center. The latter is a superbly well-written book which gives one of the clearest explanations anywhere of the essential relationship of communication to societal structures.

But the Schramm reputation in the communication field was not made by books alone. As significant as his written contribution was the influence of a group of well-trained "disciples" who went out from Stanford during those years. In themselves a dramatic demonstration of the "rippling effect" of communication, they carried the Stanford, and Schramm, reputation to all parts of the world and in turn added to the knowledge and usefulness of this new branch of learning.

To list some of these former students without mentioning them all is difficult, and perhaps unfair. Wilbur's standards were high and his requirements demanding. As a result, virtually all Ph.D.'s who bore the Schramm/Stanford imprint had a special kind of status and almost immediately moved into leadership roles in developing new centers for study and new fields for research.

At the risk of overlooking some who have made—and others who are likely to make—important contributions, the following Schramm students come immediately to mind: Paul Deutschman, whose career was unfortunately cut short before he could make his most important contributions; Steve Chaffee, Willard G. Bleyer Professor of Journalism and Mass Communication at the University of Wisconsin; Wayne Danielson, dean of the school of Communication at the University of Texas at Austin; Jack Lyle, director of the Communication Institute at the East-West Center in Hawaii; Godwin C. Chu, research associate at the same institute; Serena Wade, one of the first women to attain full professor status in the field; and Ed Parker and Bill Paisley at Stanford.

Although they did not receive their Ph.D.'s at Stanford, others who came under the Schramm influence and helped to carry his ideas worldwide were Hidetoshi Kato of Kyoto University; Y. V. L. Rao of India and later of Singapore; Vadim Golovanov, Moscow journalist; and Raad Raheem, now education officer of the International Planned Parenthood Federation, with headquarters in Nairobi.

Still a third channel through which the Schramm influence made itself felt was in Wilbur's worldwide travels and in the number of international visitors who trekked to Stanford and to the Schramm home in those years. Government after government, faced with problems of national development and aware of the key role communication could play in bringing about any change, sought out Schramm for advice and help: India, Korea, Samoa, Indonesia, Colombia, Kenya, Tanzania, Uganda, El Salvador, Niger, Pakistan, Israel, and many others.

No one could be sure in what corner of the world Wilbur would next turn up, but it usually was a safe bet that it would be at the most uncomfortable and least desirable time of the year. Wilbur seemed to have an unerring instinct for attracting the worst weather or for being in a particular country at a time of national crisis. Fate, as if to make up for the superior intellectual powers granted a single individual, seemed to decree that he should travel the world at the most unpropitious time of year.

Thus he was in Samoa in 1966 when the worst hurricane of the century hit that island and blew the roof off the hotel in which he was staying. He managed to be in India during one ten-day period when the temperature varied between the "extremes" of 104.7 and 107.4. He seemed, as well, to arrange his visits to Hawaii to correspond with tidal wave alerts, and his sabbaticals to Paris to take advantage of the rainiest summers on record.

Complementing these foreign visits, Stanford and the Schramm home in particular became the magnets which attracted an almost daily flow of scholars, teachers, planners, government officials, journalists, and others in just about every field of activity. And the discipline owes much to "Miss Betty," whose supporting role was one of major importance.

She was often called upon with only a few hours notice to add two or three plates to the dinner table, or to go out and get enough food to feed a traveling party of Samoan teachers; Betty Schramm always responded efficiently, quietly, and graciously. Of only one thing could she be reasonably certain as she set about her daily tasks: Dinner that night would seldom be for the Schramms alone. The warmth of their hospitality became legendary.

But for all the achievements and hospitable times, it would be untrue to Wilbur's basic standards of honesty and journalistic integrity to leave the impression that his years at Stanford were without their disappointments and frustrations. Never one to become enmeshed in administrative detail, Wilbur sometimes found it difficult to fathom the ways of some university officials, especially those who made promises which they subsequently ignored or conveniently forgot. He also was disappointed when some of his former students, exceptionally well trained to carry communication research to new heights, strayed into less productive lines of scholarship in search of grants or personal prestige.

He regarded as a similar personal loss those carefully designed programs intended to put communication to work to meet the needs of a group of people but later perverted to serve political purposes. The Indian Institute for Mass Communication, begun in the Stanford mold, ended up as a minor government agency concerned chiefly with such activities as training guides for international expositions. In like manner, a regional training center for mass media personnel in East Africa—which almost everyone agreed made excellent educational sense—was cut down by bureaucracy before it could get off the ground.

But perhaps the greatest disappointment came near the close of the Stanford Segment of Wilbur's brilliant and productive career. Like many in higher education, Wilbur became disheartened with the retreat from scholarship toward what was popularly termed "relevant education." Many students, and not a few faculty members, seemed no longer to share his "reverence for learning" but to be more interested in "career education" or in pushing a particular point of view to the exclusion of all others.

But these exceptions proved the rule. And the rule was that everyone who came into contact with this remarkable man left the better for the experience. It's inaccurate, as Steve Chaffee pointed out at the Association for Education in Journalism meeting at Fort Collins in 1973, to ascribe any significant movement solely to one person. But insofar as that can be done, communication research can fairly be said to be synonymous with Wilbur Schramm, first at Illinois, then at Stanford.

However, the record would not be complete, if it did not note that in one major respect—known only to a few of his closest friends and colleagues—Wilbur Schramm was one of the academic world's most successful imposters. He posed as a social scientist who applied the rigorous intellectual discipline of the hard sciences to inquiry into a new field. And he did it with great success.

But at heart he was, and is, a humanist. For the man who studied under Alfred North Whitehead and Bliss Perry and who was influenced by Emerson, Shakespeare, Robert Frost, and Gandhi reflected those associations in everything he wrote and in all that he did. In spite of the eloquence of his lectures about the importance of the discipline of science as applied to communication, Wilbur's real interest was in the social effects of communication and in its potential to better the lives of people everywhere.

Steve Chaffee summed up this view most accurately when he remarked at Fort Collins that "there is a moralistic, as well as a scientific, cast to [his] terminology. . . . His analyses became, paradoxically, more humanistic even as they became more scientific in the sense of emanating from hard empirical data."

In this light, it is understandable how the discipline's most prodigious researcher, its most prolific writer, and perhaps its busiest single individual could take time to answer a schoolgirl from Texas who wrote to question one of his early short stories.

Puzzled by the idea of a train which ran on roads, she wrote as follows: "I am a student at Aldine Senior High School in Houston, Texas. We were going over your story 'Dan Peters and Casey Jones,' and I was wondering how did the train go on the roads if it had train wheels and not tires? How could it stop when it was going on a hard top road? Could you please explain the whole story to me, so I may tell my fellow students. Would you please reply to my questions?"

The response, personally typed by Wilbur on that magic machine which served him so well, perhaps revealed more about the character of the man than all his scholarly works, all the five million plus words that he wrote at Stanford and elsewhere. He replied as follows: "That story is fantasy. That means it is realistic in every respect except one: the very one you mention. I wrote another fantasy which was real in every respect except that it had a flying tractor in it. Eric Knight wrote a famous fantasy which was real in every respect except that in it a man found out that he could fly. Now, of course, a train couldn't run very well or turn corners on paved roads. Of course, a man can't fly. But what if he could? When you read a fantasy, you have to take that point of view toward it: What would happen if this were possible? Relax a bit, and let your imagination play. Don't try to make everything hard and realistic. Enjoy it. Good luck to you."

The Hawaii Years

EVERETT KLEINJANS

I first met Wilbur in Bangkok in 1968. I had arrived from Delhi in search of a director for our new population program, and he was hosting a party to which he had invited one of the people I wanted to interview. Although he did not know me, he invited me at the request of this mutual friend. The next day I went to the airport to board Pan Am Flight Two for my return to Honolulu and met Wilbur checking in for the same flight. We arranged to sit together and spent the next sixteen hours sharing our perceptions of what the East-West Center should become, our views on communication problems in the Pacific area, and the feasibility of establishing a communication program at the East-West Center as part of our effort to establish problem-oriented programs. Our discussion was the highlight of my trip to Asia and resulted in a lengthy letter from Wilbur summarizing his perceptions for developing a communication program at the center which "will make the East-West Center a real center for the advancement of communication in Asia and the Pacific Islands, and between these areas and the United States."

In this initial letter, Wilbur not only neatly summarized our sixteen hours of talk but also sketched out a structural and programmatic outline for a communication program. His observations that we should plan for "substantive continuity" by building a core group of quality academic staff; that we should plan for "integration of activities" so that more intellectual interaction occurs between our students, scholars, and professionals; and that we should "select a few problem areas" which are manageable and currently relevant, formed the basis for planning and implementing the communication program at the East-West Center.

Wilbur's specific advice on choosing one problem area "that is of immediate and demanding importance" (the role of modern communication in economic and social development) and "one area that will develop more slowly and begin to pay off when the first one has made its chief impact" (barriers to effective communication between Asians and North Americans) were also followed.

In 1969, as we moved to specific, detailed planning for the communication program, Wilbur provided much of the inspiration and guidance, serving as a Senior Fellow along with Lakshman Rao of India and Godwin Chu. As a result of their combined planning, the East-West Communication Institute was established on July 1, 1970, with R. Lyle Webster as the first director.

Wilbur continued to maintain a close, personal interest in the emergence of the new program and agreed in 1973 to accept the directorship of the program. In his letter of acceptance he noted that "all I ask of you is a little room to run . . . and some support when we get ready to take off. Given those things, I think we together can make it an Institute of which we shall be deeply proud."

For the next two years, with Wilbur at the helm, the East-West Communication Institute continued to evolve as a significant force for improving the understanding of communication problems throughout the Pacific Basin Area. Wilbur's influence had permeated the communication program from its organization, so it may not be appropriate to say that he brought a new direction or purpose to the institute. But having him as a permanent rather than a periodic force, as the person in charge rather than the valued distinguished visitor, inevitably made a positive difference.

Perhaps his first concern was to ensure that the research and educational outreach of the institute should be firmly anchored to theory and that the institute's staff should become important contributors to the theoretical as well as the empirical literature of communication.

A second major concern had to do with a large grant which Wilbur had been instrumental in obtaining for the institute from the population division of United States Agency for International Development (US/AID). While this grant was stipulated for "institution building," its activity focus was on educational projects for family planning communication programs. Perhaps inevitably, the size of the grant relative to the total budget of the institute created the danger that the shape of the institute might become distorted. Recognizing this danger, Wilbur set out to prevent such distortion.

Both these concerns were addressed through a major reorganization of the activity structure of the institute together with a concerted effort to recruit several new staff members to bring added strength in both the theory and methodology work of the institute. Under this new structure and with new staff strength, the institute pushed ahead not only into the second three-year phase of the AID family planning communication grant, but in other areas as well.

One of the more unique of these areas was traditional media and popular culture. Wilbur encouraged development and expansion of advanced seminars, and programs were inaugurated providing an exceptional opportunity for a sharing and mutual learning on the part of scholars from East and West. Through them the institute also began a research interest in the People's Republic of China. Not only did these activities prove to be immensely popular, but they also produced a series of publications of great value both because of their high quality and because they helped fill a great void in the literature of crosscultural communciation. The prestige and affection felt for Wilbur throughout Asia undoubtedly contributed to the success of these seminars and conferences.

In 1964, Wilbur Schramm and Dan Lerner had organized for the center a major conference which led to the publication of *Communication and Change in the Developing Countries.* This book has been of great importance to the institute, for it provided it with a book which quickly became and remained a major reference in the field. And typically, Wilbur and Dan consigned the royalties from the book to provide a "discretionary fund" for the institute. Early in Wilbur's years as director, he and Dan organized a follow-up conference ("Ten Years Later") that produced a new book, *Communication and Change: The Past Ten Years and the Next,* which has now joined the earlier volume as an indispensable reference.

For many years, Wilbur has had a "love affair" with the South Pacific. Thus, not surprisingly, as the institute's director he helped stimulate a number of activities which focussed on communication in that part of the world where distance, low population density, and a variety of traditions combine to produce problems which are exotic, fascinating, and challenging. In addition to continuing his study of the instructional television program in Samoa, he gave attention to the PEACESAT program, which has attempted to expand opportunities for higher education on a multinational basis. In particular he explored possible programs of mutual undertakings between the East-West Center and the University of the South Pacific in Fiji.

But these years were not without disappointment and sadness. Wilbur had hoped to build a strong communication technology component in the institute, particularly with emphasis on educational communication technology. To this end, he tempted Ray Carpenter to join the institute: Ray's untimely death was not only a personal loss to Wilbur, but also left a vacuum in the institute's project as he had conceived it. As time passed and no appropriate replacement could be found, and as demands on his own time and resouces continued to grow, Wilbur sagely suggested that the proper course would be for the institute to concentrate on existing strength, reducing the areas of activity, working constantly to increase the quality of effort. Significantly, during the period of his service as director, the institute's publication of papers, monographs, and books became a major program effort.

In addition to his intellectual and administrative leadership during this period, Wilbur contributed a unique, never-flagging sense of humor which helped us all get through periods of difficulty and turmoil. To cite only two of countless examples, Wilbur, who is a night owl and not particularly happy with the prospect of early morning meetings, issued a directive when he was acting chancellor which abolished Tuesday morning meetings of the Council of Directors and proclaimed that "all subsequent Tuesdays will be known as King Kalakaua Day, and will be holidays." Finally, he doubled all the directors' salaries because they "will suffer the hardship of being prevented from working on Tuesday, and especially because they will be deprived of the opportunity to attend the meeting." On another occasion when space constraints in Lincoln Hall were creating a difficult and unpleasant situation for staff and scholars, Wilbur moved his desk out of his office to make room for a colleague and set up shop in the middle of the tropical garden in the courtyard. Visitors and passersby were rather disconcerted to find the distinguished director of one of our institutes holding meetings and dictating letters beneath the palm leaves in the courtyard!

In 1975 Wilbur asked to be relieved of the administrative chores of the directorship in order to devote more time to research. We asked him to become the first Distinguished Center Researcher, a position designed to recognize truly outstanding international accomplishments in areas of relevance to problem-oriented programs. Freed from the burdens of administration, Wilbur began once more to get his electric typewriter humming with his inimitable random finger style which challenges champion typists. In the first month of his "freedom" he rewrote and completed his *Big Media, Little Media* manuscript. Then he turned his attention to requests such as one from the National Academy of Science to review the research on "Sesame Street" and that sponsored by the Surgeon General's Scientific Task Force on Television and Social Behavior. He also joined a commission to investigate the alarming decline in reading scores on the SAT exams during the past decade. And again his affectionate attention went out to the South Pacific in the form of a book-length historical case study of the instructional television program there.

His writing schedule, laid out for several years, is punctuated with interruptions—requests for him to provide keynote papers and to give seminars, to receive honors from universitites and organizations the world over. Yet he is still a true member of the institute's staff, actively participating in its research and meetings. As Distinguished Center Researcher, he also serves as a resource person for the center as a whole.

In this capacity, Wilbur continues to provide valuable advice on the directions the center should be taking in the years ahead. He recently pointed out the tendencies inherent in today's academic world of collective bargaining, equal employment opportunity, and ever-increasing regulations and constraints to become overly bureaucratized. If we move too far in the direction of bureaucratic efficiency, we may find it difficult to achieve academic excellence, he feels. His specific recommendations are to work toward building top quality, flexible, short-term staff; to simplify the "complex system of administrative rules and procedures," observing that "we are too busy to do our best"; to "consolidate some of our activities into larger, more significant ones" in order to improve the quality of our efforts; and finally to develop a student program that builds meaningful involvement of students into our programmatic activities. His concerns and suggestions provide valuable insights as we continue work toward building an educational institution of quality dedicated to the promotion of understanding and better relations between East and West.

To summarize the many contributions of Wilbur to the East-West Center is difficult. I am particularly in his debt for his leadership in creating and building the East-West Communication Institute and his wise counsel over the years on the directions that the center should be taking in order to achieve its goals. Wilbur's imprint on the center is large and significant. As long as I am at the center I will remember the way he stated his vision for it: "The East-West Center must be a place where some new ideas originate and all new ideas circulate."

Bibliography of the Works of Wilbur Schramm

GODWIN C. CHU

(Note: Reviews are omitted. Translations are sampled. A number of papers written between 1932 and 1947 have been lost track of.)

THEORY AND METHODOLOGY

1945 "Reading and Listening Patterns of American University Students." *Journalism Quarterly, 22,* 23–33.

1946 Editor. "Radio Journalism." Special number of *Journalism Quarterly, 23,* 137–201.

1946 "What Radio News Means to Middleville." *Journalism Quarterly, 23,* 173–181.

1948 Editor. *Communications in Modern Society.* Fifteen studies prepared for University of Illinois Institute of Communication Research, with an introduction by editor. vi + 252 pp.

1948 "Measuring Another Dimension of Newspaper Readership." *Journalism Quarterly, 24,* 293–406.

1949 (with David M. White) "Age, Education, Economic Status: Factors in Newspaper Reading." *Journalism Quarterly, 26,* 149–159.

1949 "The Effects of Mass Communication: A Review." *Journalism Quarterly, 26,* 397–409.

1949 "The Nature of News." *Journalism Quarterly, 26,* 259–269.

1951 (with W. Danielson) "Anticipated Audiences as Determinants of Recall." *Journal of Abnormal and Social Psychology, 28,* 282–283.

1951 (with M. Ludwig) "The Weekly Newspaper and Its Readers." *Journalism Quarterly, 28,* 301–314.

1954 (with R. W. Beckman) "Manpower Needs in Radio News: AATJ and NAB Survey Results." *Journalism Quarterly, 21,* 256–257.

1954 "Procedures and Effects of Mass Communication." In *Mass Media and Education.* Fifty-third yearbook of the National Society for the Study of Education. Chicago: National Society for the Study of Education, 113–38.

1954   Editor. *The Process and Effects of Mass Communication.* Urbana, Ill.: University of Illinois Press.

1955   "Information Theory and Mass Communication." *Journalism Quarterly, 32,* 131–46.

1956   (with H. Kumata) "A Pilot Study of Cross-cultural Meaning." *Public Opinion Quarterly, 20,* 229–37.

1956   "Why Adults Read." In *Adult Reading.* Fifty-fifth yearbook of the National Society for the Study of Education, Part II. Chicago: National Society for the Study of Education, 57–88.

1957   *Responsibility in Mass Communication.* With introduction by Reinhold Niebuhr. New York: Harper & Brothers. 391 pp.

1957   "Twenty Years of Journalism Research." *Public Opinion Quarterly, 21,* 91–107.

1958   "Newspapers of a State as a News Network." *Journalism Quarterly, 35,* 177–82.

1959   Comments on "The State of Communication Research." *Public Opinion Quarterly, 23,* 5–9.

1959   (with Richard F. Carter) "The Effectiveness of a Political Telethon." *Public Opinion Quarterly, 23,* 6–17.

1960   Editor. *Mass Communications.* Urbana, Illinois: University of Illinois Press, 1949. viii + 621 pp. Revised edition, with foreword by editor. Urbana: University of Illinois Press, 1960. xi + 695 pp.

1960   "A Note on Children's Use of Television." In Schramm (editor), *Mass Communications,* 214–226.

1960   (with Jack Lyle and Edwin B. Parker) "Patterns in Children's Reading of Newspapers." *Journalism Quarterly, 37,* 149–59.

1961   (with Ruth T. Storey) *Little House: A Study of Senior Citizens.* With a foreword by Ernest R. Hilgard. Menlo Park, California: Peninsula Volunteers, Inc., and Stanford, California: Institute for Communication Research, Stanford University. xiv + 351 pp.

1961   Editor. *Case Studies in Bringing Behavioral Science into Use.* With a foreword by Wilbur Schramm. Stanford, Calif.: Institute for Communication Research, Stanford University. viii + 135 pp.

1961   "Content Analysis of the World of Confession Magazines." In J. C. Nunnaly, Jr. (editor), *Popular Conceptions of Mental Health, Their Development and Change.* New York: Holt, Rinehart and Winston, Inc., 297–307.

1961   (with Jack Lyle and Edwin B. Parker) *Television in the Lives of Our Children.* Stanford, Calif.: Stanford University Press. vii + 324 pp.

1962   Editor. *Paris-Stanford Studies in Communication.* Stanford, Calif.: Institute for Communication Research, Stanford University. vii + 137 pp.

1962   "Science and the Public Mind." In Schramm (editor), *Paris-Stanford Studies in Communication,* 17–47.

1962   "Mass Communications." *Annual Review of Psychology, 13,* 251–84.

1962   Editor. *Studies of Innovation and of Communication to the Public.* Studies in the Utilization of Behavioral Science, Vol. II. Stanford,

Calif.: Institute for Communication Research, Stanford University. viii + 286 pp.

1963 "The Challenge to Communication Research." In R. O. Nafziger and D. M. White (editors), *Introduction to Mass Communications Research,* Baton Rouge: University of Louisiana Press, 1958, and revised edition, 1963, 3-31.

1963 Editor. *The Science of Human Communication.* With foreword by editor. Second printing. New York: Basic Books, Inc. viii + 158 pp.

1963 "Communication Research in the United States." In Schramm (editor), *The Science of Human Communication,* 1-16.

1964 *The Effects of Television on Children and Adolescents.* Reports and Papers on Mass Communication No. 43. Paris: UNESCO.

1965 Introduction: "Communication in Crisis." In Bradley Greenberg and Edwin B. Parker (editors), *The Kennedy Assassination and the American Public: Social Communication in Crisis,* 1-25. Stanford, Calif.: Stanford University Press.

1966 "Information Theory and Mass Communication." In B. Berelson and M. Janowitz (editors), *Reader in Public Opinion and Communication.* Second edition. New York: The Free Press, 712-32. Also in A. G. Smith (editor), *Communication and Culture.* New York: Holt, Rinehart and Winston, 521-34.

1966 "TV as Scapegoat." In J. F. Rosenblith and W. Allinsmith (editors), *The Causes of Behavior II, Readings in Child Development and Educational Psychology.* Second edition. Boston: Allyn and Bacon, Inc., 216-18.

1966 "Two Concepts of Mass Communication." In B. Berelson and M. Janowitz (editors), *Reader in Public Opinion and Communication.* Second edition. New York: The Free Press, 206-19.

1967 (Chairman) *Report of Subcommittee on Dissemination of Scientific Information to Behavioral Scientists.* For National Academy of Sciences-National Research Council, January, 39 pp.

1967 (with Serena Wade) "Knowledge and the Public Mind." A preliminary study of the distribution and sources of science, health, and public affairs knowledge in the American public. Stanford, Calif.: Institute for Communication Research, Stanford University. 163 pp.

1967 "Communication." In *World Book Encyclopedia.* Chicago: Field Publishing Co. IV, 710-23.

1968 "Mass Communication: Control and Public Policy." *International Encyclopedia of the Social Sciences,* Vol. 3, 55-61. Macmillan and Free Press.

1969 (with Serena Wade) "The Mass Media as Sources of Public Affairs, Science, and Health Knowledge." *Public Opinion Quarterly, 33,* 197-209.

1969 (with William L. Rivers) *Responsibility in Mass Communication.* Revised edition of 1957 volume. New York: Harper & Row, Publishers. vi + 314 pp.

1971 "The Mass Media in the North American Life Cycle." In *Public et Techniques de la Diffusion Collective,* Brussels: Editions de l'Institut de Sociologie, 381-400.

1971   (with the assistance of John Mayo) *Notes on Case Studies of Instructional Media Projects.* Stanford, Calif.: Institute for Communication Research, Stanford University. 41 pp.

1971   *Notes on Instructional Cross-media Comparisons.* Stanford, Calif.: Institute for Communication Research, Stanford University. 53 pp.

1971   (with Donald F. Roberts) "Children's Learning from Mass Media." *The Encyclopedia of Education,* Vol. 6, 69–75. Macmillan and Free Press.

1971   "How Communication Works." In J. De Vito (editor), *Communication: Concepts and Processes.* Englewood Cliffs, N.J.: Prentice-Hall, Inc., 12–21.

1971   Editor. (with Donald F. Roberts) *The Process and Effects of Mass Communication.* Revised edition. Urbana: University of Illinois Press. ix + 997 pp.

1971   "Communication in Crisis." In Schramm and Roberts (editors), *The Process and Effects of Mass Communication,* 525–53.

1971   "The Nature of Communication between Humans." In Schramm and Roberts (editors), *The Process and Effects of Mass Communication,* 3–54.

1971   "What TV Is Doing to Our Children." In A. and L. Kirschner (editor), *Radio and Television, Readings in the Mass Media.* New York: The Odyssey Press, 155–63.

1972   "Mass Communication." For the *Encyclopedia Italiana.* Stanford, Calif.: Institute for Communication Research, Stanford University. 69 pp.

1973   (Editor, with Ithiel de Sola Pool, *et al.*) *Handbook of Communication.* Chicago: Rand McNally College Publishing Co. ix + 1011 pp.

1973   "Channels and Audiences." In Schramm and de Sola Pool (editors), *Handbook of Communication,* 116–40.

1973   "Mass Communication." In George A. Miller (editor), *Communication, Language, and Meaning: Psychological Perspectives.* New York: Basic Books, Inc., 219–30.

1973   (with Janet Alexander) "Broadcasting." In Schramm and de Sola Pool (editors), *Handbook of Communication,* 577–618.

1973   *Men, Messages, and Media. A Look at Human Communication.* New York: Harper & Row. 341 pp.

1973   (with Richard F. Carter) *Scales for Describing National Communication Systems.* Stanford, Calif.: Institute for Communication Research, Stanford University. (undated). 15 pp.

1973   *Motion Pictures and Real-life Violence. What the Research Says.* A working Paper for the Motion Picture Association of America. Stanford, Calif.: Institute for Communication Research, Stanford University. (undated). 52 pp.

MEDIA FOR INSTRUCTION

1962   "What We Know about Learning from Instructional Television." In Schramm (editor), *Educational Television: The Next Ten Years,* 52–76.

1962 "Learning from Instructional Television." *Review of Educational Research, 32*, 156–167.

1962 *Programed Instruction Today and Tomorrow.* New York: Fund for the Advancement of Education. 74 pp.

1964 Editor. *Four Case Studies of Programed Instruction.* With introduction by editor. New York: Fund for the Advancement of Education. 119 pp.

1964 "Appendix: Programed Instruction Today and Tomorrow" (a reprint). In Schramm (editor), *Four Case Studies of Programed Instruction,* 98–115.

1964 "Programed Instruction in Denver." In Schramm (editor), *Four Case Studies of Programed Instruction,* 30–40.

1964 *The Context of Instructional Television: Summary Report of Research Findings, the Denver-Stanford Project.* Denver, Colo., and Stanford, Calif.: Denver Public Schools and Institute for Communication Research, Stanford University. v + 160. Appendix: a-1 to a-63.

1964 *The Research on Programed Instruction. An Annotated Bibliography.* Prepared under contract with HEW Office of Education by Institute for Communication Research, Stanford University, Stanford, California. Washington: U.S. Government Printing Office. iii + 114 pp.

1967 (with Godwin C. Chu) *Learning from Television: What the Research Says.* Washington: National Association for Educational Broadcasters. v + 116 pp.

1967 (with Philip H. Coombs, Friedrich Kahnert, Jack Lyle) *The New Media: Memo to Educational Planners.* With a foreword by Rene Maheu. Paris: UNESCO, International Institute for Educational Planning. 175 pp.

1967 (with Philip H. Coombs, Friedrich Kahnert, Jack Lyle) *New Educational Media in Action: Case Studies for Planners.* With a preface by Coombs. Paris: UNESCO, International Institute for Educational Planning case studies. Three volumes, 203 pp., 226 pp., 198 pp.

1967 (with Lyle M. Nelson, William R. Odell, John Vaizey, and Seth Spaulding) "Education Television in American Samoa.: In *New Educational Media in Action,* Vol. I, 11–68.

1967 (with P. V. Krishnamoorthy, D. D. Jahdav, J. P. Bhattacharjee, Douglas Ensminger, W. Bert Johnson, R. Lyle Webster) "Ten Years of the Rural Radio Forum in India." In *New Educational Media in Action,* Vol. I, 105–34.

1967 (with Momluang Pin Malakul, Khunying Ambhorn Meesook, Prani Pookpakdi, Saising Siributr) "Educational Radio in Thailand." In *New Educational Media in Action,* Vol. I, 83–104.

1967 (with Isao Amagi, Kazuhiko Goto, Masamori Hiratsuka, Yukihiro Kumagai) "Japan's Broadcast-correspondence High School." In *New Educational Media in Action,* Vol. I, 135–68.

1968 *Communication Satellites for Education, Science and Culture.* Reports and Papers on Mass Communication No. 53. Paris: UNESCO. 23 pp.

1968 (with Lyle M. Nelson) *Communication Satellites for Education and Development—The Case for India.* Prepared for the President's task force on communication policy. Menlo Park, Calif.: Stanford Research Institute. 204 pp. Appendix A-1 to 26; Appendix B-1 to 12; Appendix C-1 to 19. References: 205–12.

1969 *Classroom Out-of-Doors.* Kalamazoo, Mich.: Sequoia Press.

1969 "Instructional Television Here and Abroad." In *The Schools and the Challenge of Innovation,* supplementary paper No. 28. New York: Committee for Economic Development, 242–269.

1969 "The New Educational Technology." In G. Z. F. Bereday (editor), *Essays on World Education: The Crisis of Supply and Demand.* New York: Oxford University Press, 133–52.

1970 "Learning from Television: What the Research Says." In *To Improve Learning, an Evaluation of Instructional Technology,* Vol. I, Part II, Instructional Technology: selected working papers on The State of the Art. New York: R. R. Bowker Co., 179–82.

1970 (with Lyle Nelson) *Report of the Educational Television Task Force.* Honolulu, Hawaii: University of Hawaii–American Samoa Contract. 88 pp.

1970 "The Future of Educational Radio and Television." The Japan Prize Lecture, 1969. In *The Japan Prize 1969.* Tokyo: NHK (The Japan Broadcasting Corporation), 77–83.

1970 (with Robert Filep) *The Impact of Research on Utilization of Media for Educational Purposes.* El Segundo, Calif.: Institute for Educational Development. vi + 66 pp. + appendix 44 pp.

1971 *The Next Ten Years: How to Look at an Exhibition of Instructional Technology.* Stanford, Calif.: Institute for Communication Research, for the Visodata Conference, Munich, October 1971. 14 pp.

1972 (Chairman, with Harold Howe and David Hawkridge) *An "Everyman's University" for Israel,* report submitted to Hanadiv, Jerusalem, Israel. 91 pp.

1972–73 *Learning in American Samoa. A Review of the Test Results.* Stanford, Calif.: Institute for Communication Research, Stanford University.

1972 Editor. *Quality in Instructional Television.* Honolulu, Hawaii: The University Press of Hawaii. 226 pp.

1972 "What the Research Says." In Schramm (editor), *Quality in Instructional Television,* 44–79.

1973 *Big Media, Little Media.* A report to the Agency for International Development. Stanford, Calif.: Institute for Communication Research, Stanford University. xiii + 333 pp.

1973 *Instructional Television in the Education Reform of El Salvador.* Washington, D.C.: Academy for Educational Development, Information Center on Instructional Technology. 89 pp.

1973 *ITV in American Samoa—After Nine Years.* Stanford, Calif.: Institute for Communication Research, Stanford University. v + 55 pp.

1973 *Some Tentative Conclusions Concerning Instructional Television.* For the National Academy of Education. Stanford, Calif.: Institute for Communication Research, Stanford University. 8 pp.

1973 (with Robert C. Hornik, Henry T. Ingle, John K. Mayo, Emile G.

McAnany) *Television and Educational Reform in El Salvador*. Research report on the Educational Reform of El Salvador prepared by members of the Institute for Communication Research, Stanford University, on behalf of AED under contract to USAID. xix +322 pp.

PUBLIC TELEVISION

1960　Editor. *The Impact of Educational Television*. Selected studies from the research sponsored by National Education Television and Radio Center. Urbana: University of Illinois Press. viii + 247 pp.

1960　The Audiences of Educational Television." In Schramm (editor), *The Impact of Educational Television*, 18–38.

1962　Editor. *Educational Television, the Next Ten Years*. With a foreword by editor. Report for U.S. Office of Education. Stanford, Calif.: Institute for Communication Research, Stanford University. xi + 375 pp.

1962　"A Note on the Audiences of Educational Television." In Schramm (editor), *Educational Television: The Next Ten Years*, 346–53.

1963　(with Jack Lyle and Ithiel de Sola Pool) *The People Look at Educational Television*. A report of nine representative ETV stations. Stanford, Calif.: Stanford University Press. 209 pp.

1967　*The Audiences of Educational Television: A Report to NET*. Stanford, Calif.: Institute for Communication Research, Stanford University. 90 pp.

1972　(with Lyle M. Nelson) *The Financing of Public Television*. With an introduction by Douglas Cater. Palo Alto, California: Communication and Society, a joint program of the Aspen Institute for Humanistic Studies and the Academy for Educational Development, Inc. x + 59 pp.

COMMUNICATION AND DEVELOPMENT

1963　Report of the mass communication study team sponsored by the Ford Foundation in cooperation with the Ministry of Information and Broadcasting. New Delhi, India. Faridabad, India: Government of India Press. 34 pp.

1964　*Mass Media and National Development. The Role of Information in the Developing Countries*. With a foreword by UNESCO and preface by author. Stanford, Calif.: Stanford University Press and UNESCO, Paris. xiv + 333 pp.

1967　(Editor, with Daniel Lerner) *Communication and Change in the Developing Countries*. With foreword by Lyndon B. Johnson. Honolulu, Hawaii: The University Press of Hawaii, 1967. xiv + 333 pp. Third printing, 1972.

1967　"Communication and Change." In Schramm and Lerner (editors), *Communication and Change in the Developing Countries*, 5–32.

1967　(with W. Lee Ruggels) "How Mass Media Systems Grow." In Schramm and Lerner (editors), *Communication and Change in the Developing Countries*, 57–75.

1969　"The Mass Media in Family Planning Campaigns." In R. Blake (editor), *Final Report, International Workshop on Communication Aspects of Family Planning Programs, Bangkok, Thailand.* Chapel Hill, N.C.: The Carolina Population Center, University of North Carolina, 9–14.

1971 "Communication in Family Planning." *Reports on Population/Family Planning,* No. 7, April 1971. 43 pp.

1971 *Family Planning Information in the Seventies.* Chicago: University of Chicago Center for Continuing Education. 12 pp.

1971 "The Things We Know about Family Planning Information." In R. Blake (editor), *Final Report, International Workshop on Communications in Family Planning Programs in Iran.* Chapel Hill, N.C.: Carolina Population Center, University of North Carolina, 12–21.

1971 *Television Reconsidered.* Singapore: First General Assembly of the Asian Mass Communication Research and Information Centre. Published, AMIC, 1972.

1974 "The Problem of Making Research Useful." *Media Asia, 1,* 5–11.

1974 (with Godwin Chu and Frederick T. C. Yu) *China's Experience with Development Communication: How Transferrable Is It?* Honolulu, Hawaii: Communication Institute, East-West Center. 24 pp.

1976 *Cross-Cultural Communication: Suggestions for the Building of Bridges.* Honolulu, Hawaii: Communication Institute, East-West Center. 13 pp.

1976 *A Western View of Planning?* Honolulu, Hawaii: Communication Institute, East-West Center. 8 pp.

1976 (Editor, with Daniel Lerner) *Communication and Change: The Past Ten Years—and the Next.* Honolulu, Hawaii: University Press of Hawaii.

INTERNATIONAL COMMUNICATION

1951 (with J. W. Riley, Jr.) "Communication in the Sovietized State, As Demonstrated in Korea." *American Sociological Review, 16,* 757–66.

1951 (with J. W. Riley, Jr., and F. W. Williams) "Flight from Communism: A Report on Korean Refugees." *Public Opinion Quarterly, 15,* 274–84.

1951 (with J. W. Riley, Jr.) *The Reds Take a City: The Communist Occupation of Seoul, with Eye-witness Accounts.* New Brunswick, N.J.: Rutgers University Press. 210 pp.

1953 (as chairman of citizens' committee) U.S. Information Agency. A program of research and evaluation for the international information administration; recommendations of a special committee to the administrator. Washington, D.C., June 15, 1953. 27 pp.

1953 (with Daniel Katz, Willmoore Kendall and Theodore Wallance) *The Nature of Psychological Warfare.* Technical Memorandum ORO-T 214, Operations Research Office of Johns Hopkins. 288 pp.

1955 *Four Working Papers on Propaganda Theory.* Written with the help of USIA, under contract 1A-W-362, between USIA and the Institute of Communications Research, University of Illinois. Urbana: University of Illinois Press. 145 pp.

1955 "Notes on the British Concept of Propaganda." In *Four Working Papers on Propaganda Theory*, 65–97.
1955 (with Hideya Kumata) "The Propaganda Theory of the German Nazis." In *Four Working Papers on Propaganda Theory*, 33–64.
1955 "The Soviet Concept of 'Psychological' Warfare." In *Four Working Papers on Propaganda Theory*, 99–145.
1956 (with Fred S. Siebert and Theodore Peterson) *Four Theories of the Press*. Essays prepared in connection with study for Department of the Church and Economic Life of the National Council of Churches. Urbana: University of Illinois Press. 146 pp.
1956 "The Soviet Communist Theory." In Siebert, Peterson and Schramm (editors), *Four Theories of the Press*, 105–46.
1958 "Propaganda Theory of the German Nazis." In W. Daugherty and M. Janowitz (editors), *A Psychological Warfare Casebook*. Baltimore: The Johns Hopkins Press, 47–57.
1958 "Soviet Concept of Psychological Warfare." In W. Daugherty and M. Janowitz (editors), *A Psychological Warfare Casebook*, 779–88.
1959 (Editor) *One Day in the World's Press: Fourteen Great Newspapers on a Day of Crisis*. Stanford, Calif.: Stanford University Press. 138 pp.

LITERARY SUBJECTS

1933 "The Cost of Books in Chaucer's Time." In *Modern Language Notes*, *48*, 139–45.
1935 *Approaches to a Science of English Verse*. With an introduction by Carl E. Seashore and Joseph Tiffin. Iowa City: University of Iowa. 82 pp.
[Papers in this field from 1935 to 1942 are missing.]
Stories
Atlantic Monthly, 1941:
　　"Windwagon Smith"
Saturday Evening Post, 1942–1947:
　　"Dan Peters and Casey Jones"
　　"The Horse that Played Third Base for Brooklyn"
　　"My Kingdom for Jones"
　　"The Flying Coffin"
　　"The Wonderful Life of Willie the Jeep"
　　"Boone over the Pacific"
　　"Death and Old Feathers"
　　"Old Professors Never Die"
　　"The Blue Air Over Kansas"
　　"Why There Are No Ordinary Men in Iowa"
　　"Grandpa Hopewell and His Flying Tractor"
　　"Grandpa Hopewell Rides Again"
　　"Voice in the Earphones"
1947 *Windwagon Smith and Other Yarns*. Illustrated by Joe Krush. New York: Harcourt, Brace. 208 pp.
1956 (with Virginia Costadosi, John K. Dunn, and Melissa Miner) *Adventures for Americans*. New York: Harcourt, Brace & Co.

A SAMPLING OF THE TRANSLATIONS

1954 (with J. W. Riley, Jr.) *Los Rojos Toman una Ciudad*. Mexico: Editorial Confidencias.

1954 (Editor) *Mass Communication*. (Japanese translation published by Sogen Sha Co., Ltd., Tokyo)

1957 (with J. W. Riley, Jr.) *Os Vermelhos Atacam Uma Cidade*. Rio de Janerio: Editora Ipanema Ltda.

1959 (with Fred S. Siebert and Theodore A. Peterson) *Four Theories of the Press*. (Japanese translation published by Tokyo-Sogensha, Tokyo)

1959 *Responsibility in Mass Communication* (in Japanese). Published in Japan by arrangement with Harper & Brothers through Charles E. Tuttle in Tokyo.

1963 *Programmierter Unterricht Heute und Morgen*. Berlin: Cornelsen Verlag.

1964 *Grundfragen der Kommunikations-forschung*. Munchen: Juventa Verlag.

1965 (with Jack Lyle and Edwin B. Parker) *Television para Los Ninos*. Barcelona, Espana: Editorial Hispano-Europea.

1966 *L'information et le developpement national*. Paris: UNESCO.

1967 "Mass Media in Developing Countries." Translated into Korean from Kappa Tau Alpha Yearbook and published in *Non Dan* (Forum), Vol. 2, No. 4, Spring 1967, 72–82.

1970 *Comunicacao de Massa e Desenvolvimento*. Rio de Janeiro: Bloch Editores.

1971 (with Jack Lyle and Edwin B. Parker) *La Televisione Nella Vita dei Nostri Figli*. Milano, Italy: Franco Angeli Editore.

1971 *Programed Instruction: Today and Tomorrow* (Arabic translation published by UNRWA and UNESCO.)

1973 (with William L. Rivers) *Responsabilidad y Comunicacion de Masas*. Buenos Aires: Ediciones Troquel.

1973 (with William L. Rivers) *Responsibility in Mass Communication* (In Korean). Seoul, Korea: Sejong Publishing Co.

1973 (with Daniel Lerner) *Comunicacao e Mudanca nos Paises em Desenvolvimento*. Sao Paulo: Editora da Universidade de Sao Paulo.

Wilbur Schramm
Curriculum Vitae

1924–1930 Reporter, desk editor, and correspondent for Associated Press

1932–1934 National Research Fellow

1934–1941 Assistant professor, associate professor, and professor of English at the University of Iowa; founder and first director of the Iowa Writers Workshop

1941–1943 (on leave) Educational director, Office of Facts and Figures and Office of War Information

1943–1947 Director, School of Journalism, University of Iowa

1947–1955 Research professor, director of University Press, director and founder of the Institute of Communications Research at the University of Illinois

1950–1955 Dean, Division of Communications, University of Illinois

1954 (on leave) Director of research project for National Security Council

1955–1973 Professor of communication, Stanford University

1957–1973 Director, Institute for Communication Research, Stanford University

1959–1960 (on leave) Fellow, Center for Advanced Study in the Behavioral Sciences

1961–1973 Janet M. Peck Professor of International Communication, Stanford University

1967–1973 Professor of education, Stanford University

1973 Professor emeritus, Stanford University

1973–1975 Director, East-West Communication Institute, East-West Center, Honolulu

1975–1977 Distinguished Center Researcher, East-West Communication Institute, East-West Center, Honolulu

Notes on Contributors

STEVEN H. CHAFFEE is Willard G. Bleyer Professor of Journalism and Mass Communication at the University of Wisconsin in Madison, where he has taught since receiving his Ph.D. from Stanford in 1965. He has published widely in the communication field with emphasis on political communication, child development, and development of general communication theory. He is the author of "Television and Adolescent Aggressiveness (Overview)" in *Television and Social Behavior*, Vol. III (U.S. Government Printing Office, 1971). Professor Chaffee is a regular contributor to *Journalism Quarterly*, *Public Opinion Quarterly*, and other scholarly publications in the communication field.

GODWIN C. CHU was born in Peking and received his education at the National Taiwan University and Stanford University, from which he holds the Ph.D. in communication research. Dr. Chu is a research associate at the Communication Institute of the East-West Center in Honolulu. His chief research interests have been in communication and change in developing countries; his most recent study, *Radical Change Through Communication in Mao's China*, will be published by The University Press of Hawaii. Dr. Chu is a frequent contributor to such publications as *Journalism Quarterly*, *International Communication*, *Intercultural Communication*, *Sociometry*, *Journal of Personality and Social Psychology*, and the *International Journal of Psychology*.

DAVID G. HAWKRIDGE is director of the Institute of Educational Technology of Britain's Open University and serves on the university's major committees and boards. Since 1970 he has been chairman of the Steering Group on Educational Technology of the Council of Europe. Dr. Hawkridge is the author of more than fifty articles, including a series of evaluations of the Open University and its applicability to other countries of the world.

HILDE T. HIMMELWEIT is professor of social psychology and director of the Communication and Attitude Change Research Unit of the London School of Economics and Political Science, University of London. Dr. Himmelweit's *Television and the Child* (1958), one of the first major scholarly works in this field, helped focus international attention on the impact, and potential impact, of television on the lives of children and young adults. Among her more than fifty books and journal articles, Dr. Himmelweit's "Adolescent and Adult Media Use and Taste: A Longitudinal Study," in the *Harvard University Program on Technology and Society* (published by Harvard University in 1972) is perhaps best known.

ROBERT B. HUDSON is one of the pioneers in the educational television movement in the United States. He was successively coordinator of programs, vice-president for programs, and senior vice-president of National Educational Television (NET) before his retirement from that organization in 1970. Prior to joining NET, Hudson was associate professor of journalism and director of University Broadcasting at the University of Illinois; prior to that, he was director of education for the Columbia Broadcasting System.

HIDETOSHI KATO is professor of sociology and director of the Research Institute for Oriental Cultures at Gakushuin University, Tokyo. He received his Ph.D. degree from Tokyo University under joint authority of the Japan Sociological Association, Japan Association of Urban Sociology, and the Japan Association of Journalism. Dr. Kato is author of eighteen books and major papers in the field of communication and popular culture. He has been a research associate or visiting scholar/professor at Kyoto University, Doshisha University, University of Kent at Canterbury, Stanford University, and Grinnell College; he is also currently associated with the East-West Communication Institute as a senior fellow.

EVERETT KLEINJANS is President of the East-West Center in Honolulu. He received his Ph.D. from the University of Michigan in 1958 and has spent most of his career in international education. Before coming to the East-West Center in 1967, he was vice-president for academic affairs and dean of the College of Liberal Arts at the International Christian University in Tokyo.

HAROLD D. LASSWELL is currently co-director of the Policy Sciences Center in New York City. A past president of the American Political Science Association, Lasswell is one of the foremost political theorists of our time. He is professor emeritus of Yale University and has taught at universities around the world. His early book *Propaganda Technique in World War I* (1927) is widely regarded as the intellectual foundation of the half-century of communication research which has followed. During these fifty years, he has continually enriched communication research by his inventions of such ideas as content analysis, configurative thinking, and the policy sciences. Professor Lasswell has published some thirty books and several hundred articles in professional journals.

PAUL F. LAZARSFELD received his Ph.D. in applied mathematics from the University of Vienna. He came to the United States in 1933 on a Rockefeller traveling fellowship and remained in America for the rest of his life. In 1939 he was appointed to the Department of Sociology at Columbia University and later became Quetelet Professor of Social Science as well as chairman of the board of the Columbia Bureau of Applied Social Research. At the time of his death, he was University Professor at the University of Pittsburgh. He published widely on problems of opinion research, mass communications, methodology, and the uses of sociology. He served as president of the American Sociological Association and of the American Association for Public Opinion Research. Among his numerous awards are honorary degrees from the University of Chicago and Columbia University.

DANIEL LERNER is Ford Professor of Sociology and International Communications at Massachusetts Institute of Technology. Author of more than twenty books in the field of the social effects of communication, he is perhaps best known for his internationally acclaimed work, *The Passing of Traditional Society* (1958). Along with Lazarsfeld,

Lasswell, Schramm, and others, Dr. Lerner is one of the small group of scholars who have set the directions for communication research in its first half-century. Honored by the French and United States governments for his work, Dr. Lerner has been professor or visiting professor at many of the world's leading universities and research institutes. In 1967 he collaborated with Wilbur Schramm on *Communication and Change in Developing Countries,* a book which has influenced most development strategies since that time.

ARTHUR A. LUMSDAINE is professor of psychology and education at the University of Washington. One of the field's most respected researchers, Dr. Lumsdaine has also taught at Stanford, Princeton, Yale, University of California at Berkeley, and UCLA. His first book, with Carl Hovland and Fred D. Sheffield, *Experiments in Mass Communication* (1949), was influential in the thinking of most communication research scholars who followed, and his subsequent works on *Learning from Films,* with Mark A. May (1958) and *Student Response in Programmed Instruction* (1961) are regarded as landmark studies in their field. His most recent book is *Evaluation and Experiment: Some Critical Issues in Assessing Social Programs* with Carl A. Bennett (1975).

JACK LYLE has combined professional experience with extensive research on the media and its impact both nationally and internationally. Now director of the East-West Communication Institute in Honolulu, he was formerly director of communication research for the Corporation for Public Broadcasting in Washington, D.C. Professor Lyle received his Ph.D. from Stanford and has taught at UCLA, University of Pennsylvania, and The American University. He also served as deputy project director of the International Institute for Educational Planning (UNESCO) in Paris. Along with Schramm, he is one of the authors of *Television in the Lives of Our Children* (1961) and *The People Look at Educational Television* (1963).

LYLE M. NELSON is Thomas More Storke Professor of Communication and chairman of the Department of Communication at Stanford University. Professor Nelson has just completed six years as a member of the Board of Foreign Scholarships (United States National Fulbright Commission), the last three as chairman. His collaboration with Wilbur Schramm began in the early days of "educational television" (1952) and has included studies and reports for national and international agencies in India, Samoa, and East Africa as well as for United States public television.

CHARLES E. OSGOOD is professor of psychology and research professor in communications at the University of Illinois, where he served for many years as director of the Institute of Communications Research. Professor Osgood is past president of the American Psychological Association, and in 1960 he received its award for Distinguished Contribution to the Science of Psychology for his research into the nature and measurement of meaning. In 1962 he received an honorary degree as Doctor of Science from his alma mater, Dartmouth College, where he received his B.A. degree in 1939, followed by a Ph.D. at Yale in 1945. In 1972 he was elected to membership in the National Academy of Sciences. He is author of *The Measurement of Meaning,* 1957, with Drs. Suci and Tannenbaum; *An Alternative to War or Surrender,* 1962; and *Perspective in Foreign Policy,* 1966, as well as numerous articles in his own scientific field.

ITHIEL DE SOLA POOL is professor of political science at Massachusetts Institute of Technology and directed its Research Program in International Communication for more than a decade. Along with Wilbur Schramm and Jack Lyle, he is one of the authors of *The People Look at Educational Television* (1963), the first comprehensive look at the status of American noncommercial television. Another of his books, *American Business and Public Policy,* won the Woodrow Wilson Award for the best political science book of 1963. Professor Pool is also one of the authors with Schramm and others of *The Handbook of Communication* (1973).

JAMES M. REID was editor-in-chief of the textbook department of Hartcourt Brace and Company when he first met Wilbur Schramm, who was then a promising young scholar. Reid quickly signed Dr. Schramm to do the literary history for *Adventures in American Literature* (1947), one of the best-selling textbooks published in the United States. Harcourt then published an anthology of Schramm's short stories for high schools. The close personal friendship which was formed between the two men at that time has lasted through the years. Reid is now retired and lives in Carefree, Arizona.

EVERETT M. ROGERS is professor of communication at Stanford University. A sociologist and former Fulbright scholar, he is a recognized authority on diffusion of innovations and the use of communication in development. His best-known book, *Diffusion of Innovations* (1962), was republished in 1971 under the title *Communication of Innovations*. His latest book, with Rekha Agarwala Rogers, is *Communication in Organizations* (1976). He is a member of the editorial board of *Human Communication Research* and *Communication* and has published regularly in those as well as other scholarly journals.

ELIZABETH SCHRAMM has endeared herself to colleagues, distinguished guests, and students of Wilbur Schramm. For forty-three years, "Miss Betty" has presided over the Schramm household with a graciousness and quiet efficiency which has become almost legendary. No one is better qualified to write about Wilbur Schramm's early years.

WALLACE E. STEGNER is one of the nation's leading novelists, perhaps best known for *Angle of Repose* (1971), for which he received the Pulitzer Prize. A classmate of Wilbur Schramm's at Iowa, Professor Stegner retired as professor of English and director of the Creative Writing Workshop at Stanford in 1974 to devote his full time to writing. Besides the Pulitzer Prize, Stegner has won the O. Henry first prize for short stories (1950), the Little Brown and Company prize for best novelette (1937), and a number of other such awards.

FREDERICK T. C. YU is professor and associate dean of the Graduate School of Journalism of Columbia University. He has taught at the University of Iowa, University of Southern California, University of Montana, and the Chinese University of Hong Kong. A former member of the editorial staff of the Springfield (Ohio) *News-Sun* and the *Washington Post,* Professor Yu is editor of *Behavioral Sciences and the Mass Media* (1968).

☿ Production Notes

The text of this book has been designed by Roger J. Eggers and typeset on the Unified Composing System by the design & production staff of The University Press of Hawaii.

The text and display typeface is Garamond No. 49.

Offset presswork and binding is the work of Vail-Ballou Press. Text paper is Glatfelter P & S Offset, basis 55.